CHILD ABUSE

A Multidisciplinary Survey

Series Editor

BYRGEN FINKELMAN, J.D.

A GARLAND SERIES

SERIES CONTENTS

VOLUME
8

VICTIM AS WITNESS

LEGAL AND PSYCHOLOGICAL ISSUES

Edited with introductions by

BYRGEN FINKELMAN, J.D.

GARLAND PUBLISHING, INC.
New York & London
1995

Library of Congress Cataloging-in-Publication Data

Child abuse : a multidisciplinary survey / series editor, Byrgen
Finkelman.
    p.   cm.
    Includes bibliographical references and indexes.
    Contents: v. 1. Physical and emotional abuse and neglect
— v. 2. Sexual abuse — v. 3. Causes, prevention, and remedies
— v. 4. Short- and long-term effects — v. 5. Treatment of child
and adult survivors — v. 6. Treatment of offenders and
families — v. 7. Protecting abused children — v. 8. Victim as
witness — v. 9. Perpetrators, victims and the courts — v. 10.
Child abuse legislation.
    ISBN 0-8153-1813-8 (v. 1 : acid-free paper). — ISBN
0-8153-1814-6 (v. 2 : acid-free paper). — ISBN 0-8153-1815-4
(v. 3 : acid-free paper). — ISBN 0-8153-1816-2 (v. 4 : acid-
free paper). — ISBN 0-8153-1817-0 (v. 5 : acid-free paper).
— ISBN 0-8153-1818-9 (v. 6 : acid-free paper). — ISBN 0-8153-
1819-7 (v. 7 : acid-free paper). — ISBN 0-8153-1820-0 (v. 8 :
acid-free paper). — ISBN 0-8153-1821-9 (v. 9 : acid-free paper). — ISBN 0-8153-1822-7 (v. 10 : acid-free paper)
    1. Child abuse—United States.   I. Finkelman, Byrgen.
HV6626.52.C54   1995
362.7'62'0973—dc20   95-753
                                          CIP

Printed on acid-free, 250-year-life paper
Manufactured in the United States of America

CONTENTS

SERIES INTRODUCTION

In 1960 Elizabeth Elmer said of child abuse "little is known about any facet of the problem and that methods for dealing with it are random and inadequate." She spoke of a "professional blind-spot" for abuse and of "the repugnance felt by most of our society for the entire subject of abused children."[1] Two years later, Dr. C. Henry Kempe and his colleagues brought national attention to the problem of child abuse with their article, "The Battered-Child Syndrome."[2] Prior to the publication of that landmark article, the literature on child abuse was almost non-existent. In the three decades since its publication, the research and literature on child abuse have become vast and daunting.

Social workers, psychologists, psychiatrists, counselors, and doctors have studied child abuse in great detail. As a result, we know that child abuse includes physical, emotional, and sexual abuse as well as neglect. Researchers have studied the causes of abuse from both the individual and societal perspectives. There are effective interventions for tertiary remediation of the problem, and there are many prevention models that hold out hope that child abuse can be stopped before it starts. Studies of the short- and long-term effects of child abuse show a range of maladies that include infant failure-to-thrive, learning disabilities, eating disorders, borderline personality disorders, violent behavior, delinquency, and even parricide. We now recognize the need for treatment of child victims, adult survivors, and adult perpetrators of all forms of abuse. Lawyers, legislators, and judges have grappled with the profusion of legal problems raised by protective services and proceedings, foster care, and the termination of parental rights to free abused children for placement in permanent homes. Legislatures have passed and amended statutes requiring various health, education and child care professionals to report suspected abuse, and they have dealt with the difficult problem of defining abuse and determining when the state should intervene to protect children from abusive parents. They have also struggled with the legal and psychological issues that arise when the child victim becomes a witness against his or her abuser. Even the Supreme Court has been called upon to sort out the constitutional rights of victims and criminal defendants and to determine the extent of government liability for failure to adequately protect children from abuse.

The articles in this series document our passage through five of the six stages that C. Henry Kempe identified in his 1978 commentary "Recent Developments in the Field of Child Abuse" as developmental stages in addressing the problem of child abuse:

> Stage One is denial that either physical or sexual abuse exists to a significant extent . . . Stage Two is paying attention to the more lurid abuse . . . Stage Three comes when physical abuse is better handled and attention is now beginning to be paid to the infant who fails to thrive . . . Stage Four comes in recognition of emotional abuse and neglect . . . and Stage Five is the paying attention to the serious plight of the sexually abused child, including the youngster involved in incest . . .

In spite of the voluminous research and writing on child abuse, the sixth and final of Kempe's stages, "that of guaranteeing each child that he or she is truly wanted, is provided with loving care, decent shelter and food, and first class preventive and curative health care," remains elusive.[3] There are many explanations for our inability to conquer the problem of child abuse. In reality, the explanation for our continued inability to defeat this contemptible social problem is as complex as the problem itself.

We continue to sanction the use of violence in the name of discipline. We put our societal stamp of approval on "punishment inflicted by way of correction and training" and call it discipline. But discipline also means "instruction and exercise designed to train to proper conduct or action."[4] It is not difficult to see the inherent conflict in these two definitions when applied to child-rearing. How can we "train to proper conduct or action" when we use physical punishment as a means of training, punishment that we would not inflict upon an adult under the same circumstances?

The courts and legislatures have been unable to find the correct balance between a family's right to privacy and self governance and the need of children for protection. We are unable or unwilling to commit sufficient revenue to programs that combat abuse.

There is also the tendency among many professionals working with abused children and abusive parents to view the problem and solution through specialized cognitive lenses. Doctors, social workers, lawyers, psychologists, psychiatrists, counselors, and educators are all striving to defeat child abuse. However, for the most part, these professionals focus on the problem of child abuse from the perspective of their own field of expertise. The literature on child abuse is spread throughout journals from these fields and in more specialized journals within these fields. It would be impossible for any single person to remain abreast of the developments in all other disciplines working toward a solution to child abuse. But it is also patently clear that the solution to the problem of child abuse is not going to come from any one individual or discipline. It is going to take professionals and lay people from all disciplines, working with knowledge from all disciplines.

An interdisciplinary examination is important in the fight against child abuse. The more professionals know about all aspects of the problem of child sexual abuse, the better equipped they will be to do work within their area of expertise. It is important, for example, for lawyers, working in the midst of the current backlash against child sexual abuse claims, to understand that there is a long history of discovery and repression of childhood sexual abuse. With a full understanding of why this backlash is occurring, lawyers and social service professionals can continue to effectively work against child sexual abuse.

Child abuse is a complex social problem. The issues confronted in these volumes are interconnected and overlapping. It is my hope that bringing together the articles in this series will aid in the fight against child abuse by facilitating a multidisciplinary search for a solution.[5]

NOTES

1. Elizabeth Elmer, M.S.S., "Abused Young Children Seen in Hospitals," *Social Work* 5(4), pp. 98–102 (October 1960).

2. C. Henry Kempe, M.D., F.N. Silverman, M.D., Brandt F. Steele, M.D. and others, "The Battered-Child Syndrome," *JAMA* 181, pp. 17–24 (1962).

3. C. Henry Kempe, M.D., "Recent Developments in the Field of Child Abuse," *Child Abuse & Neglect* 3(1), pp. ix–xv (1979).

4. *The Random House Dictionary of the English Language*, unabridged edition.

5. The articles in this collection may give the impression that child abuse and neglect and child sexual abuse are uniquely American

phenomena. They are not. There is a wealth of similar articles from almost every country imaginable. American sources have been used mainly because of the space limitations and because understanding the American child welfare system is vital to developing a cure for the problem.

VOLUME INTRODUCTION

A report of child sexual abuse is often followed by court proceedings against the offender. The purpose of these proceedings is not to protect the child but to punish the offender. Courtrooms are not child-friendly, and for many children facing their abusers can be difficult. The dramatic rise in the number of children testifying at criminal cases against their abusers has forced judges, lawyers, social workers, psychologists, and other professionals to grapple with the legal and psychological issues raised by these child victim/witnesses.

The articles in this volume address several issues: (1) the effect of various legal proceedings on children; (2) the question of their competence to give testimony against their abusers; (3) legal reforms enacted in various states to minimize the courtroom trauma suffered by abuse victims; and (4) the responses of courts, including the United States Supreme Court, to some of these reforms.

Desmond K. Runyan and his colleagues (1988) undertook to study victims of sexual abuse with a five-month follow-up. They concluded from their study that "testimony in juvenile court may be beneficial for the child, whereas protracted criminal proceedings may have an adverse effect on the mental health of the victim."[1]

Many different modifications have been suggested and/or tried in order to help minimize the trauma to child victims/witnesses including modified courtrooms, videotaped depositions or interviews, extensive pretrial preparation of children for the courtroom experience, use of specially trained court workers or advocates for children, relaxation of the hearsay rule, faster disposition of sex abuse cases, and closed courtrooms.

John F. Tedesco and Steven V. Schnell (1987) re-examined the investigation procedures in such cases and suggested a reduction in the number of interviewers of child victims of abuse. They also found that "when children were required to testify in court, they more often viewed the process as harmful. This finding would suggest that a thorough study of courtroom procedures is in order.

The purpose of the studies would be to determine exactly what aspects of the courtroom procedures are most traumatic."[2]

Gary P. Melton (1985) reviewed several proposals for reform of criminal procedures and evidentiary rules to protect child victims from the trauma that the trial process is presumed to engender."[3] He acknowledged the necessity of examining legal procedures "with respect to their effect upon the child's emotional well-being." He concluded however, that "there is insufficient evidence to justify substantial modifications of criminal procedure on psychological grounds." He felt that there was "a need for a substantial research initiative to examine the effects of legal procedures on children, both to ensure that sexual abuse victims are not doubly victimized and, more generally, to provide the information needed to assist children in making use of, and adjusting to, legal procedures."[4]

Josephine A. Bulkley discussed special hearsay exceptions for complaints of child sexual abuse and videotaping or closed-circuit television procedures for taking a child's testimony outside the courtroom. Conflicts have arisen from these attempts to alleviate trauma to a child victim/witness by use of devices (screens or video or closed circuit television) that prevent the witness from seeing the accused/defendant.[5]

In *Coy v. Iowa*[6] the United States Supreme Court held that the use of a one-way mirror to screen the defendant from the victims'/witnesses' line of vision at trial was a violation of the defendant's sixth amendment right to confront witnesses against him. The decision was very controversial and received much attention in legal and other literature. Many scholars writing about *Coy* have concluded that the outcome of the decision was correct based on the specific facts of the case. However, they feel that the Court should have made it clear that the sixth amendment does not require face-to-face confrontation in all cases. Rather a case-specific showing of the necessity of the screening device to avoid trauma should be made before permitting its use.

Charles L. Hobson (1990) acknowledged that "our criminal justice system is geared toward guaranteeing a fair trial for the defendant, not towards minimizing the trauma to the victim" and suggested that "the harm our system does to the child can be minimized . . . while preserving the defendant's constitutional rights."[7] One major way that a child victim can be protected is through the appointment of counsel for a child victim whose "sole goal is to prevent psychological harm to the child."[8]

In addition to the question of the impact of testifying on the child witness, there has also been much written about the competence and credibility of child witnesses. Competency refers to the ability of a witness to provide reliable testimony. Credibility refers to whether or not the testimony is believed. Historically, the tendency has been to treat child testimony with skepticism.

> The law is skeptical of the capacity of children to observe and recall events accurately, to appreciate the need to tell the truth, and to resist the influence of other people. Children are commonly thought to have great difficulty distinguishing fantasy from reality, and to be readily confused by an exaggerated curiosity about sexuality. . . . For these reasons, the judge may assess the testimonial competence of the prospective child witness before the trial begins (voir dire).[9]

Gary P. Melton also presented the psychological issues and research underlying children's competency to testify. He concluded that "the developmental psychology literature gives little reason to be especially concerned about the reliability of children's testimony."[10]

Laura Lane (1987) discussed the abolition of the corroboration requirement for the testimony of sexually abused adult females in 1975 and the abolition of the corroboration requirement for child complainants in 1985. She applauded the legislature and courts for having abolished the corroboration requirement "and, in doing so, hav[ing] dismissed a discriminatory and antiquated rule based on faulty assumptions about the nature of sex related cases and complaints."[11] However, "despite formal abolition, corroboration remains an essential element in the successful prosecution of child sexual abuse cases because of the nature of the offense."[12]

Judy Yun (1983) discussed the use of a child's out-of-court or hearsay statements in sex abuse prosecutions. She argued "that the various approaches that have been taken by the courts to child hearsay statements in sex abuse cases are unsatisfactory," because these "approaches inadequately assess the probative value of child hearsay statements in sex abuse cases." Yun proposes instead "the adoption of an analysis similar to that embodied in a recently enacted Washington statute. The statute admits a child's out-of-court declaration if the time, content, and circumstances of the statement provide sufficient indicia of reliability."[13]

Despite all of this attention to these issues, however, we are a long way from finding that perfect balance that will protect children, preserve the constitutional rights of defendants, and serve the interests of society and justice.

NOTES

1. Desmond K. Runyan, Mark D. Everson, Gail A. Edelsohn, Wanda M. Hunter, and Martha L. Coulter, "Impact of Legal Intervention on Sexually Abused Children," *Journal of Pediatrics* 113(4), pp. 647–53, 647 (Oct 1988).

2. John F. Tedesco, and Steven V. Schnell, "Children's Reactions to Sex Abuse Investigation and Litigation," *Child Abuse & Neglect* 11(2), pp. 267–72, 271 (1987).

3. Gary P. Melton, "Sexually Abused Children and the Legal System: Some Policy Recommendations," *American Journal of Family Therapy* 13(1), pp. 61–67, 61 (Spr 1985).

4. Id. at 66.

5. Josephine A. Bulkley, "Evidentiary and Procedural Trends in State Legislation and Other Emerging Legal Issues in Child Sexual Abuse Cases," *Dickinson Law Review* 89, pp. 645–668 (1985).

6. *Coy v. Iowa*, 487 U.S. 1012 (1988).

7. Charles L. Hobson, "Representation of Victims," *Pacific Law Journal* 21, pp. 691–730, 691–92 (1990).

8. Id. at 728.

9. Barry Nurcombe, "The Child as Witness: Competency and Credibility," *Journal of the American Academy of Child Psychiatry* 25(4), p. 473 (Jul 1986).

10. Supra. n. 3 at 66.

11. Laura Lane, "The Effects of the Abolition of the Corroboration Requirement in Child Sexual Assault Cases," *Catholic University Law Review* 36, pp. 793–808, 808 (1987).

12. Id. at 794.

13. Judy Yun, "A Comprehensive Approach to Child Hearsay Statements In Sex Abuse Cases," *Columbia Law Review* 83, pp. 1745–66, 1746 (1983).

FURTHER READING

Berliner, Lucy, and Mary Kay Barbieri. "The Testimony of the Child Victim of Sexual Assault." *Journal of Social Issues* 40(2), pp. 125–37 (1984).

Goodman, Gail S. "The Child Witness: Conclusions and Future Directions for Research and Legal Practice." *Journal of Social Issues* 40(2), pp. 157–75 (1984).

Goodman, Gail S., et al. "The Emotional Effects of Criminal Court Testimony on Child Sexual Assault Victims: A Preliminary Report." *Issues in Criminological and Legal Psychology* 13, pp. 46–54 (1988).

Goodman, Gail S., and Vicki S. Helgeson. "Child Sexual Assault: Children's Memory and the Law." *University of Miami Law Review* 40, pp. 181–208 (1985).

Jones, David P. "The Child Witness in Court: Implications for Clinical and Legal Practice." *Issues in Criminological and Legal Psychology* 13, pp. 67–69 (1988).

Krieger, Marilyn J., and Julie Robbins. "The Adolescent Incest Victim and the Judicial System." *American Journal of Orthopsychiatry* 55(3), pp. 419–25 (1985).

Labai, David. "The Protection of the Child Victim of a Sexual Offense in the Criminal Justice System." *Wayne Law Review* 15, pp. 977–1031 (1969).

Melton, Gary B. "Child Witnesses and the First Amendment: A Psychological Dilemma." *Journal of Social Issues* 40(2), pp. 109–23 (1984).

Runyan, D.K., et al. "Impact of Legal Intervention on Sexually Abused Children." *Journal of Pediatrics* 113(4), pp. 647–53 (1988).

Slicer, et al. "Guidelines for Videotape Interviews in Child Sexual Abuse Cases." *American Journal of Forensic Psychology* 7(1), pp. 61–74 (1989).

Spodnick, Jonathan. "Competency of the Child Witness in Sexual Assault Cases: Examining the Constitutionality of Connecticut General Statute Section 54–86h." *University of Bridgeport Law Review* 10, pp. 135–63.

Watkins, Sallie A. "The Double Victim: The Sexually Abused Child and the Judicial System." *Child and Adolescent Social Work Journal* 7(1), pp. 29–42 (1990).

Preparation of the Sexually Abused Child for Court Testimony

HERBERT BAUER, MD

In the case of a sexually abused child, the main purpose of court intervention is not protection of the child but conviction and punishment of the offender. Trials are usually conducted in open, adult court, and the child's testimony is often a crucial part of the procedure. It has often been stated that the legal part of the whole drama, consisting of not only the court hearing but also the preceding interrogations by police, prosecuting attorney, defense attorney, and others, does more harm to the child than the actual sexual event.

On the other hand, virtually all of us acknowledge the fundamental right of the accused to face the accuser in open court; few, if any, would condone conviction on the basis of statements made by a "faceless" accuser. Attempts have been made in other countries to circumvent the use of children as witnesses in open court. In the United States, however, indirect testimony such as a taped or televised interview is largely unacceptable. The reason is obvious. The accusation is grave, such offenses are usually felonies, and punishment is severe, particularly if a young child is involved. Children are often incapable of resistance and also often incapable of distinguishing clearly between a demonstration of physical affection and sexual molestation. In view of these factors, every precaution must be taken to protect the rights of the defendant.

After pubescence, children are usually better able to judge propriety and impropriety of physical contact. Nevertheless, few of them are aware of the consequences of bringing a charge, particularly the role they will have to play in the legal proceedings. Furthermore, they often are distressed about the outcome, such as possible removal from home, breakup of family, and imprisonment of the offender.

As long as the present system prevails, it is safe to assume that children will continue to play an important role as witnesses in a trial that decides the guilt or innocence of a person who is usually well known to the child, frequently a close relative. Invariably, the trial adds procedural assault to the initial sexual assault, with the child carrying considerable responsibility for its outcome. Subsequent guilt feelings, distortions, and denials are frequently encountered; such psychiatric residuals require treatment and emotional support.

Rather than wait for such ill-fated consequences, there is one preventive step that is often helpful in forestalling what may be called posttrial disease, namely adequate preparation of the sexually abused child for testimony. Obviously, such preparation must be adjusted according to the level of

---

Dr. Bauer is Clinical Professor, School of Medicine, University of California, Davis, California.

1

development of the involved child, from the prelogical toddler to the mature adolescent.

Reports of molestation of infants are infrequent, and usually no direct testimony is required; medical testimony is applicable only in cases where physical injuries are noticeable, and psychiatric support focuses on the family as a whole. Therefore, no special preparation of the child is needed.

In preschool children and those attending primary grades, a detailed description of courtroom procedures is helpful. Fear and avoidance of the unfamiliar setting can be averted by taking the child to the building in which the hearing is to be held. If possible, the child should meet in an informal atmosphere the persons who will do the questioning, although the subject to be discussed need not be mentioned on that first visit. The main purpose is to acquaint the child with the principal participants in the trial.

Many judges are willing to meet a child in chamber for a friendly chat, to demonstrate their black robe, and to assure the child of the protection of the court whenever needed. The judge also has the prerogative of interviewing the child alone rather than in open court, and the judge may certainly clear the courtroom of spectators and other persons not directly involved in the case. For this reason, it is of inestimable value for psychiatrists and other professional persons supporting the child to be personally acquainted with attorneys and judges involved in the case. None of them want to harm the child, and most of them will be glad to receive suggestions on behalf of the child as long as they do not interfere with the rules of the court and have no prejudicial implications.

Latency age children are much more frequently involved in "sex cases." With them, role playing in preparation for the court procedure is of great value. In posing the questions likely to come up during the hearing, either in court or an attorney's office, it is necessary to avoid any intimation, however subtle, about what the "right" answers might be. Any such intrusion on the part of the "helper" could be discovered later and might invalidate the child's statement.

During role play, both the child and the person assisting with preparation should change roles so the child has the opportunity to look at the situation "through the other person's eyes." Thus, the child should be asked to play the role of the alleged offender and of other persons, particularly family members whose action or lack of action may be significant for the child. Similarly, the person conducting the "mock trial" should assume the role of defense attorney as well as that of prosecuting attorney; this technique may avoid some of the confusion often resulting from the child being asked the same question in a different way in an effort to elicit different answers or descriptions of the alleged event.

Because matters of sexual content are to be discussed, it is important to use the child's own anatomical vocabulary; at the same time, it is helpful to mention "adult" synonyms that may be used during cross-examination. Children are reluctant to admit that they do not understand some expression and are likely to respond as though they understood what was said. There-

2

fore, it is helpful during role playing to interject occasionally the phrase "I don't understand what you mean, please explain it to me." If the child can be taught to use this inquiry whenever needed, and without fear, many a misunderstanding can be avoided.

Adolescent witnesses, although they are still legal minors, will be treated essentially like adult witnesses in court or during a deposition in an attorney's office. In preparation, it helps to explain that, for legal purposes, detailed questions will be asked and specific answers will be expected of them. They need to know that their statements may be challenged and that their truthfulness will be judged by their consistency. Role play might include a hypothetical dialogue with the defendant pleading good intentions and pointing out the dire consequences for all concerned if the jury renders a verdict of guilty.

Obviously, there may be serious objections to this recommended procedure. If the person preparing the child is a physician, a nurse, a psychologist, a social worker, or any other kind of child advocate, the legal objection might be that in an effort to protect the child from unpleasantness, such preparation tends to modify the child's original statements and may put the testimony into a different focus. For example, a young girl initially enraged over her father's sexual advances and willing to testify against him, might change her attitude after role playing during which she gains better insight into the motivation of his or her own behavior and might choose to modify her testimony accordingly. A young male victim of a homosexual attack may experience a change of sentiment when the interviewer, playing the role of the assailant, asks mockingly, "But we did have fun doing it, didn't we?"

Role playing by the victim does carry the risk of a change in attitude during the trial. Even if an attorney, aware of the legal pitfalls, were to undertake such preparation, there is a possibility that a child's testimony might be swayed.

What, then, is the proper course? Leave the child unprepared and allow the trial to proceed, regardless of consequences? Many would contend that this is the more desirable course because attorneys and judges will treat children with tact and understanding and will make every effort to avoid undue hardship; in any case, untainted testimony is paramount, and the child's emotional well-being, important as it is, has to be of secondary priority.

Or should we prepare the child in the manner outlined, giving emotional support before and after the court appearance, even at the risk of modifying the child's attitude and thereby tampering with a previously unbiased, or at least differently biased, testimony? I support this second approach and contend that interference with due process of law as a result of such preparation is exceedingly unlikely, as long as it is clear the knowledge imparted is informational only, and under no circumstances would the "right" answers be imputed. This procedure would safeguard the principle that should underlie any such event: Support of the child's best interests. □

3

When Systems Fail: *Protecting the*

Victim of Child Sexual Abuse

by VINCENT J. FONTANA

Child fatalities, retardation syndromes and psychological damage resulting from child maltreatment provide glaring evidence that systems have failed these innocent victims. Children are being victimized by our human frailties, and by our lack of commitment and concern.

What is the "system"? As used here, the system consists of a conglomerate of people with various responsibilities and expertise. When we speak of a child protective system in a community, we think of a child protective agency, or an office of Special Services for Children, or the Society for the Prevention of Cruelty to Children. In reality, the child protective system of any community encompasses the board of education, the police department, the district attorney, the medical establishment, voluntary private child care agencies, the foster care system, the family court and last, but not least, the child protective agency. The entire system is manned by people—some more caring, trained and dedicated than others. Failures in the system result as a natural consequence of large caseloads, too much paper work, faulty supervision and poor judgement.

If the inadequacies and failures of the system are to be analyzed and documented, the entire child protective system must be appraised. To criticize and find remedies for one part of the system while ignoring the others is an unfulfilling exercise in futility, besides being a waste of money and effort.

The daily frustrations encountered in dealing with the protection of young children clearly indicate that blame should be placed on all parts of the system. The lack of coordination, communication and cooperation between and among responsible agencies is the source of the trouble.

In the area of child sexual abuse, the failures in the system are insidious but nonetheless damaging. Unfortunately, these failures are not due to lack of knowledge but to failure to act and to make basic changes based on what is known.

Disagreement over the definition of child sexual abuse, problems involved in observing and documenting private events and the stigma associated with sexual abuse impede efforts to intervene and effectively assist. In addition, sexual abuse is substantially different from physical abuse of children in etiology, occurrence and reporting. There is a lack of clarity regarding what is reportable as suspected sexual abuse. Laws speak of "reasonable cause"—a standard legal phrase implying a lower threshold of information on which to act than the "probable cause" standard governing police intervention in suspected crime.

Professionals in the fields of medicine, education and social work require operational definitions of "reasonable cause" for suspected child abuse situations. Working out clearly defined criteria for reporting sexual abuse will assist in the prevention of some of the failures attributed to the system.

Although there is a tendency to equate intrafamilial child sexual abuse and the sexual victimization of children by strangers, the two are very different and require very different intervention approaches. In intrafamilial cases, which is the focus here, the relationship between the child and the offending adult exists in a far wider and deeper context than the victimization act itself, and violence or threats of violence are rare. This adds enormously to the complexity of the situation, and it means that the event and the intervention are likely to have a greater impact on the child and family

14

4

By definition, an obvious and important goal of intervention is amelioration of the consequences of intrafamilial child sexual abuse and the future protection of its victims. Achieving this goal depends upon the ability to alter the personal or environmental factors that were the cause of the abuse. Unfortunately, there is no consensus on treatment goals or treatment approaches. There is considerable disagreement about the basic issue of punishment or treatment of the abuser, with a growing emphasis on a combination of both approaches in a modified form. The long-term effect of these approaches upon the child is unclear and unknown.

Many clinicians and researchers assert that punishment through the criminal justice system is ineffective. They note that an offender may be returned home untreated and that the emphasis on proving the case in criminal court overlooks the child's needs and subjects him or her to the dictates of prosecutory advocacy. Even worse, criminal prosecution subjects an older child to greater stress and tends to make the child feel personally responsible for the parent's imprisonment.

Although some report that criminal prosecution creates resistance in the family as family members rally to the father's defense, others state that prosecution encourages the offender to seek change, thus strengthening his commitment to treatment. Giarretto advocates the use of the criminal justice system in a controlled way that avoids destruction of the family and does not lead to imprisonment.[1] In this approach, the parent is encouraged to turn himself or herself over voluntarily to law enforcement officials and to submit to criminal jurisdiction with the knowledge that imprisonment usually will be avoided through cooperation and adherence to the treatment regimen. To accomplish this purpose, other researchers advocate the use of a family, juvenile or other civil court.

Related to issues surrounding the use of the criminal justice system are the strong feelings usually expressed by social work and medical professionals that the criminal justice system is not sensitive to the needs of the child. Schultz points out that most police and prosecutors have no training in non-damaging ways to interview children, lack understanding of the child's psychosexual stage of development and tend to use adversary approaches appropriate for adults.[2] Sgroi notes that "this is, unfortunately, equally true of child protective service agencies—the workers who investigate sexual abuse cases usually lack the specialized skills, experience, and supervision required to deal with the delicate, volatile, and highly demanding child protective problem yet to be identified."[3] Similarly, Brandt notes that the trauma experienced by children and families can be exacerbated in hospitals or clinics.[4] This issue of interrogation is critical because of its impact on the child victim; interventions which add to the victimization of the child have no true protective value or function.

The need for sensitive handling of the child applies to all systems, but its importance has not yet reached everyone who is likely to respond to a child victim of intrafamilial sexual abuse. While this issue has been raised by the handful of professionals who specialize in the treatment of sexual abuse or incest, such specialists are likely to be among the last to see the child, often some time after identification or discovery of the incident and the initiation of legal intervention. Many more must be reached with information on normal psychosexual child development and correct, age-appropriate ways to talk to a child who may be a victim of sexual abuse.

While there is probably general agreement on the techniques to use, a major difficulty is the uncertainty or disbelief that many feel when a child reports being sexually abused, either directly or indirectly. This is understandable, but it must be overcome. If a child reports being sexually abused, the person in whom the child confides should make a report and give the protective service professionals a chance to assess the child's statements. Under the requirements of state reporting laws, such a statement is sufficient to make a report—to give one reasonable cause to suspect that abuse occurred. A child's statement about being sexually abused is almost universally true; children generally do not lie, fantasize or hallucinate about being sexually abused.

Moreover, there is a simple test that can be applied in many cases, especially with children below the age of puberty. Very young victims of sexual abuse tend to possess a level of detailed knowledge about sexual practices beyond the norm for their age; their sexual awareness is "age inappropriate," a sign that someone has initiated them. Sexually provocative mannerisms in young children are usually an

Vincent J. Fontana, M.D., is medical director and pediatrician-in-chief, New York Foundling Hospital Center for Parent-Child Development, New York City, and professor of clinical pediatrics, New York University School of Medicine. His article is based on a presentation at the Third National Conference on Sexual Victimization of Children, held in Washington, D.C. last April.

5

example of age inappropriate behavior. Young children who report sexual abuse should not be dismissed when they act sexually provocative. We have begun to be aware of the bias such behavior frequently creates when adults report being raped. It is even more impermissible in cases involving children. It is important that this point of view be accepted by those who are in a position to deal with children who may be the victims of sexual abuse.

Sensitive handling of the child includes any medical examination that may be performed in an attempt to document and diagnose the possibility of sexual abuse. I am confident that the professionalism of physicians and other medical workers, if supported by adequate training, will assure that the examination does not in itself become another trauma for the child victim. We cannot assume, however, that such training has been provided, and steps must be taken to make sure that it is given as part of medical training in school, in residency and in continuing educational settings.

The literature on the effects of intrafamilial child sexual abuse indicates a strong need for mental health services. Indeed, most of the effects reported are psychological or emotional, with behavioral rather than physical consequences. There seems to be little possibility of long-range physical consequences, but a great possibility of long-range emotional and behavioral damage. There is no debate on whether mental health services are needed—the debate is limited to the type, such as individual, group, conjoint or family therapy, and the correct sequence.

Family therapy has been recommended as the treatment of choice. However, some objections raised to using this approach as the primary one include parental refusal to cooperate, the impact of raising some issues—such as sexual problems between the parents—in front of the child, and the traditional stance of family therapists that all are equally responsible for the situation under treatment. Individual therapy is strongly supported by a number of clinicians, sometimes in conjunction with other types, because it gives a child the greatest chance to ventilate those feelings which might later engender the most trouble.

The difficulties of providing mental health services to victims of intrafamilial child sexual abuse, however, are no different from those encountered in obtaining such services for child protective cases in general. A study conducted for the National Institute of Mental Health pointed out that "mental health professionals are accustomed to working with individuals who are 'motivated' and who actively seek help"; they generally do not have outreach strategies for highly resistant families, and their scheduling practices cannot handle families who frequently miss appointments or come late.[5] Another study of mental health services for abused children found that improvements were dependent upon two conditions: parents who were willing to allow the child to change and to change themselves, and a therapist who was able to influence the environment, such as the school setting and relationships with others, and help the child within the playroom.[6]

Such obstacles to treatment must be understood and corrected if the mental health system is to help child victims of abuse. The likelihood that such treatment will be long-term may conflict with the current emphasis on "cost-effective"—that is, cheap—short-term approaches.

Another issue that impacts heavily on the child is whether he or she is removed from the home as a result of the interventions that follow disclosure of the abuse. Clinicians and researchers disagree on whether or not the child or the adult offender should be removed

16

6

from the home during treatment, or for longer thereafter. Some advocate separation of the offending parent from the child, usually forcing the parent to live elsewhere during initial treatment. Although, as Coleman notes, the police usually remove the child to preserve evidence and to prevent the child from being pressured to change his or her story,[7] a number of researchers recommend against removing the child unless there is some compelling reason because it may be difficult to reunite the child and the family later. Zaphiris, who believes that removal of the child may contribute to his or her victimization by exacerbating feelings of blame for the incest, recommends removal only if the incest is a symptom of other serious pathology, which he believes is seldom the case, or if it is concurrent with physical abuse.[8] Still others believe that removal of the child is ineffective under any circumstances, hence of no purpose.

The debate over the best or most appropriate intervention into intrafamilial child sexual abuse cases makes at least one thing clear: the chance that the intervention, and the system offering it, may fail, or even harm, the child victim is greater than we wish to acknowledge.

The literature offers conflicting advice on the relative merits of the social service and criminal justice approaches to intrafamilial child sexual abuse, and it offers equally conflicting advice on the most appropriate or necessary immediate intervention. While the best answer might be that such decisions should depend upon the specifics of each case, policy decisions in many states are increasing the involvement of the criminal justice approach.

A recent California case, for example, has received widespread attention. Media accounts gave the impression that a child was sent to jail for refusing to testify against her stepfather, who was reported for sexual abuse after voluntarily seeking therapy. California is one state that uses the criminal justice system to "encourage" an offending adult to seek treatment. However, the fact that it was necessary to "encourage" the stepfather *after* he sought treatment indicates that the intent of the California system was not carried through. But the case has wider implications in all states that are promoting greater use of the criminal justice system to gain leverage over offending adults.

The California child was "sent to jail" because the criminal justice system followed one of its usual procedures for dealing with recalcitrant material witnesses, who are usually incarcerated to "encourage" them to be more cooperative. Unfortunately, in this case the witness was a child and the victim of the "criminal complaint." Clearly, what is an appropriate method of dealing with an adult became a savagely inappropriate method of responding to a terrified child.

Law enforcement officials have an obligation to define and create safeguards to protect children from techniques which have been developed to deal with adults but which result in serious damage when applied to a child. This will not be an easy task because it confronts established methods that reflect standard practices which have evolved from dealing with adult defendants and witnesses in criminal trials.

Methods must be found to protect child victims from further emotional abuse. Testimony videotaped for later replay or taken in the judge's chambers with key participants present are techniques well worth exploring.

A long delay between steps in the judicial process seriously limits a child's ability to testify and inflicts further hurt to the child. Children have difficulty remembering. With the passage of time, details become indistinct. Investigations must be handled with speed and without interruption in an effort to minimize the effects of the failures of our difficult and complicated legal system. With a speedy, coordinated investigatory and prosecutory effort, further psychological trauma to the child and family will be decreased.

In formulating a set of guidelines for investigating child sexual abuse, two distinct lines of approach must be considered: law enforcement and child protective services. In law enforcement, the purpose of the investigation is to obtain evidence for criminal prosecution; in child protective services, the purpose is to assess the risk to the child in order to take protective action and offer treatment. There is an urgent need for cooperation between law enforcement and child protective agencies to integrate their approach toward both the child victim and the adult offender.

The attention given to child sexual abuse is recent. It is, perhaps, the last type of child abuse to be recognized for the serious problem it is. This attention comes at a time of dwindling resources for treatment services—an experience unlike the growth in services which paralleled the increased attention to child abuse and neglect in the 1970s. This is unfortunate, because it increases the likelihood that the new attention will not result in increased resources for treatment. In fact, it may serve to further impede efforts as resources for dealing with child abuse and neglect in general are stretched to respond to increased reports of child sexual abuse.

Nationally, the protective service caseload is burgeoning, and evidence is accumulating that resources for staff and services have not kept pace, causing child protective services in this country to be

functioning at less than acceptable levels. Yet we must continue efforts to improve the protection of all neglected and abused children, regardless of the problems we adults encounter in providing and securing the help they need. Limitations of fiscal resources or lack of knowledge must not become another source of victimization for the children in need of our protection.

These matters are far from cut and dried—they are real problems and issues; they are the reasons why systems fail. They must be systematically studied in order to develop standardized medical, legal and social procedures for dealing with child sexual abuse. A unified effort at networking by these involved groups is urgent if we are to prevent further hurt to child victims. ■

¹H. Giarretto, "Humanistic Treatment of Father-Daughter Incest," in R. R. Helfer and C. H. Kempe (Eds.), *Child Abuse and Neglect: The Family and the Community*, Cambridge, Ballinger, 1976.

²L. G. Schultz, "The Child Victim: Social, Psychological, and Legal Perspectives," *Child Welfare*, Mar. 1973.

³S. M. Sgroi, "Introduction: A National Needs Assessment for Protecting Child Victims of Sexual Assault," in A. W. Burgess, A. N. Groth, L. L. Holmstrom and S. M. Sgroi (Eds.), *Sexual Assault of Children and Adolescents*, Lexington, Mass., Lexington Books, 1978.

⁴R. S. T. Brandt, "Manual on Sexual Abuse and Misuse of Children," Boston, Mass., Judge Baker Guidance Center, undated.

⁵M. B. Holmes, et al., *Child Abuse and Neglect Programs: Practice and Theory*, National Institute of Mental Health, U.S. Dept. of Health, Education and Welfare, Pub. No. (ADM) 77-344, Washington, D.C., 1977.

⁶P. Beezley, et al., "Psychotherapy," in H. Martin (Ed.), *The Abused Child: A Multi-Disciplinary Approach to Developmental Issues and Treatment*, Cambridge, Ballinger Publishing Co., 1976.

⁷P. F. Coleman, "Incest: Family Treatment Model," Pierce County Child Protective Services, Washington State Department of Social Services, undated.

⁸A. G. Zaphiris, "Incest: The Family with Two Known Victims," Denver, American Humane Association, undated.

The Adolescent as a Witness in a Case of Incest: Assessment and Outcome

LAWRENCE CLAMAN, M.D., JANICE C. HARRIS, A.C.S.W., BARTON E. BERNSTEIN, J.D., AND ROBERT LOVITT, PH.D.

Children who have been victimized by sexual abuse are being asked regularly to testify against their sexual perpetrator. It is important to know whether some sexually abused children can testify competently without long-term negative psychological effects. This paper is a case study of a 14-year-old adolescent girl who suffered repeated sexual abuse from her grandfather. She was evaluated in a child witness project and given trial preparation. Her performance as a witness was assessed at her two trial appearances. She was evaluated after each court appearance and by phone 15 months later. A discussion of the legal and psychological assessment issues in the use of such children as witnesses is included. *Journal of the American Academy of Child Psychiatry*, 25, 4:457–461, 1986.

With the increasing reported incidence of child sexual abuse, children are being asked regularly to testify before a grand jury, in criminal trials against their sexual perpetrator, and in civil suits relative to termination of parental rights. What is the effect of a child testifying in court on his or her psychological adjustment? What is the risk of long-lasting emotional trauma? Bernstein et al. (1982) suggested that children as young as 6 years of age may have the cognitive, moral and psychosocial maturity to testify competently. They stated that such children, with the help of trial preparation and appropriate legal support in the courtroom, may be able to testify without experiencing undue stress or negative psychological effects. This would certainly apply to adolescents.

Although there are reports in the literature of children testifying competently in court, there are no reports of children who have been evaluated specifically as prepared child witnesses, e.g., who received preparation to testify and who were assessed in the courtroom regarding their performance. Nor are there reports of child witnesses seen in a follow-up evaluation to determine the effect of this experience.

This report will present the case of a 14-year-old

Received Feb. 11, 1985; accepted with revisions Mar. 27, 1985.

Dr. Claman is Associate Professor of Clinical Psychiatry, University of Texas Health Science Center at Dallas. Mrs. Harris was formerly Child Placement Caseworker, Dallas County Department of Human Resources. She is currently Director, Victim Services, Mothers Against Drunk Drivers. Mr. Bernstein is Adjunct Associate Professor of Psychiatry, University of Texas Health Science Center at Dallas; and Adjunct Associate Professor, Graduate School of Social Work, University of Texas at Arlington. Dr. Lovitt is Associate Professor of Clinical Psychology, University of Texas Health Science Center at Dallas.

Reprints may be requested from Dr. Claman, Psychiatry Department, UTHSCD, 5323 Harry Hines Boulevard, Dallas, TX 75235.

0002-7138/86/2504-0457 $02.00/0 © 1986 by the American Academy of Child Psychiatry.

adolescent girl who suffered incest from her grandfather. She was evaluated in a child witness assessment project, assessed in terms of her performance when she testified in two separate trials, and seen in follow-up evaluation. A discussion of the legal and psychological assessment issues involved in evaluating the child as a witness in cases of sexual abuse as well as a review of the relevant literature follows.

Legal Assessment Issues

Is there a basis in law for recommending the child as a possible witness? Can a child be qualified as a witness? Early common law disqualified witnesses from testifying for reasons of infancy, mental derangement and marriage relationship. These disqualifications were eliminated by the model code of evidence (Ladd, 1942). No rule now excludes children of any specific age from testifying (McCormick, 1972). The traditional test for the competency of a witness (oath capacity) is:

1. Does the child have the intelligence and capacity to provide facts about a case? (*Jackson* v. *Commonwealth*, 1946).

2. Does the child feel a duty to tell the truth, and can the child separate truth from falsehood? (McCormick, 1972).

The judge will decide whether the child is competent to be a witness. This is usually assessed within the contexts of age and mental maturity.

Melton (1980) has written that the state's interest in prosecuting child molesters "may come into conflict with its obligation as *parens patriae* to protect dependent minors" from undesirable psychological trauma. Within this context, a district attorney must decide on the value of using a child's testimony to win a case. Where the child's testimony will provide credible evidence, the district attorney must then decide if the child can be an effective, persuasive and believable witness.

Melton (1981) suggested that adherence to the truth is not sufficient to establish legal competency. The child must also have the cognitive skills adequate to comprehend the event witnessed and to communicate memories of the event in response to questions at a trial. The trial often occurs many months after the event. Furthermore, the child must be able to maintain her verbal skills under the stress of responding to questions from adult authority figures who may try to shape her responses. Thus level of suggestability is an important factor.

Other factors the district attorney must consider in assessing the child as a possible witness include the child's personal appearance, ability to relate positively, capacity to talk and express self clearly, and willingness to testify. In addition, the willingness of the managing conservator (custodial parent, state agency or guardian) to sanction and support the child testifying is important.

Psychological Assessment Issues

Psychological issues pertain to the question of capacity to testify and cope with the stress of testifying without additional negative psychological effects. At the time of psychological evaluation, the child will already have been exposed to the stress of interacting with the legal system. She will have described the details of the sexual abuse to police, medical and social work personnel, and sometimes to a prosecuting attorney or the grand jury. She will most likely be under the supervision of a child abuse agency with court legal support under state child abuse statutes. And she may already be involved with her family in a treatment program. Burgess and Holstrom (1975) in their extensive study of assault victims at Boston City Hospital emphasized two aspects of the stress experienced by child victims and their families. The first was the child having to tell the story of the assault repeatedly to authorities. The second was the prolonged legal process resulting in extended family preoccupation with the assault and its legal outcome.

An important factor in psychological assessment is having in mind the courtroom situation to be faced. Appearing in court and undergoing direct and cross-examination is stressful for a child even with good preparation and legal support. For example, testifying in front of a jury in a criminal trial on sexual abuse can be more stressful than testifying in front of a judge in chambers in a civil trial on physical abuse. In some states such as Texas (Texas Family Code 11.21), direct examination in court is no longer necessary since state law provides for the use of videotape testimony from the child to provide evidence. However, the child must still be available for cross-examination, which can be especially stressful. Attempts by the defense attorney to discredit the child's testimony may make the child feel guilty. An additional stress is that testimony is in front of the defendant with whom the child has had intimate, conflicted and often traumatic experiences. Finally, in testifying the child is assuming some responsibility and blame for trying to punish the offender.

Considering all of these factors, there needs to be very important reasons for the child, managing conservator and the prosecuting attorney to ask the child to face the stress of being a witness. In carrying out a child witness assessment, the mental health professionals and the lawyer must have this point of view clearly in mind, and consider the best short and long range interest of the child.

The psychological assessment of the child must focus on evaluating the child's cognitive, moral, and psychosocial maturity. In particular, it is important to assess the capacity of the child to testify in court in a factual way about the offense as witnessed or experienced. Terr (1980) has discussed the characteristics necessary for the child to be a competent and believable witness as well as cope with the stress of testifying. These include the consistency of the child's account of the events, degree of denial, degree of perceptual and cognitive distortion, ability to deal with loyalty conflicts, and articulateness.

Case Report

L.H. was evaluated in a child witness assessment project which assessed eight girls ranging in age from 3½ to 14. She was the only girl of three who testified in court with whom it was possible to carry out a follow-up evaluation. The child witness assessment team included a social worker, a psychiatrist, a psychologist and an attorney. At the initial assessment staffing conference, 12 witness-specific questions were answered (Table 1). An initial child witness rating was made based on the interviews of the three mental health professionals and the psychological testing. Trial preparation was then carried out. The child's actual testimony in court was observed and rated on a performance rating scale. A follow-up interview was carried out within a month of the court appearance to assess the psychological effect of testifying.

L.H. is a 14-year-old adolescent girl living with her natural parents who experienced fondling, oral sex (fellatio) and one event of coitus by her maternal grandfather over a 7-year-period from age 4 to 11. She was living with her natural parents but was frequently taken by her parents to visit her grandfather. She was

TABLE 1

Witness-Specific Questions

1. Child's appearance and personal appeal
2. Capacity to relate positively
3. Capacity to talk and express self clearly
4. Ability to describe child abuse experience
5. Consistency of child's verbal story of child abuse experience
6. Adequacy of child's understanding of family situation
7. Capacity to tell truth
8. Willingness to testify
9. Ability to deal with conflict of loyalty in testifying
10. Ability and willingness of managing conservator to support child testifying
11. Ability of prosecuting attorney to support and protect the child as a witness
12. Assessment of whether the child testifying is in the child's best interests

well-developed physically, had a pleasant appearance and dressed neatly. During the psychiatric assessment interview, she related consistently in an open, friendly, cooperative manner. She expressed herself clearly. Her thinking was very much at the formal operations stage. Her overall mood and attitude about life was positive. She was satisfied with her life and was reality-oriented, but constricted in utilizing or expressing fantasy. She had a good self-image and accepted being a girl. She nonetheless had some derogatory feelings about herself. She had good ego adaptive skills. These included good school performance, and good social adjustment with peers and adults both at school and at home, where she played an important housekeeping role. She also had appropriate interests and skills in sports and other activities. Her most prominent adaptive pattern was responding positively to life, which involved minimizing problems and angry feelings and using denial as a significant defense. On psychological testing, her intelligence estimate was in the average range. On the Rorschach, she evidenced significant feelings of anxiety and insecurity as well as feelings of inferiority and inadequacy. On the testing, she also appeared inhibited and constricted in her relations with others. In her witness-specific assessment, she was able to discuss her sexual abuse experience with her maternal grandfather in an adequate, reasonably open fashion, but avoided talking about the oral sex and intercourse part of it. Her DSM-III diagnosis was Adjustment Disorder with mixed emotional features. Her initial child witness rating was 1 (good prospective witness). She was strongly supported in her willingness to testify by her mother and father.

Trial preparation was carried out as a concerted effort of her caseworker and the prosecuting attorney. Her caseworker provided group therapy weekly for L.H. and approximately eight other adolescent girls her age who had been sexually abused by someone in their family. Those group members who had previously testified shared their experiences with the others. The girls were advised of "tricks" often used by defense attorneys and role played testifying with the caseworker playing the role first of the prosecuting attorney and then the district attorney. Anxieties and fears were ventilated and a rational approach was suggested for coping with these feelings. The caseworker or L.H.'s parents took her to the prosecuting attorney's office twice for trial preparation. The prosecuting attorney questioned her, gave her an idea of the scope of his questioning, and advised her on basic courtroom procedure. On the day of the trial, her parents as well as the caseworker were present for emotional support.

Following the initial criminal court jury trial, L.H. was assessed to be an effective witness in all categories of the rating scale by the project caseworker. The defense attorney did not cross-examine her and told the project caseworker afterwards that the longer she was on the witness stand, the more damage was done to his client. The project caseworker stated, "I am probably biased, but she was terrific—calm, credible, and very descriptive." L.H.'s grandfather was found guilty by the jury, but shortly thereafter a mistrial was pronounced. This was due to a legal technicality of the case having been tried under a statute that became out-of-date in terms of the sentencing requirement 1 week before the case was filed.

L.H. was seen in a follow-up interview by the project psychiatrist 13 days after the first trial. She said testifying went well, but she was upset about having to testify again. She said it was easier to tell her story in the actual trial than it had been before the grand jury. She was nervous, but the district attorney had asked questions she was prepared for. She was not cross-examined, but felt she could have answered the questions asked. She did not mind testifying in front of her grandfather. He was just there. She was angry about the mistrial, but she understood and explained the change in the law. She did not like testifying again, but felt she would do alright. She was still angry at her grandfather (for sexually abusing her), and reported having felt especially angry when he stood up in court and pleaded not guilty. She felt her parents were very supportive of her testifying. When her mother was interviewed informally after the follow-up interview, she expressed angry feelings about the unfairness of the legal technicality which forced her daughter to testify again. She felt the 6-month trial delay placed unnecessary pressure on her daughter. She reported that a month before the trial her daughter had an acute anxiety attack when she was home alone at night. L.H. had heard somebody knock on the living room window and thought it was her grand-

11

father when in fact it was her cousin. She broke down and cried for more than an hour, was held by her mother, and openly expressed her fear of her grandfather. During the period of the trial delay, L.H. also had nightmares during which she saw her grandfather's face right next to her and he said "I'm going to get you."

The second criminal court trial took place 6 weeks after the first, and was before the judge and not a jury. Her grandfather was again found guilty. His sentencing hearing occurred 4 days later and L.H. was present but did not testify. At the second trial, L.H. was assessed to be an excellent witness in all categories of the rating scale by an adult cousin, who was also present at the first trial. This person evaluated L.H. because the project caseworker was not allowed in the courtroom on this occasion. L.H. was felt to be an even more effective witness than she had been at the first trial because once on the stand she was less nervous and the very credible. She did not cry. Her grandfather was found guilty and sentenced to 7 years in prison. He eventually went to prison after an unsuccessful appeal. After the sentencing trial, L.H. wanted desperately to confront her grandfather and was allowed to see him in jail. She asked "Why did you do it?" He responded "No comment" and refused to talk further. This hurt her very much. She was also very upset a few days later when she learned that an appeal had been filed and he was out of jail again on an appeal bond.

L.H. was seen in a follow-up interview 9 days after the sentencing trial. She was assessed to be making a good overall adjustment in her life without significant negative psychological effects from her trial experiences. She said it was a relief to have the whole court experience behind her. She was tired of having to talk about the upcoming trial all the time at home. She said she was more nervous and less confident of herself in testifying the second time and uncertain why. In the first trial she felt she told the sexual abuse story without much strain. During the second trial she did not feel like telling the story again, but felt she told it alright anyway. She was less nervous testifying before the judge than before the jury. This was because there were not people in the jury looking at her and judging her. It did not bother her that her grandfather was there. She looked at him a number of times and said he seemed like anybody else in the audience. When she was cross-examined, the lawyer asked her many yes and no questions which made her mad, but she tried not to show this. He asked if she had not imagined the sexual abuse experience, or made up a story to please her mother because her mother was mad at her grandfather? She said these questions made her angry and that she would never do anything like that. She said it seemed the cross-examination lasted 15–20 minutes when it probably lasted only 6–7 minutes. When her grandfather was found guilty, she was glad he was sentenced to 7 years in prison even though at age 67 he might die in jail. She felt the whole experience of preparing to be a witness and testifying along with her group counseling had made her stronger than other girls.

Following the trial, L.H. continued to be seen in her therapy group for 2–3 months. For a short period of time she developed some adjustment difficulties including a drop in her school grades, engaged in some promiscuous sexual activity with two boys, experimented with marijuana, and started lying to her mother about her activities. However, she discussed these problems openly in her therapy group and appeared to value the input of the other girls and her caseworker. Following the closing of L.H.'s protective services case including her group therapy, she answered a letter from the project caseworker with a letter which had the following closing comments: "I'm doing fine. No more nightmares, no more pot, no more failing grades. I decided I deserve better." This appeared to indicate her restored self-confidence.

L.H. was reached by telephone 15 months after the second trial. The psychiatrist spoke first to her mother, who said L.H. was doing well in school and in the other areas of her life. She had no special problems. She still talked openly on occasion about her grandfather and her experience with him. He had died 3 weeks previously of cancer while still in jail. L.H. was said to feel more relaxed about her grandfather now since she was no longer afraid of his getting out of jail. The psychiatrist then spoke to L.H., who was now 16 years old. She said she was doing well in school academically and in her social life. She continued to play in the band. She was glad she testified against her grandfather and got him sent to jail. She planned to go to college and become a lawyer so that she "can put those people in jail." This appeared to indicate continued good adjustment, but that the experience with her grandfather and testifying against him was something she still had to defend against and that it had affected her current occupation goal.

Discussion

The case presented clearly indicates that L.H. experienced considerable stress even though she was an adolescent, assessed to have the capacity to be a competent witness, received appropriate trial preparation, and was given adequate support at the time of both trials in which she testified. The prolonged legal process resulted in continued preoccupation with the sexual abuse experience and its legal outcome. This was clearly a significant stress for L.H. and her family. Her being involved in a sexual abuse group helped prepare her to testify and helped her work out her feelings about herself. In testifying, she felt she mastered a stressful task, which enhanced her self-esteem and sense of adequacy. In particular she faced her grandfather both in court and in private after the second trial and said he had wronged her, and he was found guilty and sent to jail. She experienced some short-term adjustment difficulties after the two trials. She continued to be fearful 15 months later of her grandfather harming her, and this effected her occupation choice in wanting to become a lawyer who saw that such people were punished. The importance of her having the support of her family, her caseworker, and the district attorney was evident in her achieving a positive outcome.

This case illustrates certain psychological stresses reported in the literature which sexually abused adolescents may experience when they are involved in a trial and are used as witnesses. As Burgess and Holstrom (1975) state, a major stress for the adolescent victim and his or her family is the prolonged legal process resulting in extended family preoccupation with the assault and its legal outcome. In terms of testifying and being cross-examined, there is the stress of coping with the defense attorney's tactics, which Weiss and Burg (1982) state will most likely involve trying to prove the adolescent is unable to distinguish reality from fantasy, has a poor memory, is confused, and makes inconsistent statements. And finally there is the stress stated by Gager and Schur (1976) of the defense attorney trying to discredit the adolescent's testimony as a deliberate falsification of a story because of malice.

It is hoped that this case report will support the orientation that a sexually abused adolescent can testify competently without experiencing significant short-term negative psychological effects, but that careful evaluation, trial preparation and consistent support are needed during the usually prolonged pre-trial period and after the trial.

This study does not address the question of whether sexually abused elementary school-age children can testify without negative psychological effects. There were two older elementary school-age children in the authors' child witness assessment project who did testify adequately, but no follow-up evaluation was carried out to determine the psychological effect of this. The ability of such children to testify adequately is supported by anecdotal reports from district attorneys and child welfare workers. However, there is a need for further systematic studies of both adolescents and elementary school-age children as witnesses to provide more information about assessment, trial performance and the psychological outcome.

References

BERNSTEIN, B. E., CLAMAN, L., HARRIS, J. C. & SAMSON, J. (1982), The child witness: a model for evaluation and trial preparation. *Child Welfare* 61:95–104.

BURGESS, A. W. & HOLSTROM, L. L. (1975), Rape: the victim and the criminal justice system. In: *Victimology: A New Focus*, Vol. 3, ed. I. Drapkin & E. Viano. Lexington, Mass.: Lexington Books, pp. 31–48.

GAGER, N. & SCHUR, C. (1976), *Sexual Assault: Confronting Rape in America*. New York: Grosset Dunlop, pp. 54–57.

Jackson v. Commonwealth (1946), 301 KY 562, 192 S.W. 2nd 480.

LADD, D. M. (1942), A modern code of evidence. In: *American Code of Evidence, Model Code of Evidence*, as adopted and promulgated by the American Law Institute, Philadelphia, p. 340.

McCORMICK, R. (1972), Mental capacity and immaturity. In: *Text on Evidence*, Ed. 2. ed. E. W. Cleary. St. Paul, MN.: West Publishing Co., p. 140.

MELTON, G. B. (1980), Psycholegal issues in child victims' interaction with the legal system. *Victimology*, 5:274–284.

—— (1981), Children's competency to testify. *Law Hum. Behav.*, 5:73–78.

TERR, L. C. (1980), The child as a witness. In: *Child Psychiatry and the Law*, ed. D. H. Schetky & E. P. Benedek. New York: Brunner/Mazel, pp. 45–51.

WEISS, E. & BERG, R. (1982), Child victims of sexual assault: impact of court procedures. *This Journal*, 21:513–518.

Child Abuse & Neglect, Vol. 11, pp. 267-272, 1987
Printed in the U.S.A. All rights reserved.

CHILDREN'S REACTIONS TO SEX ABUSE INVESTIGATION AND LITIGATION

JOHN F. TEDESCO, PH.D. AND STEVEN V. SCHNELL, PH.D.

Des Moines Child Guidance Center, Inc., Des Moines, IA

Abstract—This investigation attempted to begin to quantify the extent to which children are helped or further victimized by sex abuse investigation and litigation procedures. Although there is virtually no research on the subject, frequent assumptions have been made that these procedures often further victimize children. Significant changes in state legislation have and are being considered which would protect victims from further victimization. A child victim questionnaire was sent to the presidents of all area child abuse and neglect councils in the state of Iowa as well as to other personnel working with sexually abused children. The somewhat surprising findings revealed that of the 48 questionnaires returned only approximately 21% of the victims perceived that the questioning and investigation was harmful, while approximately 53% saw it as helpful. Other analyses found that ratings of helpfulness were not correlated with the age of the victim, the presence of a supportive adult during questioning, the number of abuse incidents, whether or not the interviews were videotaped, and whether or not the perpetrator was a family member. Testifying in court and high numbers of interviewers were associated with more negative ratings. The limitations and implications of the results are discussed along with suggestions for future research.

Résumé—Les auteurs ont essayé de mesurer dans quelle mesure les enquêtes pour violences sexuelles et la procédure judiciaire aident les victimes ou aggravent leur sort. Bien qu'il n'existe pratiquement pas de données scientifiques sur le sujet, on présume souvent que ces démarches constituent en elles-mêmes une violence supplémentaire subie par les enfants. Très souvent, on considère de changer la législation relative à ces problèmes ou même on la change afin de protéger les victimes. Les auteurs ont envoyé un questionnaire aux présidents des différents Conseils locaux s'occupant de maltraitance-négligence à l'égard d'enfants dans l'Etat de Iowa ainsi qu'aux personnes qui par leur profession sont amenés à s'occuper d'enfants victimes d'abus sexuels. A leur grande surprise, les auteurs ont trouvé sur la base des 48 questionnaires revenus que seulement le 21% des victimes considéraient que les interrogatoires et les enquêtes leur avaient causé du tort alors que le 53% considéraient tout cela comme leur étant utile. Il n'y avait pas de relation entre l'estimation des interrogatoires quant à leur utilité pour la victime et l'âge de celle-ci, ou la présence d'un adulte comme soutien pendant l'interrogatoire, ou le nombre des épisodes de violences subies, ou l'enregistrement ou non des interviews sur bandes vidéo ou encore le fait que l'aggresseur était ou non un membre de la famille. Ce qui était considéré comme plus défavorable pour la victime était le fait de devoir témoigner devant le Tribunal ou de devoir subir un grand nombre d'interviews. Les auteurs discutent des limitations et des implications de leurs données et en tirent des idées pour les recherches ultérieures.

INTRODUCTION

AS SOCIETY'S KNOWLEDGE and awareness of child sexual abuse has increased, there has been a call for new laws that attempt to protect the rights of the child victim and prevent revictimization in the legal process. Within that context lawmakers have called upon the mental health profession to help them understand the effects of the legal system on sexually abused children and how the negative impact of the system can be ameliorated. Proposals currently being considered include modified courtrooms, videotaped de-

Paper presented at the annual conference of the American Association of Psychiatric Services for Children, Las Vegas, February 27, 1986.

Reprint requests to John F. Tedesco, Ph.D., Des Moines Child Guidance Center, Inc., 1206 Pleasant St., Des Moines, IA 50309.

positions, preparation of children prior to testifying, specially trained court workers, extended acceptance of hearsay evidence, quicker disposition of child sex abuse cases, closed courtrooms, and the extension of the statute of limitations.

Although there is very little research on the issue, we often assume that many investigation and litigation procedures have a negative impact on children and thereby further victimize them. Weiss and Berg [1] present a convincing case on how court procedures interfere with the resolution of emotional reactions associated with sexual abuse in children. They point out that children do not have the same rights as other parties in the litigation process and that legal proceedings often prolong or intensify the child's emotional reactions. Berliner and Barbieri [2] note that cross examination is frequently difficult for child witnesses. The attorney's job is to impeach the child's testimony. Consequently, the child may be intimidated, embarrassed, or otherwise humiliated. Burgess and Holmstrom [3] point out that the slow litigation process may result in a temporary plateau in a particular child's development. DeFrancis [4] found parents of the majority of victims feeling that the court process put too many pressures on the child and was overall bad for the child. Melton [5] concluded his testimony before a United States Senate subcommittee by indicating that there is a need for substantial research to examine the effects of legal procedures on children.

In contrast to the possible harmful effects of the legal process, some argue that the same procedures may be beneficial. While there is little research, Pynoos and Eth [6] argue that open discussion and exploration of trauma is beneficial for children. Testifying can be seen as increasing a child's sense of self-efficacy and can serve as a coping strategy. In addition, it can provide a child with a sense of psychological closure to a traumatic experience. Berliner and Barbieri suggest that "the experience of testifying in court can have a therapeutic effect for the child victim. . . . some children report feeling empowered by their participation in the process" [2:135]. Melton [5] in his testimony before a United States Senate subcommittee suggested that it is plausible that a child's response to the court and legal procedures may be less severe than that of an adult. The experience could be cathartic, provide a feeling of control, provide vindication, and symbolically put an end to an unpleasant experience.

Summarizing the current state of affairs, Melton states that "both the need for substantial modification of procedures and effectiveness of such procedures in reducing courtroom trauma are undocumented and indeed unstudied" [5:7]. Because of this, he concludes that a "substantial research initiative" is needed to explore the effects of legal proceedings on children [5:10]. Both Melton [5, 7] and Goodman [8] recommend that for future research to be useful, it must focus on specific characteristics of the child and the legal procedures that lead to the child being damaged or benefited by the legal proceedings:

Thus, we do not know whether a court experience is harmful for some but beneficial for others, or which circumstances lead to trauma and which to catharsis. Studies could investigate whether increased trauma. . . occurs for children who experience repeated questioning or testifying in court versus those who do not" [8:168].

METHOD

In November 1984 a letter and an accompanying questionnaire were sent to some 120 local child abuse councils, mental health facilities, individual therapists, and others who were in a position to provide services to victims of child abuse. The letter asked the service providers to distribute the questionnaire to child victims who had been involved in testifying in a criminal trial. The questionnaire consisted of 19 questions and was designed to learn the extent to which children suffered harm as a result of the various forms of questioning endured during the course of a child abuse investigation and subsequent litigation. Four of the questions were demographic and asked for the ages and sexes of both the abuse victim and the perpetrator. Five questions asked clarification of the nature of the investigation process. For example, the number and length of the interviews, the sex of the interviewers, etc. Five questions sought to clarify the nature and extent of the abuse (i.e., number of abuse incidents, length of time since last abuse incident). Regarding the legal process, victims were asked if the case had gone to court and whether or not the child had to testify. Victims were also asked to rate the investigation and litigation process as helpful or harmful, and then to rate the degree of helpfulness or harmfulness on a 7-point scale. The global dimension of helpfulness/harmfulness was accessed because of the disagreement in the literature over the helpfulness or harmfulness of sex abuse investigations [1-6]. A question asking victims to rate behavioral signs associated with abuse was also asked, but not seen as useful in assessing helpfulness/harmfulness. The final question asked the identity (victim, parent, therapist, etc.) of the person completing the questionnaire. The questionnaire was composed by a teacher, a child psychologist, and a child abuse investigator, all of whom had had extensive experience with issues related to child abuse.

RESULTS

Forty-eight questionnaires were returned by 10 male and 39 female victims who ranged in age from 4 to 22 years, with an average age of 13 years. They were victimized by 50 perpetrators (49 males and 1 female). The age range of the perpetrators was 9 to 58 years with an average of 34 years. Twenty-nine of the questionnaires were completed by the victims themselves; six were completed with the help of a parent. The remaining 14 questionnaires were completed with the help of the child's caseworker, attorney, or relative other than a parent.

Regarding the interview process, respondents were interviewed from 1 to 40 times by an average of 7 people. The most frequent number of interviewers per case was three. Of the interviewers, 169 were men and 133 were women. The interviews ranged in length from 15 minutes to "many" hours. The most frequent length of time noted was one hour, while the average length of time was two hours. Videotaped interviews were conducted for 11 of the children (23%); 36 of the victims (75%) had the support of an adult present during the interviews. In 26 instances (54%), the trial regarding the abuse incident was completed. In nine of those trials, children had to testify in the presence of the perpetrator. When asked how many abuse incidents occurred, the most frequent response was "a lot." Twenty-three of the cases (48%) reported 25 or fewer incidents of abuse by the perpetrator; 22 cases reported more than 50 incidents. The most frequent perpetrator was a parent of the victim (20 of 47) with only one of those being the mother of the victim. Other important relationships to the victim included older peer (7 of 47), stepparent (5 of 47), and adult roommate living with the family (4 of 47). Two victims failed to complete this question.

In response to whether or not the questioning was helpful or harmful to the child, 23 victims (48%) reported it to be helpful; 9 reported it to be harmful (19%); 9 rated it as both helpful and harmful (19%); and 2 rated it as neither helpful or harmful (5%). Five victims (10%) failed to answer this particular question. Victims were asked to rate the degree of helpfulness or harmfulness on a scale from one to seven with one being "not at all," four being "moderately," and seven being "extremely." Of those who saw it as helpful, the average rating was 4.86; of those who rated it harmful, the average rating was 4.08.

For the purpose of further data analysis, the helpful scale and harmful scale were combined. This resulted in a 14-point scale with 1 being "extremely harmful" and 14 being "extremely helpful."

The data also revealed that the number of interviewers was negatively correlated with perceived helpfulness, $r(41) = -.3$, $p < .05$. Subjects who testified in court rated the procedure as less helpful, $M = 7.33$, than those who did not testify, $M = 11.03$; $t(42) = 2.62$, $p < .05$. Of those who testified in court, 22% (2 out of 9) rated the procedure as helpful while 68% (21 out of 31) of those who did not testify rated the procedure as helpful. Those who testified in court also appeared to be more ambivalent or conflicted about the process as 55% (5 out of 9) rated it as both helpful and harmful compared with 13% (4 out of 31) of those who did not testify.

Victims of incest appeared to be either more conflicted or ambivalent about the procedures as 29% (8 out of 28) versus 8% of nonincest victims (1 out of 13) rated the procedure as both helpful and harmful. The same was true of female victims, 31% (10 out of 32) of whom rated the procedure as both helpful and harmful as compared to only 12% (1 out of 8) of the male victims. Although there were no mean differences in ratings between males and females, a greater percentage of males (75%, 6 out of 8) found the investigation to be helpful than did females (44%, 14 out of 32).

Treatment workers generally rated the procedure as harmful (71%, 5 out of 7), while it was frequently rated as helpful by parents (83%, 5 out of 6) and victims (60%, 15 out of 25). The mean of the ratings of treatment workers, $M = 5.14$, was significantly different from that of the parents, $M = 12.5$, $t(11) = 4.13$, $p < .001$, and victims, $M = 10.6$, $t(30) = 3.69$, $p < .001$. Ratings of the parents and of the victims did not differ significantly.

A significant difference was found between the number of interviewers seen by male and female victims, with the female victims seeing significantly more interviewers ($M = 5.3$) than male victims ($M = 3$), $t(45) = 2.55$, $p < .05$. In this particular sample, none of the males were videotaped or had to testify while over 18% of the females were videotaped and almost 25% of them had to testify in court.

DISCUSSION

Although small, the present sample of Iowa children appears similar to national norms. The average age of the children was approximately 13 years, and the overwhelming majority of the perpetrators were male, adult, family, or household members. Furthermore, the vast majority of the victims were females who had been repeatedly abused over a number of years.

Data obtained from the sample did not, however, support the idea that the interview and litigation process was necessarily "harmful" to children. Recent trends have sought to change child abuse laws in order to address the inequities felt to be present and the fact that children and adults differ in size, knowledge, and power. Child advocates obviously have wished to protect the child victim of sexual abuse from further victimization by the legal process.

The current data do not provide support for a wholesale change of laws. A greater percentage of the victims rated the legal process as helpful than rated it harmful. This is not to suggest that no changes are warranted. However, as Melton [5, 7] points out, it would likely be more productive to pursue changes that do not raise complicated constitutional issues.

What is more clearly warranted is a reexamination of some of the investigation procedures now in use. One change that should be considered is reducing the number of interviewers. The current data showed that the greater the number of interviewers, the more likely the procedure was to be rated as harmful. Modifications designed to limit the number of interviewers, such as videotaping interviews, would appear to be helpful. Videotaping was not found to adversely affect the harmful/helpful ratings in the current study. Secondly, when children were required to testify in court, they more often viewed the process as harmful. This finding would suggest that a thorough study of courtroom procedures is in order. The purpose of the studies would be to determine exactly what aspect of the courtroom procedures are most traumatic. This would help to identify what changes in courtroom procedures would be most helpful and offer empirical evidence to help lobby for the needed changes. For example, it may be important to train judges and attorneys so that they understand how both the child and adult cognitively process sexual abuse. Orzek [9] has outlined some developmental differences and their implications for interviewing children about abuse incidents. The current data also suggest that females may be more likely than males to see more interviewers, be videotaped, and be asked to testify in court. Whether or not some type of sex bias is present in current litigation procedures should also be examined.

The finding that treatment workers tended to rate procedures more harmful than parents and victims needs to be accepted with caution. The effect of sampling bias cannot be ruled out. However, the finding is consistent with the authors' initial expectations that victims themselves would find these procedures harmful. Exactly why workers are more inclined to take such a view needs further exploration as it may have implications for the type of treatment received by sex abuse victims. The further exploration of the comparative ratings of parents, treatment workers, and victims is warranted. The current sample needs to be enlarged and ratings from treatment workers, parents, and victims are needed on the same individuals so that within subject comparisons can be made. Another possibly confounding factor was psychological treatment. The vast majority of victims had completed or were currently in some sort of therapy. How therapy changes the victim's views also needs to be considered.

IMPLICATIONS

Based on the limitations of the current study, recommendations can be offered for future research. Future research would benefit from the use of a more objective behavior rating scale, employment of better sampling techniques, acquisition of a larger number of subjects, and multiple ratings in order to make within subject comparisons. The current results suggest that future research should also focus on the courtroom process.

Another source of direction for future research can be found in the pediatric psychology literature. Further research should examine the possibility of transferring knowledge gained in pediatric psychology settings to pediatric forensic settings. More research has been conducted on preparing children for the traumatic experience of hospitalization and surgery than the traumatic experience of testifying in court. Behavioral scientists have recently begun to employ a number of psychological principles to reduce the stress associated with hospitalization and treatment procedures and have explored means of identifying children who would be at high risk for adverse reactions to hospitalization [10-14]. This allows intervention efforts to be focused on those who need it the most.

Treatments utilizing modeling, cognitive-behavioral therapy, and other didactic input have been found to be helpful [15-19]. In addition, parents' reactions have been found to be a major determinant of children's reactions, and including parents in the interventions is helpful [11, 20-22]. These findings have obvious implications for preparing children for testifying in court and could help to guide future research.

The problem of sexual abuse has been present for a long period of time and is unlikely to disappear in the foreseeable future. Understanding the process from the child's perspective is a worthwhile and important undertaking. Hopefully, future research can help identify and deal with some of the most important issues confronting both the legal and mental health systems.

Acknowledgment—The authors wish to thank Barb Minear and Johnna Greffenius for their assistance with the study.

REFERENCES

1. WEISS, E. H. and BERG, R. F. Child victims of sexual assault: Impact of court procedures. *Journal of the American Academy of Child Psychiatry* 21:513-518 (1982).
2. BERLINER, L. and BARBIERI, M. K. The testimony of the child victims of sexual assault. *Journal of Social Issues* 40:125-137 (1984).
3. BURGESS, A. W. and HOLMSTROM, L. L. The child and family during the court process. In: *Sexual Assault of Children and Adolescents*, A. W. Burgess, A. N. Groth, L. L. Holmstrom, and S. M. Sgroi (Eds.), pp. 205-230. Lexington Books, Lexington, MA (1978).
4. DEFRANCIS, V. *Protecting the Child Victim of Sex Crimes Committed by Adults*. American Humane Association, Denver (1969).
5. MELTON, G. B. Child sexual abuse victims in the courtroom. Testimony before the United States Senate. American Psychological Association, Washington DC (1984).
6. PYNOOS, R. S. and ETH, S. The child as witness to homicide. *Journal of Social Issues* 40:87-108 (1984).
7. MELTON, G. B. Child witnesses and the first amendment: A psychological dilemma. *Journal of Social Issues* 40:109-123 (1984).
8. GOODMAN, G. B. The child witness: Conclusions and future directions for research and legal practice. *Journal of Social Issues* 40:157-175 (1984).
9. ORZEK, A. M. The child's cognitive processing of sexual abuse. *Journal of Child and Adolescent Psychotherapy* 2:110-114 (1985).
10. ACK, M. New perspectives in comprehensive health care for children. *Journal of Pediatric Psychology* 1:9-11 (1976).
11. AZARNOFF, P. The care of children in hospitals: An overview. *Journal of Pediatric Psychology* 1:5-6 (1976).
12. MOOS, R. H. (Ed.). *Coping with Physical Illness 2: New Perspectives*. Plenum, New York (1984).
13. VARNI, J. W. *Clinical Behavioral Pediatrics*. Pergamon, New York (1983).
14. ZABIN, M. A. and MELAMED, B. G. Relationship between parental discipline and children's ability to cope with stress. *Journal of Behavioral Assessment* 2:17-38 (1980).
15. MELAMED, B. G., MEYER, R., GEE, C. and SOULE, L. The influence of time and type of preparation on children's adjustment to hospitalization. *Journal of Pediatric Psychology* 1:34-37 (1976).
16. NELSON, W. M. A cognitive-behavioral treatment for disproportionate denial anxiety and pain: A case study. *Journal of Clinical Child Psychology* 10:79-82 (1981).
17. MELAMED, B. G. and SIEGEL, L. J. Reduction of anxiety in children facing hospitalization and surgery by use of filmed modeling. *Journal of Consulting and Clinical Psychology* 43:511-521 (1975).
18. FERGUSON, B. F. Preparing young children for hospitalization: A comparison of two methods. *Pediatrics* 64:656-664 (1979).
19. PETERSON, L. and SHIGETOMI, C. The use of coping techniques to minimize anxiety in hospitalized children. *Behavior Therapy* 12:1-14 (1981).
20. PETERSON, L., MORI, L. and CARTER, P. The role of the family in children's responses to stressful medical procedures. *Journal of Clinical Child Psychology* 14:98-104 (1985).
21. ROSKIES, E., MONGEON, M. and GAGNON-LEFEBURE, B. Increasing maternal participation in the hospitalization of young children. *Medical Care* 16:765-777 (1978).
22. SKIPPER, J. K. and LEONARD, R. C. Children, stress, and hospitalization: A field experiment. *Journal of Health and Social Behavior* 9:275-287 (1968).

Appointed Counsel to Protect the Child Victim's Rights

Charles L. Hobson*

INTRODUCTION

Child sexual abuse is one of the most destructive crimes society faces. One study has shown that thirty eight percent of females in randomly selected households in a large western city reported having been sexually abused before the age of eighteen.[1] A survey of college students showed that nineteen percent of the women and nine percent of the men reported having been victims of sexual abuse.[2] Sexual assault can have a profound effect on a child including "withdrawal, anxiety symptoms, enuresis (bed-wetting), guilt, school problems, delinquent or antisocial behavior and also lack of self-esteem."[3]

Unfortunately, the child's harm does not end with the molestation. Our criminal justice system is geared toward guaranteeing a fair trial for the defendant, not towards minimizing the trauma to the victim.[4] Thus, the act of prosecuting the molester can add to the trauma already suffered by the victimized child.[5]

---

*   Attorney, Criminal Justice Legal Foundation; J.D. 1987, University of the Pacific, McGeorge School of Law; A.B. 1984, University of California.
1.   Berliner & Barbieri, *The Testimony of the Child Victim of Sexual Assault*, 40 J. Soc. Issues 125, 126 (1984).
2.   *Id.*
3.   Parker, *The Rights of Child Witnesses: Is the Court a Protector or Perpetrator?*, 17 New Eng. L. Rev. 643, 649 (1982).
4.   *See id.* at 643-644.
5.   Libai, *The Protection of the Child Victim of a Sexual Offense in the Criminal Justice System*, 15 Wayne L. Rev. 977, 984 (1969).

The harm our system does to the child can be minimized. Legislatures and courts can develop procedures to minimize the harm the legal system does to the child while preserving the defendant's constitutional rights. One example of this is section 288 subdivision (d) of the California Penal Code.[6] Subdivisions (a) through (c) of Penal Code section 288 define the crime of child molestation and set its punishment.[7] Subdivision (d), added by the legislature in 1981,[8] provides the means to help molested children through the criminal justice system.

> In any arrest or prosecution under this section or under Section 288.5 the peace officer, the district attorney, and the court shall consider the needs of the child victim and shall do whatever is necessary, within existing budgetary resources, and constitutionally permissible to prevent psychological harm to the child victim.[9]

The broad wording of section 288(d) lends itself to many uses. This Article will focus on one way section 288(d) can be used—to appoint counsel for the molested child in a prosecution under section 288, and one tactic for the child's attorney to employ—using Rule 2-100 subdivision (a) of California's Rules of Professional Conduct[10] to keep defendant's attorney from interviewing the child outside of court without the consent of the child's attorney.[11] This Article will also argue that the main case interpreting section 288(d), *Hochheiser v. Superior Court*,[12] gives an unnecessarily restrictive reading of

---

6. CAL. PENAL CODE § 288(d) (West Supp. 1990).

7. CAL. PENAL CODE § 288(a)-(c) (West Supp. 1989).

8. In 1981, the legislature enacted section 288(c) which read:
In any arrest or prosecution under this section the peace officer, the district attorney, and the court shall consider the needs of the child victim and shall do whatever is necessary and constitutionally permissible to prevent psychological harm to the child victim.
1981 Cal. Stat. ch. 1064, sec. 1, at 4093 (enacting CAL. PENAL CODE § 288(c)). In 1987, the legistlature changed subdivision (c) to subdivision (d) without any change in its language. 1987 Cal. Legis. Serv. ch. 1068, sec. 3, at 443 (West) (amending CAL. PENAL CODE § 288). In 1989, the legislature amended section 288(d) to its present form, adding section 288.5 of the California Penal Code (continuous sexual abuse of a child) to the crimes covered by section 288(d), and adding the phrase "within existing budgetary resources." 1989 Cal. Leg. Serv. ch. 1402, sec. 3, at 5256 (West) (amending Cal. Penal Code § 288). To avoid confusion all references will be made to subdivision (d).

9. CAL. PENAL CODE § 288(d) (West Supp. 1990).

10. "While representing a client, a member shall not communicate directly or indirectly about the subject of the representation with a party the member knows to be represented by another lawyer in the matter, unless the member has the consent of the other lawyer." CAL. CIV. & CRIM. R., PROF. CONDUCT 2-100 (West Interim Annot. Serv. No. 1 1989). Rule 2-100 can also be found in West's separate California Rules of Court publication. CALIFORNIA RULES OF COURT, RULES OF PROFESSIONAL CONDUCT 2-100, at 865 (West Revised ed. 1989).

11. *See infra* notes 150-196 and accompanying text.

12. 161 Cal. App. 3d 777, 208 Cal. Rptr. 273 (1984).

section 288(d), and does not apply to a court appointing an attorney under section 288(d).[13] Finally, this Article will demonstrate that the child's attorney can use Rule 2-100 of California's Rules of Professional Conduct to limit contact between the child and defense counsel without violating defendant's constitutional rights.[14]

I. Appointing an Attorney for Molested Children

A. Helping the Victims

> Often many child abuse cases are not reported because of the treatment the child victim receives within the judicial process. Mental health professionals have found that legal proceedings can have a profoundly disturbing effect on the mental and emotional health of the child victim. Stigma, embarrassment and trauma to the child, sometimes with lifelong ramifications, are increased by involvement in the current judicial system. The effect can serve to perpetuate a problem which is already self-perpetuating, especially in incest cases.[15]

While our system of prosecuting criminals can be difficult for any victim of crime,[16] children face special difficulty as they lack the adult's maturity and sophistication to help them cope with the vicissitudes of the criminal justice system. The ordeal of the molested child is even more difficult as the child must bear the burden of being the primary source of testimony to a particularly repulsive crime.[17]

A criminal case can harm the molested child in many ways. "[R]epeated interrogations and cross-examination; facing the accused again; the official atmosphere in court; the acquittal of the accused for want of corroborating evidence to the child's trustworthy testimony; and the conviction of a molester who is a child's parent or relative can all afflict the molested child."[18] The harm that can be

---

13. *See infra* notes 73-149 and accompanying text.
14. *See infra* notes 150-245 and accompanying text.
15. Avery, *The Child Abuse Witness: Potential for Secondary Victimization*, 7 Crim. Just. J. 1, 3-4 (1983).
16. Villmoare & Benvenuti, California Victims of Crime Handbook 8 (1988).
17. Child abuse is one of the most difficult problems to detect and prosecute, in large part because there are often no witnesses except the victim. Pennsylvania v. Ritchie, 480 U.S. 39, 60 (1987). *See* Berliner & Barbieri, *The Testimony of the Child Victim of Sexual Assault*, 40 J. Soc. Sci. 125 (1984).
18. *Libai, supra* note 5, at 984.

693

done by the criminal justice system is so great that some see that "modern court procedure . . . renders the court both the child protector of last resort and one of the most serious perpetrators of child abuse."[19] Examples of the harms the criminal justice system can inflict on the molested child are legion.

> A child was the victim of a stranger's sexual molestation at age 12. The facts did not become known to the prosecutor (often the case) until she was 17. The case was dismissed on the basis of psychiatric advice that the child could not testify without having a total emotional breakdown. The child's approach to emotional survival, typically, had been to forget, forget, forget. Reinforcing her memory of this event would have been devastating.[20]

California provides another example of the harm the criminal justice system can do to molested children.

> The mother of eight and one-half to nine-year-old S.W. testified that when her son exited the courtroom after his 1982 preliminary hearing testimony, he was "totally distraught . . . in tears and couldn't . . . talk" and "started reverting back to baby-like behavior," such as wanting to wear diapers. When she told him the week before the June 15, 1984 hearing that he would be coming to court to testify, he burst into tears and went up to his room, indicating that there was no way he was going back to court and that if he did come back to court he would say "I don't know anything." She claimed he started to talk baby talk and picked up a diaper that his mother was using as a rag, and waived it at her.[21]

Not surprisingly, some experts believe that bringing charges in a child molestation case can actually compound the harm already done to the child victim.[22] This comports with the belief of "child psychiatrists that the degree of psychic trauma is as much, or perhaps more, dependent on the way that the child victim is treated after discovery than at the time of the offense itself."[23] Thus we are confronted with the problem that the benefits of successfully prosecuting the child molester may be outweighed by the harm our legal system does to the child victim.

The criminal justice system does not harm just the children; society also suffers as child victims become unwilling to testify in molestation

---

19. *Parker, supra* note 3, at 643.
20. State v. Sheppard, 197 N.J. Super. 411, 415, 484 A.2d 1330, 1333 (1984).
21. Hochheiser v. Superior Court, 161 Cal. App. 3d 777, 781, 208 Cal. Rptr. 273, 275.
22. *Parker, supra* note 3, at 644.
23. *Libai, supra* note 5, at 981.

cases due to the harm done to them by the criminal justice system. For example, in the New Jersey case of *State v. Sheppard*:[24]

> One attorney, who had handled 30 to 40 of these [child molestation] cases for the State, was able to complete a trial in only one. In most, while the child victim was able to provide her with information sufficient to support a prosecution and was sometimes able to appear with difficulty before a grand jury, she could not testify in court face-to-face with the accused and other relatives advanced the opinion that their child patients could not survive the trauma attending a courtroom appearance.[25]

The costs to the children associated with prosecuting molesters can result in an even greater bias by prosecutors towards plea bargaining to minimize the damage court proceedings will do to the child victims.[26] The burden the criminal justice system places on the child also adds to the problem of the child's recanting. A major difficulty in prosecuting child molestation cases is the victim recanting his original statement.[27] This problem is intimately tied to the situation where the victim is compelled to participate in the judicial process.[28] While the child victim initially may reveal the "information about the abuse to a trusted friend, non-abusing parent, counselor or teacher,"[29] this statement often leads to a "confusing and frightening array of interrogations."[30] When added to the great distress that the initial accusation of child abuse can give to the family,[31] it is easy to understand why the victim later may want to recant the initial accusation. Finally, the trauma associated with the criminal justice system can stifle the reporting of child molestation due to the trauma of pretrial and trial procedures for the victim.[32]

The courts are also aware of the problems our criminal justice system causes to child molestation victims. For example, one court noted that:

---

24. State v. Sheppard, 197 N.J. Super. 411, 484 A.2d 1330 (1984).

25. *Sheppard*, 197 N.J. Super. at 417, 484 A.2d at 1333. Another attorney in *Sheppard* testified that "[n]early 90% of the child abuse cases were dismissed as a result of problems attending the testimony of children." *Id.*

26. *Libai, supra* note 5, at 1007.

27. *Avery, supra* note 15, at 13.

28. *Id.* at 13-14.

29. *Id.* at 14.

30. *Id.*

31. *Id.*

32. *See* Mlyniec & Dally, *See No Evil? Can Insulation of Child Sexual Abuse Victims Be Accomplished Without Endangering Defendant's Constitutional Rights?*, 40 U. Miami L. Rev. 115, 137 (1985). The harm done to the child by the criminal justice system is not limited to ordeal of the trial. One particularly harmful aspect of pretrial procedures to the child is his being repeatedly required to retell to strangers the details of his molestation. *See infra* notes 151-57 and accompanying text.

695

[c]ertainly a five year old girl should be spared the necessity of testifying against her father in a rape case if at all possible. . . . We do not agree . . . that five year old girls should be dragged in to re-live the horrifying experience of being raped.[33]

In *State v. Conklin*,[34] the Minnesota Supreme Court listed the litany of problems the molested child had at trial including: "[t]he unfamiliar courtroom setting, the necessity of speaking to strangers about embarrassing events, the presence of a jury [and] the problems with language and mutual comprehension."[35] A California court also has recognized the harm the system can do to the child by requiring the child to describe the crime in "intimate detail" in front of the public, defendant and his supporters.[36]

The leading case interpreting section 288(d), *Hochheiser v. Superior Court*,[37] did not agree with this position. The *Hochheiser* court, in deciding that section 288(d) did not justify televising the molested children's testimony based its decision in part on the lack of support for the idea that testifying to their molestation harmed the children.[38]

The *Hochheiser* court found that the people had not proven that testifying in the presence of the jury and the accused was psychologically damaging to the sexually abused child.[39] The court found that the literature supporting this view "contains generalized statements to this effect"[40] and does not provide the empirical proof necessary to justify this claim.[41]

The *Hochheiser* court placed excessive emphasis on empirical verification. The court failed to realize that there is a problem with verifying whether our legal system or any one part of it harms child molestation victims. The effects the component parts of the prosecution have on the child mix together. Also, the effects the prosecution have on the children mix with the effects of the crime on each child. Thus it is difficult to determine how much harm any particular part of the criminal justice system does to the child.

As one commentator explained:

---

33. State v. Boodry, 96 Ariz. 259, 263-65, 394 P.2d 196, 200 (1964).
34. 444 N.W.2d 268 (Minn. 1989).
35. *Id.* at 273.
36. Eversole v. Superior Court, 148 Cal. App. 3d 188, 200, 195 Cal. Rptr. 816, 823-24 (1983).
37. 161 Cal. App. 3d 777, 208 Cal. Rptr. 273 (1984).
38. *Id.* at 791, 208 Cal. Rptr. at 282.
39. *Id.* at 792-93, 208 Cal. Rptr. at 283.
40. *Id.* at 793, 208 Cal. Rptr. at 283.
41. *Id.* at 792, 208 Cal. Rptr. at 283.

The studies do not as yet demonstrate a clear causal link between the legal proceedings and the child victim's mental disturbances; but no psychiatric study has attempted to prove, *or is likely to attempt to prove*, in the future, such a causal link. Psychiatrists agree that they cannot isolate the effects of the 'crime trauma' from the prior personality damage or either of the foregoing from the 'environment reaction trauma' or the 'legal process trauma.' But psychiatrists do agree that when some victims encounter the law enforcement system, for one reason or another, the child requires special care and treatment.[42]

Furthermore, some empirical support exists for the notion that criminal proceedings harm child molestation victims.[43] Finally, simple common sense agrees with "the opinions of most psychiatrists, psychologists, judges and parents that the mental health of the child should be given substantial consideration and protected where possible by the criminal justice system."[44] Litigation is an unpleasant experience for any lay participant. When the participant is a child who is the victim of one of the most atrocious crimes capable of commission, and who must repeat frequently and in graphic detail the acts committed against him, it is easy to see that the molested child can be in grave danger from our legal system.

Appointing counsel to represent the molested child is an excellent way to protect him from the emotional harm caused by the criminal action. One of the greatest problems the child molestation victim has is that he[45] has no one to stand up for him. The defendant has his own counsel and a host of constitutional protections to support him through the ordeal of litigation.[46] The child, however, has had no such protections until very recently.

While the tide has recently changed for the better, the molested child still needs more support. While he is entitled to a support person while he testifies[47] and will have the support of government agencies such as Children's Protective Services and the district attorney's office, the child molestation victim has no one who will stand up for *his* rights and enforce them. The support persons and social workers are invariably lay people and therefore incapable of fully

---

42. *Libai, supra* note 5, at 1015 (emphasis added).
43. *See id.* at 982.
44. *Id.* at 1015.
45. Both the victim and the perpetrator of child molestation can be male or female. For the sake of convenience, references will be made to the masculine pronoun.
46. *Parker, supra* note 3, at 643-44.
47. Cal. Penal Code § 868.5 (West Supp. 1989).

697

understanding and adequately protecting the child's rights and interests. The district attorney, while well-meaning, may have a conflict of interest with the child. While district attorneys will want to minimize the trauma a prosecution does to the child, the district attorney's main interest is convicting the molester. The duty of the Attorney General and the district attorneys is "to see that the laws of the State are uniformly and adequately enforced."[48] They have no duty to protect the interests of the victim, regardless of the consequences to the prosecution. Thus, the district attorney may have a conflict between his interest in helping the child and his interest in successfully prosecuting the molester.[49]

An appointed attorney, however, combines the best of both worlds. Like the social worker, he can give his undivided attention to the child's emotional welfare, and, like the district attorney, he has the legal knowledge that allows him to protect the child's interests and rights. By having an attorney to represent him, the child will have someone who understands court procedures and thus "protect the well-being of young complaining witnesses throughout the judicial process."[50] The attorney will be able to recognize what is excessively harsh or repetitious questioning, how often the child will be interviewed and what steps can be taken to prevent unnecessary interviews, how long the prosecution will take, how important the child is as a witness and how to protect the child from any unnecessary procedures that may harm him.

If the child is deprived of appointed counsel he will be left alone. No one else will have the motivation and the expertise to protect him as well as appointed counsel can. Given the tender age and tremendous vulnerability of the molested child, he deserves every constitutionally permissible protection. It would be a tragedy to allow the misinterpretation of section 288(d) in *Hochheiser*[51] to prevent courts from appointing counsel for molested children. *Hochheiser* deprives courts of an important tool for alleviating the great pain our criminal justice system can cause the child molestation victim.

---

48. CAL. CONST. art. V, § 13.
49. *See* CALIFORNIA ATTORNEY GENERAL'S OFFICE, CALIFORNIA CHILD VICTIM WITNESS JUDICIAL ADVISORY COMMITTEE, FINAL REPORT 67 (1988). While the district attorney also has a duty to help the child under section 288(d), his first duty must still be to prosecute the molester. The district attorney's duty to prosecute is a constitutional duty and thus not limited by section 288(d). *See supra* note 48 and accompanying text.
50. *Parker, supra* note 3, at 653.
51. *See infra* notes 89-149 and accompanying text.

B. Hochheiser v. Superior Court

One California case has analyzed fully the reach of section 288(d). In *Hochheiser v. Superior Court*,[52] the trial court ordered that the complaining witnesses' testimony in a child molestation prosecution be taken by closed-circuit television outside the courtroom.[53] The trial court used only its inherent power to control the courtroom and develop new procedures to justify this order.[54] The *Hochheiser* court did not accept the trial court's position, citing California's prosecutorial discovery cases[55] for the point that courts should not invent rules of criminal procedure involving important issues of constitutional law without legislative authorization.[56] The Attorney General tried to bolster the trial court's position by using section 288(d).[57]

The *Hochheiser* court gave a very narrow reading of section 288(d).[58] It found that the use of closed-circuit television could threaten defendant's due process, public trial and confrontation rights.[59] Therefore, the court felt that it should not read such a procedure into section 288(d). The court explained: "But we cannot read into this statute a legislative mandate for a closed-circuit television procedure or, indeed, any other specific procedure, which so drastically affects the rights of a defendant."[60]

In addition to the threat posed to defendant's public trial, due process and confrontation rights, the *Hochheiser* court also noted that "there are serious questions about the effects on the jury of using closed-circuit television to present the testimony of an absent witness since the camera becomes the juror's eyes, selecting and commenting upon what is seen."[61] The court felt that the lighting or

---

52. 161 Cal. App. 3d 777, 208 Cal. Rptr. 273 (1984).
53. *Id.* at 780, 208 Cal. Rptr. at 274.
54. *Id.* at 782, 208 Cal. Rptr. at 276.
55. People v. Collie, 30 Cal. 3d 43, 634 P.2d 534, 177 Cal. Rptr. 458 (1981); Reynolds v. Superior Court, 12 Cal. 3d 834, 528 P.2d 45, 117 Cal. Rptr. 437 (1974) (courts could not create rules of criminal procedure to allow the prosecution to obtain discovery from defendant).
56. *Hochheiser*, 161 Cal. App. 3d at 783-88, 208 Cal. Rptr. at 276-80.
57. At the time *Hochheiser* was decided, this subdivision was numbered 288(c), but all references will be made to 288(d). *See supra* note 8. At the time *Hochheiser* was decided 288(d) did not include the phrase "within existing budgetary resources." *See supra* note 8. This does not, however, change the analysis of *Hochheiser*'s misconstruction of 288(d). *See infra* note 121.
58. *Hochheiser*, 161 Cal. App. 3d 777, 791, 208 Cal. Rptr. 273, 282.
59. *Id.* at 785-86, 208 Cal. Rptr. at 278.
60. *Id.* at 791, 208 Cal. Rptr. at 282.
61. *Id.* at 786, 208 Cal. Rptr. at 279.

the camera angle used could "affect the jurors' impressions of the witnesses' demeanor and credibility."[62] The court analogized the effect of closed-circuit testimony on the jury's perception of defendant to that of shackling defendant at trial. The *Hochheiser* court felt that "the presentation of a witness' testimony via closed-circuit television may affect the presumption of innocence by creating prejudice in the minds of the jurors similar to that created by the use of physical restraints in the jury's presence."[63]

The *Hochheiser* court supported its reasoning by purporting to ascertain the legislative intent behind section 288(d). The court determined that the Summary of 1981 Crime Legislation Report compiled by the Joint Committee for the Revision of the Penal Code found that section 288(d) only mandated a "philosophical change focusing on the minor's needs."[64] The court also held that "[t]he flurry of legislative activity after the passage of [then] subdivision (c) of section 288, argues against the broad interpretation of the statute."[65] The court felt that the enactment of Penal Code section 868.5[66] and the amendment of section 767 of the Evidence Code[67] after the enactment of section 288(d) demonstrated that the legislature did not intend for section 288(d) to be construed broadly. The court explained that "[t]here would be no reason to pass such legislation if subdivision (c) already provided such remedies."[68]

Finally, the *Hochheiser* court relied on the rule of construction that where "language reasonably susceptible to more than one construction is used in a penal law, the construction which is more favorable to the defendant should be adopted."[69] Therefore, the court justified interpreting the broadly worded section 288(d) very narrowly because such a narrow interpretation favored the defendant in this criminal case.

In its attempt to keep from making a dramatic break from current law without more specific legislative authority,[70] the *Hochheiser* court

---

62. *Id.*
63. *Id.* at 787, 208 Cal. Rptr. at 279.
64. *Id.* at 791, 208 Cal. Rptr. at 282.
65. *Id.*
66. CAL. PENAL CODE § 868.5 (West Supp. 1989) (allowing a support person to accompany a testifying minor victim of a sex offense during the victim's testimony).
67. 1984 Cal. Stat. ch. 1423, sec. 1, at 4994 (amending CAL. EVID. CODE § 767) (permitting leading questions to a child involving prosecutions under section 288(d)).
68. *Hochheiser*, 161 Cal. App. 3d at 791, 208 Cal. Rptr. at 282.
69. *Id.* at 792, 208 Cal. Rptr. at 282.
70. *Id.*

noted its concern that televised testimony posed a serious threat to defendant's constitutional rights. "The mere presence and gravity of these significant questions and concerns render it inappropriate to create by ad hoc judicial fiat such a drastic departure from established procedures."[71] The court was unwilling to uphold the trial court's action unless giving testimony over closed-circuit television was specifically authorized by the legislature. As it felt that no such authority existed, the *Hochheiser* court refused to allow what it saw as a new, constitutionally-suspect procedure. The court explained "[a]s we have previously noted, legislative enactments should not be construed to overthrow long-established principles of law unless such an intention is clearly shown by express declaration or necessary implication."[72]

C. *Distinguishing* Hochheiser

The question has arisen in some child abuse prosecutions as to whether *Hochheiser* prohibits appointment of counsel for the victim.[73] *Hochheiser* can be factually distinguished from the procedure discussed in this article, and, to the extent *Hochheiser* forbids courts from using section 288(d) to fashion new procedures to help child victims, *Hochheiser* is wrongly decided and should not be followed.

The obvious difference between the procedure used in *Hochheiser* and appointing an attorney for the molested child is that two completely different procedures are used to protect the victims. The difference between giving testimony via closed-circuit television and appointing an attorney to represent the victims is more than superficial. The two procedures use different methods to protect the child victim, conflict with different interests of the defendant and differ in the degree to which each conflicts with a defendant's rights.

1. *Different Procedures*

The trial court in *Hochheiser* used closed-circuit television to help isolate the victim from the defendant.[74] Televising the testimony via closed-circuit television addresses the fear the victim has when testi-

---

71. *Id.*
72. *Id.* at 791-792, 208 Cal. Rptr. at 282.
73. That argument has been made in the pending case of People v. Pitts, No. F006225 (Cal. App. 5th Dist. March 27, 1989).
74. *Hochheiser,* 161 Cal. App. 3d at 781-782, 208 Cal. Rptr. at 275-276.

fying in front of defendant. Retelling to strangers the details of the crime committed against him is difficult enough for the child molestation victim.[75] The problem becomes more pronounced when the child has to give this testimony in front of the defendant and physically confront him.[76] Therefore closed-circuit television can be used to distance the child from the defendant and avoid the terror of having to meet his nemesis face to face in court.

While *Hochheiser* was not decided on constitutional grounds, it is clear where the court's sympathies stood.[77] "The issue of allowing the complaining witness to testify via closed-circuit television from a separate room, instead of being examined in the courtroom *is no less constitutionally questionable* than were the discovery issues our supreme court declined to resolve in *Reynolds* and *Collie*."[78]

The *Hochheiser* court's doubts about the wisdom of the trial court's actions motivated it to refuse to extend section 288(d) to cover televised testimony. The court felt that the legislature did not intend "such a fundamental change in organic law which would abrogate traditional statutory rights to the presence of the testifying witness in the courtroom with the defendant."[79] Because the *Hochheiser* court saw the trial court's use of closed-circuit television testimony as a radical change in courtroom procedure that endangers defendant's statutory and constitutional rights, it felt that it could not extend section 288(d) to cover such a situation.

Appointing an attorney to represent the victim's psychological interests is neither as radical nor as dangerous to defendants as was the televised testimony in *Hochheiser*.[80] Appointing an attorney to represent someone in a legal proceeding is hardly an original idea. Courts nationwide have been required to appoint counsel for accused felons for over twenty-five years.[81] California has had this rule even

---

75. *See Berliner & Barbieri, supra* note 1, at 133. For the problems a child victim of sexual abuse has in testifying, see *Libai, supra* note 5 and accompanying text.

76. *See* Coy v. Iowa, 108 S. Ct. 2798, 2809 (1988) (Blackmun, J., dissenting).

77. *Hochheiser*, 161 Cal. App. 3d at 787, 208 Cal. Rptr. at 279.

78. *Id.* at 785, 208 Cal. Rptr. at 278 (citing People v. Collie, 30 Cal. 3d 43, 634 P.2d 534, 177 Cal. Rptr. 458 (1981); Reynolds v. Superior Court, 12 Cal. 3d 834, 528 P.2d 45, 117 Cal. Rptr. 437 (1974)).

79. *Hochheiser*, 161 Cal. App. 3d at 791, 208 Cal. Rptr. at 282.

80. This Article does not take the position that using closed-circuit television to help some child victims of sexual abuse to testify is either constitutionally suspect or contrary to defendant's statutory rights. Resolving the validity of the procedure used in *Hochheiser* is not necessary to determine the validity of appointing an attorney under section 288(d). What is important is that the *Hochheiser* court believed that the use of televised testimony was suspect.

81. Gideon v. Wainwright, 372 U.S. 335, 344 (1963).

longer.[82] The appointment of counsel is not limited to the criminal law. A person is entitled appointed counsel in a variety of commitment proceedings.[83]

Appointed counsel is especially common where children are concerned. Under section 237.5 of the Civil Code, the court must appoint counsel for the minor in emancipation proceedings "[i]f the court finds that the interests of the minor require the representation of counsel . . . whether or not the minor is able to afford counsel."[84] Indigent minors have a right to appointed counsel in delinquency proceedings,[85] and, under certain circumstances, so do their parents or guardians.[86] Appointing an attorney to help protect the psychological well-being of children is not a "wholesale revision in the entire procedural format of a criminal trial."[87] Appointment of counsel under section 288 simply extends the idea that attorneys should be provided for those people who need them but are not able to obtain counsel on their own.[88] While the court's power to appoint an attorney for the children under section 288(d) is neither dependent upon nor derived from these other rights to appointed counsel, the prevalence of appointed counsel in our legal system shows that allowing one more type of appointed counsel will not cause the drastic disruption of the legal system that so concerned the *Hochheiser* court.

2. Different Interests

Appointing an attorney for the child also does not raise the second problem feared by the *Hochheiser* court; i.e. constriction of defendant's constitutional and statutory rights. The use of closed-circuit television to obtain testimony in *Hochheiser* did raise serious constitutional problems, especially with defendant's right to confronta-

---

82. *In re* Newbern, 53 Cal. 2d 786, 790, 350 P.2d 116, 119, 3 Cal. Rptr. 364, 367 (1960); CAL. PENAL CODE § 859 (West Supp. 1989).
83. *See, e.g.*, CAL. WELF. & INST. CODE §§ 5275 (habeas corpus from detention by certification for intensive treatment), 5276 (same), 5302 (petition for post-certification treatment) (West 1984 & Supp. 1989).
84. CAL. CIV. CODE § 237.5(a) (West Supp. 1989).
85. CAL. WELF. & INST. CODE § 679 (West Supp. 1989).
86. *Id.* § 634 (West Supp. 1989).
87. Hochheiser v. Superior Court, 161 Cal. App. 3d 777, 791, 208 Cal. Rptr. 273, 282 (1984).
88. *See* MODEL RULES OF PROFESSIONAL CONDUCT Rule 6.1 (1983).

703

tion.[89] Unlike the order given in *Hochheiser*, however, appointing an attorney to represent the child's psychological interests does no direct harm to the defendant. While the *actions* of the child's attorney may have the potential to harm defendant,[90] the appointment itself has no effect on defendant's interests. As the appointment itself does no harm to defendant, it is, therefore, not as inherently dangerous as the procedure attacked in *Hochheiser*.

Hochheiser also gives a very suspect reading of section 288(d).[91] Therefore courts should decline to go beyond *Hochheiser*, even by a fraction of an inch.[92] The differences between giving testimony over closed-circuit television and appointing counsel for the child provide more than the fraction of the inch necessary to distinguish *Hochheiser*.

D. Interpreting Section 288(d)

Hochheiser gives a faulty interpretation of section 288(d). While the court never gave a reason for its narrow reading of section 288(d) other than a desire to interpret statutes in favor of criminal defendants,[93] it is logical to assume that it allowed its fear of the constitutional threat to defendant posed by televised testimony to drive the *Hochheiser* court to a very narrow interpretation of section 288(d).[94] The *Hochheiser* court, in its rush to protect the defendant, forgot the basic principle of statutory construction and legislated section 288(d) into nothingness. A fair reading of section 288(d), taking into account the interests served by the statute and the best way to protect those interests, will find that section 288(d) gives the court the authority to appoint counsel to protect the victim's psychological interests.

Any interpretation of a statute must begin with the text of the statute. Section 288(d) provides:

> In any arrest or prosecution under this section or section 288.5 the peace officer, the district attorney, and the court shall consider the needs of the child victim and *shall do whatever is necessary, within*

---

89. *Hochheiser*, 161 Cal. App. 3d at 786 n.2, 208 Cal. Rptr. at 278 n.2. *See* Coy v. Iowa, 108 S. Ct. at 2802. *But see supra* note 80.

90. *See infra* note 159 and accompanying text.

91. *See infra* notes 93-149 and accompanying text.

92. *Cf.*, Silverman v. United States, 365 U.S. 505, 512 (1961).

93. *See supra* note 69 and accompanying text.

94. *See supra* notes 77-79 and accompanying text.

existing budgetary resources, and constitutionally permissible to prevent psychological harm to the child victim.[95]

Hochheiser, in determining that section 288(d) did not authorize courts to order the giving of testimony via closed-circuit television, relied on its view of the legislative history of section 288(d) to support its holding.[96] The *Hochheiser* court ignored the actual words of the statute. Instead, it looked to committee hearings that never mentioned using closed-circuit television,[97] and a statement regarding section 288 in the *Summary of 1981 Crime Legislation Report*[98] to determine that section 288(d) only required "a philosophical change focusing on the minors' needs."[99]

Legislative reports, hearings, and digests can be useful in interpreting a statute.[100] Before resorting to legislative history, however, a court must first attempt to ascertain the plain meaning of the language of the statute. As Justice Traynor stated:

> The will of the Legislature must be determined from the statutes; intentions cannot be ascribed to it at odds with the intentions articulated in the statutes . . . . ¶ An insistence upon judicial regard for the words of a statute does not imply that they are like words in a dictionary to be read with no ranging of the mind. They are no longer at rest in their alphabetical bins. Released, combined in phrases that imperfectly communicate the thoughts of one man to another, they challenge men to give them more than passive reading, to consider well their context, to ponder what may be their consequences. Speculation cuts brush with the pertinent question: what purpose did the Legislature seek to express as it strung those words into a statute? *The court turns first to the words themselves for the answer.* It may also properly rely on extrinsic aids . . . . Primarily, however, the words, in arrangement that superimposes the purpose of the legislature upon their dictionary meaning stand in

---

95. CAL. PENAL CODE § 288(d) (West Supp. 1990). While the phrase "within existing budgetary resources" was not before the *Hochheiser* court, this phrase only strengthens the argument for a broad interpretation of section 288(d). *See infra* note 121.

96. *Hochheiser*, 161 Cal. App. 3d at 790-791, 208 Cal. Rptr. at 281-82.

97. *Id.* at 790, 208 Cal. Rptr. at 281.

98. The court explained:

> S.B. 506 [the bill enacting section 288(d)] mandates that in any prosecution for child molestation the needs of the child to be protected from further psychological harm during arrest and prosecution be placed on an equal priority with the successful prosecution of the offender.

Hochheiser, 161 Cal. App. 3d at 791, 208 Cal. Rptr. at 282 (citing SUMMARY OF 1981 CRIME LEGISLATION REPORT at 17).

99. *Id.*

100. *See, e.g.*, People v. Perkins, 37 Cal. 2d 62, 64, 230 P.2d 353, 355 (1951).

immobilized sentry, reminders that whether their arrangement was wisdom or folly, it was wittingly under-taken and not to be disregarded.[101]

This principle is found throughout California law. "Also, in arriving at the meaning of a Constitution,[102] consideration must be given to the words employed, giving every word, clause and sentence their ordinary meaning. If doubts and ambiguities remain then, *and only then* are we warranted in seeking elsewhere for aid."[103] Ascertaining the plain meaning of a statute before using extrinsic legislative aids is a practice with well-respected roots.[104]

Courts first look to the text to prevent themselves from giving their own subjective evaluation of the motives behind legislation. "The judgment of the court rests upon the ruling that another purpose, not professed, may be read beneath the surface, and by the purpose so imputed, the statute is destroyed. There is a wise and ancient doctrine that a court will not inquire into the motives of a legislative body."[105] When courts use extrinsic aids to attempt to discern the motives behind legislation, statutory interpretation becomes an increasingly subjective field that brings with it the threat of judicial legislation.[106] When a court departs from the text of a statute and substitutes a "legislative intent" that it gleans from extrinsic sources, it substitutes its own views for that of the legislature.

The foremost embodiment of legislative intent is in the text of the statute. The legislature, when approving a statute, approves the text, not the legislative history. When the governor signs a bill, he signs the text into law, not the debates, hearings or commissioner's comments. When a statute is enacted it is reasonable to assume the

---

101. People v. Knowles, 35 Cal. 2d 175, 182, 217 P.2d 1, 5 (1950) (emphasis added).

102. Principles that apply to construction of constitutions should also apply to statutory construction. *See* Lungren v. Deukmejian, 45 Cal. 3d 727, 735, 755 P.2d 299, 303, 248 Cal. Rptr. 115, 120 (1988).

103. State Board of Education v. Levit, 52 Cal. 2d 441, 462, 343 P.2d 8, 20 (1959) (emphasis added). *See, e.g.,* Lungren v. Deukmejian, 45 Cal. 3d 727, 735, 755 P.2d 299, 303-04, 248 Cal. Rptr. 115, 120 (1988); People v. Craft, 41 Cal. 3d 554, 559-60, 715 P.2d 585, 588, 224 Cal. Rptr. 626, 629 (1986); *In re* Lance W., 37 Cal. 3d 873, 886, 694 P.2d 744, 752, 210 Cal. Rptr. 631, 639 (1985); Solberg v. Superior Court, 19 Cal. 3d 182, 198, 561 P.2d 1148, 1158, 137 Cal. Rptr. 460, 470 (1977).

104. "[W]hile courts are no longer confined to the language [of the statute], they are still confined by it. Violence must not be done to the words chosen by the Legislature." Frankfurter, *Some Reflections on the Reading of Statutes*, 47 COLUM. L. REV. 527, 543 (1948).

105. United States v. Constantine, 296 U.S. 287, 298-99 (1935) (Cardozo, J., dissenting).

106. "We have no alternative but to resort to judicial construction, that is, to judicial legislation." People v. Higgins, 87 Cal. App. 2d Supp. 938, 941, 197 P.2d 417, 419 (1948).

legislature intended what was written into the text of the statute. "After all, legislation when not expressed in technical terms is addressed to the common run of men and is therefore to be understood according to the sense of the thing as the ordinary man has a right to rely on ordinary words addressed to him."[107]

The first task in interpreting section 288(d) is to determine whether its words can be given a plain meaning. The majority of the text of section 288(d) is relatively straightforward.[108] The most difficult part of section 288(d) to interpret is the phrase "shall do whatever is necessary and constitutionally permissible." The *Hochheiser* court found that section 288(d) only stated a "mandate for philosophical change."[109] This renders the operative phrase "shall do whatever is necessary . . . and constitutionally permissible" superfluous as the phrase "shall consider the needs of the child victim" already gives the philosophical position of the legislature.

The word "shall" is typically given either a mandatory or directory reading by the courts.[110] The word "shall" is not always read to be mandatory, but California courts frequently have given "shall" this literal interpretation. In determining whether the word "shall" is mandatory or directory, courts have tried to discern which reading best fits the statute's purpose. "The entire statute may be resorted to in order to ascertain its proper meaning. If to construe it as directory would render it ineffective and meaningless, it should not receive that construction."[111]

A directory interpretation of section 288(d) would prevent it from accomplishing its purpose. The purpose of section 288(d) is "to prevent psychological harm to the victim."[112] If section 288(d) is viewed as directory, courts have the option of doing nothing to help the child victim. By giving "shall" a mandatory meaning, courts must address the child molestation victim's problems. Obviously, it will be easier to help child molestation victims if courts are required

---

107. Addison v. Holly Hill Fruit Products, Co., 322 U.S. 607, 618 (1944).

108. For the sake of convenience, the text of section 288(d) will be repeated: "In any arrest or prosecution under this section or under section 288.5 the peace officer, the district attorney and the court shall consider the needs of the child victim and shall do whatever is necessary, within budgetary resources, and constitutionally permissible to prevent psychological harm to the victim." CAL. PENAL CODE § 288(d) (West Supp. 1990).

109. Hochheiser v. Superior Court, 161 Cal. App. 3d 777, 791, 208 Cal. Rptr. 273, 282 (1984).

110. *See, e.g.,* Jacobs v. State Bar, 20 Cal. 3d 191, 198, 570 P.2d 1230, 1233, 141 Cal. Rptr. 812, 815 (1977).

111. Carter v. Seaboard Finance Co., 33 Cal. 2d 564, 573, 203 P.2d 758, 764 (1949).

112. CAL. PENAL CODE § 288(d) (West Supp. 1990).

to help them instead of being given the option of doing nothing for the children. "When the object is to subserve some public purpose, the provision may be held directory or mandatory as will best accomplish that purpose."[113] The construction of "shall" goes to the heart of section 288(d). "In constructing a statute matters of substance are to be construed as mandatory."[114]

Giving "shall" a mandatory reading also aligns it with its commonly understood definition. Webster's dictionary defines "shall" as expressing "determination, compulsion, obligation, or necessity in the second or third person."[115] *Black's Law Dictionary* also gives "shall" a mandatory definition.

> As used in statutes, contracts, or the like, this word is generally imperative or mandatory. In common or ordinary parlance, and in its ordinary signification, the word shall *is a word of command*, and one which *has always or which must be given a compulsory meaning*; as denoting obligation.[116]

Therefore, giving "shall" a mandatory meaning follows both the common law and common sense. The phrase "whatever is necessary" sets the scope of the duty imposed by "shall." Webster's dictionary defines "whatever" as "anything that, [such] as, tell her *whatever you like*."[117] Given the broad objective of section 288(d) to help child molestation victims, "whatever" should be given its plain meaning. The word "necessary," however, has been treated in different ways by the courts. The common definition of "necessary" is restrictive. "[T]hat cannot be dispensed with; essential; indispensable; as water is *necessary* to life."[118] Black's recognizes the different meanings courts attach to "necessary:"

> This word must be considered in the connection in which it is used as it is a word susceptible of various meanings. It may import absolute physical necessity or inevitability, or it may import that which is only convenient, appropriate, suitable, proper or conducive to the end sought. It is an adjective expressing degrees and may express mere convenience or that which is indispensable or an absolute physical necessity.[119]

---

113. Pulcifer v. County of Alameda, 29 Cal. 2d 258, 262, 175 P.2d 1, 3 (1946).
114. People v. Butler, 20 Cal. App. 379, 384, 129 P. 600, 602 (1912).
115. WEBSTER'S NEW TWENTIETH CENTURY DICTIONARY UNABRIDGED 1666 (2d ed. 1983).
116. BLACK'S LAW DICTIONARY 1223 (5th ed. 1979) (emphasis added).
117. WEBSTER'S NEW TWENTIETH CENTURY DICTIONARY UNABRIDGED 2081 (emphasis in original).
118. *Id.* at 1200 (emphasis in original).
119. BLACK'S LAW DICTIONARY 928 (5th ed. 1979).

California courts also recognize the flexibility of the term "necessary."[120] Given the broad purpose behind 288(d) the more flexible definition of "necessary" should be used. While it may be easy to determine what is necessary to achieve some physical goal such as "water is necessary to life," a child's psychological well-being, being much more abstract, is therefore much more difficult to define precisely than some physical objective. Therefore, "necessary" should be given a flexible definition to match the inherently difficult to define standard of "psychological harm to the victim."[121] Thus "necessary" should be read to mean "suitable, proper, or conducive" to give courts sufficient latitude to deal with the psychological harm that can befall the child molestation victim.

Under section 288(d) courts are therefore under a duty to do everything suitable to prevent psychological harm to the child molestation victim. The final question to answer in interpreting section 288(d) is the reach of this duty—what is "suitable" under section 288(d)? This question is answered by the phrase "and constitutionally permissible." A court's duty under section 288(d) is only limited by the constitution. Therefore, if a court's action does not violate a defendant's United States or California constitutional rights or California's separation of powers doctrine,[122] the court's action is immune from attack.

---

120. See Westphal v. Westphal, 122 Cal. App. 379, 382, 10 P.2d 119, 120 (1932); Danley v. Merced Irrigation Dist., 66 Cal. App. 97, 105, 226 P. 847, 850 (1924).

121. The phrase "psychological harm to the victim," while addressing an inherently abstract topic, the mental health of a child, does not render 288(d) so ambiguous that its plain meaning cannot be determined. The key issue of section 288(d) as *Hochheiser* recognized, is whether section 288(d) gives the courts additional authority to help child molestation victims. The phrase "psychological harm to the victim," other than stating the goal of section 288(d), has no bearing on the reach of the statute.

The phrase "within existing budgetary resources," added by the legislature in 1989, does not justify the interpretation taken by the *Hochheiser* court. See 1989 Cal. Leg. Serv. ch. 1402, sec. 3, at 5256 (West) (amending CAL. PENAL CODE § 288). By imposing a financial limit for the expenditure or resources under this section, the legislature has indicated a belief that some substantive action is expected under section 288(d). This further undercuts the *Hochheiser* court's belief that section 288(d) only mandated a "philosophical change" as philosophical changes do not cost money. *Hochheiser*, 161 Cal. App. 3d at 791, 208 Cal. Rptr. at 282. By providing for the expenditure of money, the legislature has noted that section 288(d) is meant to accomplish substantive goals such as providing for the appointment of counsel for children.

As the phrase "within budgetary resources" was not contained in section 288(d) when *Hochheiser* was decided, this new phrase also provides a means for distinguishing *Hochheiser* from any use of section 288(d) under the new statute. As this phrase is only concerned with the means provided to finance acts under section 288(d) it has no other direct bearing on a court's power under section 288(d) to appoint counsel for the child for the fiscal effects of the phrase "within existing budgetary resources." See *infra* note 231.

122. See CAL. CONST. art. V, § 13 (powers of the Attorney General).

A court should refuse "to follow the plain meaning of a statute only when it would inevitably have frustrated the manifest purpose of the legislation as a whole or led to absurd results."[123] Giving section 288(d) its plain meaning would not frustrate the legislature's plan, but would instead enhance it. It would give courts the power to help child molestation victims, an end the legislature wanted to achieve when it passed section 288(d). Giving courts the power to aid child molestation victims does not lead to any absurd results. There is nothing absurd in allowing courts to fashion curatives to help some of the most vulnerable victims of crime.

In determining a statute's meaning, courts "are required to give effect to statutes 'according to the usual, ordinary import of the language employed in framing them.'"[124] If the legislature only wanted section 288(d) to "mandate a philosophical change focusing on the minors needs,"[125] then it would have written section 288(d) differently. Section 288(d) would then read:

> It is the policy of the State of California that in any arrest or prosecution under this section the peace officer, the district attorney and the court ought to consider the psychological needs of the child victim.

Courts recognize that different words have different meanings, and that the legislature is aware of this when it writes statutes.[126] Thus, if the legislature wanted section 288(d) to have the meaning *Hochheiser* gave it, the legislature would have written section 288(d) to look like the passage above. As the legislature did not do this, the judiciary should not rewrite the section.

The chief constitutional objection that can be made to appointing an attorney for victims of child molestation is that it violates the separation of powers. The separation of powers doctrine is violated when the district attorney's decision to institute criminal proceedings is subject to the control of a private citizen.[127] The child's attorney is not a private citizen appointed special prosecutor by a court.[128]

---

123. People v. Belleci, 24 Cal. 3d 879, 884, 598 P.2d 473, 477, 157 Cal. Rptr. 503, 507 (1979).

124. Moyer v. Workmens's Compensation Appeal Board, 10 Cal. 3d 222, 230, 514 P.2d 1224, 1229, 110 Cal. Rptr. 144, 149 (1973).

125. Hochheiser v. Superior Court, 161 Cal. App. 3d at 791, 208 Cal. Rptr. at 282.

126. See Hogya v. Superior Court, 75 Cal. App. 3d 122, 133, 142 Cal. Rptr. 325, 333 (1977) (the legislature recognizes the difference between "shall" and "may").

127. People v. Shults, 87 Cal. App. 3d 101, 106, 150 Cal. Rptr. 747, 750 (1978).

128. See People v. Municipal Court (Bishop), 27 Cal. App. 3d 193, 207, 103 Cal. Rptr. 605, 656 (1972).

His job is to minimize the damage the judicial process does to the child, not decide whether charges are brought.

While it is not necessary to use legislative history to support this reading of section 288(d), the legislative history of section 288(d) provides support for a court's authority to appoint counsel for the child. Before passing section 288(d), the legislature held extensive hearings on the problem of child molestation and the failings of the legal system in dealing with it.[129] The *Hochheiser* court determined that these hearings were unfavorable to support the use of closed-circuit television under section 288(d), even though the use of closed-circuit television was never mentioned during the hearing.[130] Representation for the victims was, however, mentioned several times during the hearings.[131] While these usually addressed the need for someone to advocate the child's position, at one point the testimony did specifically mention the need for counsel for the victims.[132]

The child molestation hearings support a much broader reading of section 288(d) than the *Hochheiser* court gave it. Numerous references were made to the trauma the legal process inflicts on molested children.[133] As Senator Omer Rains, chairman of the Joint Committee for Revision of the Penal Code stated:

> California's laws in this area lag far behind other states which have revised their laws to deal more efficiently and effectively with persons who molest children. For example, there are no courtroom procedures in California designed to lessen the psychological harm done to the victim. The psychological effects on the victim caused by present courtroom procedures and prosecution methods are frequently every bit as serious and long lasting as the criminal act itself.[134]

Senator David Roberti also recognized the need to help child molestation victims.

> Studies indicate that both the initial molestation and the reliving of it as the case goes through the criminal-justice [*sic*] process have

---

129. Joint Committee for Revision of the Penal Code, Hearing on Child Molestation, December 16, 1980, April 10, 1981, April 24, 1981; Assembly Committee on Criminal Justice, Child Molestation Hearing, November 12, 1980 [hereinafter to be referred to as Child Molestation Hearings].

130. *Hochheiser*, 161 Cal. App. 3d at 790-91, 208 Cal. Rptr. at 281-82.

131. *See* Child Molestation Hearings, Nov. 12 at 78-79, 196-97; Child Molestation Hearings, Dec. 16 at 54.

132. Child Molestation Hearings, Nov. 12 at 78-79.

133. *See* Child Molestation Hearings, Nov. 12 at 196-97; Child Molestation Hearings, Dec. 16 at 1-2, 53-54, 73, 86-87, Appendix D at 4; Child Molestation Hearings, April 10 at 2, 19, 38, 56; Child Molestation Hearings, April 24 at 2, 10, 37, 41, 78.

134. Child Molestation Hearings, Apr. 10 at 2.

long-range detrimental effects on the victim, yet much of the law centers around the punishment and rehabilitation of the offender. Is enough attention being given to the needs of the victim?[135]

As the *Hochheiser* court recognized, the hearings considered many different techniques for lessening the psychological harm to the victim. These techniques included "videotaping procedures to avoid victims having to repeat their testimony, strictly prohibiting continuances, closing hearings, providing for the attendance of a supporting parent, and limiting the kind of questioning and voir dire."[136] The legislature was both acutely concerned with the problems of child molestation victims and aware of a broad spectrum of techniques that could lessen the harm the system did to the children. Section 288(d) was the legislature's response to this. In response to these problems facing the victims of child molestation, the legislature enacted section 288(d) and gave the courts the ability to engage in a variety of measures to help meet the many different needs of child molestation victims.

Hochheiser also attacks the ameliorative purpose of section 288(d) by citing subsequent legislative efforts to help child molestation victims.[137] *Hochheiser*'s emphasis on subsequent legislative acts is misplaced, however, as the relevant legislative intent is the intent of the legislature that enacted the statute. Subsequent legislation cannot change the plain meaning or legislative history of section 288(d) without amending it. As no such amendment has been made, the original interpretation of section 288(d) is still valid.

The *Hochheiser* court had two final justifications for narrowly construing section 288(d). The first, that it should not construe a statute to overthrow long-established principles of law unless such intention is clearly shown,[138] is inapplicable, as the appointment of counsel is not a new principle. Appointed counsel is a well-established procedure in criminal cases.[139] Furthermore, in California appointed counsel is particularly common in proceedings involving children.[140] Thus appointing counsel does not overthrow any long-established principles that the *Hochheiser* court wanted to protect.

---

135. CHILD MOLESTATION HEARINGS, Dec. 16 at 1-2.
136. *Hochheiser*, 161 Cal. App. 3d at 791 n.9, 208 Cal. Rptr. at 282 n.9.
137. *Id.* at 791, 208 Cal. Rptr. at 282.
138. *Id.* at 791-92, 208 Cal. Rptr. at 282.
139. *See infra* notes 81-82 and accompanying text.
140. *See infra* notes 84-88 and accompanying text.

The second reason is the rule of construction that penal statutes are to be construed in favor of the defendant.[141] This rule of construction, however, is only applicable when the language is susceptible to more than one construction.[142] Furthermore, "that rule will not be applied to change manifest, reasonable legislative purpose."[143] This rule is only a tool of construction. It cannot be invoked where the statute is unambiguous. "The rule comes into operation at the end of the process of construing what Congress had expressed, not at the beginning as an overriding consideration of being lenient to wrong-doers. That is not the function of the judiciary."[144] The *Hochheiser* court did not come up with any reasonable alternative to the plain meaning of section 288(d)—that a court must do anything practical that is not constitutionally forbidden to help protect the child molestation victim from any further psychological harm as the result of a prosecution under section 288. "[T]he canon entitles defendant only to the benefit of every *realistic* doubt. This rule of construction 'is not an inexorable command to override common sense and evident statutory purpose.'"[145] There is no realistic doubt to justify veering from the plain meaning of section 288(d).

The *Hochheiser* court was concerned with a possible violation of defendant's constitutional rights when it interpreted section 288(d).[146] While this may explain the *Hochheiser* court's narrow construction of section 288(d), it does not justify such a narrow construction. The *Hochheiser* court, in its zeal to protect defendant ignored the primary source of a statute's meaning — the text of the statute.[147] A thorough examination of the text of section 288(d) shows that the statute gives courts a broad grant of power to help molested children through the ordeal of the child molestation prosecution.[148]

---

141. *Hochheiser*, 161 Cal. App. 3d at 792, 208 Cal. Rptr. at 282.
142. *See id.*
143. People v. Banks, 53 Cal. 2d 370, 391, 348 P.2d 102, 116, 1 Cal. Rptr. 669, 683 (1959).
144. Callanan v. United States, 364 U.S. 587, 596 (1961).
145. People v. Anderson, 43 Cal. 3d 1104, 1145-46, 742 P.2d 1306, 1330, 240 Cal. Rptr. 585, 609 (1987) (emphasis in original) (quoting United States v. Brown, 338 U.S. 18, 25 (1948)). As Justice Black stated:

> No rule of construction, however, requires that a penal statute be strained and distorted in order to exclude conduct clearly intended to be within its·scope—nor does any rule require that the act be given the "narrowest meaning." It is sufficient if the words are given their fair meaning in accord with the evident intent of Congress.

United States v. Raynor, 302 U.S. 540, 552 (1938).
146. *See supra* notes 61-63 and accompanying text.
147. *See supra* notes 101-07 and accompanying text.
148. *See supra* notes 108-22 and accompanying text.

713

"There is, of course, no more persuasive evidence of the purpose of a statute than the words by which the legislature undertook to give expression to its wishes."[149] This principle, not the various rationales offered by the *Hochheiser* court, should be followed to allow section 288(d) to do what the legislature intended it to accomplish—help the molested child through the ordeal of the criminal prosecution.

II. Preventing Defense Counsel from Talking to the Victims

A. Rule 2-100

An attorney for the child molestation victim has many means to minimize the trauma of legal proceedings.[150] One of the most effective techniques to protect the child witness would be for the child's attorney to bar defense counsel from having any contact with the victim without the consent of the child's attorney. The child's counsel could then limit the number of times a child would have to repeat his story and prevent unnecessary encounters between the child and potentially hostile attorneys.

Among the greatest burdens a molested child must bear is the burden of having to incessantly repeat the story of his molestation to other people. In addition to making the initial complaint, usually to "a trusted friend, non-abusing parent, counselor or teacher,"[151] the child must go through an odyssey of retelling his experiences over and over again. First, he usually must "relate, in vivid detail, the specifics of the sexual encounter" to a police officer.[152] Then he will be transported to the local emergency room for physical examination, where he "is confronted with more strangers and the setting in all too many cases is a frightening environment."[153] In this setting he may again be required to retell his story.[154] Next, he will be interviewed by the detectives and district attorney(s) assigned to his

---

149. United States v. American Trucking Ass'ns, 310 U.S. 534, 543 (1940).
150. *See, e.g.,* CAL. ATTORNEY GENERAL, CALIFORNIA CHILD VICTIM WITNESS JUDICIAL ADVISORY COMMITTEE 69 n.5 (1988). *See also infra* notes 153-55 and accompanying text.
151. *Avery, supra* note 15, at 14.
152. *Id.*
153. *Id.* at 15.
154. *Id.*

case to determine the strength of his case.[155] This may also involve a polygraph examination.[156] If the district attorney decides to prosecute, the child, as the main witness, will have to testify at the preliminary hearing, and, if necessary, the trial.[157]

In addition to all of these interviews, the unrepresented child will frequently be interviewed by defendant's counsel. While the victim is under no obligation to talk to defense counsel, the uninformed victim is likely to be unaware that he does not have to talk to defense counsel.[158] The attorney for the child, in addition to informing the child and his guardian about his right to refuse to talk to defense counsel[159] can also prevent defense counsel from contacting the victim by virtue of the attorney-client relationship between the victim and his counsel.

Rule 2-100 subdivision (a) of the Rules of Professional Conduct of the State Bar of California[160] provides that

> while representing a client, a member shall not communicate directly or indirectly about the subject of the representation with a party the member knows to be represented by another lawyer in the matter, unless the member has the consent of the other lawyer.

The purpose of this rule is preserving the attorney-client relationship.

---

155. *Id.*

156. *Id.*

157. *See Berliner & Barbieri, supra* note 1, at 125.

158. *See* People v. Municipal Court (Runyon), 20 Cal. 3d 523, 531, 574 P.2d 425, 429, 143 Cal. Rptr. 609, 613 (1978); People v. Mersino, 237 Cal. App. 2d 265, 269, 46 Cal. Rptr. 821, 824 (1965) (defendant has no right to depose witnesses).

159. The district attorney would have a much more difficult time telling the victim that he did not have to talk to defense counsel. *See* People v. Hannon, 19 Cal. 3d 588, 601, 564 P.2d 1203, 1211, 138 Cal. Rptr. 885, 892-93 (1977) (state cannot tell witness not to talk to defense counsel).

160. CAL. CIV. & CRIM. R., PROF. CONDUCT 2-100 (West Interim Annot. Serv. No. 1 1989). The predecessor of Rule 2-100 was Rule 7-103 which provided that:

> [a] member of the State Bar shall not communicate directly or indirectly with a party whom he knows to be represented by counsel upon a subject of controversy, without the express consent of such counsel. This rule shall not apply to communications with a public officer, board, committee or body.

CAL. CIV. & CRIM. R., PROF. CONDUCT 7-103 (West Supp. 1989) (repealed). This Article also will discuss several ethical rules promulgated by the American Bar Association. The Model Code of Professional Responsibility is based upon ethical considerations ("EC") and disciplinary rules ("DR"). The ethical considerations "are aspirational in character and represent the objectives towards which every member should strive." AMERICAN BAR FOUNDATION, ANNOTATED CODE OF PROFESSIONAL RESPONSIBILITY 3 (1979). The disciplinary rules, however, "state the minimum level of conduct below which no lawyer can fall without being subject to disciplinary action." *Id.* Thus, the Ethical Considerations can be seen as providing interpretive guidance to the Disciplinary Rules. *Id.* at 4. The Model Rules of Professional Conduct designed to replace the Model Code of Professional Responsibility do not have any Ethical Considerations. They consists only of rules, with comments to each rule indicating the drafters' intent.

This rule [former Rule 12] is necessary to the preservation of the attorney-client relationship and the proper functioning of the administration of justice . . . . It shields the opposing party not only from an attorney's approaches which are intentionally improper, but, in addition, from approaches, which are well intended but misguided.

The rule was designed to permit an attorney to function adequately in his proper role and to prevent the opposing attorney from impeding his performance in such role. If a party's counsel is present when an opposing attorney communicates with a party, counsel can easily correct any element of error in the communication or correct the effect of the communication by calling attention to counteracting elements which may exist.[161]

The key to determining whether the relationship between the molested child and his appointed counsel is protected by Rule 2-100 is determining if the victim of a crime is a "party" within the meaning of Rule 2-100. If the child is a party under Rule 2-100, then his relationship with his attorney will be protected, and his attorney will be able to invoke the rule to insulate the child from the unwanted attention of defense counsel.

The objection that would be made against this use of Rule 2-100 is that the term "party" under Rule 2-100 is limited to the parties to the action. This objection, however, understates the reach of Rule 2-100 as it fails to appreciate the intent behind Rule 2-100. California's Penal Code defines the formal parties to the criminal case. Section 684 of the Penal Code states that "[a] criminal action is prosecuted in the name of the people of the state of California, as a party, against the person charged with the offense,"[162] and Section 685 provides that "[t]he party prosecuted in a criminal action is designated in this code as the defendant."[163] These do not, however, provide much help in determining the definition of "party" for Rule 2-100. The comment to Rule 2-100 specifically states that the term "party" is not limited to its litigation context. "As used in subparagraph (a) [of Rule 2-100] 'the subject of representation,' 'matter,' and 'party' are not limited to a litigation context."[164] Thus, these Penal Code sections cannot address the reach of Rule 2-100.

---

161. Mitton v. State Bar, 71 Cal. 2d 525, 534, 455 P.2d 753, 758, 78 Cal. Rptr. 649, 654 (1969).
162. CAL. PENAL CODE § 684 (West 1985).
163. *Id.* § 685 (West 1985).
164. Rule 2-100, comment (West Interim Annot. Serv. No. 1, 1989). This interpretation

The cases are similarly unenlightening. In *People v. Jung Qung Sung*,[165] the California Supreme Court determined that the parties to a criminal action were the people and the defendant.[166] But the court only needed to define the minimum extent of "parties" to hold that defendant was present throughout the trial when the trial record only stated that "the parties" were present throughout the trial.[167]

The only case that addressed the question of who is a "party" within the meaning of Rule 2-100 is *Kain v. Municipal Court*.[168] In *Kain*, the defendant attempted to disqualify the entire district attorney's office from his prosecution for molesting his daughters, as the office at the same time was representing the children in the dependency action against defendant.[169] The court of appeal did not accept defendant's argument that Rule 7-103[170] would prevent his counsel from communicating with the children concerning defendant's criminal prosecution. The court summarily rejected this argument, stating that the victims are not parties to a criminal action under Rule 7-103.[171]

Kain, however, does not prevent attorneys for child molestation victims from invoking Rule 2-100 to protect their clients because

---

of Rule 2-100 does not contradict this Article's textual interpretation of section 288(d). The comment which shows the ambiguity of the term "party," is very closely related to the text of rule 2-100. In the code containing rule 2-100, the comment immediately follows rule 2-100. *See* CAL. CIV. & CRIM. R. PROF. CONDUCT 2-100 comment (West Interim Annot. Serv. No. 1 1989). As the comment is literally on the same page as the text of Rule 2-100, it should be given substantial weight in interpreting Rule 2-100. This stands in contrast to the legislative materials used by the *Hochheiser* court in interpreting section 288(d) which were not included anywhere near the text of section 288(d). *See supra* notes 64-68 and accompanying text. Thus, the drafters of Rule 2-100, by including the comment with Rule 2-100, introduced the ambiguity into Rule 2-100 for all people to see. Therefore an interpretation of Rule 2-100 based on the comment does not contradict the text of the Rule 2-100 because the comment is effectively a part of the text of Rule 2-100.

165. 70 Cal. 469, 11 P. 755 (1886).

166. *Id.* at 472, 11 P. at 757.

167. *Id. See also* Oppenheimer v. Clifton's Brookdale, Inc., 98 Cal. App. 2d 403, 220 P.2d 422 (1950). In *Oppenheimer*, the court found that bribery of a police officer was a public offense and therefore could only be prosecuted in the name of the people. *Id.* at 404, 220 P.2d at 423. *Oppenheimer*, however, concerned the institution of a civil action, and whether alleging bribery of a public official was sufficient to state a cause of action. Oppenheimer did not determine who constituted the parties to a criminal case and thus is not applicable to determining the scope of Rule 2-100. *Id.* at 405, 220 P.2d at 423.

168. 130 Cal. App. 3d 499, 181 Cal. Rptr. 751 (1982).

169. *Id.* at 98 Cal. App. 2d at 501-02, 181 Cal. Rptr. at 752.

170. The predecessor of Rule 2-100 was Rule 7-103 which provided that:
    [a] member of the State Bar shall not communicate directly or indirectly with a party whom he knows to be represented by counsel upon a subject of controversy, without the express consent of such counsel. This rule shall not apply to communications with a public officer, board, committee or body.
CAL. CIV. & CRIM. R., PROF. CONDUCT 7-103 (West Supp. 1989) (repealed).

171. *Kain*, 130 Cal. App. 3d at 504, 181 Cal. Rptr. at 753-54.

Kain involved two different attorney-client relationships. The attorney-client relationship between the district attorney's office and the children in *Kain* arises from the dependency action.[172] The dependency action is commenced under section 300 of the Welfare and Institutions Code, and its purpose is "to protect and promote the welfare of the child, not to punish the parent."[173] The purpose of criminal law, however, is concerned with the punishment of defendant.[174] While the district attorney, as public prosecutor, may want to see that the child's best interests are served, his duty as public prosecutor is to see that the defendant is punished for his crimes.[175] Thus, as each has a different interest in the criminal action, the children have no attorney-client relationship with the district attorney's office in its role as public prosecutor.[176] Furthermore, the prosecutor already has a client in the criminal action, the people of California.[177] Therefore, as the district attorney is not the attorney for the molested children in a criminal action, he does not have standing to invoke Rule 2-100 to protect the children.[178] Thus, *Kain* can be distinguished because the *Kain* court did not deal with an attorney appointed to represent the children in the criminal case.

The Drafters' Comments present the best evidence of who is a party within the meaning of Rule 2-100. In addition to stating that the term "party" is not to be used in its litigation context,[179] the Drafters' Comments also show the intent behind the rule. "Rule 2-100 is intended to control communications between a member and persons the member knows to be represented by counsel . . . ."[180] The word "party" is conspicuously absent from this part of the Drafters' Comments. This indicates that Rule 2-100 is intended to

---

172. *See id.* at 501, 181 Cal. Rptr. at 752.

173. Collins v. Superior Court, 74 Cal. App. 3d 47, 52, 141 Cal. Rptr. 273, 276 (1977).

174. *See* HALL, GENERAL PRINCIPLES OF CRIMINAL LAW 18 (2d ed. 1960).

175. *See* CAL. CONST. art. V, § 13; City of Merced v. County of Merced, 240 Cal. App. 2d 763, 766, 50 Cal. Rptr. 287, 289 (1966).

176. *See* CAL. CIV. & CRIM. R., PROF. CONDUCT 3-310 (West Interim Annot. Serv. No. 1 1989) (representation of adverse interests).

177. *See supra* note 175.

178. California Rule of Professional Conduct Rule 2-100 states in relevant part:
[w]hile representing a client, a member shall not communicate directly or indirectly about the subject of the representation with a party the member knows to be represented by another lawyer in the matter, unless the member has the consent of the other lawyer.
CAL. CIV. & CRIM. R., PROF. CONDUCT 2-100 (West Interim Annot. Serv. No. 1 1989).

179. *See supra* note 164 and accompanying text.

180. CAL. CIV. & CRIM. R., PROF. CONDUCT 2-100 comment (West Interim Annot. Serv. No. 1 1989).

718

cover more than the formal parties to the litigation. Instead, as the Drafters' Comments suggest, it should cover any person who has retained counsel regarding a matter, regardless of whether that person is a formal party to any litigation.

This reading of Rule 2-100 follows the standards set by the American Bar Association. EC 7-18 provides that

> [t]he legal system in its broadest sense functions best when persons in need of legal advice or assistance are represented by their own counsel. For this reason a lawyer should not communicate on the subject matter of the representation of his client with a *person* he knows to be represented in the matter by a lawyer, unless pursuant to law . . . or unless he has the consent of the lawyer for that person.[181]

EC 7-18 demonstrates the purpose behind the rule against communication with represented persons. If someone is represented by counsel regarding a matter, that person's relationship with his attorney should be respected regardless of the client's status in litigation, if any, and no other attorney should interfere with it without the client's attorney's consent.

The newer Model Rules of Professional Conduct agree. Model Rule 4.2 provides:

> In representing a client, a lawyer shall not communicate about the subject of the representation with a party the lawyer knows to be represented by another lawyer in the matter, unless the lawyer has the consent of the other lawyer or is authorized by law to do so.[182]

The comment to this rule shows the broad meaning that should be given to the term "party." "This rule covers any person, *whether or not a party to a formal proceeding,* who is represented by counsel concerning the matter in question."[183] The comment to rule 4.2 gives the proper definition of party for Rule 2-100. "Party" must mean more than the formal parties to litigation.[184] Extending the definition of party to include anyone who is represented by counsel concerning the matter in question advances the goal of Rule 2-100 of preserving the attorney-client relationship while at the same time allowing attorneys to speak with represented people on matters outside the representation. "This Rule does not prohibit communication with a

---

181. MODEL CODE OF PROFESSIONAL RESPONSIBILITY EC 7-18 (1980). *See supra* note 160, for the differences between an ethical consideration "EC" and the disciplinary rule "DR."
182. MODEL RULES OF PROFESSIONAL CONDUCT Rule 4.2 (1983).
183. *Id.* Rule 4.2 comment (emphasis added).
184. *See supra* note 164 and accompanying text.

party, or an employee or agent of a party, concerning matters outside the representation."[185]

The ABA's third pronouncement on this subject, DR 7-104(A) is less certain.

> DR 7-104 Communication With One of Adverse Interest. (A) During the course of his representation of a client a lawyer shall not:
> (1) Communicate or cause another to communicate on the subject of the representation with a party he knows to be represented by a lawyer in that matter unless he has the prior consent of the lawyer representing such other party or is authorized by law to do so.[186]

The Textual and Historical Notes provide no additional information regarding the intention of the drafter's in using the term "party."[187] Given the similarity between rule 4.2 and DR 7-104 (a)(1)[188] and that rule 4.2 has a drafter's comment, while DR 7-104(a)(1) has no statement of the drafter's intent, there is no reason to interpret DR 7-104(A)(1) any differently.[189]

The broad definition of party also has academic support.

> Both DR 7-104(A)(1) and MR 4.2 prohibit contact with a represented "party." The lawyerism *party* sometimes refers only to parties in litigation but evidently is here intended to refer broadly to any "person" represented by a lawyer in a matter. Vide 'party of the first part' in ancient contracts.[190]

This view is taken as a given by some in the field of continuing legal education. "Witnesses in a criminal case who testify for the prosecution are not considered to be represented by the prosecutor and may be directly approached by defense counsel unless they are represented by another attorney concerning their testimony in that case."[191]

Allowing people other than the formal parties to the litigation to be protected by Rule 2-100 makes good law and good sense. The purpose of the rule is not just to insure that neither side of a litigation gains unfair advantage over the other; it is also designed to preserve the attorney-client relationship. "[T]he ultimate purpose of [then] Rule 7-103 is to preserve the confidentiality of attorney-

---

185. MODEL RULES OF PROFESSIONAL CONDUCT Rule 4.2 (1983).
186. MODEL CODE OF PROFESSIONAL RESPONSIBILITY DR 7-104(A)(1). *See supra* note 160, for the differences between ethical consideration "EC" and disciplinary rule "DR."
187. MODEL CODE OF PROFESSIONAL RESPONSIBILITY DR-104(A)(1).
188. *See* MODEL RULES OF PROFESSIONAL CONDUCT Rule 4.2 (1983).
189. *See* WOLFRAM, MODERN LEGAL ETHICS § 11.6.2, at 611 (1986).
190. *Id.* at 611 n.33 (emphasis in original).
191. BURR & FEFFER, PREPARATION AND PRESENTATION OF CASE AND ARGUMENT IN CALIFORNIA CRIMINAL LAW § 29.9, at 596 (Cal. Cont. Ed. of the Bar 1986).

client communications.''[192] Extending Rule 2-100 beyond the formal parties to the litigation will help preserve the attorney-client relationship wherever it is threatened by unwarranted communication from another attorney.

The relationship between the molested child and his appointed counsel is the type of attorney-client relationship that should be protected under Rule 2-100 from unwarranted intrusions from defense counsel. Counsel is appointed for the child to minimize the psychological trauma a prosecution under section 288 can do to the child.[193] Defense counsel, by interviewing the child, adds to the harm done to the child by forcing him to retell the story of his molestation.[194] Thus, defense counsel, when interviewing the child without the consent of the child's attorney, strikes at the heart of the child's attorney-client relationship. The reason behind appointing counsel for the child is to minimize the psychological harm done to the child by the legal system.[195] Given the great vulnerability of children, especially when victims of molestation,[196] it is particularly important that Rule 2-100 protect the relationship between the molested child and his attorney. While the attorney-client relationship is always important, it takes on extra meaning when the fragile psyche of the molested child is involved.

B. The Constitutionality of Using Rule 2-100

When an attorney for a molested child uses Rule 2-100 to prevent defense counsel from interviewing the child, a firestorm of protest

---

192. Bobele v. Superior Court, 199 Cal. App. 3d 708, 712, 245 Cal. Rptr. 144, 146 (1988).

193. See supra notes 108-21 and accompanying text.

194. See supra notes 151-57 and accompanying text. One cost of unnecessary contact between the child and defense counsel could be the child's testimony at trial. A child could be willing to retell his story only a limited number of times. Therefore, interviews with defense counsel could be the proverbial "last straw" and make the child unwilling to testify. See Mlyniec & Dally, supra note 32, at 137.

195. The district attorney should be equally susceptible to Rule 2-100. The comment states that "[t]here are a number of express statutory schemes which authorize communications between a member, and person who would otherwise be subject to this rule . . . . Other applicable law includes the authority of government prosecutors and investigators as limited by relevant decisional law." CAL. CIV. & CRIM. R., PROF. CONDUCT 2-100 comment (West Interim Annot. Serv. No. 1, 1989). If the prosecutor wants to interview the child and the child's attorney refuses, then the prosecutor will have to subpoena the child and have the child testify before the grand jury. CAL. PENAL CODE § 939.2 (West Supp. 1989). The child's attorney must determine whether the child's psychological interests are best served either by testifying before the grand jury or by being interviewed by the district attorney subject to whatever conditions that can be agreed upon between the district attorney and the child's attorney

196. See supra notes 15-36 and accompanying text.

from defense counsel will inevitably ensue. Protests from defense counsel should not, however, prevent the child's attorney from limiting access to his client, nor should it prevent courts from upholding such decisions, as there is nothing in either the United States or California constitutions to prohibit the child's counsel from restricting defense counsel's access to the child.

1. Confrontation

Preventing defense counsel from interviewing the child will not deny defendant his right to confront witnesses against him.[197] The right to confrontation is not a right to pretrial discovery. "The right to confrontation is basically a trial right. It includes both the opportunity to cross-examine and the occasion for the jury to weigh the demeanor of the witness."[198] The purpose of the confrontation right is not to give defendant carte blanche in preparing for his trial. "The primary object of [the confrontation clause] was to prevent depositions or ex parte affidavits . . . being used against prisoner in lieu of a personal examination and cross-examination of the witness."[199] Therefore, as long as the defendant is allowed to confront and cross-examine the child *at trial*,[200] his confrontation rights are not violated. "It was clear . . . that the 'confrontation' guaranteed by the Sixth and Fourteenth Amendments is confrontation *at trial*— that is the absence of defendant at the time the codefendant allegedly made the out-of-court statement is immaterial, so long as the declarant can be cross-examined on the witness stand at trial."[201] Therefore, as long as defendant is not prevented from cross-examining defendant at trial there will be no violation of his rights to confrontation.[202]

---

197. U.S. CONST. amends. VI, XIV; CAL. CONST. art. I, § 15.

198. Barber v. Page, 390 U.S. 719, 725 (1968).

199. Mattox v. United States, 156 U.S. 237, 242-43 (1895). Using Rule 2-100 to prevent defense counsel from interviewing the child outside of court will not prevent the early dismissal of meritless cases. The preliminary hearing is the vehicle designed to weed out meritless cases. "The purpose of the preliminary hearing is to weed out groundless or unsupported charges of grave offenses." People v. Eliot, 54 Cal. 2d 498, 504, 354 P.2d 225, 229, 6 Cal. Rptr. 753, 757 (1960). Thus, as long as defendant can cross-examine the child at the preliminary hearing, defendant should be safe from meritless cases.

200. *See* People v. Harris, 165 Cal. App. 3d 1246, 1256, 212 Cal. Rptr. 216, 221-22 (1985) (defendant entitled to confrontation at the preliminary hearing).

201. Nelson v. O'Neil, 402 U.S. 622, 626 (1971).

202. In Pennsylvania v. Ritchie, 480 U.S. 39 (1987), a plurality of the court found that the confrontation clause was only a trial right. *Id.* at 53-54. While three justices opposed this

2. Adequate Defense

Allowing the child's counsel to invoke Rule 2-100 also would not violate defendant's right to prepare an adequate defense. The prosecution has a duty not to suppress evidence favorable to the accused.[203] Furthermore, the prosecution cannot order a potential witness to refuse to speak to defendant's attorney.[204] Thus, if appointing counsel for the child is perceived as a government ploy to deprive the defendant of a chance to interview the witness, then the child's attorney's use of Rule 2-100 could be described as an intentional suppression by the government of whatever evidence defendant would get from interviewing the child.

a. Sufficient Preparation

A defendant is not prevented from interviewing the child because defendant already has an opportunity to interview the child before trial at the preliminary hearing. While the primary function of the preliminary hearing is to "weed out groundless or unsupported charges of grave offenses, and to relieve the accused of the degradation and expense of a criminal trial,"[205] the preliminary hearing can also serve as an important discovery tool for defendant. In *Hawkins v. Superior Court*,[206] the California Supreme Court recognized the important discovery function an adversarial preliminary hearing can play.[207] The *Hawkins* court recognized that one of the most important advantages given to defendants in preliminary hear-

---

holding, *id.* at 61 (Blackmun, J., concurring in part and concurring in the judgment); *id.* at 66 (Brennan, J., and Marshall, J., dissenting), two other justices did not address the confrontation clause issue, dissenting on the grounds that the case lacked finality. *Id.* at 72 (Stevens, J., Brennan, J., Marshall, J., and Scalia, J., dissenting). While California courts have been willing to extend defendant's confrontation right to the preliminary hearing, defendant will still be able to confront the child at the preliminary examination and trial, preserving his right to confrontation under the California Constitution (art. I, section 15). *See, e.g.*, People v. Harris, 165 Cal. App. 3d 1246, 1256, 212 Cal. Rptr. 216, 221-22 (1985) (confrontation right extends to preliminary hearing). Finally, the state right to confrontation may be the same as the federal right. People v. Contreras, 57 Cal. App. 3d 816, 820, 129 Cal. Rptr. 397, 399 (1976).

203. Brady v. Maryland, 373 U.S. 83, 87 (1963).
204. Walker v. Superior Court, 155 Cal. App. 2d 134, 140, 317 P.2d 130, 134 (1957).
205. Jaffe v. Stone, 18 Cal. 2d 146, 150, 114 P.2d 335, 338 (1941).
206. 22 Cal. 3d 584, 586 P.2d 916, 150 Cal. Rptr. 435 (1978).
207. *Id.* at 588, 586 P.2d at 918-19, 150 Cal. Rptr. at 437-438.

723

ings was the ability it gave defense counsel to elicit information from hostile prosecution witnesses.

> There is no other effective means [than the preliminary examination] for the defense to compel the cooperation of a hostile witness [citation]; in the unlikely event that all the prosecution witnesses agree to submit to defense interviews, the defense still must incur unnecessary expense and hardship which may be substantial.[208]

The United States Supreme Court also recognized defendant's ability to interview hostile witnesses at the preliminary examination.

> First, the lawyer's skilled examination and cross-examination of witnesses [at the preliminary hearing] may expose fatal weaknesses in the State's case that may lead the magistrate to refuse to bind the accused over. Second, in any event the skilled interrogation of witnesses by an experienced lawyer can fashion a vital impeachment tool for use in cross-examination of the State's witnesses at the trial . . . . Third, trained counsel can more effectively discover the case the State has against his client and make possible the preparation of a proper defense to meet that case at trial.[209]

Under California law, the defendant has the right to cross-examine prosecution witnesses[210] and to call witnesses on his own behalf at the preliminary hearing.[211] Given the importance of the victim's testimony to the typical child molestation case,[212] the prosecution will usually have the child testify at the preliminary examination and therefore leave him open to cross-examination by defense counsel. This cross-examination may be for the purpose of raising an affirmative defense[213] or to impeach the witness.[214] Furthermore "[i]t is not a valid objection that the examination may lead to discovery . . . or that the cross-examiner is unable to predict what the testimony will develop."[215] Given the latitude defendant has in cross-examination he should have little difficulty in conducting a thorough examination of the child at the preliminary hearing. If the prosecution decides not to call the child at the preliminary hearing then defendant can call the child as a defense witness and can examine him with

---

208. *Id.* at 589, 586 P.2d at 919, 150 Cal. Rptr. at 438.
209. Coleman v. Alabama, 399 U.S. 1, 9 (1970) (plurality opinion).
210. CAL. PENAL CODE § 865 (West 1985).
211. CAL. PENAL CODE § 866 (West 1985).
212. *See supra* note 17 and accompanying text.
213. Jennings v. Superior Court, 66 Cal. 2d 867, 877-78, 428 P.2d 304, 311, 59 Cal. Rptr. 440, 447 (1967).
214. Alford v. Superior Court, 29 Cal. App. 3d 724, 728, 105 Cal. Rptr. 713, 715-16 (1972).
215. Foster v. Superior Court, 107 Cal. App. 3d 218, 225, 165 Cal. Rptr. 701, 705 (1980).

similar thoroughness.[216] The defendant's right to a preliminary hearing,[217] when combined with the broad scope that defense counsel's questioning can take at the preliminary hearing, satisfies whatever right defendant has to interview witnesses to prepare for his defense.[218]

b. No State Action

In addition to not depriving the defendant of any rights, invoking Rule 2-100 survives constitutional scrutiny because the child's attorney's actions cannot be fairly attributed to the state. "[M]ost rights secured by the Constitution are protected only against infringement by governments."[219] The defendant's confrontation right and his right to prepare a defense, to the extent they are derived from the United States Constitution, come from the Due Process Clause of the Fourteenth Amendment.[220] As the fourteenth amendment only applies to state actions, not the actions of private individuals,[221] the attorney's action in invoking Rule 2-100 must in some way be attributed to the state for it to violate defendant's federal constitutional rights.[222]

---

216. *See* McDaniel v. Superior Court, 55 Cal. App. 3d 803, 805, 126 Cal. Rptr. 136, 137 (1976) (applying the principles of *Jennings* to direct examination by defendant at the preliminary hearing).

217. *Hawkins*, 22 Cal. 3d at 593, 586 P.2d at 922, 150 Cal. Rptr. at 441.

218. *Cf.*, Walker v. Superior Court, 155 Cal. App. 2d 134, 317 P.2d 130 (1957). In *Walker*, the defendant was indicted by a grand jury. *Id.* at 139, 317 P.2d at 134. While the court did not mention whether a preliminary hearing had taken place, as it was 20 years before defendant had a right to a post-indictment preliminary hearing, *Hawkins*, 22 Cal. 3d at 593, 586 P.2d at 922, 150 Cal. Rptr. at 441, it is logical to assume that the defendant in *Walker* had no preliminary hearing to give him the opportunity to examine the witness. *Walker* is based on defendant's right to "obtain witnesses to testify on his behalf and to prepare a defense." People v. Hannon, 19 Cal. 3d 588, 601, 564 P.2d 1203, 1210-11, 138 Cal. Rptr. 885, 892-893 (1977). This right is amply protected by defendant's ability to examine the child at the preliminary hearing.

219. Flagg Bros., Inc. v. Brooks, 436 U.S. 149, 156 (1978).

220. *See* Duncan v. Louisiana, 391 U.S. 145, 148 (1968); Brady v. Maryland, 373 U.S. 83, 86 (1963).

221. United States v. Price, 383 U.S. 787, 799 (1966).

222. California also requires state action to invoke its constitution. California's equal protection and due process provisions both require state action. CAL. CONST. art. I, §§ 7, 15. Gay Law Students' Ass'n v. Pacific Tel. & Tel. Co., 24 Cal. 3d 458, 467-69, 595 P.2d 592, 597-598, 156 Cal. Rptr. 14, 19-20 (1979) (equal protection); Kruger v. Wells Fargo Bank, 11 Cal. 3d 352, 366-67, 521 P.2d 441, 449-450, 113 Cal. Rptr. 449, 457-458 (1974) (due process). No California case discusses the relationship between state action and California's confrontation clause, California Constitution article I, section 15. As California's confrontation clause is in the same part of the constitution as California's due process clause, which does require state action, there is no reason not to require state action for California's confrontation clause. The confrontation clause's concern with criminal matters provides all the more reason to limit

725

Therefore, for any constitutional issue to be raised by the use of Rule 2-100 by the child's attorney, the actions of the child's attorney in using Rule 2-100 must in some way be attributed to the state.

When analyzing whether a person's actions can be attributed to the state, the key issue is whether the private actor exercises powers that are usually reserved to the state.[223] If the private actor exercises "power traditionally exclusively reserved to the State" such as elections or running towns, then these actions can be considered state actions.[224] The powers of the attorney are by no means exclusively reserved to the state.[225]

The public importance and heavy regulation of the practice of law does not make it a state function. "Doctors, optometrists, lawyers, Metropolitan [Edison Company], and Nebbia's Upstate New York Grocery selling a quart of milk are all engaged in regulated businesses providing arguably essential goods and services 'affected with a public interest.' We do not believe that such a status converts their every action, absent more, into that of the State."[226]

California's enactment of Rule 2-100 into law does not turn the child's attorney's use of Rule 2-100 into state action. A state must compel the action of a private actor to be responsible for the act.[227] California, in enacting Rule 2-100, does not compel an attorney to use it to prevent contact between his client and another attorney. Indeed, under certain circumstances the child's attorney may want to let the defendant's attorney talk to the child.[228] It is up to the attorney, not the state, to decide whether the client can speak to another attorney about the subject of the representation.[229] "Some-

---

its prohibitions to state action. *See* Dyas v. Superior Court, 11 Cal. 3d 628, 632, 522 P.2d 674, 676, 114 Cal. Rptr. 114, 116 (1974) (California's exclusionary rule does not apply to the actions of private citizens). While the California Supreme Court has defined state action differently from the United States Supreme Court on occasion, it has done so in the heavily regulated area of public utilities. *See* King v. Meese, 43 Cal. 3d 1217, 1229, 743 P.2d 889, 896, 240 Cal. Rptr. 829, 836-837 (1987); *Gay Law Students Ass'n*, 24 Cal. 3d at 469, 595 P.2d at 598-99, 156 Cal. Rptr. at 20-21. Since the attorney's use of Rule 2-100 does not involve such a situation, there is no reason to include the use of Rule 2-100 in a broader definition of state action than the federal courts use.

223. *See* 2 ROTUNDA, NOWAK, & YOUNG, TREATISE ON CONSTITUTIONAL LAW § 16.2, at 163 (1986).

224. Jackson v. Metropolitan Edison Co., 419 U.S. 345, 352 (1974).

225. *See, e.g.*, CAL. BUS. & PROF. CODE § 6060 (West Supp. 1989) (qualifications for admission to California State Bar).

226. *Jackson*, 419 U.S. at 354.

227. Flagg Bros., Inc. v. Brooks, 436 U.S. at 164.

228. *See* SMITH, CHILDREN'S STORY: CHILDREN IN CRIMINAL COURT 43 (1985).

229. "While representing a client, a member shall not communicate directly or indirectly about the subject of the representation with a party the member knows to be represented by

one's exercise of the choice allowed by state law where the initiative comes from [him] and not from the state does not make [his] action in doing so 'state action' for the purposes of the Fourteenth Amendment.''[230]

The closest relationship the child's attorney has with the state is in his appointment by the court under section 288(d) and whatever compensation, if any, he receives from California. While this article has not discussed whether and how the child's attorney is to be compensated for his services, it is possible that, like appointed counsel for indigent criminal defendants, the attorney appointed under section 288(d) could be paid by the government.[231] Even if the child's attorney is paid by the state or any subdivision of the state,[232] this does not make the state responsible for his actions. "The Government may subsidize private entities without assuming constitutional responsibility for their actions.''[233]

---

another lawyer in the matter, unless the member has the consent of the other lawyer." CAL. CIV. & CRIM. R., PROF. CONDUCT 2-100 (West Interim Annot. Serv. No. 1, 1989).

230. *Jackson*, 419 U.S. at 354 (footnote omitted). Thus California does not encourage the child's attorney to prevent defense counsel from interviewing the child. Rule 2-100 is a neutral statement that allows any attorney to prevent an opposing attorney from talking to his client. "The existence of a state law which recognizes the legitimacy of an action taken by an otherwise private person will not give rise to 'state action' being present in the private activity. To imbue an activity with state action there must be some non-neutral involvement of the state with the activity." ROTUNDA, NOWAK, & YOUNG, *supra* note 223, § 16.3 at 176. Therefore it is the child's attorney, not California, that keeps defense counsel away from the child.

231. The first place to start in determining how to finance the appointment of counsel under section 288(d) is with the phrase "within existing budgetary resources." CAL. PENAL CODE § 288(d) (West Supp. 1990). As this Article is concerned with the extent of a court's authority under section 288(d) and not the interpretation of financing provisions of statutes, a detailed analysis of the phrase "within existing budgetary resources" will not be provided.

The legislative counsel believes that the inclusion of the phrase "within existing budgetary resources" into section 288(d) makes section 288(d) a state-mandated local program. 1989 Cal. Leg. Serv. ch. 1402, at 5253 (West) (legislative counsel's digest). Article XIII B, section 6 of the California Constitution requests that the state provide a "subvention of funds" to local governments whenever "the legislature or any other state agency mandates a new program or higher level of service on any local government." CAL. CONST. art. XIII B, § 6 (West Supp. 1989). Therefore, the county could pay the cost of the child's counsel and seek reimbursement from the state. By adding the clause "within existing budgetary resources" to section 288(d), the legislature is attempting to avoid the application of article XIII B, section 6 to the state. 1989 Cal. Leg. Serv. ch. 1402, sec. 15, at 5276-77 (West).

The legislature's success in exempting the state from liability and the correctness of the legislative counsel's analysis of section 288(d) is beyond the scope of this article. What is clear is that legislature believes at least some funding should be provided from somewhere under section 288(d). What is also clear is that payment of the state does not change the child's counsel into an agent of the state. *See infra* notes 232-33 and accompanying text.

232. *See, e.g.,* CAL. PENAL CODE § 987.2 (a)-(b) (West Supp. 1989) (assignment of counsel chargeable to county government).

233. San Francisco Arts & Athletics, Inc. v. United States Olympic Comm., 483 U.S. 522, 544 (1987).

727

The attorney's appointment by the court does not make him a state actor either. In determining that appointed criminal defense counsel in a federal case was not absolutely immune to a state malpractice suit brought by his client, the Supreme Court stated that:

the primary office performed by appointed counsel parallels the office of privately retained counsel. Although it is true that appointed counsel serves pursuant to statutory authorization and in furtherance of the federal interest in insuring effective representation of criminal defendants, his duty is not to the public at large, except in that general way. His principal responsibility is to serve the undivided interests of his client.[234]

The child's attorney's sole goal is to prevent psychological harm to the child.[235] Like appointed defense counsel, he will achieve his goal by serving the "undivided interests of his client." Thus, like appointed defense counsel, his appointment does not make him a creature of the state.

In *Polk County v. Dodson*,[236] the Supreme Court rejected the assertion that a public defender acted under color of state law when exercising her independent professional judgment.[237] Here a full-time employee of the state[238] was not a state actor when acting in her professional capacity because public defenders act independently from the state in exercising professional judgment.[239] While the child's attorney is not in the same adversarial position as the public defender is against the district attorney,[240] his interests are not the same as the district attorney's and may conflict with them. The state is chiefly concerned with convicting the defendant, while the child's attorney's duty is to shield the child from psychological harm.[241]

When the attorney prevents the defense attorney from speaking with his client he is not doing it out of any desire to convict defendant at all costs; he is doing it out of a legitimate concern for the well-being of a particularly vulnerable client. The child's attorney does not control the prosecution.[242] His only client is the child; the people are the clients of the district attorney.[243] The role of the child's

---

234. Ferri v. Ackerman, 444 U.S. 193, 204 (1979).
235. *See* CAL. PENAL CODE § 288(d) (West Supp. 1990).
236. 454 U.S. 312 (1981).
237. *Id*. at 325.
238. *Id*. at 314.
239. *Id*. at 319.
240. *See id*. at 318.
241. *See supra* notes 48-50 and accompanying text.
242. *See supra* note 128 and accompanying text.
243. *See supra* note 175 and accompanying text.

attorney is closest to that of appointed counsel for defendant. Each represents the interests of a private individual in a criminal action. Each is solely concerned with preventing certain harms from befalling their respective clients. Neither has ultimate control over the prosecution of the case. The only connection either has with the government is the appointment as counsel and possibly the manner of compensation.[244] Both are essentially private attorneys doing a public service[245] and the state is not constitutionally responsible for the actions of either.

CONCLUSION

Penal Code section 288(d), if properly applied by the courts, can provide the molested child with a host of protections throughout the criminal case.[246] Courts should not be afraid to use section 288(d) to help the children. As long as a procedure is constitutional and beneficial to the child's psyche, a court is required by section 288(d) to implement that procedure. The *Hochheiser* court was concerned about infringing upon defendants' rights.[247] Once this hurdle is overcome there is no barrier to broad, creative uses of section 288(d) to alleviate the myriad of harms our criminal justice system can inflict upon the child. Appointing counsel to represent the child is just one of many potential uses of section 288(d). The only barriers to the use of section 288(d) should be the constitution and the hurt the child feels. While the former will place real limits on what a court can do under section 288(d),[248] the latter, unfortunately, is virtually limitless under our current criminal justice system.

Using section 288(d) to get counsel for the child is one major remedy to the child's problems. The child will be less alone in the criminal proceedings. He will have someone who can and will protect his interests. He will have a champion who will fight for his rights when he is incapable of asserting them and will protect him from the greater interests that threaten to crush him. He will have someone who is not a tool of the prosecution, the courts or defendant. He

---

244. *See supra* notes 231-34 and accompanying text.
245. *See supra* note 245 and accompanying text.
246. For a list of some of the procedures section 288(d) could be used to support, see *Hochheiser*, 161 Cal. App. 3d at 791 n.9, 208 Cal. Rptr. at 282 n.9.
247. *See supra* notes 59-63 and accompanying text.
248. *See* Coy v. Iowa, 108 S. Ct. 2798 (1988).

will have someone who knows what his rights are and how to defend them. He will have someone with a duty to act only in his interests and protect all his rights.

CRIMINAL LAW—EVIDENCE—COMPETENCY OF MINOR WITNESSES—OB-LIGATION OF OATH—The Pennsylvania Superior Court has held that in the absence of an understanding and comprehension of an oath, and the Divine punishment it implies, minor witnesses are incompetent to testify.

Commonwealth v. Rimmel, 221 Pa. Super. 84, 289 A.2d 116 (1972).

Defendant, John A. Rimmel, was criminally convicted on two charges of indecent assault. The conviction rested entirely upon the testimony of two girl victims who were eight years old at the time of the trial.[1] Prior to the trial the judge conducted an extensive voir dire examination in chambers to determine the competency of the witnesses to testify. The judge ruled both competent.

On appeal, the Pennsylvania Superior Court reversed[2] stating that neither girl was competent to testify. In its opinion the superior court declared there was no indication that either girl comprehended the difference between truth and falsehood or that they sufficiently comprehended the solemnity of the oath.[3] No appeal was taken to the Pennsylvania Supreme Court for personal reasons expressed by the parents of the female victims.

The court relied on *Rosche v. McCoy.*[4] In that case the court held that competency should be determined in the discretion of the trial judge once the fact of infancy becomes apparent to him. His discretion is not absolute but nevertheless will not be reversed in the absence of abuse.[5] In the present case the court went on to state that this issue is not to be determined merely on the ability of the witness to communicate his thoughts in terms of language. There must be a capacity to understand questions and to frame and express intelligent answers, a capacity to remember what it is one is being called to testify about and a consciousness of the duty to speak the truth.[6]

The court went on to state that the voir dire of the two girls showed no comprehension, on the part of either, of the difference between truth and falsehood. This statement is unfounded, especially in light of the testimony the court footnotes in support of this contention.[7]

---

1. Commonwealth v. Rimmel, 221 Pa. Super. 84, 85, 289 A.2d 116, 117 (1972).
2. *Id.* at 89, 289 A.2d at 118.
3. *Id.* at 87, 289 A.2d at 118.
4. 397 Pa. 615, 156 A.2d 307 (1959).
5. *Id.* at 620, 156 A.2d at 310.
6. 221 Pa. Super. at 86, 289 A.2d at 117.
7. In support of this conclusion the court cited the following portions of the voir dire examination in the footnotes to their opinion:

701

More importantly the court concluded that neither girl showed ". . . sufficient indication of a comprehension of the solemnity of the oath so that a citizen of our Commonwealth may be sentenced or convicted as a result of the testimony thereunder given."[8] This belief was based on the fact that the girls answered that they would be "beaten," as one girl stated, or "hollered at" or "punished," as the other stated, in answer to the question of what would happen to them if they told a lie.[9]

The court in its opinion quoted with approval a passage from Wigmore's treatise, *On Evidence*, which explains the reason why a witness is required to swear an oath before being allowed to testify.[10] Wigmore explains[11] that the earlier theory of the oath was an objective test in which the witness summoned Divine vengeance for lying, whereby when the witness is seen standing unharmed all present know that the Divine judgment has pronounced the witness to be a truth-teller.[12] Today, Wigmore explains, the oath is believed to be a method of reminding the witness strongly of the Divine punishment somewhere in store for lying, and thus of putting the witness in a frame of mind calculated to speak only the truth as the witness believes it to be.[13]

In regard to comprehension of truth and falsehood, Cynthya McNamara stated, "THE COURT: All right. Do you know that you are supposed to tell the truth? CINDY MCNAMARA: Yes. THE COURT: Do you tell the truth all the time? CINDY MCNAMARA: Yes." and Linda McNamara stated, "THE COURT: Linda, do you know that you are supposed to tell the truth all the time? LINDA MCNAMARA: Yes. THE COURT: Do you try to tell the truth all the time? LINDA MCNAMARA: Yes."
Id. at 86 n.1, 289 A.2d at 117 n.1.

8. *Id.* at 87, 289 A.2d at 118.

9. In support of this the court cited the following portion of the voir dire examination in the footnotes to their opinion:

In regard to understanding of the obligation of an oath, Cynthya McNamara stated: "THE COURT: Do you know [what] it means to take an oath, to raise your hand to God. Do you know what that means? CINDY MCNAMARA: No. THE COURT: Okay. Well, that means that you are asking God to witness that you are telling the truth. You are asking God to be the one who sees that you tell the truth. Do you understand that? CINDY MCNAMARA: Yes." and "THE COURT: Now, do you know what happens if you tell a lie? LINDA MCNAMARA: Yes. THE COURT: Okay. What happens? LINDA MCNAMARA: You get beaten. THE COURT: Okay. You mean your mother or your teacher gives you a beating? LINDA MC-NAMARA: Yes. THE COURT: Do you know it is wrong to tell a lie? LINDA MCNA-MARA: No. THE COURT: Well, you don't? Do you tell lies? Do you understand my question? That's all right, you are among friends. We are all friends. I told you I have a girl like you. Do you try to tell the truth all the time? LINDA MCNAMARA: Yes."
Id. at 86-87 n.2, 289 A.2d at 117-18 n.2.

10. *Id.* at 87-88, 289 A.2d at 118.

11. 6 J. WIGMORE, ON EVIDENCE § 1816 (3d ed. 1940).

12. Wigmore in a footnote cites a number of seventeenth century English cases in support of this history. *Id.* § 1816, at 285 n.1.

13. *See* note 11 *supra.*

As long ago as 1905, in *Commonwealth v. Furman*[14] the Pennsylvania Supreme Court declared that a minor witness need not know of the existence of some Divine punishment awaiting him for false swearing. In that case the lower court allowed, over the objections of the defendants, an eight-year-old boy to testify in a murder prosecution after it appeared to the satisfaction of the court that the witness was competent.[15] On appeal, the supreme court stated that in this enlightened age courts should discard the notion that a child must know about theoretical concepts of Divine punishment before being allowed to testify. A witness need only know that he is expected to tell the truth and that some punishment will follow a violation.[16] Additionally, it was in *Furman* that the court first espoused a test of competency which was to be followed in all future cases and to which the superior court in *Rimmel* gave lip service. The witness must clearly *comprehend the difference between truth and falsehood, and his duty to tell the truth.*[17]

The Pennsylvania Supreme Court next considered the question of the competency of a minor to testify in *Piepke v. Philadelphia & Reading Ry.*[18] where the court reversed and remanded[19] a lower court determination of incompetency of a minor witness to testify about a train accident in which the witness' playmate was seriously injured by a train backing up. The court, noting that there was no controlling statute in Pennsylvania disqualifying witnesses because of infancy, stated that the witness need only demonstrate a capacity to recall the incident he is to testify to, to understand the question put to him and give rational answers to these questions, and *to know that he ought to speak the*

---

14. 211 Pa. 549, 60 A. 1089 (1905).
15. The voir dire examination cited in the opinion of the court with regard to competency was as follows:
   Q. Do you know what it is to tell the truth? A. Yes.
   Q. Suppose you don't tell it, what will become of you? Do they tell you in Sunday school? What do they say, if you tell lies? Where will you go to? Do you know? A. No.
   Q. Do you know whether you must tell the truth or not? A. Yes.
Id. at 549, 60 A. at 1089.
16. *Id.* at 550, 60 A. at 1090.
17. 221 Pa. Super. at 86, 289 A.2d at 117 (emphasis added).
The substantial test of the competency of an infant witness is his intelligence, and his comprehension of an obligation to tell the truth. The truth is what the law, under the rules of evidence, is seeking, and if a full and present understanding of the obligation to tell it is shown by the witness, the nature of his conception of the obligation is of secondary importance.
211 Pa. at 550, 60 A. at 1089.
18. 242 Pa. 321, 89 A. 124 (1913).
19. *Id.* at 329, 89 A. at 126.

truth.[20] For the latter qualification the court cited the test enunciated in *Furman* as controlling.[21]

In the Delaware County case of *Sherkus v. Radbill*[22] the judge relied on the *Furman* and *Piepke* opinions in holding two boys, ages eight and ten, competent to testify about a collision involving a playmate and a passing truck. The case is interesting because of facts quite similar to the present case concerning the witnesses' answers to questions asked to determine competency. The older boy stated that he was punished for lying.[23] The younger boy while knowing nothing of the nature of the oath knew that he was expected to tell the truth, but could not explain what telling the truth meant or what would happen to a boy who did not tell the truth. He knew, however, what always happened to him when he told a lie, stating that his parents would "whip" him.[24]

In 1948 the Pennsylvania Superior Court held a six-year-old female victim of sexual assault competent to testify, citing the *Furman* and *Piepke* tests.[25] In that case the witness comprehended her duty to tell the truth knowing that she was punished for not doing so.[26]

In the following year the court decided *Commonwealth v. Carnes*[27] in which a seven-year-old was considered competent to testify as a witness to an automobile accident, utilizing the same test of competency that the courts of this Commonwealth have been using since 1905 when *Furman* was decided.[28] In *Carnes* the question of competency in the trial was not raised until cross-examination of the witness at which time the objection of plaintiff's counsel to the untimely questioning was sustained.[29] On appeal, the superior court stated that while there was not specific questioning on the witness' ability to distinguish between truth and falsity and his obligation to tell the truth the trial judge's conclusion of competency will not be disturbed since much must be left to his discretion.[30] The trial judge had made his

---

20. *Id.* at 328, 89 A. at 125 (emphasis added).
21. *Id.* at 329, 89 A. at 126.
22. 19 Del. Co. 620 (Pa. C.P. 1929).
23. *Id.* at 621.
24. *Id.*
25. Commonwealth v. Allabaugh, 162 Pa. Super. 490, 58 A.2d 184 (1948).
26. *Id.* at 492, 58 A.2d at 185-86.
27. 165 Pa. Super. 53, 67 A.2d 675 (1949).
28. 211 Pa. 549, 60 A. 1089 (1905).
29. 165 Pa. Super. 53, 59, 67 A.2d 675, 678 (1949).
30. *Id.* at 59, 67 A.2d at 678.

decision of competency based on having heard generally the questions asked of the witness and the answers given by him.

The Pennsylvania Supreme Court thoroughly summarized the law concerning minor witnesses in *Rosche v. McCoy*,[31] which, as mentioned previously, was the sole precedent relied on by the court in the present case. In *Rosche* the court synthesized and refined the decisions in *Furman* and *Piepke*, stating three requirements the trial judge should apply in exercising his discretionary power to rule on the competency of minor witnesses to testify. A child of tender years should possess:

> (1) such capacity to communicate, including as it does both an ability to understand questions and to frame and express intelligent answers, (2) a mental capacity to observe the occurrence itself and the capacity of remembering what it is the witness is called to testify about, and (3) *a consciousness of the duty to speak the truth.*[32]

The case dealt with the competency of a seven-year-old girl to testify about an accident she had witnessed when she was four years old. It was the first case in Pennsylvania in which a minor witness was asked to testify to events which happened years earlier. As a result, the court on appeal reversed the trial judge's determination of competency stating that the witness failed to qualify on the first and second criteria for determining competency.[33] Nowhere in *Rosche* was the third criterion, a consciousness of the duty to speak the truth, equated with the requirement that the witness be "aware of the responsibilities of taking an oath" or that the witness show "sufficient indication of a comprehension of the solemnity of the oath" as was required by the superior court of the two minor witnesses in *Rimmel*.[34] To the contrary, the court in *Rosche* implied that the modern trend has demonstrated a lessening of the importance of the oath in the case of infant witnesses.[35]

---

31. 397 Pa. 615, 156 A.2d 307 (1959).
32. *Id.* at 620-21, 156 A.2d at 319 (emphasis added).
33. The court stated:
It is obvious that had [the witness] been called . . . at the time of *this* occurrence, when she was but 4 years of age, she would have been incompetent. Carolyn's *memory* of the event and its details did not, indeed it could not, improve as time went on. The only thing that did improve was her capacity to communicate in terms of words. But that capacity is meaningless unless supported by the capacity to note the occurrence at the time it happened and the ability to remember it.
Id. at 621-22, 156 A.2d at 310.
34. 221 Pa. Super. at 87, 289 A.2d at 118.
35. 397 Pa. at 620, 156 A.2d at 310.

The *Rimmel* court read something into the *Rosche* decision which simply was not there.

It is suggested that the decision in *Rimmel* represents a return by the superior court, in contravention to all precedent since 1905, to a long discarded requirement that a minor witness know the nature, importance, and solemnity of the oath. Failing qualification under this test, the witness is incompetent to testify according to the superior court's holding.

The ramifications of this decision are numerous, especially in criminal cases. It would seem that defense counsel will enjoy the benefits of this decision almost exclusively. It is seriously doubted that there exist many potential witnesses of tender age that have any idea of the significance of the oath. Many children who would otherwise qualify as competent because they know that they should be predisposed to truth-telling will be prohibited from rendering intelligent testimony of what they witnessed. This will preclude not only those minors who visually perceive the occurrence to which they are testifying, but also all the unfortunate victims of crimes which are perpetrated against them, as in *Rimmel*.

In the Allegheny County Common Pleas Court, Criminal Division, a case, which remains unreported, was recently concluded where the judge, using the *Rimmel* test, held that a twelve-year-old was incompetent to testify in a murder case in which he witnessed the crime.[36] Fortunately, the prosecution secured a conviction without the aid of the minor witness' testimony but the result will not always be the same in the future.

In Pennsylvania a minor is presumed incompetent to testify until the age of fourteen.[37] It is suggested that it may be only a matter of time before an otherwise intelligent and competent fourteen-year-old will be adjudged incompetent for failing to understand the significance of the oath according to the *Rimmel* standard.

The *Rimmel* standard represents a return to an archaic idea that witnesses must know the significance of an oath. One objective of the American system of justice through the trial of a case in an adversary proceeding is the ascertainment of truth. It should be sufficient that minor witnesses be predisposed to truth-telling to allow their testimony to be given.

---

36. Commonwealth v. Bundy, Criminal Nos. 3060-61 (Pa. C.P. Alleg. Co., July 21, 1972) (argued before Judge Clark in the Allegheny County Court of Common Pleas).
37. Rosche v. McCoy, 397 Pa. 615, 621, 156 A.2d 307, 310 (1959).

706

The *Rimmel* case should be overruled so that the courts can return to the state's traditional common sense standard to adjudge competency of minor witnesses to testify.

Stephen Levin

Journal of Social Issues, Vol. 40, No. 2, 1984, pp. 9–31

Children's Testimony in Historical Perspective

Gail S. Goodman

University of Denver

Children have been testifying in courts of law for centuries, but not without raising questions about the value of their statements. Over the years, the legal system has proposed a host of rules to govern children's testimony, but today the value of many of these rules is being questioned. The scientific study of child witnesses by psychologists began around the turn of the century. Early studies tended to support some of the legal profession's stereotypes of children by claiming to show that children are "the most dangerous of all witnesses." More recent studies challenge this oversimplified view and instead indicate that children are not always more suggestible than adults. In this paper, the laws, past and present, and the development of the relevant psychological literature are reviewed, with special attention placed on the early studies.

"When are we going to give up, in all civilized nations, listening to children in courts of law?" So asked Belgian psychologist J. Varendonck in 1911.

Varendonck was not the first to question the value of children's testimony. The credibility of children's statements has been a source of controversy for centuries. Some critics emphasize children's suggestibility and possible obliviousness to the meaning and purpose of legal trials. They argue that children's testimony may retard rather than advance the cause of justice. This is not a trivial matter: People have suffered the death penalty largely on the basis of children's testimony (Collins & Bond, 1953). But there are also proponents of children's testimony; they argue that children can remember and report at least some events quite accurately, and in some cases may be the key or the only eyewitnesses to a

The writing of this article was facilitated by a grant from the Developmental Psychobiology Research Group of the University of Colorado Health Sciences Center, Department of Psychiatry. I would like to thank Caroline McKinnon for research assistance and Marshall M. Haith for comments on an earlier draft of this paper.

Correspondence concerning this article should be addressed to Gail S. Goodman, Department of Psychology, University of Denver, Denver, CO 80208.

9

crime. Prosecution is sometimes impossible if children are barred from testifying. This controversy poses a dilemma for the legal system. It forces the following restatement of Varendonck's question: When should we listen to children's testimony in a court of law?

Children have witnessed events of legal import for centuries, and they have testified in trials as momentous as the Salem witch trials. Over the years, the legal system has evolved rules and practices for dealing with child witnesses. Until recently, these laws were rarely challenged.

Psychologists are relative newcomers to the debate, since the scientific study of children's testimony only began around the turn of the century. At first a productive research endeavor, criticism from the legal profession later stymied the effort, and laboratory studies of children's testimony came to a sudden halt in the first quarter of this century. As a consequence, even current books that discuss child witnesses are forced to rely heavily on the older literature (e.g., Loftus, 1979). Until recently there has been little up-to-date research to cite. Unfortunately, the older studies suffered both from methodological flaws and from the intrusion of negative biases against children. Reliance on these studies has helped to perpetuate an oversimplified view of the child witness.

Courts and legislatures are now reassessing the laws that govern child witnesses and looking to psychologists, psychiatrists, attorneys, and social workers for information and advice. The openness of the contemporary justice system to social science research, in addition to its concern for the rights of victims as well as the accused, has helped spark new interest in the child witness. This journal issue is dedicated to recent thinking and research in this area. In order to free the field from its past biases and misconceptions, but at the same time retain what was valid in earlier work, a reexamination of the laws and psychological studies is due.

This paper surveys past and present laws and the early psychological research that concern child witnesses. It begins with the Salem witch trials, a good example of how stereotyped beliefs about children's testimony can be maintained under ambiguous conditions. Next, it reviews the major laws concerning child witnesses. Finally, it considers some of the early but still influential psychological research on child witnesses.

The Child Witness in Salem

Perhaps the most famous American example of children's testimony occurred in Salem, Massachusetts, in 1692. History books traditionally tell the following story: Several young adolescent girls, more or less as a prank, accused a slave woman of being a witch and responsible for a set of symptons they were suffering. The townsfolk mistakenly believed the girls. Hysteria resulted. Many adults feigned the same symptoms and accused others in order to escape being labeled as witches themselves. According to Morison (1972): "The 'afflicted children,' finding themselves the object of attention, and with the exhibitionism natural to young wenches, persisted in their charges for fear of being found out, and started a chain reaction" (p. 176). This traditional account has always omitted an important consideration: Why did the girls' story result in mass hysteria among the populace at that paticular time? A belief in witchcraft was common in New England both before and after 1692, yet in no other year was there such severe persecution of witches. Only three hangings for witchcraft occurred in Massachusetts Bay before 1692, but 20 people were put to death in that year alone (Morison, 1972).

An alternative interpretation of the events throws a different light on the children's motivations. Caporael (1976), a psychologist, and Matossian (1982), a historian, have argued that the symptoms experienced by children and adults in Salem are characteristic of "ergotism," a kind of food poisoning caused by ingestion of ergot, a fungus that grows on rye. The inhabitants of Salem harvested and consumed rye, and weather conditions favored the growth of ergot that year. The symptoms of ergotism match those described by the afflicted Salemites; they include formication (a feeling that ants are crawling under the skin), urine stoppage, and delirium. Ergot, chemically similar to LSD, may produce symptoms similar to those produced by psychedelic drugs; people who suffer from ergotism may be highly suggestible and likely to see hallucinatory images—of devils, for instance. Of importance to the present paper, children and teenagers are particularly vulnerable to ergotism. Thus, rather than expressing a tendency to pull pranks, displaying "exhibitionism natural to young wenches," and feeling compelled to maintain a fallacy, the adolescents may have been among the first to experience the effects of ergotism. If so, the young witnesses may have reported their sensations accurately but, like many adults who later developed the same symptoms, misattributed them to witchcraft.

Laws Concerning Child Witnesses

The traditional interpretation of the events at Salem reflects cultural beliefs about children. Similar beliefs are evident in the special laws that still govern testimony by child witnesses. Our culture holds ambivalent views about children; they are seen as innocent and truthful, but at the same time as manipulable or even devious. A child who reports a sexual assault may be seen as an innocent, truthful victim or as a creature of uncontrolled sexual fantasy. A child who witnesses a murder may be viewed as having no reason to lie, but as being highly suggestible. Largely because of this equivocal image the law has adopted a policy that permits a judge considerable discretion in screening the testimony of child witnesses.

Competence Examinations

Perhaps the most controversial law applying to child witnesses is the requirement that their competence to testify be demonstrated. While children may appear as witnesses in both criminal and civil matters, most states have laws specifying that children under a certain age (e.g., 10 years) are presumed incompetent to testify unless competence can be demonstrated.

In common law, rules concerning the competence of witnesses formed one of the most important branches of the law of evidence (Stephen, 1863). A witness could be judged incompetent for a wide variety of reasons, including religious beliefs, being a party to the dispute, being married to the accused, or being a child. Although most of these rules have been abolished, youths are still judged as either competent or incompetent to testify on the basis of rather arbitrary rules (Collins & Bond, 1953).

Historically, children below a certain age were automatically barred from testifying. Early canon law excluded witnesses who had not yet reached the age of puberty (Collins & Bond, 1953). In early common law, the age limit was lowered to 7 years of age; children below 7 years were believed to lack the capacity to commit a crime or to take an oath (Wigmore, 1935/1976)—the latter being required for legal testimony. A child 7 years and above might be permitted to testify if the court determined that he or she understood the nature of an oath. An example appears in *Rex v. Braddon and Speke* (1684), in which a 13-year-old boy's competence was determined as follows:

> *Judge:*   What age are you of?   *Witness:* I am 13, my lord.
> *Attorney:* Do you know what an oath is?   *Witness:* No.
> *Judge:*   Suppose you should tell a lie, do you know who is the father of
>   lies?   *Witness:* Yes.
> *Judge:*   Who is it?   *Witness:* The devil.
> *Judges:*   And if you should tell a lie, do you know what would become of you?
>   *Witness:* Yes.
> *Judge:*   What if you should swear to a lie? If you should call God to witness to a lie,
>   what would become of you then?   *Witness:* I should go to hell-fire.

After this interview, the boy was permitted to testify.

The age stipulation was eventually discarded. In *Rex v. Braiser* (1779), 12 common law judges were asked to decide whether the statements of a 5-year-old would be admissible as evidence in a sexual-assault trial. The judges decided that "there is no precise or fixed rule as to the time within which infants are excluded from giving evidence" but that the court must pose questions to determine if the child understands the "danger and impiety of falsehood."

This case set an important standard for competence examinations of child witnesses. The age requirement was replaced with a requirement that the witness understand "the impiety of falsehood"—an understanding to be determined by the court through questioning. Only if the court was satisfied that the child had this understanding would the child's statements be admissible. The ruling left judges wide discretionary power to determine a child's competence.

The oath. As we have seen, one of the key issues in proving competence has been determining the child's understanding of the nature of an oath. In earlier times, a child (or adult) who did not have "proper" and sufficient religious training could not take the oath and would be barred from testifying. Unless a witness believed in divine vengeance for false statements, he or she could not be trusted to speak the truth (Wigmore, 1935/1976). Typically, a "general" course of religious studies was required so that instruction could not be given exclusively for the purpose of the trial. But in the last century, this requirement was eliminated. For example, in *Rex v. Baylis* (1849), it was decided that the judge could instruct the child on the nature of an oath, and if the instruction was accepted, the child could immediately be called as a witness. Alternatively, postponement of the trial could be permitted for this purpose. Thus, an order was made for a prisoner to be detained until the 10-year-old girl he allegedly raped received religious instruction.

Today, few states require religious instruction or a formal oath. But a child must typically be able to demonstrate the ability to tell the truth from a lie and know that it is wrong to tell a lie. Of course, neither an oath nor knowledge of the difference between truth and falsehood, nor the understanding that punishment may follow a lie, guarantees honesty. Moral knowledge does not necessarily correspond to moral behavior (Damon, 1978).

Observation, Memory, and Verbal Ability

Understanding the difference between the truth and a lie, and the obligation to speak the truth, have been the main determinants of competence. But several other criteria have also been employed, as highlighted in a widely cited trial. In 1895, a 5-year-old boy testified as a witness to his father's murder. The defendant, found guilty and sentenced to be hanged, appealed to a higher court, partly on the grounds that the child should not have been permitted to take the stand. In *Wheeler v. United States* (1895), the appeals court held:

> "The boy was not by reason of his youth, as a matter of law, absolutely disqualified as a witness . . . . While no one would think of calling as a witness an infant only two or three years of age, there is no precise age which determines the question of competency. This depends upon the capacity and intelligence of the child, his appreciation of the difference between truth and falsehood, as well as of his duty to tell the former. The decision of this question rests primarily with the trial judge, who sees the proposed witness, notices his manner, his apparent possession or lack of intelligence, and may resort to any examination which will tend to disclose his capacity and intelligence, as well as his understanding of the obligation of an oath . . . . (pp. 524–525)

In addition to reemphasizing the child's understanding of the difference between truth and falsehood, this decision stressed "the capacity and intelligence" of the child, which later served to justify the criteria commonly in use today. The child must possess: (a) the mental capacity at the time of the occurrence to observe and register the event accurately, (b) the memory sufficient to retain an independent (i.e., uncoached) recollection of the event, (c) the ability to communicate this memory, and (d) the ability to understand one's obligation to speak the truth (*American Jurisprudence,* 1960). A child's demeanor may also be taken into account (*American Jurisprudence,* 1960). A judge cannot rely solely on the opinion of others or on the results of tests, but must conduct his or her own interview with the child and make the final decision concerning the child's competence. The judge could decide, for example, that the child is competent to testify about certain events but not others. If a child is at first permitted to testify but found to be incompetent during the trial, the judge may excuse the young witness and instruct the jury to disregard the child's statements.

For several reasons, a child may be judged legally incompetent at the time of the event, but competent at the time of the trial. The child may therefore testify even if many years have elapsed between the event and the competence determination. For example, in *Knab v. Alden's Irving Park, Inc.* (1964), a child who was 4 years of age at the time of an injury but 12 at the time of the trial was judged competent to testify. Other circumstances may also change a child's competence. In *Burnam v. Chicago Great Western Railway* (1937), a child was permitted to testify after forgetting the relevant facts for a while but then "remembering" them as a result of a vivid dream.

Questions have been raised about the wisdom of competency examinations. The practice could easily lead to a situation in which the same child would be deemed competent by one judge but incompetent by another. Furthermore, one must ask whether a judge can accurately ascertain the potential accuracy of a child's testimony. Wigmore (1935/1976) specifically argued against the competence examination of child witnesses because there is little reason to assume that judges can make a better decision than a jury. Why not let the jury evaluate the child's statements and attach to them whatever credibility they seem to deserve?

Several states have taken Wigmore's advice and eliminated the necessity of a competency examination for children. The legal trend is to adopt Rule 601 of the Federal Rules of Evidence, which effectively eliminates all grounds for incompetence, including age (Bulkley, 1982; Melton, Bulkley, & Wulkan, 1983). Some states, such as Colorado, have eliminated the presumption of incompetence for certain charges only, notably child sexual assault.

Although competency examinations are being removed in some jurisdictions as obstacles to children's testimony, one obstacle is difficult to remove. As a matter of practice, children 4 years and under are unlikely to be called as witnesses. Even though young children may remember people and events, their poor verbal skills and inability to withstand cross-examination often prelude courtroom testimony. Nevertheless, children as young as 3 years of age have been found competent to testify (Berliner & Barbieri, 1984).

Corroboration

For some crimes and in some states, corroboration (i.e., independent evidence) is required before a child's testimony can be admitted as evidence in a court of law. If corroboration cannot be provided, prosecution cannot proceed. Corroboration is most often demanded for children who testify about sexual assault (see Lloyd, 1983); it was not required in common law, but, as a result of statutes, became mandatory in certain states (Wigmore, 1935/1976). For example, some state statutes require corroboration of children's testimony in trials of child sexual assault, but not in trials of murder or forcible rape. Some jurisdictions also require the judge to give special cautionary instructions to the jury regarding the credibility of children.

In America, corroboration requirements are now a subject of controversy. These laws make prosecution of crimes such as sexual molestation extremely difficult, and there is little evidence to support the claim underlying these laws that children frequently make false reports of sexual abuse (Katz & Mazur, 1979). Corroboration requirements have largely been eliminated for child victims and/or witnesses. It is unknown, however, whether a judge or a jury would convict a person based on the uncorroborated testimony of a child (see Goodman, Golding, & Haith, 1984).

Leading Questions

Once a child is deemed competent to testify, the same rules apply to the child as to an adult witness—with a few exceptions. One exception is that, for an adult, leading questions (i.e., questions that suggest an answer to the witness) are generally permitted only upon cross-examination. For children, however, leading questions may be permitted even upon direct examination. If the child is frightened or refuses to answer questions, the attorney may ask permission to lead the child (*American Jurisprudence*, 1960). Although it is recommended that attorneys let the child tell the story in his or her own words (*American Jurisprudence*, 1960), using leading questions only when necessary, Thomas (1956) notes that the use of leading questions is the prevailing method of obtaining information from children. This practice, which has a long history (see Wigmore, 1935/1976), is unfortunate: Leading questions increase inaccuracies in both children's and adults' testimony (e.g., Lipton, 1977; Loftus & Davies, 1984). Such questioning may also lead the jury to discount perfectly accurate testimony. The courts may therefore weaken both the reliability and the impact of children's statements by continuing this practice.

Exceptions to Hearsay

Hearsay is generally excluded as evidence in courts of law, but exceptions may be made in cases involving child witnesses. These exceptions broaden the admissibility of children's statements (Severance, 1983). "Spontaneous utterances" overheard by another can be admitted if the child's statements are made soon after the event, when the child is still in an "excited" state. The person who heard the child can take the stand and repeat the child's statements even if the child does not testify. The presumption underlying this *rea gestae* (excited utterance) exception is that the child is not making the statements, but rather that the event is speaking through the child (Stafford, 1962). The statements derive their credibility not from the child's competence as a witness, but from the strength of the circumstances. As far back as *Rex v. Brasier* (1779), the possible necessity of invoking the *rea gestae* exception, particularly for young children, was considered. If a child was too young to take an oath, the court might accept testimony from an adult about the child's excited utterances.

In making this exception, a crucial legal condition is that the child must not have had the time or capacity to fabricate the statements. Again, the judge has considerable discretion. For example, he or she can decide how long an interval may elapse before the child's statements are no longer spontaneous. Courts have interpreted this *rea gestae* exception quite loosely, particularly in cases of child sexual assault.

There are other exceptions to the hearsay rule (Bulkley, 1983). For example, statements made during a medical examination can be admitted as evidence by the doctor. So, if in treating certain bruises the doctor asks the child what caused them, the child's answer that "Uncle Bill hit me" could be entered as evidence. At least in sexual-assault cases, psychiatrists and psychologists have been permitted to testify about statements made during therapy sessions and to present videotapes of the child reenacting criminal events with the aid of dolls and props. The therapist would then be subject to cross-examination about the child's statements. In addition, a "residual" exception is being considered in some states which would permit admittance of statements made by a child to another about sexual abuse (Bulkley, 1982).

Appeals in Cases Where Children Testify

Questions about a child's competence to testify have served as a basis for appeal. Older statistics indicate that about one in four of these cases was reversed (*American Law Reports,* 1962). More recent statistics are unavailable. Although a trial court's decision on a child's competence is not to be reversed unless there is clear abuse of discretion, several factors could contribute to the persistence of a high rate of reversals. Sometimes a judge will have prohibited a child from testifying because of age, when he or she should have evaluated the child's intelligence and understanding of the nature of an oath. At other times the child may not have been adequately interviewed. For instance, the child might be questioned concerning his or her general memory and intelligence, but not sufficiently about the difference between truth and falsehood. A reversal could also be based on a decision by the appeals court that the child was not competent after all, based on the trial record. A number of such factors can alter the initial decision.

Protection of the Child Witness

In contrast to the defendant, the child witness has no constitutional rights to protection during the investigation or the trial. The court has, however, an obligation to protect the child from undue harm. A judge may decide that the child's physical or mental health could be damaged by testifying and therefore disqualify the child (Klotter, 1980). At times the sensitive nature of the case has been used to exclude a child (*Crowner v. Crowner*, 1880), but this *parens patria* role of the court may conflict with the defendant's constitutional rights.

One major conflict is between the defendant's Sixth Amendment rights and the court's obligation to protect the child from emotional trauma. Based on the Sixth Amendment, the accused has the right to confront the accuser. This right can be interpreted to mean "face to face" confrontation, in which case the child must appear in court, face the defendant (who may have threatened the child with death if he or she ever revealed what happened), and submit to cross-examination. Even though this could be traumatic for the child, the defendant's rights have typically prevailed. Some jurisdictions provide for videotaped depositions of the child's testimony in sexual-assault cases (Bulkley, 1982), but the defendant may be present at these depositions.

Pynoos and Eth (1984) point out that, in California, a trial involving a child witness is supposed to be given priority on the docket. From the point of view of bolstering memory and decreasing emotional strain, this practice would be recommended, but the rule is rarely invoked.

Another protection concerns punishment for perjury. If a young child is permitted to testify, the child is immune from such punishment. Children may, however, be held in contempt of court. This year, for example, a 12-year-old girl refused to testify against her stepfather, a physician who admitted sexually molesting her. The girl was held in solitary confinement in a Juvenile Detention Center for over a week until public outrage and the girl's continued refusal to testify led to her release ("Girl," 1984).

Pretrial Investigations

Anyone familiar with actual cases understands the crucial role that police play in obtaining evidence, such as through the questioning of witnesses. In my experience, many cases involving child witnesses are lost or dropped because of poor techniques used during the pretrial stage. For example, the use of suggestive questioning or suggestive line-ups can later undermine prosecution. As will be seen in the following review of the psychological literature, the suggestibility of children has been a long-standing concern. Partly as a result of this concern, several countries require that only specially trained psychologists interview child witnesses (see Parker, 1982; Reifen, 1975; Trankeil, 1958). The United States has not yet followed suit.

Early Psychological Research

What does psychological research tell us about children's abilities as witnesses? Here I will examine primarily the turn-of-the-century literature addressed to this question.

Early studies of children's testimony dealt almost exclusively with children's memory and suggestibility, and a similar situation exists today. Our understanding of cognitive development is much greater than it was in 1900, however. Most developmental researchers now recognize that a child's knowledge of or familiarity with to-be-remembered information profoundly affects memory performance. A child who is quite knowledgeable about a certain domain of information may remember events within that domain better than an unknowledgeable adult (Chi, 1978; Chi & Rees, 1983). Furthermore, the child's performance is intimately related to the cognitive skills he or she brings to the particular task (Fischer, 1980). These newer theoretical notions counter claims like those of Piaget (1962) that children's thinking is entirely tied to developmental "stages." Depending on a child's knowledge and skills, he or she may show illogical or egocentric thinking on one task but not on another (Borke, 1975). In addition, a child's emotions during the event and during attempts to remember what happened are likely to influence both memory and report (Dent & Stephenson, 1979; Terr, 1979, 1983).

These issues have only recently been given the recognition they deserve. Early researchers tended to make categorical statements about children's abilities, claiming, for example, that children are always more suggestible than adults or that a child necessarily remembers less. And, as Undeutsch (cited by Sporer, 1982) points out, the early studies were designed to demonstrate the inaccuracies rather than the accuracies of memory. Moreover, standards for scientific research have improved considerably since the early 1900s. It is with these problems in mind that the reader should consider the older literature.

The Beginnings of the Scientific Study of Child Witnesses

Before the scientific study of child witnesses, a large body of fictional, popular-psychological, and medical writings contained strong biases against children (Sporer, 1982). Binet is typically credited with conducting the first systematic research on children's testimony. In *La suggestibilité* (1900), his experiments on "suggestion by moral influence" demonstrated the effects of leading questions.

In one of Binet's demonstrations, he asked children (ranging in age from 7 to 14 years) to spend 12 minutes looking at a card on which he had pasted various objects (e.g., a button, a stamp). As the children reported what they had seen, Binet asked questions about the objects. He found that some children would give a full, detailed account but that the account was false. Others would be correct about certain facts but not others. In another experiment, Binet divided children into three groups, each receiving a different set of questions that varied in the degree of suggestion. For example, the first group might be asked "How is the button fastened?" The second group was given a moderate suggestion, for example, "Is the button fastened with a thread?" The third group was given a strong suggestion: "What is the color of the thread which passes through the holes of the button and fixes it to the card?" The majority of children accepted the suggestion. A group of young adults made the same kind of errors but less frequently. Binet felt that he had measured individual differences in children's suggestibility *on his tasks*. He did not claim to measure suggestibility generally, and he recognized deficiencies in his tests.

Based on his findings, Binet recommended that authorities not ask questions of children. Instead, children should merely write out their reports. Despite the legal importance of his work, Binet did not pursue it, blaming the French justice system for their lack of cooperation (Wolf, 1973). Two years after *La suggestibilité* was published, however, Stern and his colleagues at the University of Breslau initiated research on the psychology of testimony and report (*"Psychologie der Aussage"*).

Stern and the Early European Research

Although the study of eyewitness testimony is today dominated by investigations of adult's memory, this was not so at the turn of the century. At that time a good deal of research was conducted on children's testimony. Many turn-of-the-century reviews on the "psychology of testimony" devoted considerable attention to studies with children (Stern, 1910; Whipple, 1909, 1911, 1912, 1913). One of the earliest cases of a psychologist serving as an expert witness occurred around 1903 or 1904 when Stern, the leading researcher at the time, testified about the statements of an adolescent boy in a sexual assault-case (Stern, 1926, as cited by Sporer, 1982). Sexual assault on children became the early prototype for cases in which psychologists testified (Sporer, 1982).

To study testimony, the German researchers at first used picture-tests, but criticism from the legal profession soon motivated the use of "event-tests." These were rather realistically staged events, such as the famous classroom demonstration in which a confederate pretended to assault the instructor. Regardless of the type of test, studies of children's testimony concentrated on explorations of their suggestibility, their accuracy of report, contrasts between narrative and interrogatory methods of report, and the role of practice. Unfortunately, most of this research has yet to be translated into English. Summaries in English are available, but it is difficult to evaluate the methods employed in the original studies or the correspondence between the data and the conclusions reached.

In any case, many professionals concluded from these studies that "children are the most dangerous of all witnesses" (Baginsky, as cited by Whipple, 1911). Some demanded that children's testimony be excluded from the court record whenever possible. I will summarize a small sample of the experiments supporting this conclusion.

Stern (1910, 1939) described a picture-test in which a peasant's living room was shown to children and young adults (ranging in age from 7 to 18 years). Overall, narrative questions resulted in 5–10% errors and interrogatory questions resulted in 25–30% errors. Developmental differences were not reported for these two types of questioning but were reported for suggestive questioning, which produced 50% errors in 7-year-olds but only 20% errors in 18-year-olds. In an example from this study, Stern describes how a 12-year-old girl, who was asked "Was there not a clothes press in the picture?", answered "Yes" and gave a full description of it when no such item had been presented. Stern admitted that this example was extreme, but later, examples such as this one were cited as characteristic of children. Stern also stated that one finds errors of fantasy in children's narrative reports but added that adults also blend the imagined with the experienced (Stern, 1910).

Event-tests were also conducted with children. Those conducted by Varendonck (1911) will be presented at the end of this chapter. They were (and still are) widely cited and used to exemplify the suggestibility of children, despite the fact that an adult comparison group was not included. The experiments are, however, dramatic illustrations of suggestibility. The studies were initiated when Varendonck was asked to serve as an expert witness on children's testimony in a famous murder trial. Largely on the basis of Varendonck's findings, the jury acquitted the defendant.

Actual cases were often cited to support the claim of children's unreliability. For example, Whipple (1913) cited a case reported by Marbe in which several German school children accused their male school teacher of sexual offenses. The girls' testimony was very detailed but was discredited as the result of further questioning, a medical report, and the expert testimony of Professor Marbe. The argument was made that the children's suggestibility and conformity led to the accusations.

Psychologists hoped that practice might improve the testimony of child witnesses. Lipmann (1911) believed that training for correct reporting by children should emphasize redirecting their attention to important information and the development of a critical attitude toward filling in of details. Stern (1910) reported an improvement with practice when children were repeatedly presented with pictures and asked to discover their previous errors. On the other hand, Whipple (1912) reported a lack of improvement with event-tests. Unfortunately, instead of using events about which children might be likely to testify, children were asked to repeatedly observe physical demonstrations, such as the effect of centrifugal force upon a vessel of water. This choice was justified on the basis that school children were familiar with the nature of these tasks and that they commanded the children's fullest attention. But the lack of improvement with practice may have resulted, at least in part, from the remoteness of the task from everyday life.

Regardless of practice, Stern believed that in pathological cases or during certain developmental phases such as puberty, the likelihood of mixing fantasy and reality was increased. Young adolescent girls were supposed to be particularly affected at puberty (Stern, 1939). But in the end, Stern, like Binet, concluded that the falsification of testimony is typically the result of questioning, and that the questioner is responsible for the child's false report (Stern, 1939).

The deleterious effects of questioning were also emphasized by two British researchers. Pear and Wyatt (1914) examined the testimony of 11- to 14-year-old normal and "mentally defective" children about a visit by two strangers to the children's classroom. The day after the visit, the children were asked to recount the event. About the children's narrative accounts, Pear and Wyatt state: "It [can] be seen that in every group the degree of accuracy attained is remarkably high, and hence the *spontaneous* account of an event is exceedingly reliable, even in the case of mental defectives. In many respects, not a single deviation from the actual situation was to be found. Thus when the testimony of children is unaffected by questions or suggestions, it is worthy of the utmost consideration" (p. 397). In contrast, when children were questioned about the event, "Over one-third of the replies of the normal children and over one-half of the replies of the mentally defective [were] incorrect. Thus the interrogatory of the latter group is very unreliable, and the corresponding testimony of the normal children must be treated with great reserve" (p. 401). It should be noted, however, that the children answered some questions quite accurately; for example, 84% of the normal children's answers to questions about the visitors' actions were correct. Normal children were less susceptible to suggestive questions than were the mentally defective but, when asked again about the event 7 weeks later, both groups showed an increase in suggestibility.

Some writers emphasized the positive aspects of children's testimony. Gross (1910, as cited by Whipple, 1912) staked his 30 years of court experience on the claim that a "healthy half grown boy" is the best possible witness for

simple events. He claimed that children make *different* errors than do adults—
but not necessarily worse ones—and he suggested the idea of developing a
category system for the types of errors most commonly found as a function of
age, sex, temperament, etc. (Gross, 1910, as cited in Whipple 1911). Heindl
(1909, as cited in Whipple, 1912) asked children to estimate the stature, age,
color of hair, etc., of a familiar and an unfamiliar person seen for 4 minutes.
Heindl concluded that children are perfectly good observers—perhaps more
objective than adults—but have greater difficulty translating their observations
into verbal reports. Nevertheless, Stern (1910) stated that the more common,
negative view about children caused their testimony to be less highly valued in
Germany than formerly.

The picture of the child witness that emerges from these early studies is of a
potentially accurate witness, one who can recount events and answer nonleading
questions reasonably correctly, but whose report can easily be contaminated by
suggestion. As Binet and Stern both noted, the inaccuracies in children's reports
are largely produced by questioning. Although the view of children as the most
"dangerous of all witnesses" prevailed, a review of the early research suggests
that the argument could also be made that untrained interviewers pose as great a
danger to justice as do child witnesses.

Stern, as early as 1910, argued that special investigators should interview
children and that the interviews should be conducted only once, as soon as
possible after the incident. Leading questions would not, of course, be permitted.
"Above all," he claimed, "the expert must be a child psychologist." Germany
largely accepted his suggestion, as has Israel (Reifen, 1975; Sporer, 1982). Most
other countries have not.

The Decline of Research

Psycholegal research diminished after this initial burst of effort. Psychologists criticized the legal profession for, among other things, their reliance on
eyewitness testimony, and, as Loh (1981) describes, these attacks prompted
counterattacks by the legal profession (see Munsterberg, 1908; Wigmore, 1909).
Many psychologists retreated from the study of testimony at this point. Psychologists in Europe continued laboratory studies for a while, but their psycholegal
research turned more toward evaluations of individual witnesses in actual cases.

At the end of the 1920s and during the 1930s, interest in legal psychology
temporarily reawakened (Loh, 1981), promoted this time mostly by lawyers. In a
chapter entitled "The Child and the Woman," Brown (1926) presented quite a
negative view: "It is never safe to depend either on the memory or the reason of
a child. Practically the only value in a court of law of any testimony that a child
might give, is that which re-enforces or is re-enforced by other testimony" (p.
140). He presented what he considered "an excellent rule" regarding sug-

gestibility: "women are more suggestible than men, and children are more suggestible than adults." McCarty (1929) was somewhat kinder to the child, claiming that older children, being more alert than adults, make better witnesses. But he also said that the statements of children should be scrutinized carefully since, for the child, imagination and reality are not well differentiated. Burtt (1931) also commented on the suggestibility of children and on the inability of young children to differentiate fantasy from reality. He did concede, however, that if the possibility of suggestion can be ruled out, children may occasionally give better, more objective testimony than adults. He argued for the use of standardized intelligence tests to ascertain testimonial competence and pointed out the courts' reluctance to use them. For example, in an assault case, the court objected to testimony concerning the IQ of a 10-year-old child witness on the basis that the jury could judge her intelligence better than could a test. Fortunately, the court was probably justified in this decision. Recent studies have shown no relation between IQ (within the normal range) and accuracy of report for a staged event (Goetze, 1980) or for the accuracy of face recognition (Chance & Goldstein, 1984).

Books published in the 1920s and 1930s presented virtually no new data on children's testimony, although some studies of suggestibility for less realistic events continued (e.g., Marple, 1933). In Germany, once the center of research on testimony, the replacement of the laboratory study with individual evaluations (e.g., Trankell, 1972) was reinforced in the 1930s and 1940s by laws making it a requirement that child witnesses be examined by psychological experts (Sporer, 1982). Laboratory studies of child witnesses and reviews hardly appeared again until the 1970s (but see Rouke, 1957). This time they made their emergence in North America and the British Isles.

Psycholegal Research in the '80s

Today's burst of research on psychology and law can be traced to several factors (see Loh, 1981). The activism of the 1960s, the courts' changing attitudes toward civil and criminal rights, and an increased openness of the courts to testimony of psychological experts all contributed to the revival.

The reawakening of research in psychology and law inevitably fosters a reemergence of research on child witnesses. But society's increased concern with children's rights and protecting children from abuse also spurs this endeavor. Moreover, advances in developmental theory should enable researchers to approach the study from a more enlightened perspective.

Many important questions were left untouched by the early researchers. Society's recent interest in the rights of crime victims encourages investigation of the emotional effects on children of witnessing or being victimized by crime and of testifying in court. Methods for obtaining the most accurate and least trauma-inducing testimony from children (during pretrial and trial stages), children's understanding of court procedures, and jurors' reactions to child witnesses are all worthy topics about which little systematic research exists.

There are several conclusions to be derived from this history of the laws and psychological research concerning the child witness. One is that the present laws, based on questionable assumptions and standards from the past, are in a state of transition. Hopefully, a new system, based on less questionable premises, will emerge. Another conclusion is that the psychological study of child witnesses is less cut and dried than Varendonck (1911), in the following sections of his classic paper, would have had us believe. Much more work needs to be done before we have an accurate understanding of the child witness.

References

American Jurisprudence Proof of Facts. (Vol. 6). (1960). San Francisco: Bancroft-Whitney Co.

American Law Reports. (1962). Rochester, New York: Lawyers Cooperative Publishing Co.

Berliner, L., & Barbieri, M. K. (1984). The testimony of the child victim of sexual assault. *Journal of Social Issues, 40*(2), 125–137.

Binet, A. (1900). *La suggestibilité.* Paris: Schleicher-Frères.

Borke, H. (1975). Piaget's mountains revisited: Changes in the egocentric landscape. *Developmental Psychology, 11,* 240–243.

Brown, M. R. (1926). *Legal psychology.* Indianapolis: Bobbs-Merrill Co.

Bulkley, J. (1982). *Intrafamily child sexual abuse cases.* Washington, DC: American Bar Association.

Bulkley, J. (1983). Evidentiary theories for admitting a child's out-of-court statement of sexual abuse at trial. In J. Bulkley (Ed.), *Child sexual abuse and the law* (pp. 153–165). Washington, DC: American Bar Association.

Burnam v. Chicago Great Western Railway, 340 Mo. 25, 100 S.W. 2d 858 (1937).

Burtt, H. E. (1931). *Legal psychology.* New York: Prentice-Hall, Inc.

Carporael, L. R. (1976). Ergotism: The Satan loosed in Salem? *Science, 192,* 21–26.

Chance, J. E., & Goldstein, A. G. (1984). Face-recognition memory: Implications for children's eyewitness testimony. *Journal of Social Issues, 40*(2), 69–85.

Chi, M. T. H. (1978). Knowledge structures and memory development. In R. Siegler (Ed.), *Children's thinking: What develops?* (pp. 73–96). Hillsdale, NJ: Erlbaum & Associates.

Chi, M. T. H., & Rees, E. T. (1983). A learning framework for development. In M. T. H. Chi (Ed.), *Trends in memory development* (Vol. 9, pp. 71–107). New York: Krager.

Collins, G. B. & Bond, E. C. (1953). Youth as a bar to testimonial competence. *Arkansas Law Review, 8,* 100–107.

Crowner v. Crowner 44 Mich. 180, 6 N.W. 198 (1880).

Damon, W. (1978) Moral development. *New Directions for Child Development* (No.2). San Fransisco: Jossey-Bass Publishers.

Dent, H., & Stephenson, G. M. (1979). Identification evidence: Experimental investigations of factors affecting the reliability of juvenile and adult witnesses. In D. P. Farrington, K. Hawkins, & S. M. Lloyd-Bostock (Eds.), *Psychology, law, and legal processes* (pp. 195–206). Atlantic Highlands, NJ: Humanities Press.

Fischer, K. (1980). A theory of cognitive development: The control of hierarchies of skill. *Psychological Review, 87,* 477–531.

Girl, 12, on coast held in contempt. (1984, January). *New York Times,* p. 10.

Goetze, H. (1980). *The effect of age and method of interview on the accuracy and completeness of eyewitness accounts.* Unpublished doctoral dissertation, Hofstra University, New York.

Goodman, G. S., Golding, J. M., & Haith, M. M. (1984). Jurors' reactions to children's testimony. *Journal of Social Issues, 40*(2), 139–156.

Katz, S., & Mazur, M. A. (1979). *Understanding the rape victim.* New York: Wiley.

Klotter, J. C. (1980). *Criminal evidence* (3rd ed.). Washington, DC: Anderson Publishing Co.

Knab v. Alden's Irving Park, Inc., 49 Ill. App. 2d 371, 199 N.E. 2d. 815 (1964).

Lipmann, O. (1911). Pedagogical psychology of report. *Journal of Educational Psychology, 2,* 253–261.

Lipton, J. P. (1977). On the psychology of eyewitness testimony. *Journal of Applied Psychology, 62,* 90–93.

Lloyd, D. (1983). The corroboration of sexual victimization of children. In J. Bulkley (Ed.), *Child sexual abuse and the law* (pp. 103–124). Washington, DC: American Bar Association.

Loftus, E. F. (1979). *Eyewitness testimony.* Cambridge, MA: Harvard University Press.

Loftus, E. F., & Davies, G. M. (1984). Distortions in the memory of children. *Journal of Social Issues, 40*(2), 51–67.

Loh, W. D. (1981). Psycholegal research: Past and present. *Michigan Law Review, 79,* 659–707.

Marple, C. H. (1933). The comparative suggestibility of three age levels to the suggestion of group versus expert opinion. *Journal of Social Psychology, 4,* 176–184.

Matossian, M. K. (1982). Ergot and the Salem witch affair. *American Scientist, 70,* 355–357.

McCarty, D. G. (1929). *Psychology for the lawyer.* New York: Prentice-Hall.

Melton, G., Bulkley, J., & Wulkan, D. (1983). Competency of children as witnesses. In J. Bulkley (Ed.), *Child sexual abuse and the law.* Washington, DC: American Bar Association.

Morison, S. E. (1972). *The Oxford history of the American people* (Vol. 1). New York: Oxford University Press.

Munsterberg, H. (1908). *On the witness stand.* New York: Doubleday.

Parker, J. (1982). The rights of child witnesses: Is the court a protector or a perpetrator? *New England and Law Review, 17,* 643–717.

Pear, T. H., & Wyatt, S. (1914). The testimony of normal and mentally defective children. *British Journal of Psychology, 3,* 388–419.

Piaget, J. (1962). *Play, dreams, and imitation.* New York: Norton.

Pynoos, R. S., & Eth, S. (1984). The child as witness to homicide. *Journal of Social Issues, 40*(2), 87–108.

Reifen, D. (1975). Court procedures in Israel to protect child-victims of sexual assault. In I. Drapkin & E. Viano (Eds.), *Victimology: A new focus* (Vol. 3, pp. 67–72). Lexington, MA: Lexington Books.

Rex v. Baylis 13 L. T. (o.s.) 509 (1849).

Rex v. Braddon and Speke 9 How. St. Tr. 1127, 1148 (1684).

Rex v. Braiser 11 Leach 199, 168 Eng. Rep. 202 (1779).

Rouke, F. L. (1957). Psychological research on problems of testimony. *Journal of Social Issues, 13* (2), 50–59.

Severance, L. (1983, August). *Eliciting evidence from children: Pretrial interviews and courtroom testimony.* In G. Goodman (Chair), *The child witness: Psychological and legal issues.* Symposium conducted at the American Psychological Association Convention, Anaheim, CA.

Sporer, S. (1982). A brief history of the psychology of testimony. *Current Psychological Reviews, 2,* 323–340.

Stafford, C. (1962). The child as witness. *Washington Law Review, 37,* 303–324.

Stephen, J. F. (1863). *A general view of the criminal law of England.* London: Macmillan and Co.

Stern, W. (1910). Abstracts of lectures on the psychology of testimony and on the study of individuality. *American Journal of Psychology, 21,* 273–282.

Stern, W. (1939). The psychology of testimony. *Journal of Abnormal and Social Psychology, 34,* 3–30.

Terr, L. (1979). Children of Chowchilla: A study of psychic trauma. *Psychoanalytic Study of the Child, 34,* 552–623.

Terr, L. (1983). Life attitudes, dreams, and psychic trauma in a group of "normal" children. *Journal of the American Academy of Child Psychiatry, 22,* 221–230.

Thomas, R. V. (1956). The problem of the child witness. *Wyoming Law Review, 10,* 214–222.

Trankell, A. (1958). Was Lars sexually assaulted? A study in the reliability of witnesses and of experts. *Journal of Abnormal and Social Psychology, 56,* 385–395.

Trankell, A. (1972). *The reliability of evidence.* Stockholm: Beckmann.

Varendonck, J. (1911). Les témoignages d'enfants dans un procès retentissant. *Archives de Psychologie, 11*, 129–171.

Wheeler v. United States, 159 U.S. 523 (1895).

Whipple, G. M. (1909). The observer as reporter: A survey of the 'psychology of testimony.' *Psychological Bulletin, 6*, 153–170.

Whipple, G. M. (1911). The psychology of testimony. *Psychological Bulletin, 8*, 307–309.

Whipple, G. M. (1912). Psychology of testimony and report. *Psychological Bulletin, 9*, 264–269.

Whipple, G. M. (1913). The psychology of testimony and report. *Psychological Bulletin, 10*, 264–268.

Wigmore, J. (1909). Profesor Munsterberg and the psychology of testimony. *Illinois Law Review, 3*, 399–445.

Wigmore, J. H. (1935/1976). *Evidence in trials at common law* (revised by J. Chadborn) (Vol. 6). Boston, MA: Little, Brown & Co.

Wolf, T. H. (1973). *Alfred Binet.* Chicago: University of Chicago Press.

Appendix

The Testimony of Children In a Famous Trial
J. Varendonck

Translated by Cindy Hazan, Robert Hazan, and Gail S. Goodman

From the 23rd to the 28th of January, 1910, a celebrated case in the county of eastern Flanders, Belgium, was called before the Assize Court. The court was asked to determine the innocence or guilt of a man accused of the murder and rape of a child. Six days before the opening of the trial, the defense attorneys asked me to write a report on the value of the testimony to be heard. . . . For the reader's convenience, I have reproduced a newspaper article that appeared on the eve of the opening of the trial. . . . "Next Monday Mr. Amand Van Puyenbroeck, married, 36 years of age . . . will appear before the Assize Court in response to a summons. He is currently being detained while awaiting trial, under the charge of having voluntarily killed and afterwards of having or having attempted to rape Cecile De Bruyeker, 9-years-old, at 300 meters from her house, last Sunday, 12 June 1910, in the afternoon."

On Sunday, June 12, Cecile De Bruyeker had gone to play with playmates in the vicinity of her house. . . . She played hide-and-seek in the yard of the accused, and in areas surrounding his house, with the accused's 8-year-old daughter and with Louise Van der Stuyft, 9-years-old. Towards 4 o'clock the victim was seen with the same children at the village chapel. From there, it was said, she went towards a small path that led behind Van Puyenbroeck's yard.

By evening, Cecile had not returned home. Her mother became worried and began to search for her child. After many unsuccessful attempts to find Cecile, Madame De Bruyeker talked to the two friends with whom her daughter last played. They were already in bed but were awakened. Both of them gave approximately the same answer: "Cecile played with us, but we have not seen her since."

The whole town became agitated. All the inhabitants began the search, but no one found the least trace of the lost child. Finally, the police were called. It was Monday morning at 3 a.m. when Superintendent of Police Lambert, accompanied by agent Dierens, arrived at the home of Louise Van der Stuyft (who had played with the absent child the day before), woke her up, and took her to the path where the victim had been last seen. One of the officers followed a small route that led through the hedge of Van Puyenbroeck's garden into a field. And there, at a distance of thirty to forty feet from the hedge, in a dry ditch, he discovered the corpse of the missing child. . . .

At that moment, Louise Van der Stuyft declared approximately the following: "After having prayed the rosary in the chapel, we went to play behind Van Puyenbroeck's garden. A tall man with a black moustache, dressed with a black jacket and pants and a cap of the same color, came here and promised me one cent if I would go with him. Then he offered the same proposition to Cecile who accepted it. She told us that 'if not he would not like her anymore.' They went through this path. I watched him, he pulled Cecile with him, and after a while, I went to look and found her dead in the ditch.

"It is impossible for me to say whether he was wearing clogs or boots, but I heard it said his name was Jan and that he was from Laerne. Filled with fear, I went to bed and did not dare talk to anyone about it . . . ."

Since my first reading of the record, I was convinced of poor Van Puyenbroeck's innocence. . . . The accusation was based solely on the testimony of children, as we will see from my report.

But everyone accused of crime based on children's testimony does not encounter a psychologist to counter the indictment that lies heavy upon them. . . . When are we going to give up, in all civilized nations, listening to children in courts of law?

Psychological Observations of the Testimony of Children

Those who are in the habit of living with children do not attach the least value to their testimony because children cannot observe and because their suggestibility is inexhaustible. The observations reported below give an idea of these two principal defects. . . .

Experiments Conducted On January 20th, 1912

. . . To prove how dangerous it is to ask tendentious questions, I asked questions similar to those asked of the actual child witnesses to 108 students from our school, aged 7 to 13 years. I had the police report right in front of me, and I duplicated as much as possible the questions of interest in the report.

87

But first I shall describe a few experiments that demonstrate how poorly children observe and how suggestible they are:

(1) In the second grade (average age of students: 7 years), the teacher wrote the following sentence on the blackboard, but before doing so he drew the children's attention to the person in question, teacher H. This is how he proceeded: "You know Monsieur H., don't you? The teacher of the fourth grade?" The children see him many times a day; each time the students line up before entering class, Monsieur H., because of the arrangement of lines, is immediately next to them. . . .

It is quite certain then that the students know who is in question. Afterwards, the teacher rubs strongly on his chin, pronouncing the word "beard." Now here is the question that appears on the blackboard: "What is the color of Monsieur H.'s beard?" The children write down their answer to this question. Of 18 students, 16 wrote: "black"; the 2 others wrote nothing. In reality, Monsieur H. does not have a beard and the children could have observed this fact every day.

(2) In 3rd grade, we proceed with the same experiment, with the exception that it is now Monsieur Th. who is in question. There equally, a conversation preceded the exercise. It was superfluous because we knew that the young children knew Monsieur Th. very well, and they knew immediately who was in question when they heard this name mentioned. The students of his class were on the average 8-years-old. The question was conceived as follows: "What is the color of Monsieur Th.'s moustache?"

According to 19 students, Monsieur Th. had a moustache of a given color. But Monsieur Th. is completely beardless. Only one student out of 20 declared that Monsieur Th. does not have a moustache.

(3) The same question, asked under identical circumstances in the 4th grade, produced the following results: Sixteen students out of 20 declared that Monsieur Th. has a moustache of a certain color and, among them, there were six 11-year-olds, and two others were even older. The six remaining were not susceptible to the suggestion.

Conclusion: A question asked badly can result in erroneous information about a person that children see several times a day. . . . The series of experiments hereafter tends to show that we cannot depend on any of the perceptions of children.

In 4th grade, where the previously reported incident took place, I submitted the students to another examination. (The teacher had taken care not to discuss the first experiment.) A colleague of another class, Monsieur B., went to the 4th grade, and kept his hat on during the whole time he stayed in the classroom. It is a rare event, because according to custom all who enter a class take off their hat. From the smallest student to the director, none disregarded this custom. It could be presumed then with good reason that for the well-raised children of the upper or middle bourgeoisie, of whom our students' population is almost exclusively composed, this impoliteness did not go unnoticed.

With his hat on, Monsieur B. talked for about five minutes, agitating at certain times in an aggressive manner with his hands and his legs, and pointing with his finger. Afterwards, he left the class and the door was hardly closed when the teacher said: "I want now to know who among you is a good observer," and wrote on the blackboard the following question, to which the students had to respond in writing: In which hand was Monsieur B. holding his hat?

The students, aged 9- to 12-years, answered as follows: (a) Seventeen students declared that Monsieur B. was holding his hat in his right hand: (b) Seven students declared that Monsieur B. was holding his hat in his left hand. In total, 24 of the answers were false and 3 were true. . . .

Conclusion: I assert that the above experiments suffice to establish: (1) That we can hardly trust the declarations of children when they claim to have observed certain details that they describe; (2) That their imaginations play nasty tricks on them; (3) That it suffices to have a person who has power over them (i.e., parents, teachers, and in general all persons enjoying a certain prestige) to be convinced of a thing, and this conviction will immediately be shared by children; and (4) that by badly posed questions—whether voluntary or involuntary—we can obtain answers that stupefy. . . .

Another Experiment

I also attempted to demonstrate the lack of value of children's testimony in criminal affairs in another series of experiments that I have not yet discussed. The experiments took place in my class where the students were on the average 8 years old. The director was present as a silent witness. I said: "My boys, this morning, while you were in line before me at the school playground, a gentleman approached me, didn't he?" (In reality, no one approached me.)

Afterwards I used literally the words that the examining magistrate said to Louisa Van der Stufyt, during his first interrogation: "You certainly know this gentleman and tell me, by writing it on your paper, who he is." The students looked at me with a surprised look. I added: "Anyone who does not know him should write down a zero . . . ." Seven boys out of 22 accepted my suggestion at first sight.

I pursued the experiment by reproducing as much as possible the circumstances in which Louisa Van der Stuyft and Elvire Van Puyenbroeck declared that Van Puyenbroeck was the culprit. In fact, it was not until Sunday, June 19th, eight days after the crime, that these children accused the defendant under the following circumstances: (1) Public opinion had already accused him, and his name was certainly pronounced in their presence; (2) The nuns at the girls' school lectured their students that they must tell the truth; (3) They received gifts from Alice Dierens and from the wife of the superintendent of police so that they would accuse Van Puyenbroeck; and (4) The superintendent's wife asked suggestive questions of the two principal witnesses indicating that they knew the murderer.

As far as I was concerned, I did not even need to say as much as the people who interviewed the children in the actual affair. I was satisfied with asking: "Wasn't it Monsieur M. who came close to me?" The director added: "I want to know the truth!"

Here is the result of my less suggestive question: Seventeen students wrote Monsieur M.; one student maintained that it was Monsieur W.; four students wrote nothing.

Afterwards I asked about the following details: (1) The color of Monsieur M.'s clothes; (2) If he had or did not have a beard; (3) What gesture Monsieur M. made.

There were only two students out of 22 whom I could not make do what I wanted; and among these two, one later told me he had come very late to class after we had already entered the school building.

I concluded that I succeeded in convincing the great majority of students in my class, by nothing but pronouncing his name, that Monsieur M. came to see me in their presence. And these children described a person that they had not even seen. Can it be astonishing, consequently, that the name of the accused was obtained from Louisa Van der Stufyt and Elvire Van Puyenbroeck?

I wanted to prevent an objection that I had tested the children in groups, whereas the witnesses of the actual affair had been interrogated separately. To avoid exposing myself to the least criticism, I continued the interrogation in the manner of an examining magistrate in the presence of witnesses. . .

The student M.
Q: When did Monsieur M. come?   *A:* In the morning.
Q: What time?   *A:* At eight twenty-five.
Q: Where was I?   *A:* At the school playground.
Q: And the students?   *A:* In line at the school playground.
Q: You did see Monsieur M. well? What was he like?   *A:* He was lively.
Q: Don't you think that he was a little angry with Monsieur Varendonck?   *A:* Yes.

[Here Varendonck explains how it is that Monsieur M. had the angry look. This declaration was imagined as was the rest:—Eds.]

Monsieur M. lives in a country-house at L—and consequently his grandson, who lives with him, your colleague M., comes everyday to school by train. But yesterday there was a thick fog; all the trains were delayed, and M. had to hurry to arrive at school on time. His grandfather, who was accompanying him, being no longer a young man, had difficulties keeping up with his grandson . . . and thence his anger.

[After this explanation, which every child received at a desired moment, Varendonck continued his interrogation.—Eds.]

Q: Did Monsieur M. make any gestures?   *A:*   Yes.

Q: Which ones?   *A:*   He lifted his arms up.

Q: Are you sure of all you are saying there?   *A:*   Yes, of course.

Q: It is, thus, entirely the truth?   *A:*   Yes, yes, yes.

   The student G.

Q: Have you seen Monsieur M.?   *A:*   Yes.

Q: Did he gesture?   *A:*   Yes.

Q: If I recall correctly, you were first in line, the closest to Monsieur M. Didn't you hear what Monsieur M. was saying?   *A:*   I heard the words, but I could not repeat them.

Q: Didn't he say: 'Monsieur Varendonck, I am angry with you!'   *A:*   No.

Q: Or: 'Monsieur Varendonck, you made me run!'?   *A:*   Yes, that is it.

Q: That's fine. You saw the gestures of Monsieur M., you said?   *A:*   Yes. He was furious. . . .

Q: You also saw the gestures of Monsieur M. before his departure?   *A:*   Yes, he left without saluting you.

Q: Then you saw that he pushed me like this (on the shoulder)?   *A:*   Yes, sir, I saw it well. . . .

I came to the end of my task. During many days and long nights, I examined and studied the report. Alone with my conscience, in the calm of my office, I finished expressing my profound conviction "that the children who testified in this case had seen nothing, absolutely nothing of the murder, nor the murderer; and that consequently, we cannot set the least value in their declarations . . . ."

91

SEXUALLY ABUSED CHILDREN AND THE LEGAL SYSTEM: SOME POLICY RECOMMENDATIONS

GARY B. MELTON
University of Nebraska-Lincoln

There are two broad types of questions raised by sexually abused children's involvement in the legal system: 1) competency to testify; and 2) procedural and evidentiary reforms to protect child witnesses. Relevant psychological research is reviewed. It is recommended that children be permitted to testify without prior qualification. There is insufficient evidence to justify substantial modifications of criminal procedure on psychological grounds. The federal government should launch a research initiative to examine the effects of legal procedures on children.

This article is intended to present the psychological issues and research underlying two broad questions of legal policy relevant to the participation of sexually abused children in the legal system. First, children's competency to testify will be discussed. Second, attention will be given to the several proposals for reform of criminal procedures and evidentiary rules to protect child victims from the trauma which the trial process is presumed to engender.

CHILDREN'S COMPETENCY TO TESTIFY

Although there is usually a rebuttable presumption of children's incompetence to testify, it is well established in Anglo-American jurisprudence that the question of whether children's testimony is sufficiently reliable to enhance justice is

---

This article is based on testimony by the author on behalf of the American Psychological Association and the Association for the Advancement of Psychology before the Senate Subcommittee on Juvenile Justice on May 22, 1984. Portions of the testimony were derived from Melton (1981a, 1981b, 1984a).

In part as a result of the testimony, the Missing Children's Assistance Act (1984) was recently amended to give the Justice Department express authority to support research on child victims' involvement in the legal system.

Thanks are due Ellen Greenberg of the APA Office of National Policy Sudies for her assistance in preparing the testimony.

For reprints, write Gary B. Melton, Law/Psychology Program, University of Nebraska-Lincoln, 209 Burnett Hall, Lincoln, NE 68588-0308.

The American Journal of Family Therapy, Vol. 13, No. 1, 1985 © Brunner/Mazel, Inc.

to be decided on a case-by-case basis. The traditional view is reflected in the Supreme Court's 1895 decision in *Wheeler v. United States*. In that case, the Court held that the five-year-old son of a murder victim was properly qualified as a witness. Rather than invoking a *per se* rule that young children are, by reason of their immaturity, incompetent to testify, the Court held that the admissibility of a child's testimony is dependent upon the trial judge's determination of the "capacity and intelligence of the child, his appreciation of the difference between truth and falsehood, as well as his duty to tell the former" (*Wheeler v. United States*, 1895, pp. 524–525). Concretely, children's competency to testify is usually assessed through a wide-ranging voir dire focused on a variety of moral, cognitive, and social skills: the child's ability to differentiate truth from falsehood, to comprehend the duty to tell the truth, and to understand the consequences of not fulfilling this duty; the child's cognitive capacity to form a "just impression of the facts" at the time of the alleged offense and to communicate memories of the event in response to questions at trial; the child's ability to organize the event cognitively and to differentiate it from his or her other thoughts and fantasies; the child's ability to withstand suggestions by parents, attorneys, and other adult authority figures. In cases of sexual abuse, the child is also required in some courts to demonstrate an understanding of the meaning of sexual terms and behavior.

Although there are some qualifiers, the available research generally supports the potential of children as young as age four to present testimony which is reliable, or at least as reliable as that produced by adult eyewitnesses (cf. Loftus, 1979). Research on children's memory is illustrative. In general, laboratory studies, including simulations of eyewitness tasks (e.g., Marin et al., 1979), suggest that four-year-old children's recognition memory is comparable to that of adults (Brown, 1973; Brown & Campione, 1972; Brown & Scott, 1971; Corsini et al., 1969; Nelson, 1971; Perlmutter & Myers, 1974, 1975, 1976; Standing et al., 1970). There is, however, a developmental trend in the amount of information produced on free recall (Emmerich & Ackerman, 1978; Kobasigawa, 1974; Perlmutter & Ricks, 1979; Ritter et al., 1973). Nonetheless, that information which is elicited on free recall is especially likely to be accurate, perhaps as a result of the relative lack of interpolation into memory by young children of what they think they should have seen, heard, or experienced in a given situation. In sum, then, the available data suggest that even young children generally have sufficient memory skills to respond to the recall demands of testimony. However, their lack of productivity on free recall may mean that more extensive questioning is needed to elicit their memories than would be true of adult witnesses.

Young children's cognitive abilities are more problematic (see Melton, 1981a). They typically have difficulty in conceptualizing complex events and ordering them in time and space. In particular, they tend to center their attention on one aspect of a stimulus rather than on multiple factors in conceptualization and reasoning. However, this difficulty may not be very relevant to the nature of the testimony which a child may be required to give in cases of sexual abuse. That is, the child may be able to give a concrete description of what happened, provided that questions are direct and in language familiar to the child. In such an instance, the child's difficulty in conceptualizing the event may not be very important. The significance of such skills is especially likely to be minimized if the child is able to use concrete means of communication (e.g., pointing to parts of an anatomically correct doll) so that verbal fluency is less important.

Even if children can adequately relate their experiences, there still may be concerns about whether they will do so truthfully. In fact, there is little correlation between age and honesty (Burton, 1976). Where there is a pronounced developmental trend is in the *reasons* children give for moral decisions, a trend which is arguably irrelevant to the probative value of children's testimony. However, young children's immaturity of moral and social reasoning may make them more vulnerable to adult suggestions.

Young children tend to conceptualize the morality of an act in terms of the probability of punishment by adult authorities. Hence, they may perceive little actual freedom in decision making. The directly relevant research is admittedly scan and removed from the problem of "telling on" parents or other adults important to the child. However, at least one study (Marin et al., 1979) found that children in kindergarten and first grade were no more swayed by the suggestions embedded in a leading question than were adult witnesses.

In actuality, children may be less easily influenced than adults by suggestions implicit in subtle changes of wording. On the other hand, when chidlren lack the cognitive skills or experience to organize a perception, they may be especially vulnerable to adults' explanations of what may have occurred. The child may be dependent upon adults to clarify the meaning of an event foreign to the child's previous experience. Thus, there may be reason to be concerned about children's vulnerability to suggestion, but even here the age trends may be weaker, or at least more complex, than might be expected. That is, a blanket statement that children are more suggestible than adults is not justified by the available research (see Loftus & Davies, 1984, for review).

Given the amount of time consumed by voir dire of child witnesses, there may be reason, as Dean Wigmore (1940) argued, to admit children's testimony without establishing their competency. In most cases where there is a real question of the child's competency to testify, the validity of the inquiry on voir dire is questionable. For example, the series of questions commonly asked about the child's religious beliefs and understanding of the significance of an oath probably has little, if any, correlation with the child's predisposition to tell the truth (see Melton, 1981b, p. 74, note 1, and pp. 79–80). Especially given the relatively minor effects which developmental factors are likely to have on the veracity of children's testimony, a reasonable policy might be simply to allow the trier of fact to judge the credibility of the child in the same way that any witness's testimony must be evaluated.

Two qualifiers must be made to this conclusion, however. Both are caveats about misconceptualizing the question of children's competency to testify as an internal attribute of the child. In fact, such competency might be better understood as an *interactive* construct. First, the issue of competency to testify is as much an issue of judges' and jurors' capacities as that of the child (cf. Goodman et al., 1984). Even if children's testimony were influenced by childish logic, the admission of such testimony would still enhance justice if the trier of fact could validly interpret the reality underlying the child's account of the event. Second, the level of competency of the child is likely to vary with the situation. High levels of anxiety adversely affect recall and cognitive funtioning. Thus, interventions designed to reduce ambiguity about the situation (e.g., visiting the courtroom prior to testimony) and the scariness of testimony itself (e.g., a friendly word from the judge) may improve the quality of children's testimony.

PROCEDURAL AND EVIDENTIARY REFORMS

Concern with the level of stress engendered (or alleviated) by legal procedures is not, of course, simply a matter of increasing children's productivity as witnesses. There is also a need to minimize stress for the child's own sake. Child advocates wish to ensure that the child victim of sexual abuse is not victimized again by the legal process itself. With that goal in mind, there have been a number of proposals for procedural and evidentiary reforms intended to reduce the risk of children being traumatized by the legal process, while also permitting alleged child molestors to be brought to justice. In general, these proposals provide for limiting the audience during child victims' testimony and/or preventing direct face-to-face confrontation by the defendant. Among the procedural reforms suggested are permitting the child to testify in front of a one-way mirror outside the physical presence of the defendant (e.g., Libai, 1969; Parker, 1983) and admitting videotaped depositions in lieu of testimony at trial (e.g., Arizona Revised Statutes, 1978/1982; Florida Statutes, 1979/1983; Montana Code, 1977/1981; New Mexico Statutes, 1978). Alternatively, some have argued that the courtroom testimony of child victims of sexual abuse should not be necessary. In that vein, Kansas (1982) and Washington State (1982/1984) have recently enacted statutes permitting admission of hearsay about child victims' statements (see Skoler, 1984, for commentary).

These proposals all raise serious constitutional issues (Melton, 1981b). Each arguably invades one or more of the following fundamental rights: the defendant's sixth amendment rights to a public trial and to confrontation of witnesses and the public's first amendment right, through the press, to access to the trial process. Although most of these issues have yet to be litigated, the Supreme Court's decision in *Globe Newspaper Co. v. Superior Court* (1982; see Melton, 1984a) gives a clear message that *mandatory* procedural aberrations in cases involving child sexual abuse are unlikely to withstand strict scrutiny. In *Globe*, the court struck down as violative of the first amendment a Massachusetts statute providing for mandatory closure of the courtroom to the press (and others not having a direct interest in the case) during testimony by a minor victim of a sex offense. Writing for the majority, Justice Brennan acknowledged that protection of minor victims is a compelling state interest, but he found the Massachusetts statute to be insufficiently narrow in its scope. Justice Brennan argued that some minor victims might *want* publicity of the trial so that they could expose the heinous behavior of the defendant; others might simply not be bothered by presence of the media. Moreover, the incremental protection of witnesses' privacy offered by the statute was minimal in that Massachusetts already permitted publication of the victims' names in the court record.

The *Globe* majority was also unpersuaded that mandatory closure would increase reporting of sex offenses against children. Even if empirical evidence to that effect were available—as it is not—it is hard to imagine research which would be so overwhelming as to permit mandatory closure. Justice Brennan argued that a mandatory-closure statute would be justified on the ground of enhancing the frequency and quality of children's testimony only if it could be shown that "closure would improve the quality of testimony of *all* minor victims" (p. 2622, note 26), an impossible task.

Globe indicates that broad procedural reforms to protect child witnesses are unlikely to pass constitutional scrutiny. Regardless, such reforms are premature. Both the need for substantial modifications of procedure and the effectiveness of such procedures in reducing courtroom trauma are undocumented and indeed unstudied. The assumption by the *Globe* dissenters and others that "certainly the [traumatic] impact [of trial procedures] on children must be greater" (p. 2626, note 7) than on adult victims of sexual offenses is plausible. Children are less likely than adults to have the cognitive and emotional resources for understanding the experience, and legal authorities not used to communicating with children may find it difficult to allay their concerns. However, particularly for young children, it is equally plausible that children's responses are *less* severe on average than those of adults. Provided that parents and others do not overreact and that they are supportive of the child during the legal process, it may well be that the trial experience will cause little trauma. At least for some child victims, the experience may be cathartic (Berliner & Barbierei, 1984; Pynoos & Eth, 1984; Rogers, 1982); it provides an opportunity for taking control of the situation, achieving vindication, and symbolically putting an end to the episode.

Even assuming that the legal process is psychologically harmful for some child victims, there is essentially no research literature on which to base interventions to prevent such harm or, as *Globe* (1982, p. 2621) permits, to identify particularly vulnerable child victims so that trial procedures (e.g., access of the press) may be modified to protect them. At present, the literature is virtually barren on these points,* as it is with respect to children's involvement in the legal system generally.** Although there is a rapidly burgeoning literature about children's competence as legal decision makers (Melton, 1984b; Melton et al., 1983), basic research is lacking on their understanding of the legal process. We do not know, for example, how young children understand the role of an attorney and the nature of the adversary process.

Although research on sexually abused children's responses to testimony in criminal trials is hampered by the small number of children who actually testify in such cases, it would be useful to "debrief" children after testimony to obtain at least a subjective appraisal of the experience and the thoughts it provoked. Such data gathering seems to be a first step in developing techniques of allaying children's anxiety while at the same time meeting the needs of the legal system. Research of this sort would likely be useful to police investigators, prosecutors, and mental health and social service professionals who work with sexually abused children, as well as to policy makers. Moreover, such knowledge would be helpful in preparing sexually abused children and others, especially those involved in emotionally charged disputes (e.g., contested custody), to testify in court.

There is also a need to test the efficacy of particular procedural reforms. At least until such time as the constitutionality of state statutes providing, for example, a special hearsay exception is successfully challenged, there is the opportunity for direct study of the effectiveness of such reforms in increasing the frequency of reports of sexual abuse, enhancing the quality of testimony, and diminishing whatever trauma is engendered by the trail process. Such state reforms might legitimately be viewed as "natural experiments" enabling us to learn ways of ensuring humane treatment of child victims by the legal system.

In addition, the federal Victim and Witness Protection Act of 1982 and analogous state victim-protection statutes provide opportunities to test the efficacy of special procedures to protect child victims which are supplements to, rather than funda-

---

*There are two studies directly on point (Burgess & Holmstrom, 1978; De Francis, 1969). However, both studies have significant methodological limitations (Melton, 1984a) and may best be viewed as pilot clinical interview studies useful primarily for formulating hypotheses for more rigorously designed research.

**Significant modifications of criminal procedure and rules of evidence are more likely to be defensible if they are narrowly drawn, especially if fundamental interests of the defendant or the press are affected. This principle implies that data are needed to indicate which groups are especially vulnerable in the courtroom. In this regard, it must be determined whether special vulnerability is an attribute of child witnesses generally or only those of a particular age, sex, or type of victimization (e.g., incest), for instance. Necessarily, then, studies or reforms to protect sexually abused children will also involve different groups of children and adults for the purpose of comparison. Well-designed research on the involvement of sexually abused children in the legal system thus may help to fill the large gaps in knowledge about the diverse roles of children in the legal system—as witness, as object of custody dispute, as respondent in delinquency proceedings, etc.

mental changes of, existing criminal procedure.* Some of these interventions designed to provide assistance to victims and their families (e.g., special efforts to explain the process) are intuitively helpful and require little alteration of typical procedures. Other possible interventions (e.g., modification of the physical layout of the courtroom; involvement of the child or the family in prosecutorial decision making) are less clearly desirable, although they may be useful for some children. Careful development and evaluation of such interventions is needed, with particular attention to the appropriateness of various procedures for the specific case involved. Research would also be helpful to determine the most effective methods of training for police, prosecutors, and judges and counseling for parents in preparing sexually abused children for participation in the legal process and identifying and alleviating any psychological ill effects which may arise.

In conclusion, the developmental psychology literature gives little reason to be especially concerned about the reliability of children's testimony. Accordingly, a sound policy might be to admit children's testimony without respect to their competency to testify. Attention needs to be given, however, to fact finders' comprehension of children's testimony and to the interaction between children's developmental level and the courtroom context in determining the quality of their testimony. Legal procedures also need to be examined with respect to their effect upon the child's emotional well-being. At the present time, however, there is insufficient evidence to justify substantial modifications of criminal procedure on psychological grounds. There is a need for a substantial research initiative to examine the effects of legal procedures on children, both to ensure that sexual abuse victims are not doubly victimized and, more generally, to provide the information needed to assist children in making use of, and adjusting to, legal procedures. The federal government could play a very useful role in facilitating an assessment of the effects of various state procedural innovations to facilitate the participation of children as witnesses in courtroom proceedings.

REFERENCES

Ariz. Rev. Stat. Ann. § 12-2312 (1982) (enacted 1978).

Berliner, L., & Barbieri, M. K. (1984). The testimony of the child victim of sexual assault. *Journal of Social Issues, 40*(2), 125-137.

Brown, A. L. (1973). Judgments of recency for long sequences of pictures: The absence of a developmental trend. *Journal of Experiemental Child Psychology, 15*, 473-481.

Brown, A. L., & Campione, J. C. (1972). Recognition memory for perceptually similar pictures in preschool children. *Journal of Experimental Child Psychology, 14*, 55-62.

Brown, A. L., & Scott, M. S. (1971). Recognition memory for pictures in preschool children. *Journal of Experimental Child Psychology, 11*, 401-402.

Burgess, A. W., & Holmstorm, L. L. (1978). The child and family in the court process. In A. W. Burgess, A. N. Groth, L. L. Holmstrom, & S. M. Sgroi (Eds.), *Sexual assault of children and adolescents* (pp. 205-230). Lexington, MA: Lexington Books.

Burton, R. V. (1976). Honesty and dishonesty. In T. Lickona (Ed.), *Moral development and behavior: Theory, research, and social issues* (pp. 173-197). New York: Holt, Rinehart & Winston.

Corsini, D. A., Jacobus, K. A., & Leonard, D. S. (1969). Recognition memory of preschool children for pictures and words. *Psychonomic Science, 16*, 192-193.

DeFrancis, V. (1969). *Protecting the child victim of sex crimes committed by adults.* Denver: American Humane Association.

---

*The Victims of Crime Assistance Act of 1984 also provides significant funds—perhaps as much as $100 million—to help states in assisting victims. The legislation requires that states receiving grants provide psychological services to victims as one of the program components. The states have an excellent opportunity to test the efficacy of various innovations in assistance to child victims.

Emmerich, H. J., & Ackerman, B. P. (1978). Developmental differences in recall: Encoding or retrieval? *Journal of Experimental Child Psychology, 25,* 514–525.

Fla. Stat. Ann. §918.17 (West. Supp. 1983) (enacted 1979).

Globe Newspaper Co. v. Superior Court, 102 S.Ct. 2613 (1982).

Goodman, G. S., Golding, J. M., & Haith, M. M. (1984). Jurors' reactions to child witnesses. *Journal of Social Issues, 40*(2), 139–156.

Kan. Stat. Ann. § 60-460(dd) (Supp. 1982).

Kobasigawa, A. (1974). Utilization of retrieval cues by children in recall. *Child Development, 45,* 127–134.

Libai, D. (1969). The protection of the child victim of a sexual offense in the criminal justice system. *Wayne Law Review, 15,* 977–1032.

Loftus, E. F. (1979). *Eyewitness testimony.* Cambridge, MA: Harvard University Press.

Loftus, E. F., & Davies, G. M. (1984). Distortions in the memory of children. *Journal of Social Issues, 40*(2), 51–67.

Marin, B. V., Holmes, D. L., Guth, M., & Kovac, P. (1979). The potential of children as eyewitnesses: A comparison of children and adults on eyewitness tasks. *Law and Human Behavior, 3,* 295–306.

Melton, G. B. (1981a). Children's competency to testify. *Law and Human Behavior, 5,* 73–85.

Melton, G. B. (1981b). Procedural reforms to protect child victim/witnesses in sex offense proceedings. In J. Bulkley (Ed.), *Child sexual abuse and the law* (pp. 184–198). Washington, DC: American Bar Association.

Melton, G. B. (1984a). Child witnesses and the First Amendment: A psycholegal dilemma. *Journal of Social Issues, 40*(2), 109–123.

Melton, G. B. (1984b). Developmental psychology and the law: The state of the art. *Journal of Family Law, 22,* 445–482.

Melton, G. B., Koocher, G. P., & Saks, M. J. (Eds.). (1983). *Children's competence to consent.* New York: Plenum Press.

Missing Children's Assistance Act of 1984, 98 Stat. 2125.

Mont. Code Ann. §§ 46-15-401 to -403 (1981) (enacted 1977).

Nelson, K. E. (1971). Memory development in children: Evidence from nonverbal tasks. *Psychonomic Science, 25,* 346–348.

N.M. Stat. Ann. § 30-9-17 (1978).

Parker, J. Y. (1983). The child witness versus the press: A proposed legislative response to *Globe v. Superior Court. Albany Law Review, 47,* 408–465.

Perlumutter, M., & Myers, N. A. (1974). Recognition memory development in 2- to 4-year-olds. *Developmental Psychology, 10,* 447–450.

Perlumutter, M., & Myers, N. A. (1975). Young children's coding and storage of visual and verbal material. *Child Development, 46,* 215–219.

Perlmutter, M., & Myers, N. A. (1976). Recognition memory in preschool children. *Developmental Psychology, 12,* 271–272.

Perlmutter, M., & Ricks, M. (1979). Recall in preschool children. *Journal of Experimental Child Psychology, 27,* 423–436.

Pynoos, R. S., & Eth, S. (1984). The child as witness to homicide. *Journal of Social Issues, 40*(2), 87–108.

Ritter, K., Kaprive, B. H., Fitch, J. P., & Flavell, J. (1973). The development of retrieval strategies in young children. *Cognitive Psychology, 5,* 310–321.

Rogers, C. M. (1982). Child sexual abuse and the courts: Preliminary findings. In J. Conte & D. A. Shore (Eds.), *Social work and child sexual abuse* (pp. 145–153). New York: Haworth Press.

Skoler, G. (1984). New hearsay exceptions for a child's statements of sexual abuse. *John Marshall Law Review, 18,* 1–48.

Standing, L., Conezio, J., & Haber, R. (1970). Perception and memory for pictures: Single-trial learning of 2500 visual stimuli. *Psychonomic Science, 19,* 73–74.

Victim and Witness Protection Act, Pub. L. 97-291, 96 Stat. 1248 (1982).

Victims of Crime Assistance Act of 1984, 98 Stat. 2170.

Wash. Rev. Code Ann. § 9A.44.120 (Supp. 1984) (enacted 1982).

Wheeler v. United States, 159 U.S. 523 (1895).

Wigmore, J. H. (1940). *On evidence* (Vol. 2, 3rd ed.). Boston: Little, Brown.

The Child as Witness: Competency and Credibility

BARRY NURCOMBE, M.D., F.R.A.C.P.

The terms *competency* and *credibility* are defined as they relate to child witnesses. The criteria employed by the courts in assessing a child's competency to testify are discussed, and research into the effect on children's testimony of limitations of memory, and of suggestibility, susceptibility to external influence, emotional arousal and long delay, is summarized. A systematic approach to the clinical evaluation of credibility is described, and the concept of a specific biopsychosocial syndrome associated with sexual abuse critically discussed.

Journal of the American Academy of Child Psychiatry, 25, 4:473–480, 1986

A child who claims to have been sexually abused may have convinced the police, the social worker and the prosecuting attorney involved in the case; but the same child may be treated as a fantasist or liar by one or both parents, and the counsel for the defense. From the evidence presented, and subject to various biases, judge or jury will ultimately determine the child's credibility. In the meantime, the witness is trapped between opposing forces: the expectation that he or she should tell the truth; guilt about disrupting the family; shame at repeated public exposure; uncertainty about personal responsibility for what happened; the threats, accusations or insinuations of one or both parents and their attorney; and bewilderment at the protracted adversarial proceedings his or her revelations have entrained. In these circumstances, it is not surprising that many complaints either never come to light or are falsely retracted.

This paper will deal with the concepts of juvenile testimonial competency and credibility and discuss how a clinician can help a Department of Protective Services or prosecuting attorney decide whether a child will be a reliable, honest and resolute witness. It is not enough to dismiss the matter by contending that clinicians are disqualified from being expert witnesses in questions of credibility, or that children never lie about being sexually abused. This paper contends that if clinical opinion is derived from systematic data and scientific knowledge, it can serve the interests of both child and justice system.

Competency

The testimonial competency of a witness is his capacity to provide reliable testimony. The credibility

Received Dec. 9, 1985; revised Feb. 27, 1986; accepted Mar. 19, 1986.

Dr. Nurcombe is Professor of Psychiatry and Human Behavior, Program in Medicine, Brown University, and Clinical Director, Emma Pendleton Bradley Hospital, 1011 Veterans Memorial Parkway, East Providence, RI 02915, where request for reprints may be sent.

of a witness refers to the extent to which a judge or jury believe that the witness is providing honest and accurate testimony. Though competency and credibility are interwoven, it is instructive to consider them separately.

The competency of a minor to testify has been reviewed from a legal standpoint by Stafford (1962) and Siegel and Hurley (1977), and from a psychological point of view by Melton (1981). In those states which have relevant statutes, there is a rebuttable presumption that children below the age of 10 years are incompetent to testify unless the judge can convince him or herself to the contrary. In other states, case law puts the age of competency at 14 years. In fact, children as young as 3 years of age have been qualified as witnesses.

The rules of evidence are customarily relaxed to accommodate qualified minors: leading questions are permitted and, in some circumstances, hearsay evidence is admissible. For example, another witness may be allowed to testify concerning the child's excited utterances shortly after a traumatic event. The event is thus regarded as "speaking through the child" (*rea gestae*) (Stafford, 1962).

The law is skeptical of the capacity of children to observe and recall events accurately, to appreciate the need to tell the truth, and to resist the influence of other people. Children are commonly thought to have great difficulty distinguishing fantasy from reality, and to be readily confused by an exaggerated curiosity about sexuality. Although it is often contended that false accusations of sexual molestation are prevalent, it is also thought that fact-finders tend to be biased against adult defendants in favor of female or child witnesses.

For these reasons, the judge may assess the testimonial competency of the prospective child witness before the trial begins (*voir dire*). It is not necessary that the child understand the full legal implications of taking an oath; but the court must ascertain that the child has the capacity (1) to register, recall and describe events reliably; (2) to distinguish truth from falsehood; and (3) to appreciate his or her obligation to tell the truth.

Unless the child's capacity is patently defective, expert consultation may be helpful to determine if the child had the capacity to register an event and if he or she will be able to recall it accurately when examined in court. The ultimate determination of credibility then rests with the judge or jury. As Melton (1981) points out, competency and credibility are interactive matters related to the psychology of memory, suggestibility, confabulation, fabrication and moral development. A review of recent research throws light on some of these issues.

Development of Memory

Short-term memory has low capacity and short duration, whereas long-term memory is a more permanent record of past events. The durability of memory depends upon the transfer of information from short-term to long-term storage and its consolidation, retention and ultimate retrieval.

Memory is either episodic or semantic. Episodic memory refers to the automatic storage and reproduction of spatially located, temporally ordered, personal experience. In contrast, semantic memory, which is coextensive with cognition, involves the storage and utilization of words, symbols, rules and concepts. Ordinarily, the child must appreciate that semantic material should be remembered ("meta-memory") before it is retained. With maturation, the child acquires more efficient strategies for recording, storing, recalling and reproducing episodic memories; and, as hierarchically organized cognitive structures develop, semantic memory becomes more complex. New experiences are assimilated according to the child's organized preconceptions of the world, or entrain the accommodation of preexisting structures. Recall, in turn, is influenced by preconception (Brown, 1975; Kail and Hagen, 1982).

Episodic and semantic memory interact. A child's capacity to store, recall and reproduce an event is influenced by the construction that was or can be placed on the event. Did it make sense? What sense did or does it make? Can the subsequent semantic reconstruction of an event reduce the reliability of its memory? The answers to these empirical questions are not clear. They are obviously relevant to the predicament of the child witness who must recount events from the distant past.

Of particular interest to the forensic clinician is the maturation of episodic memory for personal experience that has been recorded and must be retrieved in circumstances of heightened emotional arousal. As a young child is both relatively ignorant of sexuality, and relatively unable to attribute motivation to others, the effect of naivete on the memory of an adult's actions is also a relevant question.

The child of 4–6 years is better able to locate events spatially than to order them temporally. The concept of historical time and sequence, as opposed to speed and distance, is not usually acquired until 10 years of age or later (Goldstone and Goldfarb, 1966). The younger child is likely to have trouble dating events or accurately recalling a series of discrete occurrences. Nevertheless, children of 4–5 years perform as well as adults on tasks of recognition memory, particularly when verbal recall is deemphasized (Perlmutter and Myers, 1976), though they are markedly less able to recall events spontaneously unless prompted by direct questions (Perlmutter and Ricks, 1979).

To what degree do these observations reduce the credibility of a minor's testimony? Given the probability that they will be interrogated by parents, police and attorneys before a trial, and asked leading or direct questions in court, what is the evidence that children are particularly susceptible to suggestion or influence?

Suggestibility and Susceptibility

Recent memory research has employed naturalistic experimental situations rather than the traditional lists of nonsense syllables or words. Dawson (1981), for example, found that both adults and children are readily biased by leading questions concerning their memory of events viewed in motion pictures. Goetze (1980) examined the capacity of black children of different ages to recall a live purse-snatching experience in two circumstances: free narrative and structured questionnaire. Free recall resulted in more accurate, but less complete, information. Older children responded more accurately and completely to the questionnaire, but there was no effect of age on free recall. Neither sex nor intelligence appeared to influence either free or questionnaire recall.

Dale et al. (1978) investigated the effect of the form of questions on the memory of preschoolers after they had viewed short films. They found that the syntax of the question had no effect if the query concerned something which was actually present in the film. However, if the entity was not present in the film, children were more likely to answer "yes" incorrectly when questions were worded thus:

1. "Did you see the ...?"
2. "Did you see any ...?"
3. "Didn't you see some ...?"

The implication for clinical interviewers, police investigators and counsel is that the following kind of question is less likely to induce a false positive response:

4. "Did you see (a) ...?"

The potentially biasing effect of suggestive intonation has not been investigated.

Cohen and Harnick (1980) investigated the capacity of children and college students to recall events from a film in the face of misleading questions. Third grade children accepted false suggestions more readily and were less observant of detail than sixth grade or college students (who were roughly equivalent in suggestibility and recall of detail).

Marin et al. (1979) exposed subjects from kindergarten, third grade, seventh grade and college to a staged event, and examined them with regard to the completeness and accuracy of free recall, prompted recall and susceptibility to suggestion. Older subjects were superior on free recall. However, younger subjects were not significantly inferior in answering yes-no questions or identifying photographs; nor were they more likely to be misled by leading questions.

Hoving et al. (1969) found an interesting relationship between task difficulty, age and susceptibility to the influence of peers. Conformity increased with age in complex tasks, but it decreased with age if the task was less ambiguous. In other words, when careful judgment was required, younger children were less susceptible to peer pressure than older children. Allen and Newtson (1972) found that susceptibility to adult influence decreased from first to fourth grade, but increased slightly in tenth grade. Fodor (1971) found an association between susceptibility to influence and level of moral judgment.

Compared to children, adults cite less egocentric and more sociocentric, relative and abstract justifications for behavior (Kohlberg, 1976). However, the concordance between moral judgment and moral behavior is uncertain. Whatever their reasons, children are apparently no less honest than adults (Melton, 1981), and there is no evidence that they are more likely than adults to make false accusations.

Impact of the Courtroom on the Child

Benedek (1982) and Weiss and Berg (1982) have described the plight of the child sexual abuse victim in the courtroom. It is likely that the child is already psychologically disturbed as a result of emotional deprivation in a disturbed home, the trauma of sexual molestation, and guilt about his or her own part in the offense. He or she may view him or herself as the agent of the exposure of an incestuous parent and the potential cause of the dissolution of the family. Before the trial, the child is expected to recount the details

of the alleged offense, again and again, to strangers. Repeated court appearances may be required. In court, the child will eventually be confronted by the accused who is exercising his or her constitutional rights. In contrast to the accused, the child has no advocate. His or her testimony is open to direct challenge on the grounds of incompetence, confabulation or fabrication. These considerations deter victims from reporting offenses, lead to false retractions, and erode the apparent credibility of honest witnesses.

There has been no formal research into the effect upon memory of extreme emotional arousal at the time of experiencing or recalling a psychologically traumatic event. Although the clinical literature is replete with case reports that illustrate the repression of traumatic events, and although ego-defensive distortion is potentially of great significance in forensic evaluation, little is known about its effect upon memory in a courtroom situation. Furthermore, there has been no research into the effect of long delay on the reproducibility of episodic memory in childhood.

Clinical Evaluations of the Child Witness

Most research into the credibility of adult witnesses has come from German investigators. Arntzen (1970), for example, proposed four criteria by which the credibility of evidence might be evaluated: constancy over time, amount of detail, expressive format and underlying motivation. Kohnken and Wegner (1982) found that the amount of evidential detail discriminated between honest and fabricated testimony. Herbold (1977) and Berger (1979) have also investigated the characteristics of false evidence. Goodman (1984), Goodman et al. (1984), Johnson and Foley (1984), and Loftus and Davies (1984), have reviewed these issues in relation to children.

Although the courts accord mental health clinicians no special expertise in distinguishing truth from falsehood, a Department of Protective Services or prosecuting attorney may request mental health consultation on the following related questions: (1) Does the child have the cognitive and emotional competence to testify? (2) Is the child's story credible? (3) Is the child emotionally disturbed? (4) If so, will the stress of appearing in court aggravate the disturbance or cause lasting damage? (5) If the child is to testify, what psychological preparation will be required?

Credibility is a relative matter. Honest testimony may be incredible for a number of reasons, whereas bare-faced fabrications can be quite convincing. When the clinician is requested to advise the Department of Protective Services whether a child's account of an alleged event is credible, it is helpful to follow a systematic decision pathway. Needless to say, unless reasonable rapport is achieved, the procedures to be described are invalid.

Guidelines for interviewing children suspected of having been sexually abused have been presented by a number of authors (e.g., Jones and McQuiston, 1985). This paper will present the deductive reasoning which should direct the enquiry process.

When a child or adolescent alleges sexual abuse or molestation, the following logical possibilities apply:

1. The child does not have the mental capacity to distinguish between fact and fantasy, or to give a reliable account of the alleged event.
2. The child is truthful but has misinterpreted an innocent incident.
3. The child is truthful but deluded.
4. The child is confabulating or fabricating sexual abuse either spontaneously or as a result of indoctrination by another person.
5. The child is truthful and credible.

The implications of this series of hypotheses for clinical evaluation will now be considered.

Developmental Immaturity

Under the mental age of 4 years, a child may not have the maturity to recall events in detail completely, or in correct sequence. Do not assume this is so: assess each case on its merits. The psychological testing of intelligence and memory will provide confirmation on this matter. Between the ages of 4 and 6 years, suggestibility appears to be relatively high though marginal reliability is counterbalanced by the inability of a preschooler to concoct elaborate lies.

It is sometimes contended that normal preschoolers are so prone to fantasize that they cannot discriminate between imagination and reality. This is almost certainly an overstatement. Children's fantasies are generally rehearsals for, or attempts to assimilate, real events. When a 5-year-old provides a clear-cut verbal description, dramatic enactment, or pictorial representation of an erect, discharging penis, or of vaginal or anal penetration, it is unlikely that such a memory has been spontaneously invented. In this context, it is important to remember that younger children are better able to reproduce events with dolls, or portray them graphically, than to convey them in words.

Demonstrating what his mother had done to him, a 7-year-old boy of borderline intelligence placed the head of a female doll over the genitals of an anatomically explicit male doll, giggled conspiratorially, and made eager rhythmic movements and sounds. After placing a pencil in such a way that it protruded horizontally from the crotch of a male doll, he rammed the pencil point-first into the hindparts of a female doll, representing, thus, what he alleged he saw his father do to a female cousin.

Misinterpretation and Indoctrination

The misinterpretation of an innocent experience is an outside possibility. It should be considered in the case of single ambiguous experiences, as when a teacher puts his arm around a pupil. Misinterpretation is likely to be activated or aggravated by parental suggestion or indoctrination.

A 5-year-old girl whose mother had been killed in an automobile accident was due to inherit substantial insurance damages. Following her mother's death, the child lived with her single, unemployed father. The father's right to custody of the child was disputed by the maternal grandparents who claimed that the father, who had never married or supported the mother, was a drug dealer and a wastrel. The father, in turn, countered that the maternal grandfather had had an incestuous relationship with the child's deceased mother.

After visiting the grandparents one weekend, the child alleged that her grandfather had molested her sexually. When interviewed, she said that her grandfather had taken a hammer upon which white paint had been spilled, and tapped her on the genitals with it. Demonstrating what the grandfather had done on an anatomical doll, she was clearly able to distinguish between a hammer and a penis.

At a separate interview, the grandfather conceded that there was indeed a paint-splattered hammer in his house but he denied that he had molested the child in any way.

Allegations of sexual abuse have become increasingly common in custody disputes during or following divorce. The custodial parent, usually the mother, accuses the noncustodial parent of having molested the child and seeks to block further visitation. The noncustodial parent, in turn, asserts its ignorance of the alleged event. Considerable pressure may be exerted on the child by the mother to lodge a complaint against the father. The possibility of parental indoctrination of the child should be considered in such cases.

Delusion

Children rarely, if ever, have delusions of a type involving a false, immutable conviction of having been physically or sexually abused. Such a symptom would be more feasible during adolescence as part of a schizophreniform, paranoid or manic psychosis. However, even in such adolescents, delusions of sexual abuse are rare and would always be associated with characteristic signs of psychotic thought disorder, derangement of mood or social eccentricity.

In exceptional cases, a susceptible child may be induced by a psychotic adult, usually a mother, to share delusional beliefs. Since most children of psychotic parents eventually become aware that their parents are deluded, a shared delusion implies an unusually intense, dependent relationship between child and adult.

Confabulation and Fabrication

"Confabulation" refers to personal fantasy which the subject regards as real. "Fabrication" denotes deliberate lying. Confabulation and fabrication merge. The fabulist is prone to falsehood, whereas what once were lies may eventually seem to the fabricator to be truth. Some children spin such an intricate web of deceit, fantasy and fact that they forget where one begins and the other ends.

Persistent confabulation is most likely in those who have a histrionic personality. Driven by the fear of being abandoned or ignored, such children seek the center of the stage with dramatic displays of emotion and imagination. Past confabulation is likely to be reported by teachers and parents, along with a tendency to elicit the concern of other by presenting somatic complaints.

A 10-year-old girl was noticed at school to have a bruise over one eye. Questioned by her teacher, she revealed that it had been caused by her father. The incident was reported at once to the child abuse section of the Department of Protective Services who, in turn, requested a forensic evaluation.

The family situation was different from that which is commonly associated with child abuse. The father, a professional man, was divorced from the child's mother, a chronic schizophrenic, and had recently married the stepmother. The child had no desire to visit her mother who had previously neglected and frightened her, and was genuinely fond of her stepmother. However, she was quite envious of the close bond between her father and his new bride.

On the morning of the alleged abusive incident, the father had remonstrated with his daughter for waking him by making too much noise. In the course of the argument, he struck a table, disloding a spoon which bruised the child above the eye. The child had thought little about the bruise until it was noticed by the teacher and subjected to official investigation.

Fabrication can be motivated by malevolence felt toward the accused or displaced from another person onto the accused.

A 10-year-old boy accused his "big brother," a college student, of sexually molesting him. He alleged that, while his mother was washing up after dinner, the "big brother" sat next to him on a couch and "pinched" his "rectum" through his jeans.

Neither the police, to whom the incident was reported, nor the child's clinician, who was already involved in the case, found the story credible. The boy eventually retracted his allegations following a clinical interview.

It transpired that the child was enuretic, encopretic, and had numerous somatic complaints. He had no friends and was doing poorly in school. His mother was exasperated with him and his father, who had separated from his wife, visited the family infrequently. Shortly before the boy's allegations

of abuse, the father had visited the home and been openly critical of his son's fecal soiling.

Fabrication can be motivated by a malicious enjoyment of the mischief created by a well-placed lie. A more transparent motive involves the need to escape from unhappy circumstances.

Given the possibility of confabulation or fabrication, the veracity of a child's allegations can be assessed according to the following criteria: (1) external consistency; (2) internal consistency; (3) internal detail; (4) the child's affect while relating the story; (5) the child's susceptibility to suggestion; (6) the child's reaction to challenge in regard to confabulation, fabrication and external influence; and (7) evidence of histrionic, malicious or escapist motivation.

External Consistency. Check the transcripts of the police interrogation and subsequent interviews. Does the child give substantially the same account to different people, or are there serious inconsistencies in detail or time sequence between different versions of the same incident or incidents?

Internal Consistency. Does the child's story make sense? Are the time sequence, location and other descriptive details stable, or do they change as the interview proceeds and the child is asked to go back and recount different aspects of the incident?

Internal Detail. Does the child provide sufficient detail? Where, when and in what surroundings did the incident take place? Children can often give extremely accurate descriptions, for example, of the furniture and decor of rooms, the clothing worn by the accused, or the music that was playing on the radio at the time of the alleged incident. The particularities of the incident are very important. Does the child present only a generalized accusation ("He raped me")? Can the child provide specific details about what took place?

A hospitalized 5-year-old child from a chaotic family remarked to a pediatric resident that "Puckie," a man who drove an ice-cream van, had "made love" to her. She could provide no more details of the encounter other than, "It was wonderful."

Does the child's account contain convincing, idiosyncratic details throwing light upon the accused's personality? Though this feature carries less weight in the case of sexually active adolescents who can adapt their memory of other experiences for deceitful or fantastic purposes, it can be quite telling in the case of younger children.

A 9-year-old girl gave a detailed history of paternal incest which had taken place over several years. She described how the father would wait until her mother went to work at night and then take her to his bedroom. Among numerous other details, she described how her father would make her suck his nipples, and how he would ejaculate into kleenex tissues which he kept beside the bed.

The Child's Affect. While describing the alleged incident, does the child display emotion congruent with the material being discussed? Is the child embarrassed, upset, resentful, depressed, angry, fearful or, on the other hand, inappropriately vigilant, shifty, suspicious, faintly smiling or overeager to tell the tale? Remember that some children appear numb, flat or remote as a result of exhaustion, denial or dissociation.

Susceptibility to Suggestion. Can the child be induced to change the story or adopt ideas and symptoms when the interviewer applies pressure?

Interviewer: I see lots of children who've been in situations like this. Many of the kids I've seen get aches and pains in the legs and feet. How about you?
Child: Yes.
Interviewer: Where?
Child: (Pointing to the soles of the feet.) In the ankles. In the feet.

Check the transcript of the police interrogation. Is there evidence that the interrogator has led, or applied undue pressure to, the child?

Reaction to Challenge. Toward the end of the interview, the interviewer should gently suggest the possibility of confabulation to test the child's response. For example:

Interviewer: Sometimes kids make up stories in their minds. Like daydreams. After a while they think the stories are true when they were really only daydreams. Maybe that's what you did. Maybe you made that story up and then began to believe it yourself.
Child: (*Hotly*) No. I never made it up. It's true.

The possibility of fabrication should also be gently confronted. For example:

Interviewer: I know you weren't happy at home. Some people might think you made that story up so you could get out of the home. The attorney might ask you that in court and you would have to tell the truth. What would you say?
Child: I'd tell him it happened like I said it did.

In order to test the possibility that someone had induced the child to allege abuse, the following challenge could be effective:

Interviewer: It occurred to me that your mother might have told you to say those things about your father. Maybe she put the idea in your head.
Child: Who told you that?
Interviewer: It occurred to me. Is that what happened?

After any of these three challenges the child may quietly disagree, vigorously reject the suggestion, be-

come tense and confused, or admit that the challenge represents the truth. The child should not be challenged in this manner unless reasonable rapport has been achieved.

Histrionic, Malicious or Escapist Motivation. Distorted motivation may also be revealed after one or more of the three previous challenges, when the child breaks down and further exploration is possible. It is important to help the child seek a reason for a confabulated or fabricated story.

Interviewer: How come you invented that story about the big brother? I wonder why you needed to do that?
Child: I don't know why.
Interviewer: Maybe you were angry about something?
Child: I didn't like him. I didn't want him to come.
Interviewer: Can you tell me about that?

A Biopsychosocial Syndrome?

A number of authors have proposed that a particular pattern of symptoms and signs is especially prevalent in children who have been sexually assaulted. Weiss and Berg (1982) describe an emotional disorder following a single incident of molestation, similar to that often observed in adult victims. The child exhibits generalized anxiety, nightmares, emotional lability and phobias. Younger children regress, with separation fears and infantile clinging. Depression and suicidal ideation may be encountered in adolescents. Female victims may question their own responsibility for the event. Male victims may describe a compulsion to perpetrate the same offense on other boys.

A number of authors have described a characteristic symptom pattern in cases of incest (Browning and Boatman, 1977; Finch, 1967). Physical complaints may be elicited of enuresis, encopresis, and urogenital irritation or infection. The child may present other somatic symptoms, especially abdominal pain, fatigue, and headache. Teachers or foster parents may note anxiety, depression and episodes of mental abstraction. The child may be petulant, manipulative, and withdrawn at different times. An excessive interest in, and unusual knowledge of, sexual matters may be manifest in play and artistic expression. Frequent masturbation, indiscriminate seductive behavior, and gender role confusion have also been described.

When her daughter told her of the matter, the child's mother may have taken no action, disbelieved the child, or told her that it happens to everyone. The father may show no concern, complain of blackouts, or accuse the girl of promiscuity or seductiveness. The child sometimes demonstrates maternal role reversal. Older victims commonly exhibit shame, guilt, hostility to both parents, and social withdrawal. Anxiety, nightmares, phobias, feelings of helplessness, fear of sexuality and a sense of inner badness are typical. Sexual promiscuity, prostitution and marital maladjustment have been described as later outcomes of childhood incest.

It has been proposed that these clinical features are so characteristic that a "sexually abused child syndrome" could be clinically identified and introduced by counsel into court as *res ipsa loquitur* (self-evident) proof that sexual abuse has occurred. The burden would then be shifted to the accused to prove that the abuse was not caused by him (Mele-Sernovitch, 1979). It is doubtful if this doctrine would be admissible in criminal cases. Many of the symptoms described are so nonspecific that, in the absence of allegations by the victim, the occurrence of sexual abuse could not be sustained with confidence. Furthermore, it is not clear how complete the symptom pattern should be for the hypothetical syndrome to be diagnosed. It must be concluded that the symptom pattern described above is consistent with, but not pathognomonic of, sexual abuse.

Conclusions

Children under 9 years of age have less capacity than older children to recall past events without prompting. There is also evidence that younger children are more likely than older children, adolescents and adults to be influenced by suggestive questions, though research has been inconsistent on this point. Nevertheless, if prompted, children as young as 3 years of age can recall past events quite well, although they will have difficulty under 10 years of age dating the events or attributing the appropriate motivation and intention to other people. Despite conventional wisdom, there is no evidence that children are more prone to lie than adults, and no evidence that they are more prone to confabulate or fabricate complex allegations. There has been little research into the susceptibility of children to adult influence; indeed, level of moral judgment may be a more important factor than age in this regard. The possibility of parental indoctrination should, however, be considered in all cases involving disputed custody or visitation rights. Unfortunately, little is known about the effect of high emotional arousal on the registration and retrieval of memories of personal experience. This is clearly of great importance in the context of traumatic sexual molestation and potentially disturbing courtroom confrontations.

Given these research findings, and the dubious validity of judicial *voir dire* evaluations of children's competence, it has been recommended that children be allowed to testify, and the jury left to determine competency and credibility (Melton et al., 1984). This more liberal attitude to the juvenile witness seems appropriate to children older than 8 years of age. However, since the rules of evidence are relaxed for minors, and since children must be asked many direct or leading questions, pretrial clinical evaluation of competency would seem advisable for very young witnesses. The clinician may also be asked to examine the child before legal action is taken, in order to determine whether the child is credible and psychologically strong enough to cope with repeated appearances in court, whether psychological preparation would enable the child to give evidence, and whether psychiatric treatment would prevent further emotional trauma as a consequence of the legal process.

It is important to follow a logical pathway when evaluating a child's potential credibility as a witness, first excluding mental incapacity, misinterpretation and delusion, and then probing for confabulation, fabrication or indoctrination. Verbatim recordings of such interviews can provide telling evidence in court.

Although many children exposed to sexual abuse exhibit emotional disturbance, the symptoms which have been described as characteristic of incest are largely nonspecific. It is doubtful that a true "sexual abuse syndrome" can be supported. It has been suggested that expert opinion about the presence of the hypothetical syndrome could be used strategically in court to shift the burden of proof onto the accused, but this maneuver does not appear to be legitimate from either a clinical or legal standpoint. The pattern of symptoms and signs associated with sexual abuse must be regarded as suggestive, rather than pathognomonic, of sexual abuse.

Greater awareness of the plight of the child victim and the danger of "legal process trauma" has suggested modification of courtroom procedures. Audiotape or videotape recordings have been proposed as substitutes for adversarial confrontation. Libai (1969) has promoted the concept of a special courtroom for the hearing of child witnesses, a practice which has been adopted in Israel. Libai also discusses the use of specially trained police interrogators, the admission into evidence of pretrial testimony as an exception to the hearsay rule, the scheduling of special sessions when the case is unduly protracted, and limitations on the size of the audience in the courtroom.

A number of states have already adopted the procedure of videotaping the testimony of the child victim in a special court from which all people have been excluded other than the judge and the opposing counsel. However, the right of the accused to a public trial and to be present throughout the trial (in order to confront the accuser and consult counsel) are protected by the sixth and fourteenth amendments. The

extent of flexibility in these constitutional safeguards
has not yet been fully tested.

References

ALLEN, V. L. & NEWTSON, D. (1972), Development of conformity
and independence. *J. Pers. Soc. Psychol.*, 22:18–30.

ARNTZEN, F. (1970), *Psychologie der Zeugenaussage*. Gottingen:
Gogrese.

BENEDEK, E. P. (1982), Editorial: The role of the child psychiatrist
in court cases involving child victims of sexual assault. *This
Journal*, 21:519–520.

BERGER, M. (1979), Zur Glaubwürdigkeitbegutachtung von Kindern
und Jugentlichen in Sitlichkeitsprozessen. *Monatsschr. Kriminol.
Strafrechtsreform*, 62:149–156.

BROWN, A. L. (1975), The development of memory: knowing, knowing about knowing, and knowing how to know. *Adv. Child Develpm. Behav.*, 10:103–152.

BROWNING, D. H. & BOATMAN, B. (1977), Incest: the child at risk.
Amer. J. Psychiat., 134:69–72.

COHEN, R. L. & HARNICK, M. A. (1980), The susceptibility of child
witnesses to suggestion: an empirical study. *Law Hum. Behav.*,
4:201–210.

DALE, P. S., LOFTUS, E. F. & RATHBON, L. (1978), The influence
of the form of the question on the eyewitness testimony of
preschool children. *J. Psycholing. Res.*, 7:269–277.

DAWSON, P. (1981), The psychology of eyewitness testimony: developmental study of long term memory for film. Doctoral dissertation. New School for Social Research, New York.

FINCH, S. (1967), Sexual activities of children with other children
and adults. *Clin. Pediat.*, 3:102–108.

FODOR, E. M. (1971), Resistance to social influence among adolescents as a function of moral judgment. *J. Soc. Psychol.*, 85:121–
126.

GOETZE, H. J. (1980), The effect of age and method of interview on
the accuracy and completeness of eyewitness accounts. Doctoral
dissertation. Hofstra University, Department of Psychology,
Long Island.

GOLDSTONE, S. & GOLDFARB, J. L. (1966), The perception of time
by children. In: *Perceptual Development in Children*, ed. A. H.
Kidd & J. L. Rivoire. New York: International Universities Press.

GOODMAN, G. S. (1984), The child's testimony in historical perspective. The child witness: conclusions and further directions
for research. *J. Soc. Issues*, 40:1–176.

—— GOLDING, J. M. & HAITH, M. M. (1984), Jurors' reaction to
child witnesses. *J. Soc. Issues*, 40:139–156.

HERBOLD, H. (1977), The psychology of evidence. *Polygraph*, 6:2;
252.

HOVING, K. L., HAMM, J. & GALVIN, P. (1969), Social influence a
a function of stimulus ambiguity at three age levels. *Develpm.
Psychol.*, 1:631–636.

JOHNSON, M. K. & FOLEY, M. A. (1984), Differentiating fact from
fantasy: the reliability of childrens' memory. *J. Soc. Issues*, 40:33
50.

JONES, D. P. H. & MCQUISTON, M. (1985), *Interviewing the Sex-
ually Abused Child*. Denver: The C. Henry Kempe Nationa
Center for the Prevention and Treatment of Child Abuse and
Neglect.

KAIL, R. & HAGEN, J. W. (1982), Memory in childhood. In: *Handbook of Developmental Psychology*, ed. B. B. Wolman & G
Stricker. Engelwood Cliffs, N.J.: Prentice-Hall.

KOHLBERT, L. (1976), Moral stages and socialization: the cognitive
developmental approach. In: *Moral Development and Behavior
Theory, Research and Social Issues*, ed. T. Lickona. New York
Holt, Rinehart & Winston.

KOHNKEN, G. & WEGNER, H. Z. (1982), Glaubwürdigkeit von
Zeugenaussagen. *Z. Exp. Angew. Psychol.*, 24:92–111.

LIBAI, D. (1969), The protection of the child victim of a sexual
offense in the criminal justice system. *Wayne Law Rev.*, 15:977–
1032.

LOFTUS, E. F. & DAVIES, G. M. (1984), Distortions in the memory
of children. *J. Soc. Issues*, 40:51–68.

MARIN, B. V., HOLMES, D. L., GUTH, M. & KOVAC, P. (1979), The
potential of children as eyewitnesses: A comparison of children
and adults on eyewitness tasks. *Law Hum. Behav.*, 3:295–305.

MELE-SERNOVITZ, S. (1979), Parental sexual abuse of children. The
law as a therapeutic tool for families. In: *Legal Representation of
the Maltreated Child*. Washington, D.C.: National Association of
Counsel for Children.

MELTON, G. B. (1981), Children's competency to testify. *Law Hum
Behavior*, 5:73–85.

—— BULKLEY, J. & WULKAN, D. (1984), Competency of children
as witnesses. In: *Child Sexual Abuse and the Law*, ed. J. Bulkley.
Washington, D.C.: American Bar Association, National Legal
Resources Center for Child Advocacy and Protection.

PERLMUTTER, M. & MYERS, N. A. (1976), Recognition memory in
preschool children. *Develpm. Psychol.*, 12:271–272.

—— & RICKS, M. (1979), Recall in preschool children. *J. Psychol.*,
27:423–436.

SIEGEL, D. M. & HURLEY, S. (1977), The role of the child's preference in custody proceedings. *Family Law Quart.*, 11:1–58.

STAFFORD, C. F. (1962), The child as witness. *Washington Law
Rev.*, 37:303–324.

WEISS, E. H. & BERG, R. F. (1982), Child victims of sexual assault:
impact of court procedures. *This Journal*, 21:513–518.

Paul Lees-Haley is a Board-certified vocational expert and a licensed psychologist with offices in Huntsville, Alabama. Dr. Lees-Haley has provided consulting services for major corporations and many government agencies. He has served as an expert witness and litigation consultant from coast to coast, in personal injury and workers' compensation cases. He is the author of numerous articles for psychological journals and for legal publications.

Innocent lies, tragic consequences: the manipulation of child testimony

PAUL R. LEES-HALEY, Ph.D.*

"Let's give him a fair trial this evening, and hang him in the morning."
Anonymous

Surely everyone agrees on the desperate need for help for child abuse victims, and on the need for vigorous child advocates. But in court, child advocates should not be confused with unbiased independent experts. Child advocates are fighting for the child, and some of them may fight with a philosophy of "Damn the defendant, full speed ahead."

*The author would like to thank Theodore Blau, Ph.D. and William McIver, Ph.D. for the original inspiration for this article. Neither is responsible for its contents or shortcomings.

Zealous advocacy is for lawyers, not for objective interviewers and researchers. Preconceptions and interviewing styles that shape children's perceptions and reports are reckless and potentially vicious in their impact on persons entitled to due process and to the children themselves.

> Preconceptions and interviewing styles that shape children's perceptions and reports are reckless and potentially vicious in their impact on persons entitled to due process and to the children themselves.

This article will describe certain preconceptions about child abuse that are assumed by some helping professionals. It will argue that these assumptions are erroneous, and that they can cause innocent victims to suffer from false accusations as child abusers. It will then describe a procedure by which any experienced interviewer can demonstrate the risk of such assumptions when they are held by a therapist who is testifying in a child abuse case.

In 1986 an alleged child abuser was sentenced to 99 years in prison based on the testimony of a 5-year-old child. Children who were as young as three years of age have been found to be competent to testify,[1] and as Berliner and Barbieri observed, "Prosecution of child sexual assault often rests largely on the child victim's testimony."[2] At least 20 states have abolished special competency requirements for children, and they have created a presumption that they are competent witnesses.[3] Let us examine a few of these preconceptions . . .

ASSUMPTION: The current methods that are being used by therapists to interview children are appropriate and sufficient for gathering evidence about alleged child abuse. For example, according to a report by the Child Sexual Abuse Clinical Consultation Group, in conjunction with the Sexual Assault Center,[4] "An informed professional opinion about sexual abuse can be made by evaluation of the child. It is not necessary to interview the accused offender."

ASSUMPTIONS: Children need to be "helped" in special ways to talk about the crime. As James K. Stewart, Director of the National Institute of Justice, put it, "innocent children are often reluctant to speak out against those upon whom they depend both emotionally and physically."[5]

"All child victims of sexual abuse can be expected to be fearful of the consequences of . . . disclosure."[6]

Some children give "clues" through play or oblique references . . . but are unwilling to share this information directly with you."[7]

ASSUMPTION: Children don't lie. Consider these quotes:

It is "a maxim among child sexual abuse intervention counselors and investigators that children never fabricate the kinds of explicit sexual manipulations they divulge in complaints or interogations"[8]

"the child is the best and usually the only reliable reporter of the event(s). The accused individual has a strong motivation to lie . . ."[9]

"Very few children . . . have ever been found to exaggerate or to invent claims of sexual molestation."[10]

"In other words, there is no reason to doubt a child's report of sexual assault . . ."[11]

These advocates actually go so far as to say that, unlike adults whose eyewitness testimony is notoriously unreliable,[12] children probably don't even make errors in their abuse reports:" It is unlikely that a child would lie *or be mistaken*" (emphasis added).[13]

ASSUMPTION: A "special" adult is needed to elicit the child's "true" views—not just any adult can do it. This special adult must be supportive and encouraging of the child and suspicious of adults, believing that the latter are good suspects even if they appear to be normal people.

One physician, for example, says that it is "countertherapeutic and unjust" to use therapists who will not *suspect* "apparently normal adults" or who are not *believers* in the possibility of "unilateral sexual victimization" of children by such "apparently normal" adults.[14]

"Each child should have a victim advocate or other supportive adult for assistance and accompaniment throughout the investigation and adjudication processes."[15]

ASSUMPTION: Although the children need to be protected during these interviews, no one needs to worry about the needs and rights of the defendants who are alleged to be child abusers.

Some of the above-mentioned authors begin by reminding us that "when an offender is acquitted . . . it does not mean that the child was not abused."[16] Then these authors have the excruciating callousness to claim that "no binding consequence accrues to the adults who are involved as a result of a mental health opinion that a child is the victim of abuse."

If responsible professionals act on false assumptions, are the results any better than the work of irresponsible parties?

Has their zeal to prosecute blinded them to the consequences of false accusations of child abuse? Have they never noticed that, as *Women's Day*[17] so aptly put it, "On the mere suspicion of mistreatment, social workers have the power to take your child away" with all of the concomitant emotional and social and financial consequences? Is it "no binding consequence" to have one's career wrecked by false allegations of child abuse?

The problem

These assumptions and the interviews that are inspired by them are dangerous weapons. If responsible professionals act on false assumptions, are the results any better than the work of irresponsible parties? This question must be addressed to the social workers, psychiatrists, psychologists, and police investigators who are conducting these interviews. These groups are not lacking in confidence in their own importance and abilities. Even the least academically trained of the three licensed professional groups (social workers) tell us that "the values and generic skills of social work make it an obvious and competent profession to address the societal and individual problems of child sexual abuse."[18]

Unqualified "authorities" sometimes jump to breathtaking conclusions: an Abt Associates consultant, *writing in a publication of the U.S. Department of Justice*, made the remarkable statement that, "when a 7-year-old girl spontaneously asks her father . . . about details of erection and ejaculation, there can be little doubt that this child was sexually abused. . . ."[19] If that 7 year old has been alone with only one male in the recent past, are we then to conclude that there is little doubt that he is guilty of child abuse? Are we also to assume without doubt that a little girl, in the United States, in 1987, has never seen or inadvertently overheard a conversation about an X-rated movie, book, or magazine, or an animal mating in a children's zoo, or the topic of sex, and that she would not ask about such things if she had not been sexually abused?

In the same article the Abt Associates consultant cited, as evidence of the alarming frequency of child abuse, The National Center on Child Abuse and Neglect estimate that approximately 72,000 children were reported as sexually maltreated by a parent or household member in 1983.[20] What the same agency also found—and the consultant did not bother to mention—is that "over 65 percent of all reports of suspected child maltreatment proved to be unfounded."[21]

Procedure: Is Big Bird a criminal?

In a staged demonstration, interviews were conducted with two girls, ages 5 and 7, and one boy age 6. The interviewer used assumptions and practices that therapists are using throughout the country, but used these assumptions and practices deliberately to manipulate the children into testifying to patent nonsense. This investigator played the part of a therapist who:

1. has a "gut feeling" (clinical intuition) that the alleged perpetrator is guilty,
2. senses that the child wants to tell but is afraid, or has been told to keep it secret, or finds it difficult to express because it was painful, or for other reasons is reluctant to tell, and therefore,
3. feels that the child needs support and

encouragement to "open up" about this painful topic and to express these hard-to-express truths, and finally,

4. knows that children do not lie or make mistakes.

In these interviews, answers in the desired direction met with smiles and warmth and remarks like "good for you." When a child answered in the undesired direction, she was met with facial expressions of scepticism and disappointment, questioning looks, and frowns, along with a parallel tone of voice and remarks such as, "It's o.k. to tell me," "Are you sure?" and "You're safe here." An effective way to induce alarm in a perfectly calm child is to say, "Don't worry, this won't hurt. You are safe here." They've heard it before.

Readers who imagine that such practices are not occurring in real settings are referred to McIver's[22] videotaped interview between a child social service worker and a 4½ year old child whose testimony led to the conviction of a 38 year old man for molesting her. In this interview the child was led to say that the defendant had touched her genital area with his hands and mouth, by smiling and hugging her when she made such allegations and by being cold and nondemonstrative when she did not. McIvery cites cases in which interviewers congratulated children for making desired allegations and became perturbed when the child did not.

The point is not that therapists are trying to frame anyone. The point is scientific knowledge versus sloppiness: the actions of well-meaning, concerned therapists can lead a child to testify falsely. As McIver[23] pointed out, these interviews are highly stressful experiences for a child, especially a very young one.

Prosecutors are well aware of the fact that the nonverbal behavior of adults influences what the child says. Prosecutors deliberately manipulate nonverbal behavior toward obtaining convictions. In the courtroom some prosecutors, during direct examination, stand between the defendant and the child so that the child cannot see the defendant. Others instruct children to look at a victim advocate or supportive family member and not to look at the defendant while testifying. According to Whitcomb, "one victim advocate encourages children to tell the judge if the defendant is making faces."[24] How is a falsely accused child abuse defendant expected to look? Impartial? Unconcerned? Enthusiastic and supportive?

In the experiment with these three children, no attempt whatsoever was made to ask sensible, reasonable questions or to use concepts and words the child understood. The point of this experiment was to demonstrate that a child's answers are often the result of the interviewer's behavior, not the child's experience. The interviewer paid rapt attention to the answers that he wanted, and he was inattentive to the wrong answers, which he suspected were innocent fibs inspired by the perpetrators' threats against the child. The findings below are flagrant examples of events that are happening in more subtle ways wherever children are being interviewed.

> The point is scientific knowledge versus sloppiness: the actions of well-meaning, concerned therapists can lead a child to testify falsely.

Testimony by manipulated children: How Big Bird was framed

Each child was sworn in with the following oath, "Do you swear or affirm to tell the truth, the whole truth and nothing but the truth, so help you God?" After a few minutes of rapport-building chit chat, each child was presented with an anatomically incorrect paper doll—one with three heads, six arms, and four legs. Only a few smiles and expectant looks were required to obtain the agreement of both the seven year old and the six year old that their fathers had touched all six of their hands, all four of their feet, and all three of their heads. The five year old, a more independent thinker, flatly denied that her father had ever touched her anywhere at all, in her entire life.

All three children gleefully agreed that Big Bird has repeatedly "behaved in a lewd and lascivious manner" in their presence. Big Bird "presented his genitalia in a lascivious manner" to the five year old and the six year old on Saturn, Mars and Venus. The seven year old maintained that even though Big Bird did this on earth, he never did it on another planet. Sensing the interviewers disappointment, however, she volunteered that her dog may have done so.

The five and six year old agreed that psychotic psychosexual hermaphroditism was probably the basis for Big Bird's behavior, but when the seven year old was offered this explanation, she ventured, "I don't think so." She found more plausible the theory that it might be fractured yellow feathers or bird measles that caused this outburst of pathological exhibitionism. She also agreed that it could be related to the North Alabama intergalactic religious wars of 1986.

Commentary:

A typical example of one factor that controlled answers in these interviews is the responses the children made to questions about the running speed of "diddle-dees" versus "kubunga kubungas." They consistently agreed that a "diddle-dee" (spoken quickly in a higher pitcher with a smile) can run faster than a "kubunga kubunga" (spoken in a low pitch with a slow, ponderous tone and a frown). Perhaps many adults would have also agreed that a "diddle-dee" can run faster too, but the reason for our decision would be found in the sounds and style of asking, not in an accurate definition of the terms.

It is extremely significant and typical that the children answered "yes" or "no" or some synonym for "I think so," and not "I don't know," when asked completely incomprehensible questions. From kindergarten forward children are taught that questions have answers.[25] In other words, when asked ludicrous questions in terms that they had never heard, the children guessed. Children aren't trying to be accurate scientists when they answer questions; they are trying to please the adults.

Children's answers cannot only be influenced and slanted, they can be turned around 180 degrees. When the answer wasn't the desired one, a simple but powerful technique reversed the child's original answers (follow these six steps):

1. Frown and look hurt when the child answers.
2. Tilt your head and assume a stern, somewhat accusing look, while staring at the child's eyes.
3. Ask, "Are you sure?"
4. Continue staring in complete silence until the child responds.
5. As the child begins to reverse the answer, begin to look relieved.
6. Upon reversal, breathe a sigh of relief and smile warmly.

This technique is extremely effective in reversing answers. A typical example of the result is the reply of one of the little girls in this study, who had firmly and clearly said, "No" to a question, and then, after a moment of the reversal technique, said, "Ah, I mean . . . yes."

Conclusion

What does a demonstration like this prove? That Big Bird must be stopped? A scientific survey would have had adequate samples, controlled procedures, and peer review. This study involved merely three times the number of child witnesses most defendants get, with only as much peer review and control of procedures as you usually get in a psychotherapist's office, i.e., none. No claim is made that this study has any scientific merits, but is it any less valid than what we are doing to alleged child abusers?

The average 5 year old cannot tell you his phone number, does not know what day of the week it is, and cannot accurately answer the question, "What is your address?"[26] The average six year old doesn't know how many units make a dozen, doesn't know in which direction the sun sets, and can't name the four seasons.[27] Yet young children are considered to be sufficiently knowledgeable to take an oath and to testify on complex matters that can lead to imprisonment of an innocent defendant.

While this article was being written, it was discovered that a 15-year old girl had been deceiving authorities for six months with fantasies of an international white slavery ring. These authorities included local, state, federal and international (IN-TERPOL) experts with many years of experience. In a neighboring state, an 8-year old testified as an eye-witness in a capital offense trial, and after the trial the child admitted that she had fabricated her entire testimony. In another case, it was discovered that a nine year old child had persuaded a four year old to frame her stepfather.

Memories are creations made by people, not videotapes of events.[28] Once told, and then repeated—especially with adult encouragement—a child's fictitious memory becomes more believable to that child.[29] The child can come to believe a new "memory." Children make human errors, they tell fibs, they are overwhelmed by adults, and they act out unconscious motivations. And then if their testimony is accepted in adult court, it becomes a powerful event in the life of the alleged offender.

Excepting George Washington, all of us, having been children, should know that only an expert could believe that children don't fib. And as Mark Twain observed, "George Washington evidently was a backward boy. He lacked skills common to

every American child—he couldn't even tell a lie."

Recommended action:

The attorney whose client is falsely accused of child abuse can find experienced interviewers in every city who can demonstrate how easily children can be led to testify inaccurately as a consequence of behaviors irrelevant to the legal matters at hand. This author recommends using a carefully selected, well-trained interviewer from a background such as psychology, medicine, or early education for their relevant experience and witness value. However, a bright attorney will not feel limited to these professions. For example, an absolutely spectacular person for demonstration purposes would be a magician with a lot of experience performing before children. Try it, and you'll see for yourself—and for your client.

Children aren't trying to be accurate scientists when they answer questions; they are trying to please the adults.

Notes

1. G. Goodman, "Children's Testimony in Historical Perspective," *Journal of Social Issues,* vol. 40, no. 2, 1984, p. 15.
2. Lucy Berliner and Mary K. Barbieri, "The Testimony of the Child Victim of Sexual Assault," *Journal of Social Issues,* vol. 40, no. 2, 1984, p. 125.
3. Debra Whitcomb, "Prosecuting Child Sexual Abuse—New Approaches," *National Institute of Justice Reports,* May, 1986.
4. Child Sexual Abuse Clinical Consultation Group in conjunction with Sexual Assault Center. Evaluations of Children. Seattle, Washington: Harborview Medical Center, 1983.
5. James K. Stewart, "Directors Notes," *NIJ Reports,* May 1986.
6. F. S. Porter, L. C. Blick, and S. M. Sgroi, "Treatment of the Sexually Abused Child," in S. M. Sgroi, *Handbook of Clinical Intervention in Child Sexual Abuse.* (Lexington, Massachusetts: Lexington Books, 1982), p. 117.
7. C. L. Bridges, "The Nurse's Evaluation," in S. M. Sgroi, *Handbook of Clinical Intervention in Child Sexual Abuse.* (Lexington, Massachusetts: Lexington Books, 1982), p. 67.
8. Roland C. Summit, "The Child Abuse Accommodation Syndrome," *Child Abuse and Neglect,* vol. 7, 1983, pp. 190-191.

9. Child Sexual Abuse Clinical Consultation Group, pp. 1-2.
10. Summit, p. 190.
11. Child Sexual Abuse Clinical Consultation Group, p. 2.
12. E. F. Loftus, *Eyewitness Testimony* (Cambridge, Massachusetts: Harvard University Press, 1979), and R. Buckout, "Eyewitness Testimony," *Scientific American,* v. 231, 1974, pp. 23-31.
13. Child Sexual Abuse Clinical Consultation Group, p. 2.
14. Summit, p. 190.
15. Whitcomb, p. 5.
16. Child Sexual Abuse Clinical Consultation Group, p. 1.
17. *Women's Day,* May 6, 1986, p. 30.
18. Berliner and Stevens, 1982, p. 93.
19. Whitcomb, pp. 4-5.
20. Whitcomb.
21. Glenn P. Joyner, "False Accusations of Child Abuse—Could It Happen to You?" *Women's Day,* May 6, 1986, p. 30.
22. William F. McIver, "The Case for a Therapeutic Interview in Situations of Alleged Sexual Molestation," *The Champion,* January-February, 1986, vol. x, no. 1, pp. 11-13.
23. McIver.
24. Whitcomb.
25. T. Blau, "The Credibility of the Child Witness in Sexual Abuse Cases: Workshop for the Expert Witness." Presentation at the Second Annual Symposium of the American College of Forensic Psychology, Sanibel Island, Florida, 1986.
26. S. S. Sparrow, D. A. Balla, and D. V Cicchetti, *Vineland Adaptive Behavior Scales Survey Form Manual, Interview Edition* (Circle Pines, Minnesota: American Guidance Service, 1984).
27. D. Wechsler, *Manual for the Wechsler Intelligence Scale for Children-Revised* (New York: The Psychological Corporation, 1974).
28. E. F. Loftus, "Reconstructive Memory Processes in Eyewitness Testimony," in B. D. Sales, ed., *The Trial Process* (New York: Plenum, 1980).
29. McIver.

Additional references

Blau, T. (1985) *The Psychologist as Expert Witness.* New York: John Wiley.

Buckout, R. (1974) "Eyewitness testimony." *Scientific American,* v. 231, 23-31.

Loftus, E. F. (1979) *Eyewitness Testimony.* Cambridge, Mass.: Harvard University Press.

U.S. Department of Health and Human Services, National Center on Child Abuse and Neglect, *National Study on Child Neglect and Abuse Reporting,* Denver: American Humane Association, 1984, cited in Whitcomb, 1986.

Wechsler, D. (1974) *Manual for the Wechsler Intelligence Scale for Children–Revised.* New York: The Psychological Corporation.

Whitcomb, Debra. (1986) Prosecuting child sexual abuse—new approaches. *National Institute of Justice Reports,* May, 1986. ━●

CORROBORATION OF INFANT'S TESTIMONY IN SEX CRIMES

State v. Porcaro

6 N.Y.2d 248, 160 N.E.2d 488 (1959)

Defendant was indicted for first degree sodomy, second degree assault and impairing the morals of a minor, his ten year old stepdaughter. The child's sworn testimony of regular sexual intercourse, both in the usual manner and orally, for the previous four years was uncorroborated by other evidence. The jury convicted defendant of impairing the morals of a minor.[1] Timely and repeated demands by the defendant for a physical examination of the prosecutrix were refused. The trial court entered judgment on the verdict convicting defendant of impairing the morals of a minor which the appellate division of the supreme court affirmed.[2] The court of appeals reversed by a 4-3 decision on the ground that the sworn testimony of the alleged victim was insufficient to sustain conviction, especially in the absence of findings from a physical examination.[3] The court in recognizing the policy behind an express statutory provision requiring corroboration of the *unsworn* testimony of a minor in any criminal case,[4] preferred to rely on the insufficiency of the evidence in the case rather than to construct a rule requiring corroboration of an infant's *sworn* testimony in sex crimes.[5]

At common law, the testimony of the injured person in a sex offense was alone sufficient to sustain a conviction, corroboration was not required[6] and the rule remains the same today unless changed by statute.[7] The rule

---

[1] N.Y. Pen. Law § 483(2) "A person who wilfully causes or permits such child (actually or apparently under the age of sixteen) to be placed in such a situation . . . (where) . . . its morals (are) likely to be impaired is guilty of a misdemeanor."

[2] 6 App. Div. 2d 680, 174 N.Y.S.2d 447 (1958).

[3] People v. Porcaro 6 N.Y.2d 248, 189 N.Y.S.2d 194, 160 N.E.2d 488 (1959).

[4] N.Y. Code Crim. Proc. 392. Rules of Evidence; Evidence of Certain Children, How Received . . . ". . .Whenever in any criminal proceedings, a child actually or apparently under the age of twelve years, does not in the opinion of the court . . . understand the nature of the oath, the evidence of such child may be received though not given under oath. . . . But no person shall be held or convicted of an offense upon such testimony unsupported by other evidence."

[5] See Fuld, J. concurring opinion in State v. Porcaro (supra note 3) which argues for a rule requiring corroboration in sex crimes.

[6] Boddie v. State, 52 Ala. 395 (1875); State v. Ellison, 19 N.M. 428, 144 Pac. 10 (1914); 7 Wigmore, "Evidence" § 2061 (3d ed. 1940); 20 Am. Jur. "Evidence" § 1222 (1939); and extensive annotation in Annot., 60 A.L.R. 1124 (1929). *Contra,* State v. Bowher, 40 Idaho 74, 231 Pac. 706 (1924); Matthews v. State, 19 Neb. 330, 27 N.W. 234 (1886); see also *infra* note 13.

[7] See for example, N.Y. Pen. Law § 71 (abduction), § 103 (adultery), § 1091 (compulsory prostitution of wife), § 1455 (compulsory marriage), § 2013 (rape), § 2177 (seduction), § 2460 (compulsory prostitution). Compare with above for a different statutory treatment, Ohio Rev. Code § 2945.63 concerning seduction under promise of marriage or seduction by a teacher, which provides that ". . . a conviction shall not be

applies to all sex offenses including rape,[8] statutory rape,[9] seduction,[10] bastardy,[11] and incest.[12] However, some courts require the testimony to be "clear and convincing"[13] or else be corroborated; and others, remembering the admonition of Lord Chief Justice Hale that rape "is an accusation easily to be made and hard to be proved; and harder to be defended by the party accused, tho never so innocent,"[14] reverse convictions of sex crimes regularly when there is no corroboration of *sworn* testimony, but rely on the ground that the "evidence is insufficient to sustain the finding of guilt beyond a reasonable doubt."[15]

The principal case, *State v. Porcaro,* was decided the same day as *People v. Oyola,*[16] a very similar case; and both decisions noted the absence of corroboration of the prosecutrix's sworn testimony. The importance of both decisions is that they did not establish a technical rule of law requiring corroboration in infant sex crimes, but rather relied in the opinions on the rule that the evidence was insufficient to sustain a conviction beyond a reasonable doubt. Judge Fuld in his concurring opinion wished to make an explicit rule always requiring corroboration in sex offenses,[17] but Van Voorhis J., Conway C. J., and Froessel J., refused to do this. A technical rule of corroboration is justly criticized by Wigmore as a "crude and childish" measure[18] and completely inadequate to safeguard the defendants who are victims of fraudulent complaints. The court is to be commended for their due caution in refusing to allow the conviction to stand, yet steering carefully away from an artificial rule which obstructs justice in a clear case. A safer protection for defendants is Wigmore's suggestion[19] of a required psychiatric examination of the female complainant in a sexual crime at the

---

had on the testimony of such female, unsupported by other evidence. . . ."; however, no other requirement of corroboration by statute or decision exists in sex crimes. 15 Ohio Jur. 2d "Criminal Law" § 463-5 (1955); 28 Ohio Jur. 2d "Incest" § 13 (1958); 10 Ohio Jur. 2d "Abortion" § 17 (1954). Collection of statutes in Wigmore as cited in *supra* note 6 at 346 *et seq.*

[8] Boddie v. State, *supra* note 6; People v. Keith, 141 Cal. 686, 75 Pac. 304 (1904).

[9] Lear v. Commonwealth, 195 Va. 187, 77 S.E.2d 424 (1953).

[10] State v. Seiler, 106 Wis. 346, 82 N.W. 167 (1900).

[11] McGuire v. State, 84 Ariz. 342, 326 P.2d 362 (1958).

[12] People v. Gibson, 301 N.Y. 244, 93 N.E.2d 827 (1950). For comprehensive listing of cases see citations to Wigmore and A.L.R. *supra* note 6.

[13] People v. O'Conner, 412 Ill. 304, 106 N.E.2d 176 (1952), Brown v. State, 127 Wis. 193, 106 N.W. 536 (1906).

[14] L.C.J. Hale, 1 Pleas of The Crown 633, 635 (1680).

[15] New York is an excellent example of this in the following cases, all of which were rendered without opinion and reversed convictions of various sex crimes against minors. People v. Myers, 309 N.Y. 837, 130 N.E.2d 622 (1955); People v. Rosen, 293 N.Y. 683, 56 N.E.2d 297 (1944); People v. Derner, 288 N.Y. 599, 42 N.E.2d 605 (1942); People v. Slaughter, 278 N.Y. 479, 15 N.E.2d 297 (1938).

[16] 6 N.Y.2d 259, 189 N.Y.S.2d 203, 160 N.E.2d 494 (1959).

[17] 160 N.E.2d 488, 490.

[18] 7 Wigmore, "Evidence" § 2061 (3d ed. 1940).

[19] 3 Wigmore, "Evidence" § 924a (3d ed. 1940).

request of the defendant. Numerous medical authorities[20] and other writers[21] have advocated this because they "know how frequently sexual assault is charged or claimed with nothing more substantial supporting the belief than an unrealized wish or unconscious, deeply suppressed sex-longing or thwarting."[22] Decidedly, statutory treatment is needed for a mandatory psychiatric examination of complainants in sex offenses. This is especially true in cases like the principal one, where the credibility of the prosecutrix is questionable because of her age and immaturity. A recent Indiana case,[23] illustrates the necessity of a statute by affirming a conviction of assault and battery on no other evidence than the uncorroborated testimony of an admitted perjurer, and holding that the court had no power to require a prosecutrix to submit to a physical or psychiatric examination.

James R. Miles

---

[20] See citations in Wigmore above.

[21] 1937-38 A.B.A. Committee on the Improvement of the Law of Evidence as cited in Wigmore above; McKinney, "Pre-Trial Psychiatric Examination as Proposed Means for Testing the Complainant's Competency to Allege a Sex Offense," 1957 U. Ill. L.F. 651.

[22] Dr. W. F. Lorenz as reported in 3 Wigmore, *supra* note 19, at 465.

[23] Wedmore v. State, 237 Ind. 212, 143 N.E.2d 649 (1957).

THE EFFECTS OF THE ABOLITION OF THE CORROBORATION REQUIREMENT IN CHILD SEXUAL ASSAULT CASES

The nation's growing awareness of sexual abuse of children has resulted in an increase in the number of reported cases of abuse throughout the country.[1] Child protection agencies nationwide report that an estimated 1.5 million alleged child abuse cases were reported in 1983 and approximately 71,961 of these abuse cases involved allegations of child sexual maltreatment.[2] The true incidence of child sexual abuse, however, remains difficult to measure as it is the most under-reported form of abuse.[3] Moreover, even though more cases of child sexual assault are going to court than ever before,[4] it is estimated that approximately 90% of all child abuse cases across the country are never prosecuted.[5]

In the District of Columbia, the statistics are equally alarming. In the first six months of 1986, the Metropolitan Police Department investigated 347 sexual assault cases and 39.7% of these cases involved a child alleging sexual maltreatment.[6] Between 1978 and 1985, Children's Hospital Medical

---

1. D. WHITCOMB, E. SHAPIRO & L. STELLWAGEN, WHEN THE VICTIM IS A CHILD: ISSUES FOR JUDGES AND PROSECUTORS 8 (1985) [hereinafter D. WHITCOMB].

2. *Id.* at 2.

3. NATIONAL LEGAL RESOURCE CENTER FOR CHILD ADVOCACY AND PROTECTION, CHILD SEXUAL ABUSE: LEGAL ISSUES AND APPROACHES 2 (1981) [hereinafter CHILD SEXUAL ABUSE]. The available statistics are sketchy because only recently have states included a provision for separating child sexual abuse statistics from the aggregate statistics of other forms of abuse. *Id.* See D. WHITCOMB, *supra* note 1, at 2, "The Bureau of Justice Statistics estimates that only one-third of all crimes, and 47 percent of violent crimes, are reported to the police. Moreover, young victims are only half as likely as the total population to report crimes to the police." *Id.*

4. D. WHITCOMB, *supra* note 1, at 8. This is due to a higher level of reports resulting from "high levels of media attention and public outrage over sexual crimes against children." *Id.*

5. *Id.* at i. "In many of these cases, the decision not to proceed is based on concerns about the child's possible performance on the witness stand or the impact of the court process on the victim's recovery." *Id.* The reason for the high percentage of cases which are not prosecuted has gone virtually unexplained. "Both community members and criminal justice professionals are increasingly concerned about [the] apparent ineffectiveness in dealing adequately with the crime of child sexual abuse." *Id.*

6. Metropolitan Police Department, Sex Offense Investigation Report 1 (June 30, 1986). In 1985, there were 789 cases of sexual assault reported in the District of Columbia. Two hundred and sixty-three of these cases, or 33%, were victims under the age of 16. Metropolitan Police Department, Sex Offense Investigation Report 1 (Dec. 31, 1985).

Center counseled 2,376 cases involving sexually abused children through its victim's assistance project.[7]

Historically, the District of Columbia has imposed the legal requirement of corroboration on all sex-related crimes.[8] After the District's case was presented, the judge could, at the request of the defense, direct a verdict of acquittal based on lack of corroborative evidence.[9] In 1975, the District of Columbia Court of Appeals abolished this requirement for cases involving sexually abused adult females.[10] In 1985, the District of Columbia City Council followed the judiciary's lead and abolished the corroboration requirement for child complainants.[11]

This Note will trace the evolution and the demise of the legal requirement of corroboration as it was applied in the District of Columbia. An analysis of the evolution will reveal that the courts have become more flexible in applying the corroboration requirement in the last decade than in the past. This Note will conclude that, despite formal abolition, corroboration remains an essential element in the successful prosecution of child sexual abuse cases because of the nature of the offense. Consequently, the legislative abolition, although meritorious, will probably have few practical benefits.

I. THE EVOLUTION AND ABOLITION OF THE CORROBORATION REQUIREMENT

In *Lyles v. United States,*[12] the earliest known reference to the need for corroboration in District of Columbia sex crime cases, the Court of Appeals

---

7. D. LLOYD, LEGAL OUTCOME OF CHILDREN'S HOSPITAL NATIONAL MEDICAL CENTER CHILD SEXUAL ABUSE CASES 1/10/78-12/31/85, at 2 (1986).

8. *See infra* note 20 and accompanying text.

9. Lloyd, *The Corroboration of Sexual Victimization of Children,* in CHILD SEXUAL ABUSE AND THE LAW, A REPORT OF THE AMERICAN BAR ASSOCIATION 103 (J. Bulkley ed. 1982). "The corroboration requirement in sex crimes is analogous to the government having the burden of refuting an implied charge of recent fabrication." Fitzgerald v. United States, 443 A.2d 1295, 1305 (D.C. 1982). The District of Columbia statutes that the corroboration requirement pertained to included: rape, D.C CODE ANN. § 22-2801 (1981); sodomy, D.C. CODE ANN. § 22-3502 (1981); assault with intent to rape, D.C. CODE ANN. § 22-501 (1981); indecent acts with a child, D.C. CODE ANN. § 22-3501 (1981); incest, D.C. CODE ANN. § 22-1901 (1981); lewd, indecent, or obscene acts, D.C. CODE ANN. § 22-1112 (1981).

10. Arnold v. United States, 358 A.2d 335, 344 (D.C. 1976) (en banc). The court noted that the requirement was to protect the defendant from a conviction based on false charges. However, the court was "persuaded that the requirement . . . presently serves no legitimate purpose" because the defendant has adequate constitutional safeguards. *Id.* at 343.

11. D.C. CODE ANN. § 23-114 (Supp. V 1986). "For purposes of prosecutions brought under title 22 of the D.C. Code, independent corroboration of a child victim is not required to warrant a conviction." *Id.*

12. 20 App. D.C. 559 (1902). The corroboration requirement did not exist at common law. 7 WIGMORE ON EVIDENCE § 2061, at 342 (3d ed. 1940).

for the District of Columbia Circuit[13] suggested in dictum that corroboration was necessary for a conviction if the complainant's testimony was not credible.[14] The court, however, did not create a legal requirement of corroboration in sex crime cases.[15] In the next relevant case, *Kidwell v. United States*,[16] the United States Court of Appeals for the District of Columbia Circuit reversed a conviction which was supported solely by the complainant's testimony.[17] In reversing the conviction, the court observed that in sex offense cases where the courts had sustained convictions, "the circumstances surrounding the parties at the time were such as to point to the probable guilt of the accused, or, at least, corroborate indirectly the testimony of the prosecutrix."[18] Although the cases decided immediately after *Kidwell* did not interpret that case as imposing a corroboration requirement,[19] subsequent cases misread *Kidwell* as holding that corroboration was a legal prerequisite to conviction in sex offense cases.[20]

---

13. This case and others cited in this Note were decided prior to the Home Rule Act of 1983, D.C. CODE ANN. §§ 1-201 to 1-295 (1981).

14. 20 App. D.C. at 562. The court stated, "[t]he crime of rape is not always easy to establish. It most generally depends upon the testimony of a single witness to the actual or alleged commission of the crime, and unless her testimony is beyond question or doubt, *or* made so by surrounding circumstances, there is danger in conviction." *Id.* (emphasis added).

15. *Id.* In fact the court indicated that a conviction could be obtained solely on the testimony of the complainant if that testimony was believable beyond a reasonable doubt. *Id.*

16. 38 App. D.C. 566 (1912). The defendant was charged and convicted of carnal knowledge committed against his niece who was under the age of 16. *Id.* at 568.

17. *Id.* at 574. The prosecutrix testified that she lived in defendant's home and that he had been having intercourse with her for three years "whenever an opportunity was afforded." *Id.* at 573.

18. *Id.* This was not the sole reason why the court reversed the conviction. The court emphasized that the prosecutrix's allegations were not credible in view of her "incorrigible character" and the "respectable standing" of the defendant. *Id.*

19. Mears v. United States, 55 F.2d 745 (D.C. Cir. 1932); Weaver v. United States, 299 F. 893 (D.C. Cir. 1924). In *Weaver* the Court of Appeals for the District of Columbia found the complainant's testimony "so directly discredited, as to be unworthy of belief." 299 F. at 897. This passage indicates that the court was applying the requirement that the government present sufficient evidence so that a jury could find the defendant guilty beyond a reasonable doubt. The court cited a portion of *Kidwell* which suggests that a conviction for rape can be obtained without corroboration on the *"unassailed* testimony of a single witness." *Id.* (emphasis in original). In *Mears,* the defendant's conviction for carnal knowledge of a fifteen year old girl was sustained. No reference was made to any legal requirement of corroboration. 55 F.2d at 745. *See* McKenzie v. United States, 126 F.2d 533 (D.C. Cir. 1942) (although the conviction was reversed on other grounds, there was no suggestion of a requirement of corroboration to establish a prima facie case).

20. *Kidwell* often has been cited for the proposition that corroboration is a legal requirement. *See, e.g.,* United States v. Huff, 442 F.2d 885, 888 (D.C. Cir. 1971); United States v. Bryant, 420 F.2d 1327, 1330-31 (D.C. Cir. 1969); Coltrane v. United States, 418 F.2d 1131, 1134 (D.C. Cir. 1969); Allison v. United States, 409 F.2d 445, 448 (D.C. Cir. 1969); Dade v. United States, 407 F.2d 692, 694 (D.C. Cir. 1968); Barber v. United States, 392 F.2d 517, 519 (D.C. Cir. 1968); Borum v. United States, 409 F.2d 433, 437 (D.C. Cir. 1967), *cert. denied,* 395

Lyles and *Kidwell*[21] were both rape cases involving adult female complainants. In *Kelly v. United States,*[22] the District of Columbia Circuit extended the corroboration requirement to sex offenses which were lesser sex offenses than rape, and in *Wilson v. United States,*[23] the court explicitly extended the corroboration requirement to cases in which the complainant was a child.[24] The court of appeals reasoned that cases of sexually abused children required corroboration because a child's testimony lacked the reliability of an adult's.[25] Therefore, the court concluded, if an adult's testimony must be corroborated, then surely, a child's must be corroborated.[26]

In *Borum v. United States,*[27] the court clarified the procedure to be followed in sex crime prosecutions. The court stated that "[w]hile the matter of corroboration is initially for the trial court, like any other question as to the legal sufficiency of the evidence to warrant submission of the case to the jury, it is the latter's function to decide whether the standard of corroborative proof has been met."[28] The court, citing *Kidwell,* indicated that corroboration was required as to both the corpus delecti and the identification of the accused,[29] and the jury must be instructed that to convict they must find

---

U.S. 916 (1969); Miller v. United States, 207 F.2d 33, 35 (D.C. Cir. 1953); Ewing v. United States, 135 F.2d 633, 635 (D.C. Cir. 1942), *cert. denied,* 318 U.S 776 (1943).

21. In *Kidwell,* although the prosecutrix was under sixteen when the alleged incident occurred, she was past the age of consent when she testified. 38 App. D.C. at 573.

22. 194 F.2d 150, 156 (D.C. Cir. 1952) (Defendant was charged with inviting one to accompany him for lewd and immoral purposes contrary to D.C. CODE ANN. § 22-2701 (1940). This offense was a misdemeanor, while previously the corroboration requirement was applied only to felonies.).

23. 271 F.2d 492 (D.C. Cir. 1959) (defendant convicted of taking indecent liberties with an 11 year old girl).

24. *Id.* at 493. The court noted that the "[a]ppellant was guilty if anyone was, for he alone was with the child at the time of the alleged offense. But there was no evidence of any sort, except the testimony of the child herself . . . ." *Id.* at 492. "[W]e now hold that the *corpus delecti* . . . may not be established by the child's uncorroborated testimony on the witness stand." *Id.* at 493.

25. *Id.* at 493. The court relied on M. GUTTMACHER & H. WEIHOFEN, PSYCHIATRY AND THE LAW 374 (1952). 271 F.2d at 493. "It is well recognized that children are more highly suggestible than adults. Sexual activity, with the aura of mystery that adults create about it, confuses and fascinates them. Moreover, they have . . . no real understanding of the serious consequences of the charges they make. . . . [M]ost courts show an admirable reluctance to accept the unsubstantiated testimony of children in sexual crimes." *Id.* at 493 (citation omitted).

26. *Id.* at 493. The court stated that "[a] woman's uncorroborated tale of a sex offense is not more reliable than a man's. A young child's is far less reliable." *Id.* at 492-93.

27. 409 F.2d 433 (D.C. Cir. 1967), *cert. denied,* 395 U.S. 916 (1969). The defendant broke into a home by striking the 80 year old resident over the head with a pistol. Shortly thereafter a female neighbor came into the house and the defendant forced her to undress and submit to sexual intercourse. *Id.* at 435.

28. *Id.* at 438.

29. *Id.* at 438. The court found sufficient corroborative evidence in the following: the

corroboration of each element.[30]

As the court expanded the corroboration requirement to encompass more factual situations,[31] it applied the requirement more stringently. In *Allison v. United States,*[32] the appellant was convicted of intent to gain carnal knowledge of an eleven year old female.[33] Although the complainant's younger brother witnessed the defendant "on top of" the complainant and two witnesses testified as to the victim's report and demeanor immediately after the incident,[34] the court concluded that the story lacked sufficient corroboration and reversed the conviction.[35] The court explained that the corpus delicti must be corroborated in addition to the identification of the accused.[36] Sufficient corroboration of the corpus delicti entails corroboration of every element of the offense[37] and in this case, the court found that the element of intent was not sufficiently corroborated.[38]

The District of Columbia courts, perhaps recognizing that this stringent standard at times produced unrealistic and unjust results,[39] began to retreat

complainant called the police immediately following the intruder's exit; medical evidence of intercourse was presented; a laundryman overheard the initial conversation between the complainant and the defendant, and appellant's fingerprints were found at the scene of the crime. *Id.* at 438.

30. *Id.* at 437 n.16.

31. *See* Wilson v. United States, 271 F.2d 492 (D.C. Cir. 1959); Kelly v. United States, 194 F.2d 150 (D.C. Cir. 1952); *see also supra* notes 23-30 and accompanying text.

32. 409 F.2d 445 (D.C. Cir. 1969).

33. *Id.* at 447. The defendant was also charged with taking indecent liberties with a minor child in violation of § 22-3502(a) but was acquitted. *Id.*

34. *Id.* at 448. At trial, testimony revealed that the complainant was walking with her younger brother and cousin when the defendant coaxed them into his house. *Id.* at 447. He then sent the young boys to the store and when he was alone with complainant he threw her onto the couch, pulled down his zipper, got on top of her, and tried to pull her pants down. *Id.* at 447-48. When the boys returned they could hear the complainant screaming and through the keyhole of the door could see the appellant on top of the complainant. *Id.* at 448. The complainant escaped, ran home, and immediately, in a hysterical state, told a friend that "some man had pulled her in the house." *Id.* An officer testified that the complainant told him that the appellant "tried to put his private in her." *Id.*

35. *Id.* at 452. The court remanded to the district court to enter judgment of guilty to the charge of taking indecent liberties with a minor child. *Id.*

36. *Id.* at 448. *See Borum,* 409 F.2d at 437 n.16 (indicating that both the identity of the accused and the corpus delecti must be corroborated).

37. Allison, 409 F.2d at 449.

38. *Id.* at 449-50. "Putting aside for a moment the matter of corroboration, we have no doubt that the Government's case established an intent to commit carnal knowledge." *Id.* "If this testimony were corroborated it would surely support a jury finding that, beyond a reasonable doubt, appellant entertained the intention to carnally know the prosecutrix." *Id.* at 450. "Since . . . the *corpus delicti* was uncorroborated, appellant's conviction . . . cannot stand." *Id.*

39. *See* United States v. Gray, 477 F.2d 444, 445 (D.C. Cir. 1973); United States v. Terry, 422 F.2d 704, 708 n.6 (D.C. Cir. 1970) (criticizing the *Allison* standard). The strict rule of corroboration, that every element of the offense must be corroborated, "compel[s] the Govern-

from this standard.[40] In *Gray v. United States,*[41] the United States Court of Appeals for the District of Columbia Circuit, held that the corroboration requirement had been met and stated that "corroborative evidence [is] sufficient when it would permit the jury to conclude beyond a reasonable doubt that the victim's account of the crime was not a fabrication."[42] The court reasoned that the rule should be flexible and the quantum of proof should depend on the facts of each case.[43] The District of Columbia Court of Appeals subsequently adopted this standard and its reasoning in *Moore v. United States.*[44] The result was that the strict standard of *Allison* no longer controlled while the new standard of *Gray* and *Moore* applied to sexual offenses in the District of Columbia.[45]

Three years after *Gray* and *Moore,* in *Arnold v. United States,*[46] the District of Columbia Court of Appeals, sitting en banc, abolished the requirement in cases with a "mature female" prosecutrix.[47] *Arnold* involved two adult females who alleged that the defendant raped them on separate occa-

---

ment to prove virtually its entire case twice: once by the victim's testimony and again by independent evidence." *Gray,* 477 F.2d at 445.

40. *See Gray,* 477 F.2d at 445 (corroboration requirement is flexible and quantum of proof depends on facts of each case); *Terry,* 422 F.2d at 704 (corroboration is any evidence outside of the victim's testimony that has probative value); Fitzgerald v. United States, 443 A.2d 1295, 1301 (D.C. 1982) (sufficient corroboration need only consist of factual circumstances which tend to support the victim's testimony); Moore v. United States, 306 A.2d 278 (D.C. 1973) (sufficient corroboration exists if trier of fact could reasonably believe victim's story); Evans v. United States, 299 A.2d 136 (D.C. 1973) (circumstantial evidence may be used to corroborate victim's testimony).

41. 477 F.2d 444 (D.C. Cir. 1973). The appellant, who was convicted of rape and burglary, argued that, according to *Allison,* every element of the offense had to be corroborated. He urged that penetration, an element of rape, had not been corroborated. *Id.* at 445.

42. *Id.*

43. *Id.* Factors which the court indicated should be considered in determining whether the standard of corroboration had been met include: the age of the victim; impressionability; and motivation to falsify or exaggerate. *Id.*

44. 306 A.2d at 278. The defendant summoned the complainant, a 10 year old female, into his apartment where he subsequently pulled down her pants. *Id.* at 279-80. The court of appeals applied the standard set forth in *Gray;* that there is sufficient corroboration "if it would permit the jury to conclude beyond a reasonable doubt that the victim's account of the crime was not a fabrication." *Id.* at 280 (citing United States v. Gray, 477 F.2d 444, 445 (D.C. Cir. 1973)).

45. Under the new standard, both the identity of the accused and the corpus delicti still required corroboration. *See Gray,* 477 F.2d at 445-46. However, there still may be corroboration under this standard, if, in the totality of the circumstances, one element is uncorroborated while the others are strongly corroborated.

46. 358 A.2d 335 (D.C. 1976) (en banc).

47. *Id.* at 344. "[W]e abrogate the requirement in future rape and lesser included sex related cases, insofar as mature females may be involved . . . ." *Id.* The court cautioned that the issue of credibility of the prosecutrix would still remain important. *Id.*

sions.[48] In both cases the complainants claimed that the defendant lured them into his car and then threatened them with bodily harm and death until they submitted to sexual intercourse.[49] Medical evidence confirmed intercourse in both situations but the defendant relied on consent as a defense.[50] There was no evidence demonstrating that the women resisted.[51] At trial, the prosecution requested that the jury not be instructed as to a legal necessity of corroboration.[52] The court granted the motion[53] and did not instruct the jury as to the legal necessity of corroboration.[54] The jury found the defendant guilty and he appealed.[55]

The District of Columbia Court of Appeals noted that the trial court, by disregarding a long line of precedent,[56] erred in failing to give the instruction,[57] but because sufficient corroboration existed, the error was harmless and conviction was upheld.[58] The court reasoned that the corroboration requirement protected defendants against false accusations,[59] but concluded that the defendants have the benefit of other adequate procedural safeguards and, therefore, the corroboration was unnecessary in this case.[60] Despite the

---

48. *Id.* at 336-38.

49. *Id.*

50. *Id.* at 339.

51. *Id.* at 340.

52. *Id.* at 339.

53. *Id.* The judge commented:

I see no reason under the sun in this day and age . . . to say that on the uncorroborated testimony of a victim a defendant can be convicted of kidnapping while armed, armed robbery arising out of the same transaction and . . . where he then commits a rape he can be convicted of the kidnapping while armed on the uncorroborated testimony of the complainant . . . but cannot be convicted of assault with intent to commit rape on her uncorroborated testimony . . . .

Id.

54. *Id.* at 340. The judge instructed the jury as follows: "You may consider whether or not the witness has been corroborated by other independent evidence, or whether the witness lacks corroboration with respect to any relevant issue . . . ." *Id.*

55. *Id.*

56. *Id.* "A long line of decisions in this jurisdiction hold that the accused [charged with a sexual offense] may not be convicted without some evidence . . . corroborating the testimony of the victim." *Id.* "By its refusal to give the instruction on corroboration . . . the trial court defied established precedent . . . ." *Id.* at 341.

57. *Id.*

58. *Id.* at 342. "Satisfied that appellant had a fair and impartial trial and that the trial court's refusal to give the required instruction did not affect any substantial right, we conclude that the error was harmless." *Id.* (citing Schneble v. Florida, 405 U.S. 427 (1972)).

59. *Id.*

60. *Id.* at 344. The court noted that "proof beyond a reasonable doubt is sufficient for a conviction." *See* Estelle v. Williams, 425 U.S. 501 (1976); Cool v. United States, 409 U.S. 100 (1972) (per curiam); *In re* Winship, 397 U.S. 358 (1970) (all discussing proof beyond a reasonable doubt). The court implied that this standard of proof was adequate to protect the defendant against false accusations. 358 A.2d at 343-44. The court also stated that the requirement

broad language, the court only abolished the requirement in cases involving "mature females."[61] While *Arnold* left many questions unanswered,[62] it was quite clear that its holding would not be applied to cases involving child victims.[63]

In its application of *Arnold,* the District of Columbia Court of Appeals in *Davis v. United States* [64] faced the question of which victims would be considered "mature" for the purpose of determining whether the corroboration requirement would be applied.[65] The prosecutrix was a female who alleged that the defendant had raped her.[66] The trial court concluded that the *Arnold* exception applied because she was found to be "mature." The jury was not instructed as to the necessity of corroboration.[67] On appeal, the court of appeals considered whether the trial court had the discretion to decide the issue of maturity, and if not, whether the victim was "mature" within the meaning of *Arnold.* The court of appeals upheld the conviction stating that the trial court acted well within its discretion in determining that the complainant was mature.[68] The court emphasized that age does not determine maturity and the trial court, which may observe the complainant's demeanor, is in the best position to decide the issue.[69]

---

serves no legitimate purpose because it probably has little effect on the jurors' minds because they are normally suspicious of such charges anyway. Also it serves little practical purpose because the judge has the power to set aside the verdict. *Id.* at 343 (quoting 7 WIGMORE ON EVIDENCE § 2061, at 354 (3d ed. 1940)). The court also pointed out that the requirement was not known at common law and recognized that the rule did not stem from constitutional or statutory provisions. *Id.*

61. 358 A.2d at 344. *See supra* note 10 and accompanying text. The court concluded, "[W]e mandate that in the future no instruction directed specifically to the credibility of any mature female victim of [a sex offense] and the necessity for corroboration of her testimony shall be required or given in the trial . . . ." 358 A.2d at 344.

62. The court limited its holding to cases where "mature females may be involved." 358 A.2d at 344. The court never indicated why mature females were any different from other classes of possible victims. Other dicta indicated that the court was unhappy with this rule in all cases. The court stated that the rule "serve[d] no legitimate purpose." *Id.* at 343. *See supra* note 61. Finally, the court stated that "we know of no good reason why . . . we should not now purge from our jurisprudence the requirement and all of its demeaning implications." 358 A.2d at 344.

63. *See In re* L.A.G., 407 A.2d 688 (D.C. 1979); *In re* J.W.Y., 363 A.2d 674 (D.C. 1976); Robinson v. United States, 357 A.2d 412 (D.C. 1976). All hold that the *Arnold* rule did not apply in cases with child victims.

64. 396 A.2d 979 (D.C. 1979).

65. *Id.* at 980. The court indicated that the defendant correctly observed that the *Arnold* court did not define "maturity." *Id.*

66. *Id.*

67. *Id.*

68. *Id.* The court observed that age alone is not determinative of maturity. *Id.* (citing 7 WIGMORE ON EVIDENCE § 2061, at 451-53 (1978)).

69. *Id.* The reviewing court must give the trial court's determination of maturity "consid-

Six years after *Arnold, Fitzgerald v. United States*[70] questioned the corroboration requirement as applied to children. The prosecution charged the
defendant with assault and intent to commit rape.[71] Evidence at trial indicated that the girl entered the defendant's car for a ride to the store. Under
the pretext of visiting a friend, the defendant pulled into an alley, stopped
the car and attempted to rape the complainant.[72] She escaped by opening
the car door and slipping out of the car onto the ground.[73] Defendant then
told her that if she told anyone "he would climb through her window and
kill her."[74] The victim was visibly upset when she returned home but reported the crime to no one until she told a friend the next day.[75] The attempted rape was not reported to authorities until eleven days later.[76] The
medical examination by this time revealed no evidence of the assault.[77] Consequently, at trial, the defendant moved for judgment of acquittal for lack of
corroborative evidence.[78] The court denied the motion because it found sufficient corroboration in "the crying, . . . the running to her room, and the
other things . . . ."[79] After determining the legal sufficiency of the corroboration, the court failed to instruct the jury as to the necessity of corroboration, thus treating the victim as an adult under *Arnold.*[80] The jury convicted

---

erable latitude" because he has the opportunity to see and hear the victim at trial. *Id.* at 980-
81.

70. 412 A.2d 1 (1980), *reh'g en banc,* 443 A.2d 1295 (D.C. 1982).

71. *Id.* at 1297. Appellant was also charged with taking indecent liberties with a minor in
violation of D.C. CODE ANN. § 22-3501(a) (1981) and enticing a minor child contrary to D.C.
CODE ANN. § 22-3501(b) (1981). The defendant was acquitted on these two counts. *Id.* at
1297 n.1.

72. 443 A.2d at 1297-98. Complainant initially entered the defendant's car to accompany
him to the store. He had been a friend of the complainant's step-father and she had known
him since she was young. *Id.* at 1297.

73. *Id.* at 1298.

74. *Id.*

75. *Id.* "Upon their return to Mrs. Geathers' house, complainant ran into the house crying. Mrs. Geathers asked what was wrong. Complainant said that her head hurt and ran
upstairs. Further inquiry by Mrs. Geathers was fruitless." *Id.*

76. *Id.*

77. *Id.*

78. *Id.* Defense counsel stated, "You have nothing here other than the statement of the
girl claiming an allegation of oral sodomy. You have a delay in the report . . . no medical
[evidence], no bruises, no cuts or anything and I submit that this is just insufficient to send to
the jury." *Id.*

79. *Id.*

80. *Id. But see* Borum v. United States, 409 F.2d 433 (D.C. Cir. 1967) *cert. denied,* 395
U.S. 916 (1969); Arnold v. United States, 358 A.2d 335 (D.C. 1976) (en banc). The court, by
considering the sufficiency of the corroborating evidence, was applying the corroboration requirement, but then under *Borum* the judge should have instructed the jury as to the necessity
of corroboration for the conviction. Since the jury was not instructed in this manner, it was
actually instructed as if the victim were "mature" under *Arnold.*

the defendant.[81]

The District of Columbia Court of Appeals reversed the conviction, holding that the failure of the court to instruct the jury as to corroboration was reversible error.[82] On the issue of the corroboration requirement as applied to children, the court of appeals stated that a child's testimony was less reliable than that of an adult.[83] It reasoned that since children are more susceptible to suggestion and curious about sex while not fully cognizant of the consequences of the charges that they make, proper protection of the defendant requires corroboration in these cases.[84]

The dissent argued that the reasons the *Arnold* court gave for abolishing the requirement as to adult female complainants applied equally to child victims.[85] It faulted the majority for concluding that child witnesses are less reliable than adults[86] and argued that psychological reports indicated otherwise.[87] It maintained that the rule was discriminatory and should be abolished in all cases.[88]

In 1985, the District of Columbia City Council passed the Child Abuse Reform Act of 1984.[89] This Act abolished the corroboration requirement

---

81. 443 A.2d at 1298.

82. *Id.* at 1303. "We are unable to say here . . . that the absence of a corroboration instruction was not 'so clearly prejudicial to substantive rights as to jeopardize the very fairness and integrity of the trial.' " *Id.* (citing Watts v. United States, 362 A.2d 706, 709 (D.C. 1976) (en banc)). *But see Arnold,* 358 A.2d at 341 (holding that the failure of the court to give the corroboration instruction was not reversible error).

83. 443 A.2d at 1299. "Courts have traditionally been skeptical of sexual charges by children . . . ." *Id.*

84. *Id.* The court relied, as *Wilson* did, on M. GUTTMACHER & H. WEIHOFEN, *supra* note 25 and accompanying text.

85. 443 A.2d at 1308. The dissent noted that "this archaic obstacle to prosecution has been maintained in cases involving children—the victims most in need of protection." *Id.*

86. *Id.* The dissent observed, "The majority's justification for distinguishing between 'mature' females and other complainants lies in its apparent belief that there is a greater danger of false accusations in sex offense cases involving child victims." *Id.*

87. *Id.* The dissent relied on Peters, *Children Who Are Victims of Sexual Assault and the Psychology of Offenders,* 30 AM. J. PSYCHOTHERAPY 398 (1976), Rosenfeld, *Fantasy and Reality in Patients' Report of Incest,* 40 J. CLINICAL PSYCH. 159, 161 (1979).

88. 443 A.2d at 1308. The dissent noted that "the corroboration requirement in its present form only serves to perpetuate discrimination against children of both sexes as well as adult male victims." *Id.* at 1308-09.

89. D.C. CODE ANN. § 23-114 (Supp. V 1986). Prior to this Act, in 1981, the District of Columbia City Council passed the District of Columbia Sexual Assault Reform Act of 1981, Act No. 4-69, which was signed by the Mayor on July 21, 1981 and transmitted to Congress pursuant to § 602(c)(2) of the District of Columbia Self-Government and Government Reorganization Act, Pub. L. No. 93-198, 87 Stat. 774, 814 (1973). The United States House of Representatives disapproved the Act on October 1, 1981. If this Act had passed it would have abolished the corroboration requirement in 1981. *See* H.R. RES. 208, 97th Cong., 1st Sess. (1981), *reprinted in* 28 D.C. Reg. 4526 (1981).

prospectively for prosecutions brought under title 22 of the District of Columbia Code.[90] The abolition of the corroboration requirement was intended to eliminate the obstacles hindering prosecution, enabling the city to try more cases on the merits and bring more sex offenders to justice.[91]

In *Gary v. United States,*[92] a case that arose after the Child Abuse Reform Act of 1984 was passed but before its effective date, the District of Columbia Court of Appeals abolished the corroboration requirement.[93] The defendant, who was found guilty of raping the sixteen year old complainant, argued that the trial court committed reversible error under *Fitzgerald* by not instructing the jury on the legal requirement of corroboration.[94] In abolishing the requirement, the court of appeals observed, as discussed in *Arnold* and the dissenting opinion of *Fitzgerald,* that corroboration served no useful purpose because the defendant had adequate protection regardless of who the victim may have been.[95] The court concluded that there was no valid basis to distinguish a child's testimony from an adult's.[96] It added that children's reports of sexual attacks had been discounted too long by the courts.[97]

---

90. *See supra* note 11. Note that title 22 of the District of Columbia Code is titled Criminal Offenses under part IV, Criminal Law and Procedure.

91. *See infra* note 98.

92. 499 A.2d 815 (D.C. 1985), *cert. denied,* 106 S. Ct. 3279 (1986). The defendants argued that they were charged under the wrong statutes. They were charged under the code that existed before the District of Columbia Sexual Assault Reform Act of 1981. *See supra* note 89. The defendants claimed that since the one house veto was held to be unconstitutional under INS v. Chadha, 462 U.S. 919 (1983), the Reforms under the 1981 act were valid, and consequently, they were charged under the wrong statute. The court disagreed, holding that the *Chadha* decision applied prospectively only. *Id.* at 817-32.

93. The Act was adopted by the District of Columbia City Council on October 23, 1984 and signed by the Mayor on November 8, 1984. 31 D.C. Reg. 5977 (1984). It became law on May 3, 1985. D.C. CODE ANN. § 23-114 (Supp. V 1986).

94. *Gary,* 499 A.2d at 833.

95. *Id.*

Since the reasons for this court's holding in *Arnold v. United States,* . . . where we abolished the requirement for corroboration when a mature female is involved, are equally applicable to all sex offenses, regardless of the sex or age of the victim or perpetrator, we now abolish the requirement entirely.

The constitutional protections provided the defendant are adequate in a sex case and the corroboration requirement no longer serves a useful purpose. . . . The asserted purpose of the corroboration requirement was to support and test the credibility of the complaining witness. There is no reason to distinguish between a mature female and a mature male sex offense victim. Nor is there any logical reason to raise barriers to the jury evaluation of the credibility of a minor in a sex offense where we do not require it in other situations.

Id. (citations omitted).

96. *Id.*

97. *Id.* at 833-34.

II. The Practical Effects of Abolishing the Corroboration Requirement

Since the legal necessity of corroboration has been abolished, it is possible, although unlikely, for convictions in sex related offenses to be based upon the uncorroborated testimony of a single child witness, provided that the witness' credibility has not been impeached. The legislature and the court's decision to abolish the antiquated and discriminatory requirement is praiseworthy because it attempts to remove obstacles to prosecution. However, while it is true that more child sex abuse cases will now be tried on the merits,[98] it is unlikely in practice to have many practical benefits.[99] Although corroboration is no longer a legal necessity, it remains of utmost importance to the prosecution and yet it is difficult to obtain. Thus, it is doubtful that the absence of the legal requirement of corroboration will facilitate prosecution.

When corroboration was required, the court moved away from the unrealistically strict standards of the earlier cases[100] toward a less rigid totality of the circumstances test as applied in the later cases of *Gray, Moore, Arnold,* and *Fitzgerald.*[101] Under this test, if the complainant's testimony was credible and the identity of the perpetrator and most elements of the corpus delicti were corroborated, the case would withstand defendant's motion for acquittal and ultimately the case would be sent to the jury.[102] This, however, was not the only aspect of sex crime cases in which the court became more tolerant. The court also exercised greater leniency in the area of evidence admissiblity.[103] For example, in *Arnold* the court admitted the testimony of the victims' confidants including a friend, a minister, and an attorney who each testified about conversations that took place the day following the rape.[104] Perhaps because of the difficulty of obtaining corroborative evidence in sex crime cases, the court in *Arnold* admitted evidence which

---

98. W. Rolark, Report of the D.C. City Council on Bill 5-426 (June 25, 1984) (unpublished report). "With this requirement eliminated, it is expected that more child abuse cases will be papered, and more cases will be tried on the merits." *Id.*

99. Arnold v. United States, 358 A.2d 335, 348-49 (D.C. 1976) (en banc) (Mack, J., dissenting) (indicating that the abolishment of the requirement without a restructuring of the penal code would do more to hinder the prosecution).

100. *See supra* notes 33-39 and accompanying text.

101. *See supra* notes 40-46 and accompanying text.

102. *See supra* note 45; *see also* United States v. Gray, 477 F.2d 444, 444-46 (D.C. Cir. 1973); Moore v. United States, 306 A.2d 278 (D.C. 1973).

103. *Arnold,* 358 A.2d at 348 (Mack, J., dissenting). Generally, this would not have been admissible under the spontaneous declaration exception to the hearsay rule because the complainants had time to reflect between the rape and the various conversations. *See infra* note 106 and accompanying text.

104. *Arnold,* 358 A.2d at 337-38.

otherwise may have been inadmissible hearsay.[105] In child sexual assault cases, the court has relaxed evidentiary standards such as the spontaneous declaration exception to the hearsay rule[106] and the complaint of rape exception.[107]

In the future, without the requirement, the court may tend to restrict its current view of admissible evidence. In some cases, the complainant's testimony will be the sole evidence that goes to the jury.[108] Realistically, this

---

105. 358 A.2d at 348 (Mack, J., dissenting).

106. The spontaneous declaration exception to the hearsay rule allows a declaration made by a victim to another to be admitted as substantive evidence of the truth of the matter asserted. *Fitzgerald v. United States*, 443 A.2d 1295, 1303 (D.C. 1982). *See generally* Bulkley, *Evidentiary Theories for Admitting a Child's Out-of-Court Statement of Sexual Abuse at Trial* in CHILD SEXUAL ABUSE AND THE LAW 154 (1981). The court has recognized that in the absence of medical evidence "[t]he purpose of admitting fresh complaint testimony is . . . to meet in advance a charge of recent fabrication [which is implicit in the corroboration requirement] . . . ." *Fitzgerald*, 443 A.2d at 1303 (citing State v. Tirone, 64 N.J. 222, 227, 314 A.2d 601, 604 (1974)). *See supra* note 9. The spontaneous declaration must be made within a short time after the incident while the victim is in an emotional state. It may not be the product of a calm narrative where the victim has had the chance to reflect and possibly fabricate the whole story. *Fitzgerald*, 443 A.2d at 1303-04. *See, e.g., In re* Lewis, 88 A.2d 582 (D.C. 1952) (4 year old child's statement to mother admissible since child made statements while under the influence of recent sexual assault); Snowden v. United States, 2 App. D.C. 89, 94 (1893) (spontaneous utterance exception to the hearsay rule extended in cases of child sexual abuse so that a distraught young victim's statement to her grandmother upon arriving home was admissible).

The District of Columbia courts have generally relaxed this hearsay exception where the declarant was a child both in cases where the child was too young to testify and where the child appeared as a witness. Beausoliel v. United States, 107 F.2d 292 (D.C. 1939), expressly indicated that relaxed standards should be applied to child sexual assault cases. *See* Wheeler v. United States, 211 F.2d 19 (D.C. Cir.), *cert. denied,* 347 U.S. 1019 (1953) (suggesting a relaxed standard although not expressly indicating the effect of declarant's age). *But see* Brown v. United States, 152 F.2d 138 (D.C. Cir. 1945) (indicating the dangers inherent in relaxing the rules).

107. Another evidentiary exception is the complaint of rape. Under this exception evidence that a report of the abuse was made is admissible solely to show that the victim was not silent. The content of such a report is not admissible. *Fitzgerald*, 443 A.2d at 1305; 29 McCORMICK ON EVIDENCE § 297, at 709 (1972); WIGMORE ON EVIDENCE § 1135, at 297-314 (1972). The evidence that the report was made is admissible only if the report was made promptly or there is an explainable delay in reporting. *Fitzgerald*, 443 A.2d at 1305. "This theory is premised on the *necessity* for admitting the fact of the complaint in sex crimes, because of the unique requirement that the sex crime be corroborated." *Id.* at 1303 (emphasis in original). This is almost always applicable in cases involving child victims because a delay in reporting may occur as a consequence of a threat or bribe to keep silent. *Id.* at 1305. *See* Testimony of David W. Lloyd on Behalf of the Child Sexual Abuse Assistance Program before the D.C. City Council, Public Hearing No. 4 on the District of Columbia Basic Criminal Code Act of 1979 (Feb. 21, 1980). Therefore, in the District of Columbia, "if a child sex complainant tells a parent, friend, a police officer, or almost anyone about the sex incident, that is some evidence of corroboration as a matter of law . . . ." *Fitzgerald*, 443 A.2d at 1303 n.12.

108. CHILD SEXUAL ABUSE, *supra* note 3, at 16. If the child's testimony is the sole evidence to go to the jury, the defendant will also be less likely to plead guilty. *Id.*

implies that the defense must work harder to place the complainant's testimony in doubt. As a result, the complainant will be subjected to closer scrutiny during the investigatory stages and perhaps a more rigorous cross-examination.[109]

Clearly, the absence of the requirement confers an immediate benefit upon prosecutors by alleviating their concern over the possibility that the court will direct a verdict and acquit the defendant due to lack of corroborative evidence.[110] However, the prosecutor must still concern himself with obtaining enough corroborative evidence to avoid the judge setting aside the verdict or having the conviction reversed on appeal due to the insufficiency of the evidence.[111] In addition, the prosecutor must obtain sufficient evidence to overcome the jury's suspicion of the child's testimony.[112]

With a legal corroboration requirement absent, the issue of whether the evidence corroborates the child's testimony is totally within the province of the jury. Juries are suspicious of allegations that are sex related[113] and additionally may believe certain prevalent myths about children such as their suggestibility, curiosity, and tendency to fantasize about sex.[114] These assumptions, which may automatically place the child's credibility in doubt, are erroneous. Psychological studies demonstrate that children only fantasize about circumstances within their experience and observation.[115] Although children are likely to be curious, they are unlikely to make false reports about sex.[116] Finally, studies show that children are no more sug-

---

109. *Arnold,* 358 A.2d at 348 (Mack, J., dissenting) (indicating that the abolishment of the corroboration requirement without further reform will make the trial more difficult on the victim).

110. *See supra* note 9 and accompanying text.

111. Lloyd, *supra* note 9, at 103.

112. *Id.* Jurors' preconceived beliefs about children may have a powerful impact on their evaluation of the child's credibility. J. BULKLEY, RECOMMENDATIONS OF IMPROVING LEGAL INTERVENTION FOR INTRAFAMILY CHILD SEXUAL ABUSE CASES 33 (1982); D. Shackleton, Chairperson, Comm. on Human Services, Committee Comments on Bill 5-425 (June 29, 1984); Goodman, Golding & Haith, *Jurors' Reactions to Child Witnesses,* 40 J. SOCIAL ISSUES 139, 141 (1984) [hereinafter Goodman].

113. Annotation, *Modern Status of Rule Regarding Necessity for Corroboration of Victim's Testimomy in Prosecution for Sexual Offense,* 31 A.L.R. 4th 120 (1986). There are three false presumptions concerning sex crime cases in general: (1) a great number of cases are false reports; (2) the jury is prejudiced against the defendant; and (3) rape is an accusation which is difficult to defend against. J. BULKLEY, *supra* note 112, at 31; L. HOLMSTROM & A. BURGESS, THE VICTIM OF RAPE 238 (1978); H. KALVEN & H. ZEISEL, THE AMERICAN JURY 70-71 (1966); S. KATZ & M. MAZUR, UNDERSTANDING THE RAPE VICTIM 213-14 (1979); D. LLOYD, *supra* note 9, at 103-04.

114. *See supra* note 25 and accompanying text.

115. *See supra* note 112.

116. *See supra* note 112.

gestible than adults.[117] Therefore, jurors should not be any more skeptical about a child's testimony than that of an adult. Studies show, however, that jurors are more skeptical.[118]

These fallacies, which may place the child's credibility in doubt, may be reinforced in the minds of the jurors if the judge gives a discretionary instruction which states in relevant part: "Children are likely to be more suggestible than adults. Moreover, children may not have a full understanding of the serious consequences of [the testimony they give] [the charges they make] . . . ."[119] This cautionary instruction, which is based on fallacious assumptions,[120] underscores the importance of corroboration from the prosecutorial standpoint.

Unfortunately, corroboration is an element found lacking in many of these cases. Due to the nature of the crime, there are rarely any eyewitnesses.[121] Medical evidence is also found lacking as well because in many cases the sexual contact falls short of penetration.[122] Also, in 80% of the sex related crimes committed against children in the District of Columbia, there is no medical evidence of resistance because the child victim is generally not forcibly raped but rather is threatened or bribed.[123] Finally, many times a child does not show signs of emotional distress immediately following the assault but instead the child's behavior may change in subtle and often misunderstood ways.[124]

III. CONCLUSION

The legislature and courts admirably have abolished the corroboration re-

---

117. *See supra* note 112.
118. Goodman, *supra* note 112, at 143-44. "In sum, jurors are likely to enter the courtroom with biases against children's credibility, but these biases can be overcome by sufficient evidence. If the evidence is ambiguous, jurors' attitudes about children's credibility may be one important influence on the final verdict." *Id.; see* J. BULKLEY, *supra* note 112, at 33; Note, *The Rape Corroboration Requirement: Repeal Not Reform,* 81 YALE L.J. 1365, 1382-83 (1972) (suggesting that even absent the corroboration requirement, prosecutors rarely pursue a case relying solely on complainant's testimony).
119. H. GREEN & T. GUIDOBONI, CRIMINAL JURY INSTRUCTIONS FOR THE DISTRICT OF COLUMBIA (3d ed. 1978), instruction 2.21.
120. *See supra* notes 115-18 and accompanying text.
121. Lloyd, *supra* note 9, at 107. If there is eyewitness testimony in these cases corroboration is rarely an issue anyway because the defendant will normally plea bargain. *Id.*
122. CHILD SEXUAL ABUSE, *supra* note 3, at 16.
123. *Id.* Testimony of David W. Lloyd on Behalf of the Child Sexual Abuse Assistance Program before the D.C. City Council, Public Hearing No. 4 on the District of Columbia Basic Criminal Code Act of 1979 (Feb. 21, 1980). Also, in cases of intra-family sexual abuse cases, reports are made long after abuse has occurred and, therefore, physical evidence may be nonexistent. *Id.*
124. *Id.* at 4, *reprinted in* Fitzgerald v. United States, 443 A.2d 1295, 1308 (D.C. 1982).

quirement and, in doing so, have dismissed a discriminatory and antiquated rule based on faulty assumptions about the nature of sex related cases and complainants. While this may be one step toward bringing sex offenders to justice, it is doubtful that this step will bring about many practical benefits. Corroboration with the rule in place or in its absence is still essential to prosecution and is a severe detriment where it is lacking.

Laura Lane

Behavioral Sciences and the Law, Vol. 9, 3–20 (1991)

The Corroboration Requirement in Child Sex Abuse Cases

Murray Levine, J.D., Ph.D. and
Lori Battistoni, J.D.

The sharp rise in reports of child abuse has led to efforts
to protect children in family courts in child protective proceedings. Hearsay evidence of a child's prior statements
may be admitted in child protective proceedings, but such
evidence is legally insufficient to support an adjudication
of abuse without corroborative evidence. Courts have
admitted expert psychological, psychiatric or social work
testimony about the child sex abuse syndrome as sufficient
corroborative evidence. The testimony is called "validation" testimony. The scientific basis for such validation
testimony in the absence of a disclosure by the child is very
weak. Courts have also tended to accept the most minimal
evidence as corroboration of the child's out-of-court statements, including other hearsay evidence. The socially valu-
able policy of protecting children by admitting weak
evidence, such as validation testimony, or other hearsay,
should be reviewed to ensure the evidence meets criteria
of reliability in order to minimize erroneous determinations.

INTRODUCTION

The sharp rise in reports of child sexual abuse[1] accompanying federal legislation
and mandated reporting of child abuse[2] has led to increased problems of protecting
children, and prosecuting alleged offenders. Sex abuse offenses against children may
be pursued through either the child protective system and the juvenile or family
courts, or through criminal prosecution, or both. In many states, the offenses are
defined by reference to the criminal code whether the allegation is pursued in criminal

---

Murray Levine, J.D., Ph.D., is Professor of Psychology and Law at the State University of New York
at Buffalo. Lori Battistoni, J.D., is an attorney with the law firm of Crowell & Moring in Washington,
D.C. The authors wish to acknowledge support in the form of a Baldy Center for Law and Social
Policy research assistantship granted to Lori Battistoni, and for general support from the Research Center
for Children and Youth, SUNY, Buffalo. Correspondence and requests for reprints should be addressed
to Dr Murray Levine, Psychology Department, 228 Park Hill, State University of New York at Buffalo,
NY 14260, USA.
[1] American Association For Protecting Children, Highlights of Official Child Neglect and Abuse Reporting 1986 (1988); American Association for Protecting Children, Highlights of Official Child Neglect
and Abuse Reporting 1985 (1987). For a discussion of the rediscovery of child abuse see S. J. Pfohl,
(1977). *The Discovery of Child Abuse.* SOCIAL PROBLEMS 24, 310.
[2] Title XX, Social Security Act; Child Abuse Prevention and Treatment Act, 1974; M. H. Meriwether
(1986). Child abuse reporting laws: Time for a change. FAMILY LAW QUARTERLY, 20, 141; J. Eckenrode,
J. Powers, J. Doris, J. Mansch, & N. Balgi (1988). *Substantiation of child abuse and neglect reports.* JOURNAL
OF CONSULTING AND CLINICAL PSYCHOLOGY, 56, 9.

0735-3936/91/010003-18$09.00

courts or through the child protective system.[3] Although it is difficult to establish precise figures on the incidence and prevalence of child sexual abuse, many females and probably a lesser number of males experience some form of sexual abuse as children. Most sexual abuse probably goes unreported.[4] About 10 to 12% of all reports of maltreatment involve sexual abuse; these are substantiated by child protective service workers in about 40% of the cases.[5] The pursuit of a proportion of these cases,[6] through either of the courts, has created new issues of proof, both because of the characteristics of the offense, and concern about the child as a witness.[7] This paper used New York law for its major illustrations. However, because of legislation governing federally reimbursable child protection programs, many aspects of the laws are similar from state to state.[8]

In response to the women's movement,[9] many states amended their rape laws to remove corroboration requirements.[10] Those protections were later extended to child witnesses in sex abuse cases. For example, before 1984, New York State law included strict corroboration requirements for the child victim's testimony in child sexual abuse cases in criminal and family court proceedings. Recognizing that in many such cases the victim is the only witness (often providing the only evidence) upon which to base prosecution,[11] the state legislature in 1984 eliminated these corroboration requirements.[12] Thus today in New York, no additional evidence is required in criminal court to support childrens' *sworn* testimony regarding sexual

---

[3] Younes, Besharov, Peterson & Wrubel (1988). State child abuse and neglect laws: a comparative analysis. In PROTECTING CHILDREN FROM ABUSE AND NEGLECT. POLICY AND PRACTICE, edited by D. J. Besharov.

[4] Peters, Wyatt, & Finkelhor (1986). Prevalence. In A SOURCEBOOK ON CHILD SEXUAL ABUSE, edited by D. Finkelhor.

[5] *supra* note 1 AAPC (1987); note 2, Eckenrode *et al.*

[6] In 1987, Erie County, NY, a county with urban and rural areas and a population of just under 1 million, received, 5,258 reports of maltreatment. They indicated about 30% of the reports and petitions were filed in family court for about 30% of the indicated cases of maltreatment. Erie County DSS, Consolidated Services Plan, 1 January 1988–31 December, 1990. Buffalo, NY: Erie County Department of Social Services.

[7] D. Whitcomb, E. R. Shapiro, & L. D. Stellwagen (1985). When the victim is a child: issues for judges and prosecutors; G. S. Goodman (Issue Editor) (1984). *The child witness.* JOURNAL OF SOCIAL ISSUES, *40*, 1.

[8] See Younes *et al*, note 3.

[9] S. Brownmiller (1975). AGAINST OUR WILL.

[10] For example, before November 1984, New York Penal Law 130.16 required that prosecutors present: 'independent corroborative evidence (which) harmonize(d) with the victim's testimony in such a manner as to furnish the necessary connection between the defendant and the crime'. See People v. Emmons, 135 A.D.2d 557, 522 N.Y.S.2d 23 (2nd Dept. 1987), citing People v. Keindl, 117 A.D.2nd 679, 679, 498. N.Y.S.2d 417, 418 (2nd Dept. 1986).

[11] The memorandum filed with New York State Assembly Bill 9016, entitled: "AN ACT to amend the penal law, in relation to certain offenses requiring corroboration", proclaimed that, "By their nature, sex offenses against children are usually committed in secret, under circumstances in which corroboration is simply not available". S. A. Bill 9016, Chapter 89, Approval 6, 1984 N.Y. Laws. The Bill Jacket contained over 100 letters of support from public agencies and private individuals around the state.

[12] Corroboration is defined as "evidence of such substantial facts and circumstances as will produce in a sound and prudently cautious mind a confident conclusion that the testimony of the complainant is true in all essentials... additional evidence of a different character to confirm the same point..." BALENTINE'S LAW DICTIONARY, 3rd edn. (1985). The requirement of corroborating evidence dates back further than one might believe: "A single witness may not validate against a person any guilt or blame for any offense that may be committed; a case can be valid only on the testimony of two witnesses or more". DEUTERONOMY *19:15*. The conditions under which corroboration is required as a matter of law will differ issue by issue and state by state.

assault. A defendant may be convicted,[13] or an adjudication of sex abuse may be made in family court,[14] on the child's testimony alone.

Acknowledging that some children may not be psychologically able to testify, and desiring to protect potentially vulnerable children from the rigors of the court-room, hearsay evidence[15] is admitted in many states in either criminal or family/juvenile court proceedings or in both.[16] However, while a child's out-of-court state-ments may be admissible as evidence, in many states such statements are not legally sufficient to make a fact-finding of sex abuse either in family/juvenile court or in criminal court absent some form of corroboration.[17] Supplementary evidence is required to establish the reliability of the child's statements.[18]

The Sixth Amendment confrontation clause rights of criminal defendants pre-cludes the admissibility of hearsay involving a child's out-of-court statements in many cases.[19] However, child protective proceedings in family or juvenile court are brought to protect a child, and are not criminal in nature. The respondent parent or other caretaker of the child is not called a defendant and cannot be imprisoned as a direct consequence of an adjudication of child sexual abuse. Thus the respondent has

---

[13] There is presently no corroboration requirement where a competent child provides the only evidence. See New York State Penal Law, Section 130.16 (McKinney's, 1984).

[14] Article 10 of the Family Court Act allows a fact finding of abuse to be made based solely on the child's word. See New York Family Court Act, Article 10, Section 1046 (McKinney's 1987).

[15] "'Hearsay' is a statement, other than one made by the declarant while testifying at the trial or hearing, offered in evidence to prove the truth of the matter asserted". Fed. R. Evid. 801(c). Hearsay statements are not admissible unless the actual declarant testifies, or one of the 28 exceptions to the hearsay rule applies. In addition, there is a residual exception in which hearsay statements may be admitted if they have sufficient indicia of reliability. Fed. R. Evid. 803(24).

[16] *supra* Younes *et al.*, note 3. In criminal cases, a defendant's Sixth Amendment confrontation right may arise when the child's hearsay statements are introduced into evidence.
   In Idaho v. Wright 58 LW 5036 (1990) the U.S. Supreme Court held that some hearsay is admissible under a residual hearsay exception, provided there is a showing of the unavailability of the declarant, and particularized guarantees of the trustworthiness of the statements.

[17] Many states have moved to allow hearsay in child sexual abuse criminal trials under specified circum-stances, but these statutes often include a corroboration requirement. See Whitcomb, Shapiro and Stellwa-gen, *supra* note 6 at 12–14. In a child protective hearing: "previous statements made by the child relating to any allegations of abuse... shall be admissible in evidence, but if un-corroborated, such statements shall not be sufficient to make a fact-finding of abuse ... Any other evidence tending to support the reliability of the previous statements, including, but not limited to the types of evidence defined in this subsection shall be sufficient corroboration". New York Family Court Act, Article 10, Section 1046(a) (vi)(McKinney's 1985).

[18] See J. Yun, (1983). *A comprehensive approach to child hearsay statements in sex abuse cases.* COLUMBIA LAW REVIEW 83, 1745. "The policy served by requiring corroboration of a victim's out-of-court statements in a child protective proceeding is to assure that a fact-finding determination is not being made based on hearsay evidence alone". Matter of Ryan D., 125 A.D.2d 160, 165, 512 N.Y.S.2d 601, 604 (4th Dept. 1987). The justification of non-admissibility of hearsay emanates from the belief that cross examin-ation of a witness in court is an effective method for determining truths from falsehoods. See 5 Wigmore, EVIDENCE IN TRIALS AT COMMON LAW, 12.
   If a child below the statutory age at which competency is presumed (age 10, 12 or 14 in different states) is found competent to testify after a *voir dire* conducted by the judge, then the child may be sworn and its testimony may be received and weighted just as any other witness' testimony. New York Penal Law Sec. 130.16. A child who is not competent to be sworn may still testify. However, when a child gives unsworn testimony, corroboration requirements are imposed to ensure the trustworthiness of the child's statements. Thus, a criminal defendant in a child sex abuse case cannot be convicted if the sole evidence is the child's uncorroborated, unsworn testimony. New York CPL Sec. 60.20. In People v. Murphy 526 N.Y.S. 2d 905 (1988) the trial judge examined a child witness under the age of 12, and found the witness competent to testify. However, based on a child witness' performance on the stand, the judge found the witness incompetent, and set aside a jury verdict because the conviction was based on the uncorroborated testimony of an unsworn child witness.

[19] But see Idaho v. Wright, *supra* note 16.

very limited Sixth Amendment confrontation rights, and out-of-court statements (hearsay) by children are regularly admitted. Still, an adjudication of child sexual abuse may not be made on the basis of a child's uncorroborated out-of-court statements introduced as hearsay.

A review of current case law in New York's Family Court suggests that the evidence necessary to corroborate children's out-of-court statements in child sexual abuse cases is very minimal. Courts are liberally interpreting the statute permitting "any other evidence" to corroborate a child's out-of-court statements. In 1987, the New York Court of Appeals, the state's highest court, held that testimony by an expert witness, termed a "validator", was sufficient to meet the statutory requirements of corroboration in a sex abuse case heard in Family Court.[20] The justification for such a liberal interpretation of the corroboration requirement is invariably stated as protection of child victims of sexual abuse.

In this article, the types of evidence that family/juvenile courts are accepting as meeting the corroboration requirement are reviewed. We agree with the goals espoused by the courts, but we raise questions about some types of evidence accepted by the courts in attempting to reach those goals.

APPLICATION OF THE HEARSAY RULE IN FAMILY COURT PROCEEDINGS

Child protective cases are heard in family or juvenile courts. The process generally begins with a report of suspected maltreatment. The initial report, whatever its source, initiates an investigation by the child protective agency. The investigating worker may "unfound" the case if he or she finds there is "no credible evidence" of child sexual abuse, or "indicate" when there is some credible evidence.[21] The worker may then recommend a treatment program to the family which the family may accept voluntarily. A petition alleging child sexual abuse is brought in family court by a child protective service agency when the subject of an indicated child maltreatment report refuses a treatment plan, or when the agency seeks the court's authority to remove either the child-victim or the alleged perpetrator from the home.[22] The allegation is adjudicated in an adversary hearing in which rules of evidence appropriate to a civil procedure are employed; the Family Court judge has great discretion in applying the rules.[23]

Serious consequences may follow an adjudication of maltreatment. The family court judge may order the child placed in a foster home or an institution. The judge may order additional remedies such as limiting parental visitation, granting only supervised visitation, or requiring family members to enter counseling.[24] An adjudication of maltreatment may result in a temporary, or even permanent loss

---

[20] Matter of Nicole V., 71 N.Y.2d 112 (1987).

[21] Even though no criminal penalties follow, an indicated report can have serious consequences for the subject of the report. If a person has a record with an indicated report of abuse or maltreatment, the person may be barred from adopting children, or from working with children. See New York Social Service Law Art. 6 Sec, 424-a. Licensed professionals may be subject to disciplinary proceedings for professional misconduct. See Title VIII, New York Education Law, Art. 130(3), Sec. 6509.

[22] See New York Family Court Act, Article 10, Section 1032 (McKinney's, 1987).

[23] See New York Family Court Act, Article 10, Section 65 (McKinney's, 1987).

[24] See Uniform Family Court Rules, Subchapter A, Sec. 2510.3.

of custody order.[25] A parent may lose the child's custody to the state[26] or to the child's other parent.[27] An adjudication of abuse in relation to one child can be used as evidence of abuse against another child, with the consequent loss of custody of that child as well.[28]

Eventually the children may be restored to the parent, but two adjudications of abuse within a five-year period provide legally sufficient cause to terminate parental rights.[29] Moreover, if a family fails to follow through a treatment plan after the child has been taken into custody, that failure may be sufficient to support an adjudication that the child is permanently neglected and parental rights may be terminated in order to release the child for adoption.[30]

In family court proceedings the determination itself can be a sanction because of the stigma attached.[31] Orders of protection can be enforced against an alleged abuser.[32] These orders force the alleged abuser to stay away from the child for any 'specified time' the family court judge decides is necessary.[33] In many jurisdictions the district attorney's office monitors child protective proceedings in order to determine whether criminal charges should be filed against the alleged perpetrator.[34] Even if a case is merely indicated by child protective worker, the alleged abuser can be barred from certain work with children or from adopting a child.[35]

In all fact-finding hearings except for termination of parental rights, the applicable standard of proof is preponderance of the evidence.[36] This less rigorous standard

---

[25] See New York Family Court Act, Article 10, Sec. 1055 (b)(i) (McKinney's 1937).

[26] See *In Re* Ruth McI., 528 N.Y.S.2d 385 (1st Dept. 1988)(custody of a five-year old girl given to Commissioner of Social Services for 18 months based on medical evidence that child was sexually abused while she was in her father's custody, although the court admitted that it had not been established by a preponderance of evidence that the father was the perpetrator). See also Matter of Kimberly K., 123 A.D.2d 865, 507 N.Y.S.2d 654 (2nd Dept. 1986) (custody of girl awarded to Commissioner of Social Services based on child's out-of-court statements, medical evidence of an enlarged introitus and the testimony of a social worker that the child had been abused).

[27] See Matter of Ryan, D., 125 A.D.2d 160, 512 N.Y.S. 2d 601 (4th Dept. 1987) (four-year old boy placed in mother's custody as a result of a factfinding that the father sexually abused the boy). This is commonplace in divorce cases, since FCA, Article 10, Section 1046(a)(vi) has been held to apply to custody proceedings involving allegations of child sexual abuse.

[28] New York Family Court Act, Article 10, Section 1046(a)(i).

[29] See New York Social Services Law, Article 6, Sections 384–b:(4)(e) & (8)(b) (McKinney's 1987).

[30] See New York Social Services Law, Sec. 384-b 7.

[31] See Matter of Linda K., 132 A.D.2d 149, 521 N.Y.S.2d 705 (2nd Dept., 1987).

[32] See Family Court Act, Article 10, Section 1056 (McKinney's 1985).

[33] *Id.* There is no statutory limit on the duration of an order of protection. For example in Matter of Erin G., 527 N.Y.S.2d 488 (2nd Dept., 1988), after determining that the three-and-a-half year-old child had been sexually abused by her father, the court ordered him to stay away from the child until she turned 18, constituting a 15-year order of protection. The Appellate Court found that the order was not unreasonable in light of the discretionary statute. See also Matter of Fawn S., 123 A.D.2d 871, 507 N.Y.S.2d 651 (2nd Dept., 1986) (temporary order of protection granted covering the time during which the remanded proceedings take place).

[34] As an example, in Erie County, the District Attorney's office opens a case file on all family court petitions when they are filed with the family court. Subsequently, a representative from the "CAAR Unit" (Comprehensive Assault Abuse & Rape Unit) may attend family court proceedings involving these cases, taking notes that will be used to help make the prosecutorial decision.

[35] See New York Social Services Law, Article 6, Section 422; 424-a(d) (McKinney's 1987).

[36] Prior to 1982, a state could terminate parental rights by proving by a preponderance of evidence that the child was permanently neglected. In Santosky v. Kramer, 455 U.S. 745, 746 (1982), the Court held that before the State can completely sever the rights of the parents "due process requires that the State support its allegations by at least clear and convincing evidence". The New York State Court of Appeals later ruled that the preponderance standard would apply to fact-finding involving temporary placement of the child. See Matter of Tammie Z., 66 N.Y.2d 1, 494 N.Y.S.2d 686 (1985).

of proof is applied because there is no criminal sanction, and because the court's purpose is to protect the child.[37] The admission of hearsay and the corroboration requirement work in concert with this less rigorous standard of proof.[38] The family court judge is given great discretion[39] to determine what evidence satisfies the corroboration requirement. The requirement is said to be "not unduly stringent".[40] The meaning of "not unduly stringent" can be articulated by exploring the evidence accepted as corroboration of a child's out-of-court statements. Such evidence generally takes one or more of several forms, including expert testimony, physical evidence and even other hearsay statements.

Expert Testimony

On the assumption that testifying in court is psychologically harmful,[41] children, especially younger children may be excused from testifying. Evidence of the alleged abuse is introduced in the form of testimony repeating an out-of-court statement made by the child alleging the abuse and identifying the perpetrator. The person who heard the statement (e.g., parent, teacher, police officer, child protective worker etc.) is permitted to testify to it.[42] That testimony is hearsay, but is admissible and it is subject to cross examination.

---

[37] See Matter of Linda K., 132 A.D.2d 149 (2nd Dept., 1987). Family Court Act, Article 10 is frequently referred to as a "Children's Bill of Rights," nourishing the already strong propensity for judges to lean toward favoring the interests of the child in these cases. See Matter of Michael G., 129 Misc.2d 186, 492 N.Y.S.2d 993 (Fam.Ct.,1985).

[38] "... previous statements made by the child relating to any allegations of abuse... shall be admissible in evidence, but if uncorroborated, such statements shall not be sufficient to make a fact-finding of abuse.... Any other evidence tending to support the reliability of the previous statements, including, but not limited to the types of evidence defined in this subsection shall be sufficient corroboration". NY Family Court Act, Art. 10, Sec. 1046(a)(vi).

[39] The Court of Appeals has acknowledged for more than a decade that the sensitive quality of these cases requires family court judges to take a very personal approach when dealing with them. See Matter of Cecilia R., 36 N.Y.2d 317, 367 N.Y.S.2d 770 (1975).

[40] Matter of Linda K., 132 A.D.2d 149, 154 (1987). In an Appellate Division decision this pronouncement was made: "we conclude that due process requirements are met by permitting a finding of abuse to be made on the basis of a child's out-of-court statement which is corroborated by any competent, nonhearsay, relevant evidence...". Matter of Nicole V., 123 A.D.2d 97, 105 (1985). The Court of Appeals affirmed in Matter of Nicole V., 71 N.Y.2d 112 (1987), but indicated in a companion case that under some circumstances hearsay in the form of an out-of-court statement by a second child would provide adequate corroboration. Matter of Francis Charles, 69 N.Y.2d 611, 517 N.Y.S.2d 1026 (1987).

[41] Because there is a very limited confrontation right in child protective proceedings, the judge may take a child witness' testimony in chambers, and out of sight of the respondent. Although testifying in court, enduring cross examination and confronting a defendant or respondent is undoubtedly stressful for anyone, there is reason to belive that participation in a criminal trial in which the child victim confronts the alleged perpetrator may be especially harmful to some vulnerable children or may result in inadequate testimony. See American Psychological Association Amicus Brief Maryland v. Craig, U.S. Supreme Court No. 89–478, (October term, 1989). One study reports that participation in a juvenile court proceeding may be anxiety relieving for some children, but there is no necessary right to confrontation with the defendant in juvenile or family court. See Runyan, Everson, Edelson, Hunter, & Carter (1988). *Impact of legal intervention on sexually abused children*, THE JOURNAL OF PEDIATRICS, *113*, 647. The U.S. Supreme Court recently held that a particularized showing of possible trauma to the child/victim witness caused by testifying in front of the alleged abuser, and that the child would not be able to testify, was sufficient in a criminal trial to outweigh the defendant's 6th Amendment right to confrontation. See Maryland v. Craig 58 LW 5044 (1990).

[42] See *supra* note 17.

Where a child does not testify, expert testimony[43] may be essential because it can be offered to establish the prima facie case; the expert provides the corroborative evidence necessary to support the child's out-of-court disclosure to another person.[44] Psychologists,[45] social workers[46] or psychiatrists provide such expert testimony which is often referred to as "validation" testimony.[47]

Expert testimony is introduced as evidence in two ways. First, the mental health professional may testify about what is called the "sexually abused child syndrome".[48] The expert witness may discuss behaviors identified as indicators of this syndrome, that he or she has observed in the child, or which have been reported to the expert in the course of taking a history. The implication of the testimony is that the child has indeed been sexually abused. Second, the expert may testify on aspects of the "sexually abused child syndrome" without making specific reference to the particular child in question. The thrust of the testimony is to explain aspects of the child's behavior which may appear puzzling or inconsistent, such as delay in reporting the alleged abuse.[49]

Some courts have accepted both types of expert testimony to corroborate children's

---

[43] Expert testimony is defined as "opinion evidence of some person who possesses special skill or knowledge in some science, profession or business which is not common to the average man and which is possessed by the expert by reason of his special study or experience". BLACK'S LAW DICTIONARY 712 (5th edn., 1979). Before a person is allowed to give expert testimony, the court decides whether she or he is a qualified expert and whether the expert testimony will aid in the factfinder's decision. See Cacciola (1986). *The admissibility of expert testimony in intrafamily child sexual abuse cases*, UCLA LAW REVIEW, 34, 175 (1986). It should be noted that a professional can offer evidence as a lay witness as well. In this instance the person may be allowed to give testimony regarding the child's statements made to them. See Matter of Dana F., 113 A.D.2d 939, 493 N.Y.S.2d 837 (2nd Dept., 1985).

[44] See Cacciola, *supra* note 43. See also Bell (1988) *Working with child witnesses: The caseworker's support of a sexually abused child is of critical importance.* PUBLIC WELFARE, 5.

[45] See Matter of Linda K., 132 A.D.2d 149 (1987).

[46] See Matter of Michael G., 129 Misc.2d 186 (1985).

[47] See Matter of Nicole V., 71 N.Y.2d 112 (1987). In this type of "validation" testimony, the expert testifies, based on her or his experience and interactions with the child, as to whether or not she or he is convinced that the child was sexually abused. Although experts are allowed to give this type of validation testimony, they may not be allowed to vouch for the credibility of the child. Matter of Sanchez, 535 N.Y.S.2d 937 (Fam.Ct., 1988) held that there is no proof that a psychologist is a better judge of whether or not someone is telling the truth, and because of that, the "ultimate issue of credibility" should be left to the trier of the facts. *Id.* at 939.

[48] This syndrome is defined by the behaviors exhibited by the child who has been sexually abused. The theory supporting its development is based on the clinical experience of several mental health professionals who have worked with victims of sexual abuse. Sgroi, Porter & Blick (1982). Validation of sexual abuse. In Handbook of clinical intervention in child sexual abuse, edited by S. M. Sgroi. See G. Harcourt (1986). *Child sexual abuse*, In PSYCHIATRIC SEQUELAE OF CHILD ABUSE, edited by Jacobson. See also Cacciola, *supra* note 43.

[49] This type of expert testimony, based on general issues in the scientific literature, is compared to that regarding the "battered child syndrome" and the "rape trauma syndrome", both of which have been found to be admissible. See Cacciola, *supra* note 43, at 192–193. The expert testifies based on an assumption that the lay person would not understand the "ins and outs" of the syndrome. For example, it is not uncommon for children to retract and later reconfirm the accusation of abuse. The expert may testify that such behavior is part of the "Child Sex Abuse Accommodation Syndrome". See Summit (1983). *The child abuse accommodation syndrome.* CHILD ABUSE & NEGLECT, 7. See also J. Haugaard & N. Dickon Reppucci, THE SEXUAL ABUSE OF CHILDREN (1988). It is assumed that without expert testimony explaining that such inconsistency is an aspect of the syndrome, the jury would view inconsistency as discrediting the witnesses' testimony.

out-of-court statements in child protective proceedings.[50] Normally these cases do not depend solely on the testimony of an expert for corroboration of the child's out-of-court statements. Other evidence is often available.[51]

In only one case has a New York court held that expert "validation" testimony is sufficient corroboration in and of itself.[52] In *Matter of Linda K.*, the child's psychologist testified that the alleged abuse did occur and that the child's father was the abuser.[53] The doctor based his opinion on several months of weekly sessions. He based his expert opinion on his observation of these behaviors: the child avoided conversations about her father, she arranged her dolls and toy animals in "different kinds of oral sexual activities",[54] and she expressed that her father touched and licked her vaginal area.[55] The appellant challenged the lower court's holding that mere validation testimony was sufficient corroboration, arguing that given the opprobrious stigma attached to child abusers, due process demands that more substantial proof be offered before a fact-finding of abuse is made.[56] The appellate court noted the flexibility in the corroboration requirements and the widespread acceptance of expert testimony in child sexual abuse cases.[57] The court concluded that only the quality of the expert testimony itself could restrict sole reliance upon such evidence as sufficient corroboration. In this case, the court found that the quality of the expert testimony was satisfactory.[58]

---

[50] See Matter of Nicole V., 71 N.Y.2d 112 (1987) (a social worker hired by the child's mother, after 10 sessions with the child, testified that the child's withdrawn demeanor and age-inappropriate knowledge of sexual activity were behavioral signs of sexual abuse); See Matter of Kerri K., 135 A.D.2d 631, 522 N.Y.S.2d 210 (2nd Dept. 1987) (child's therapist and CPS caseworker testified that the child's regression from toilet training, possessive attitude toward mother, increased frequency of changing clothes, together with her use of anatomically detailed dolls portraying sexual contact while stating her dad hurt her, were all signals of child sexual abuse); See Matter of Ryan D., 125 A.D.2d 160 (1987) (a child psychologist who worked with the boy, concluded that child sexual abuse was a possibility based on the boy's anxiety, increase in aggressive behavior paired with feelings that he couldn't protect himself, and avoidance of others he had previously interacted with; and a psychiatric social worker testified as to the general characteristics of the sexual abuse syndrome although the child had not disclosed sexual abuse to her).

[51] See Matter of Nicole V., 71 N.Y.2d 112 (1987) (The court noted that the fact-finding was also supported by evidence that the child "suffered from vaginal rashes, depression and sleep disturbances, that blood was found in her vaginal area and by a certified medical report which said she had no hymen").

[52] Matter of Linda K., 132 A.D.2d 149 (2nd Dept., 1987). The only other court to address this proposition is the New York County Family Court which ruled that validation testimony "itself and standing alone" meets the corroboration requirements of Section 1046(a)(vi). See Matter of E.M., 137 Misc.2d 197, 520 N.Y.S.2d 327 (Fam. Ct., 1987).

[53] 132 A.D.2d 149, 151 (2nd Dept., 1987). Should the expert testify as to his or her belief that the respondent is the abuser, or should the expert be limited to testifying that the child's behavior is consistent with the hypothesis that abuse occurred? Experts may not be allowed to testify as to their belief that the child is credible. Such testimony may invade the fact finder's province. See Matter of Sanchez, 535 N.Y.S.2d 937 (Family Court, 1988).

[54] Matter of Linda K., *supra* note 41.

[55] *Id.*

[56] *Id.*

[57] *Id.* The Court noted that in 1985, Section 1046(a)(vi) was amended to allow "any other evidence" to substantiate the child's out-of-court statements. The Court concluded that this legislative intent, together with the "unequivocal language of Family Court Act Section 1046(a)(vi)" denote flexibility, in keeping with the statutory objective universally accepted — the protection of the child.

[58] *Id.* A more stringent test for qualification of experts was recommended in Matter of E.M. The opinion recommended a requirement that validation evidence, when it is the solitary source of corroboration, be "highly credible". Whether the expert's testimony is "highly credible" is determined by using the third Frye criterion, that is, "the proper application of the technique on a particular occasion". [Frye v. United States, 293 F. 1013 (D.C. Cir. 1923) (test for the reliability of evidence derived from a scientific principle — here a lie detector test)]. See Matter of E.M., 137 Misc.2d 197, 199 (1987).

Courts evaluate the corroborative weight of expert testimony in terms of the expert's professional credentials and experience. Normally the expert's credentials are not the only relevant factor. In addition, as established in *Frye v. United States*,[59] courts should also examine whether the method used by the expert is reliable, and accepted by the scientific community.[60] The *Frye* test is normally applied when evidence is based on a new scientific technique, not when expert testimony is based on standard examining procedures. Still, it is instructive to examine the *Frye* criteria in this context. In determining the reliability of scientific evidence three factors are considered: "the validity of the underlying principle", "the validity of the technique applying that principle", and "the proper application of the technique on a particular occasion".[61] In addition, in order to be the basis for expert testimony, a scientific method must enable the expert to add insight to the topic which a layperson could not.[62]

When the "sexually abused child syndrome" is subjected to this analysis, the result is not impressive. The non-specific nature of the syndrome, as well as the lack of empirical data relating to its validity in distinguishing abused from non-abused children, raises serious questions as to the validity of the underlying principle. This explains why there is little agreement among mental health professionals supporting the use of the syndrome to reach conclusions that children have been sexually abused.[63] Thus if evaluated against *Frye* criteria, expert "validation" testimony regarding the "child sexual abuse syndrome" may not meet the criteria of scientific validity necessary for its admissibility. New York courts have not assessed validation testimony in a manner which would allow them to reach this conclusion.[64] Instead, as noted in *Matter of E.M.*:

> it appears that what the courts in New York have done ... is to implicitly ... endorse the validity of factor 1 [of the 3 factors in *Frye*] ... that is, the underlying principle that the intrafamilial child sexual abuse syndrome is a recognizable psychological phenomenon and that the syndrome may be measured by factor 2 ... namely the "validation process".[65]

In the interests of protecting the child, the New York Court of Appeals generally

---

[59] 293 F. 1013 (D.C. Cir. 1923). The standard is still applicable today. See Matter of E.M., 137 Misc.2d 197(1987).

[60] See M. Levine (1984). *The adversary process and social science in the courts:* Barefoot v. Estelle. THE JOURNAL OF PSYCHIATRY & LAW SUMMER, 147. Although the Frye standard remains good law, the Supreme Court seems to have weakened it in Barefoot v. Estelle, 463 U.S. 880, 103 S.Ct. 3383 (1983). Here, the Supreme Court held that the willingness of one mental health professional to tesify to a given point can be sufficient to establish acceptance in a segment of the scientific community, even in the face of contrary opinion offered by the national professional association.

[61] Matter of E.M., 137 Misc.2d 197, 199 (1987). Implicit in the analysis of the first two factors is the qualification of the person utilizing the scientific method (lie detector test or validation interview). Included is whether that person followed correct procedures, and whether the data obtained were interpreted correctly.

[62] See *supra* note 43

[63] In a recent book, which comprehensively addresses the subject of child sexual abuse, two noted experts refuse to support the use of a specific syndrome to predict abuse. See J. Haugaard & N. D. Reppucci *supra* note 43. See also, Cf., Matter of E.M., 137 Misc.2d 197 (1987).

[64] See *supra* note 58 and accompanying text.

[65] Matter of E.M., 137 Misc.2d 197, 199–200 (1987). The opinion goes on to note that courts should also carefully address the third factor in order to ensure that the techniques utilized by the expert were applied with appropriate professional care, thereby ensuring that the conclusions reached were sufficiently reliable. *Id.* See also Matter of Linda K., 132 A.D.2d 149 (1987).

accepted the clinical indications of child sexual abuse described by Sgroi and her colleagues. Sgroi lists 20 such indicators, including: "overly compliant behaviors", "agressive behavior", "pseudomature behavior", "persistent and inappropriate sexual play with peers or toys", "detailed and age-inappropriate understanding of sexual behavior", "arriving early at school and leaving late with few, if any, absences", "sleep disturbances", and "withdrawal". These are not conclusive indicators of sexual abuse, but Sgroi asserts that some combination of them "may be observed in children who are sexually abused".[66]

Since there is no standard procedure to elicit these indicators, and little indication that children's behavior can be reliably classified on the basis of the indicators, it is impossible to determine whether an expert has followed "the correct procedures" and thus met one of the main tests in *Frye*. Because of the lack of empirical data, the rate of false positive identifications of children as sexually abused through the use of these indicators is unknown. In other words, no study has determined how often reliance upon the syndrome has falsely identified a child as having been sexually abused.[67]

It is far from established that any of these indicators, in any combination, are valid in the absence of a more or less direct statement by the child revealing some sexual involvement or sexual knowledge. Conte & Schuerman[68] compared 369 sexually abused children with normal children recruited from the community on a voluntary basis. They obtained data from parents who completed forms and from social workers who had interviewed the parents. Some items on the scales filled out by social workers and by parents statistically differentiated normal children from sexual abused children, but the results show substantial overlap between the normal and the abused children on items similar to those specified by Sgroi.

Friedrich undertook several studies of differences between sexually abused children, children seen clinically for other problems, and normal children. He concluded that, "It is apparent that very few differences existed between the conduct disordered and the sexually abused boys with the exception that the conduct disordered boys were true to their diagnosis and significantly more aggressive, and the sexually abused boys were significantly more sexualized".[69] Based on an additional study which included sexually abused children, children seen at mental health out-patient clinics, and normal children, Friedrich conclude: "Both the outpatient and the sex abuse groups differed significantly from the normal comparison group on all variables, but the outpatient group differed from the sex abuse group most clearly on the sex item variables. That was the only variable where the sexual abuse group was significantly elevated with respect to the outpatient sample".[70] Similarly, Wheeler & Berliner have concluded: "no psychological measures currently assess the impact of CSA [child sex abuse]".[71]

A recent proposal for a diagnostic category to be added to the *DSM-IIIR* is called

---

[66] See *supra* note 48, Sgroi, Porter & Blick at 40–41.
[67] See J. Haugaard, & N. D. Reppucci, *supra* note 49.
[68] J. Conte & J. Schuerman (1988). *The effects of sexual abuse on children. A multidimensional approach.* In LASTING EFFECTS OF CHILD SEXUAL ABUSE, edited by G. E. Wyatt & G. J. Powell.
[69] W. Friedrich (1988). Behavior problems in sexually abused children. An adaptational perspective. In G. E. Wyatt & G. J. Powell, eds., 181.
[70] *Id.* at 182.
[71] J. Wheeler & L. Berliner (1988). *Treating the effects of sexual abuse on children.* In G. E. Wyatt & G. J. Powell, ed., 235.

"Sexually Abused Child's Disorder". The proposal is explicit on the point that the only truly differentiating characteristic involves a report of sexual experience or sexual knowledge: "The primary feature of the Sexually Abused Child's Disorder is an age-inappropriate increased awareness and altered emotional reaction to neutral inquiry about genital anatomy or exposure to differentiated sexual experiences such as exhibitionism, sexualized kissing, fondling, vaginal or anal penetration, child pornography, and oral copulation".[72] Some expert witnesses acknowledge that the only significant feature in sexually abused children is the specificity and detail with which they will discuss sexual activity.[73]

Often psychologists and/or social workers use play activity with either a standard doll or anatomically detailed dolls in the clinical setting to evaluate the child's report of the sexual involvement. This procedure is then used by the expert as part of the basis for his or her validation testimony regarding the syndrome.[74] There does not, as yet, exist a standardized method for using these dolls, and little is known about reliability of the behavior, nor about the validity of the inferences that are drawn from observations using such procedures.[75]

The procedures experts use to ascertain whether a child has been sexually abused have also come under intensive criticism. Based on reviews and videotapes of interviews with allegedly abused children by experts, critics charge that:

> the techniques used by interviewers are intrusive and suggestive, tainting the interview and rendering the information produced unreliable. The techniques most frequently criticized include the interviewers' use of dolls, toys and drawings-which, it is pointed out, children commonly use to create fantasies-for the purpose of eliciting truthful accounts of reality. The use of leading questions to focus attention on sexual abuse, especially following a child's repeated denials, has been sharply criticized. And critics have attacked interviewers' asking children if they have been threatened, reassuring them that they are safe and that it is "okay to tell," and then praising them if they disclose any abuse. According to this theory, the interviewers who use these techniques may be well-intentioned and the children may have no intention of lying, but the effect is that children are taught what to say. In the end, they do not lie but rather grow so confused that they can no longer distinguish between what they have been taught to believe and what actually occurred.[76]

However, there is no evidence that children can be "brain washed" or "programmed" to make up a whole event. Children can be lead to give incorrect responses in tests of memory for events in which they have participated, but they are more

---

[72] D. Corwin (1988). *Early diagnosis of child sexual abuse. Diminishing the lasting effects.* In G. E. Wyatt & G. J. Powell, eds., 254.

[73] See Matter of Linda K., 132 A.D.2d 149, 521 N.Y.S.2d 705 (1987) (Tuthill's testimony); see also Matter of Ryan D. 125 A.D.2d 160 (4th Dept., 1987) (Schiff's testimony).

[74] See Matter of Michael G., 129 Misc.2d 186 (1985) (The qualified therapist testified that Michael's placing the "baby doll" and "daddy doll" in bed together, after removing their clothing and stated "Daddy hurts him", was an indication that the child suffered from "intrafamilial child sex abuse syndrome").

[75] See S. White, G. Strom, G. Santilli, & K. M. Quinn (1986). *Interviewing young children with anatomically correct dolls.* CHILD ABUSE AND NEGLECT, *10*, 519.

[76] D. Hechler (1988). *The battle and the backlash.* THE CHILD SEXUAL ABUSE WAR, 154–155. See also R. Reinhold (1990). *McMartin Case: swept away by panic about molestation.* NEW YORK TIMES (24 January), at A-1, A-18, col 1.

likely to be incorrect about events peripheral to the experience (e.g., color of the room) than about key aspects of the experience (e.g., where the child was touched).[77]

There is another dilemma stemming from the use of expert testimony to validate sexual abuse. To protect the child from the possible trauma of repeating the story of abuse yet another time,[78] the courts have generally been unwilling to order the child to be examined by respondent's expert(s).[79] These decisions limit the use of the adversarial process as a corrective against error. A respondent's expert is limited to testifying on the basis of a review of the State's expert's record,[80] and/or stating the limits of the underlying scientific base for validation testimony.

Given the requirement that the child demonstrate sexual knowledge or repeat the story to the validator, and given that no other signs or symptoms appear to add to the differentiation between sexually abused and other emotionally disturbed children, validation testimony is no more than a second recounting of an out-of-court statement made by the same child to another person. Thus validation testimony seems to be an example of hearsay corroborating hearsay. New York courts, however, are accepting repeated out-of-court statements as adequate corroboration of each other when the statements are made to different people on separate occasions.[81]

The New York Court of Appeals has approved the use of validation testimony and has accepted the child sex abuse syndrome and (by implication) the Child Sex Abuse Accommodation Syndrome as recognized diagnoses. It is unlikely that the Court of Appeals will soon reverse its position. However, we may anticipate challenges to the underlying scientific base for validation testimony as the defense bar becomes increasingly attuned to weaknesses in the approach. For example, if an expert diagnoses the Child Sex Abuse Syndrome on the basis of some combination

---

[77] Goodman, Aman & Hirschman (1987). *Child sexual abuse and physical abuse: children's testimony.* In CHILDREN'S EYEWITNESS TESTIMONY, edited by Ceci, Toglia & Ross. Sink (1988). Studies of true and false allegations: A critical review. In SEXUAL ABUSE ALLEGATIONS IN CUSTODY AND VISITATION CASES, edited by E. B. Nicholson & J. Bulkley, 37.

[78] When children are victims of sexual abuse they may repeat their stories to: a parent, friend, teacher, police officer(s), social worker(s), district attorney(s), judge(s), psychologist(s), nurse(s), physician(s), etc. Children fear and dislike repeating the story, but it is not clear that one more repetition to defendant's experts who presumably would be sensitive to a child's needs would add that much additional stress. See J. Haugaard and N. D. Reppucci, *supra* note 49.

[79] See Matter of Tara H., 129 Misc.2d 508, 494 N.Y.S.2d 953 (Fam.Ct., 1985); Matter of Maria F., 104 Misc.2d 319, 428 N.Y.S.2d 425 (Fam.Ct., 1980). Matter of Vanessa and Aretha R — A.D.2d — (4th Dept., 1989). According to Family Court Act Section 165: "the provisions of civil practice law and rules shall apply to the extent that they are appropriate to the proceedings". New York Family Court Act, Article 10, Section 165 (Mckinney's, 1985). This Section allows family court judges to choose, based on their assessment of the potential impact to the child, whether or not respondents' expert(s) will be allowed to interview the child. The courts have also rejected respondents' requests for examinations before trial (EBT), or for oral depositions of children or other witnesses. See Matter of Maria F. 104 Misc. 2d 319 (Fam.Ct.,1980); In Matter of Diane B. 96 Misc. 2d 798 (Fam. Ct., 1978), the court ruled that children were subjects of Article 10 proceedings and not parties, and therefore the disclosure provisions of CPLR 3101 (a)(1) did not apply to them. However, the court held that CPLR 3101(a)(4) authorizes disclosure if on a motion, the court finds special circumstances. See Schwartz v. Schwartz 23 A.D.2d 204 (1st Dept., 1965). One of these is the hostility of the witness to the respondent. Another is the witnesses' special knowledge of the facts. In Diane B., the children were 18, 17 and 16, and were represented by a law guardian. The father was excluded from the examination. His due process rights were held to be adequately protected by the presence of his attorney. *Id.*

[80] New York Family Court Act, Article 10, Section 1046(a)(vii) (McKinney's 1985) states that the physician-patient, psychologist-client and social worker-client privileges are not applicable in Family Court proceedings. Family Court Act, Section 1038 makes hospital and public or private agency records relating to abuse or neglect available upon subpoena. See New York Family Court Act, Article 10, Section 1038 (McKinney's, 1987).

[81] See Matter of Fawn S. 1234 A.D.2d 871 (2nd Dept., 1986).

of factors that Sgroi[82] mentions, the defense would be entitled to inquire as to the scientific evidence showing that combination of factors differentiated sexually abused children from non-sexually abused children. Such testimony may result in scientific experts appearing in opposition to clinical experts, and may result in some clarification for the courts of the limits of expertise in these cases. The testimony describing symptoms in addition to the child's disclosures of abuse to the expert is probably not probative and may well be prejudicial.

Medical Evidence

Most children who have been sexually abused do not show physical signs of the abuse, such as lacerations, contusions or swelling or stretching of the introitus (vaginal or anal openings).[83] In fact, only a minority of child sexual abuse cases are confirmed by physical findings.[84] For this reason, even the most minimal traces of medical evidence are considered significant evidence in child protective proceedings.[85]

Minimal medical evidence can have a conclusive effect. For example, in *Matter of Nicole V.*, the Court of Appeals affirmed a finding of abuse based on a child's out-of-court statement because there was also evidence that the child's hymen was not intact.[86] Just how much weight is given to this type of evidence depends on the circumstances of the case. As the Family Court noted in Matter of Michael G., "while far from conclusive in and of itself, this child's physical condition is a corroborative factor".[87] However, in the extreme circumstance where no other explanation exists for the medical condition (i.e.. pregnancy or venereal disease) the "conditions" are given a *res ipsa loquitur*[88] effect.[89]

In a child protective proceeding, if there are physical findings indicating abuse, there is no necessity to establish the identity of the alleged abuser as there would

---

[82] See *supra* note 48.

[83] The external and internal genitalia of non-abused children may well contain normal anatomical variations that can erroneously be the basis for an inference of sexual abuse. See report by Dr John McCann, University of California San Francisco, associate clinical professor of pediatrics in D. Nathan (1989). Child abuse evidence debated. New data may aid in sex-crime cases. THE MS REPORTER, March, 81–82; See also M. T. Haslam (Harrogate Clinic, North Yorkshire, UK) (1989). Child sexual abuse—the Cleveland experience. Paper read at the meeting of the International Law and Psychiatry Association, Jerusalem, Israel, June.

[84] Physical injury or trauma is found in only 20–35% of suspected child sexual abuse victims, and those signs do not necessarily constitute clear medical evidence. See J. Haugaard & N. D. Reppucci, *supra* note 49. From the examination of other estimates the 20–35% figure may be somewhat high. See S. Sgroi, *supra* note 36 at 75–78. Depending on how physical trauma is defined, the statistics can vary greatly.

[85] See Matter of Kerri, K., 135 A.D.2d 631 (1987) (child's pediatrician noted redness in the vaginal area).

[86] See Matter of Nicole V., 71 N.Y.2d 112, 524 N.Y.S.2d 19 (1987).

[87] See Matter of Michael G., 129 Misc.2d 186 (1985) (child's pediatrician testified that examination of the child revealed "a swollen irritated penis and trauma to the anus, and that this condition could have been caused by sexual abuse"). *Id.* at 997.

[88] The Latin phrase means "the thing speaks for itself" is taken from the law of negligence. It is a rule of evidence which presumes the defendant was the wrongdoer based on the fact the accident occurred and that the defendant was in control of the situation when it occurred. See W. Prosser, On Torts (W. Keeton, 5th edn, 1984).

[89] See New York Family Court Act, Article 10, Section 1046 (a)(iv) (McKinney's, 1985). See also Matter of Tara H., 129 Misc.2d 508, 494 N.Y.S.2d 953 (Fam. Ct., 1985) (five-year-old girl contracted gonorrhea while in her father's custody); Matter of Joli M., 131 Misc.2d 1088, 502 N.Y.S.2d 653 (Fam. Ct. 1986) (child found to be pregnant).

be in a criminal proscution.[90] If there is evidence of injury to the child, the respondent caretaker may be subject to adjudication for neglect[91] on the basis that the caretaker failed to protect the child from that injury.[92] In a variation of the *res ipsa loquitur* effect, once apparently non-accidental injury is shown, a prima facie case is made; the burden then shifts to the respondent caretaker to provide an explanation of how the injury occurred.[93]

The Fifth Amendment privilege has very limited applicability in a child protective proceeding.[94] If the respondent fails to testify, the court is permitted to draw any adverse inference warranted by that fact[95] in contrast to the criminal trial in which jurors are given instructions that they may not draw an adverse inference if the defendant chooses not to testify.[96] Thus the respondent in a child protective proceeding is placed in a bind. If the respondent fails to testify, an adverse inference may be drawn from that failure. On the other hand, if the respondent does testify, the statements may be used against the respondent in a criminal proceeding unless he or she is granted testimonial immunity.[97]

"Other" Out-of-Court Statements

Although New York Family Courts have deemed the Child Protective Statute flexible,[98] until recently such flexibility had not allowed hearsay statements to corroborate each other. In *Matter of Cindy*, the court firmly held that it would violate the fundamentals of due process and the intent of the Legislature to allow "such testimonial bootstrapping".[99] Similarly, while acknowledging the wide spectrum of acceptable forms of corroboration, the court in *Matter of Nicole V.*, concluded that "due process requirements are met by permitting a finding of abuse to be made on the basis of a child's out-of-court statement which is corroborated by any competent, *non-hearsay*, relevant evidence ...".[100]

In light of this previously strong tendency not to allow hearsay to corroborate hearsay, the decision by the Court of Appeals in *Matter of Francis Charles, Jr., Samuel*

---

[90] Even in Family Court evidence of abuse to the child is not necessarily evidence that the respondent was the abuser. See Matter of Dara R., 119 A.D.2d 579 (2nd Dept., 1986).

[91] See New York Family Court Act, Article 10, Section 1012 (e)(i) (McKinney's 1985).

[92] Even given a finding that there was not a preponderance of evidence to show that respondent father was the perpetrator, a child could be placed in the custody of the commissioner and placed out of the home. See *in re* Ruth McI, 528 N.Y.S.2d 385 (1st Dept., 1988).

[93] See New York Family Court Act, Article 10, Section 1046 (a)(ii) (McKinney's 1985). See also Matter of Jacinta J., 140 A.D.2d 990 (4th Dept., 1988).

[94] See M. Levine & E. Doherty (1990). The tension between the Fifth Amendment and the therapeutic requirement that abusers acknowledge their responsibility for the abuse. Paper read at the meeting of the American Psychology Law Society, Division 41, American Psychological Association, Williamsburg, Virginia, March.

[95] See Commissioner of Social Services o/b/o Patricia A. v Philip d. G. 59 NY2d 137.

[96] See Griffin v. California 380 U.S. 609 (1965).

[97] See Family Court Act, Article 10, Section 1014 (d) (McKinney's 1985) See Levine, *supra* note 94.

[98] Family Court Act, Article 10, Section 1046(a) (vi)(McKinney's 1985). See Matter of Nicole V. 71 N.Y.2d 112, 119 (1987).

[99] 122 Misc.2d 395, 396, 471 N.Y.S.2d 193, 194 (Fam. Ct. 1983) (the written statement submitted to the court by one sister could not corroborate a second sister's written statement). (Emphasis added.).

[100] Matter of Nicole V., 123 A.D.2d 97. However, the Court of Appeals reversed. 71 N.Y.2d 112, 115 (1987).

W. and David C.[101] is surprising. Relying on the flexibility of the corroboration requirement, the Court held that the out-of-court statements made by two brothers to a police investigator were sufficient corroboration for each other.[102] The Court initially noted that if the corroborating statement was merely a repetition by the same child, then the statements would not be considered adequate.[103] The Court further justified its decision by reference to the fact that the boys consistently described detailed aspects of the abusive incidents.[104]

The Court of Appeals' holding allows the same type of evidence which requires corroboration—i.e., the out-of-court statement—to provide that corroboration.[105] The holding is especially noteworthy because the second hearsay statement was the only corroborating evidence offered in the case. This decision by the Court abandons the principle basis for the hearsay rule in that it allows evidence which is not subject to cross-examination to substantiate a finding against the respondent.

Unsworn In-Court Testimony

Unsworn in-court testimony, offered by a child in support of earlier out-of-court statements he or she has made, has also been held to be adequate corroboration.[106] In *Matter of Christina F.*, a five-year-old girl testified unsworn, in chambers,[107] without the defendants but in the presence of counsel and the court.[108] The child's unsworn testimony was held to be sufficient corroboration of the statements she had made to a police officer earlier in the investigation, despite the fact that it was the only other evidence of the abuse.[109] Noting that the child, when asked specific questions about the abuse, provided the court with more detail about the sexual contact than she had the police officer, the court stressed the believability or credibility of the child's story as the central focus in deciding the case.[110] The court's subjective impression of the child's cognitive abilities helped formulate the decision.

---

[101] This case was decided with Matter of Nicole V., 71 N.Y.2d 112 (1987). See Matter of Francis Charles, Jr., Samuel W. and David C., 69 N.Y.2d 611, 517 N.Y.S.2d 1026 (1987).

[102] *Id.*

[103] *Id.* Note, however, this is essentially the situation that prevails when a validator is permitted to testify to a child's out-of-court statement or to provide corroboration for another out-of-court statement.

[104] See Matter of Francis Charles, Jr., 69 N.Y.2d 611 (1987).

[105] *Id.* There have been cases in the past in which other hearsay statements have been allowed as corroboration, but in these cases the other hearsay statements were not the sole additional form of proof in the proceeding. See Matter of Tantalyn TT., 115 A.D.2d 799, 495 N.Y.S.2d 740 (3rd Dept., 1985) (testimony regarding child's behavior); See also Matter of Cindy JJ., 105 A.D.2d 189, 484 N.Y.S.2d 249 (3rd Dept., 1984) (abuser's admission).

[106] See Matter of Christina F., 135 Misc.2d 495, 516 N.Y.S.2d 383 (Fam. Ct., 1987).

[107] The testimony that was taken in chambers did not constitute what is commonly termed "in camera testimony". In camera testimony simply means that the regular procedure of the hearing is followed, qualified only by the fact that it is in private. Here, the judge merely asked the child questions in his chambers. None of the usual procedure applied. Id. Under Family Court Act Sec. 153(b), the judge has discretion to dispense with the oath before taking the testimony of a minor. See New York Family Court Act, Article 10, Section 153(b) (McKinney's, 1987).

[108] See Matter of Christina F., 135 Misc.2d 495 (Fam. Ct. 1987) (the child testified that her father had masturbated in front of her as well as touched her vagina).

[109] *Id.*

[110] *Id.*

ANALYSIS

In Family Court, there are several types of evidence which in and of themselves are sufficient to corroborate children's out-of-court statements. They include certain medical conditions,[111] validation testimony,[112] other hearsay statements,[113] and unsworn testimony.[114] The justification offered by the courts for the acceptance of each differs. For example, courts reason that because medical evidence and validation interviews are based in scientific work, they are inherently trustworthy.[115] The rationale for allowing hearsay statements to corroborate each other is not clearly articulated.[116] Finally, the courts have relied on their assessment of a particular child's abilities as a justification for allowing his or her unsworn testimony to corroborate out-of-court statements.[117]

These decisions indicate a tendency of Family Court judges to adjust the rules of evidence in order to protect children who may be victims of abuse. Thus, family court judges accept a very expansive definition of the corroboration amendment allowing virtually "any other evidence" to serve to corroborate out-of-court statements.[118] The extreme example is allowing hearsay statements to act as corroboration for other hearsay statements.[119] Here, evidence requiring substantiation receive substantiation from exactly the same type evidence which required its own substantiation (the second hearsay statement). Validation testimony, to the degree it relies on a child's out-of-court disclosures of sexual abuse, is also hearsay. Considering the theoretical underpinnings of the hearsay rule,[120] it is difficult to understand how hearsay can be sustained as appropriate corroboration for other hearsay in that the respondent is twice denied the opportunity to cross examine the hearsay declarant.

Although the Sixth Amendment confrontation right is not an issue in family court, the power of the state with all its resources versus the individual still remains. Even though the potential consequences of an adjudication of maltreatment carries no criminal penalties, other impairments of liberty interests clearly follow. Similarly, these proceedings may not be without harm to the child, who may be separated

---

[111] See *supra* note 83 and accompanying text.
[112] See Matter of Linda K., 132 A.D.2d 149 (1987). See also *supra* notes 37–45 and accompanying text.
[113] See *supra* notes 98–105 and accompanying text.
[114] See Matter of Christina F., 135 Misc.2d 495 (1987). See also *supra* notes 106–110 and accompanying text.
[115] See Matter of E.M., 137 Misc.2d 197 (1985). Obviously for the former of the two, this is clearly acceptable. For example, outside of artificial insemination, there is only one medical explanation for pregnancy. On the other hand, validation testimony is based on clinical procedures which have, as yet, little, if any, scientific grounding. See *supra* notes 59–81 and accompanying text.
[116] See Matter of Francis Charles, Jr., 69 N.Y.2d 611 (1987).
[117] See Matter of Christina F., 135 Misc.2d 495 (1987).
[118] The amendment was an addition to the statute—the phrase "any other evidence" was added. See New York Family Court Act, Article 10, Section 1046 (a)(vi) (McKinney's, 1985).
[119] See Matter of Francis Charles, Jr., 69 N.Y.2d 611, 517 N.Y.S.2d 1026 (1987).
[120] See *supra* note 15 and accompanying text. The hearsay rule's history begins as early as 1500. During this early period hearsay statements were received, albeit against opposition. The exacting development of this principle paralleled that of trial by jury, thus it was not until the 1700s that the hearsay rule gained its precision. See 5 Wigmore on Evidence, Section 1364 (1974).

from family members. In order to afford adequate due process protections,[121] the constitutional rights of the parents[122] who are accused in these proceedings should be balanced against the need to protect the child.[123]

One of the main principles of due process is the avoidance of error.[124] In these cases it appears that family court judges will err on the child's side in order to protect the child. Undoubtedly, the goal for the liberal standard of proof in child protective proceedings—i.e., protecting the best interests of the child—is valid.[125] Indeed, the inherent difficulties that accompany adjudication of these cases makes the child protective worker's and the judge's dilemma even more understandable.[126] Yet it is important to recognize the problem that accompanies allowing, and indeed relying on, evidence which would normally be subject to exclusion as hearsay or as a prejudicial invasion of the province of the trier of fact.[127] Experts have been allowed to offer opinions as to whether the child is credible, was abused and whether the accused was the abuser.[128,129] The Court in *Matter of Nicole V.*[130] implied that such evidence has been accepted in New York[131] and by courts in other jurisdictions, even in criminal cases, either to bolster credibility of child victims[132] or to corroborate their testimony.[133]

---

[121] One of the fundamental concepts of due process is that it is flexible and that each circumstance does not call for the same types of protections. See Mathews v. Eldridge, 424 U.S. 319 (1976). When applying this concept one court concluded that, "due process requirements are met by permitting a finding of abuse to be made on the basis of a child's out-of-court statement which is corroborated by any competent, nonhearsay, relevant evidence...". Matter of Linda K., 132 A.D.2d 149 quoting Matter of Nicole V., 123 A.D.2d 97, 105 (2nd Dept., 1985). This is interesting in light of the cases cited throughout this article which allow hearsay statements to corroborate children's out-of-court statements. See Matter of Francis Charles, Jr., 69N.Y.2d 611 (1987).

[122] In many intrafamilial sexual abuse cases the alleged abuser is either the father or the stepfather of the victim, and so it is being assumed here. The percentage of cases involving another relative, i.e. an uncle or a brother, is lower. See Peters, Wyatt, Finkelhor, *supra* note 4.

[123] This is often the argument used by appellants when appealing adverse family court decisions. In Matter of Linda K., 132 A.D.2d 149 (1987), the appellant argued unsuccessfully that validation testimony by itself did not constitute corroboration of the child's out-of-court statements. He argued that, 'in view of the stigma attached to being labeled a child abuser, due process mandates that more substantial proof must be adduced before a finding of abuse can be affirmatively established'. *Id.* at 709.

[124] See Mathews v. Eldrige, 424 U.S. 319 (1976).

[125] See *supra* note 37 and accompanying text.

[126] See *supra* note 11 and accompanying text.

[127] Even the hearsay exceptions most typically applied to sexual assault cases—excited utterances, medical complaints, and complaint of rape—have limited merit in child sexual abuse proceedings because of the unusual nature of the offense. See D. Whitcomb (1985). When the victim is a child: issues for judges and prosecutors. U.S. Department of Justice (August). See also People v. Riggio, WL 121201 (4th Dept., 1988) (conviction reversed in part because of the prosecutor's use of the excited utterance exception to admit mother's testimony about child's out-of-court statement). When there is not a well-rooted hearsay exception applicable to a circumstance such as this, FRE 803 the "catch-all" residual exception would be used. The test in these cases is whether the probative value of the evidence outweighs any prejudicial effect that it may cause to the person against whom it is being offered. See Fed. R. Evid. 803.

[128] See Matter of Linda K., 132 A.D.2d 149 (1987). But see Matter of Sanchez 535 N.Y.S.2d 937 (Family Court, 1988).

[129] Family court judges will distinguish evidence that the child has been abused from evidence showing the respondent was the abuser. See Matter of Dara R., 119 A.D.2d 579 (2nd Dept., 1986).

[130] 71 N.Y.2d 112 (1987).

[131] See People v. Keindl, 68 N.Y.2d 410, 509 N.Y.S.2d 790 (1986) (court allowed use of expert in criminal proceeding since the testimony did not go to the ultimate question of whether the defendant was guilty, but rather referred to the psychological reactions of children who are sexually abused).

[132] The Court cited State v. Kim, 64 Haw 598, 645 P 2d1330; State v Middleton, 294 Ore 427, 657 P2d 1215, at 121.

[133] The Court cited State v. Sandberg, 392 NW2d 298 (Minn), at 121.

In some jurisdictions, courts have been quite restrictive in the purposes for which expert testimony on the child abuse syndrome may be admitted in a criminal trial. Such expert testimony on the child sex abuse accommodation syndrome, for example, may be limited to rebuttal of myths or misconceptions about victims of child abuse that would challenge a witness' credibility, but not to establish that the child has been the victim of abuse.[134] In *People v. Bowker*, for example, the California court noted: "It is one thing to say that child abuse victims often exhibit a certain characteristic or that a particular behavior is not inconsistent with a child having been molested. It is quite another to conclude that where a child meets certain criteria, we can predict with a reasonable degree of certainty that he or she has been abused. The former may be appropriate in some circumstances; the latter is clearly not".[135] In California criminal courts, expert testimony may not be admitted on the question of whether the defendant committed the alleged sexual abuse, or in the case of an expert testifying to other than a medical examination, as to whether the abuse occurred. It may be that experts do have special skills in eliciting disclosures from children, and the court should not be deprived of that testimony. However, the courts should consider whether expert testimony in sex abuse cases should be limited to reports of disclosures. In the absence of disclosures, testimony concerning the child's credibility, whether the child has been abused, and whether the respondent was the abuser probably should not be admitted. The scientific basis for such testimony at present appears to be too weak. On the other hand, expert testimony might be very helpful in assisting the court to understand puzzling aspects of a child's behavior or to develop dispositions and treatment plans.

CONCLUSIONS

The dilemma faced by lawmakers when addressing the issue of child sexual abuse is difficult. The lack of evidence beyond the word of the child, the large number of cases involving familial relations, and the particularly repugnant nature of the act, all contribute to the frustration and distress experienced by everyone involved. Courts and policy-makers have attempted to deal with these difficulties by allowing less stringent evidentiary standards. Presumably children are protected from abusive circumstances and the difficulties associated with prosecution are ameliorated. In light of the history of the deficient treatment of child sexual abuse cases, these benefits are precious indeed. However, as with most policy changes, the intended benefits may be accompanied by unforeseen costs. In this instance the costs stem from the admittance of questionable evidence which may sometimes lead to erroneous findings of abuse, even when the fact finders are judges who are trained to sift evidence. The safeguards that are introduced by carefully examining the balance between probative and prejudicial values may be weakened. Perhaps we do wish to adjust the equities to protect children, and we certainly do not wish to bring all the formality of a criminal trial into a child protective proceeding, but that policy should be reviewed with due regard for existing knowledge.

[134] See People v. Bowker, 249 Cal. Rptr. 886 (Cal. App. 4 Dist. 1988). (The expert testimony was admitted when the two-year-old victim gave inconsistent accounts of what happened, and denied that some episodes of abuse has occurred. The expert testified that inconsistency was to be expected, is commonplace and should not invalidate a child's response.)
[135] *Id.* at 891.

A Comprehensive Approach to
Child Hearsay Statements in Sex Abuse Cases

The incidence of sexual abuse of young children has increased dramatically in recent years.[1] The crimes committed are predominantly nonviolent in nature[2] and almost always occur in secrecy, with the child usually being the only witness.[3] No particular age group is immune to sexual abuse,[4] nor are the offenders confined to any particular class of persons.[5] Indeed, more often than not, the offender is a parent, relative, or an acquaintance of the child.[6]

Detecting sex abuse, as well as convicting its perpetrators, is exceptionally difficult,[7] due to the lack of witnesses[8] and corroborative physical evidence,[9] and to the reluctance or inability of the victim to testify against the defend-

---

1. The American Humane Association's national study of state child-protection statistics showed a 200% increase in the reporting of sexual abuse since 1976. By 1980, there were 25,000 reported cases of child sex abuse per year. Collins, Studies Find Sexual Abuse of Children is Widespread, N.Y. Times, May 13, 1982, at C1, col. 1, C10, col. 2.

These statistics may, in fact, understate the problem, for a substantial number of the cases are never reported. Either the child does not report the incident, see National Center on Child Abuse and Neglect, Child Sex Abuse: Incest, Assault and Sexual Exploitation 2 (1981); Landis, Experiences of 500 Children with Adult Sexual Deviation, 30 Psychiatric Q. Supp. 91, 99 (1956), or the parents refuse to go to the authorities, see Collins, supra, at C10, cols. 5-6.

Estimates of the actual number of sexual assaults have varied widely. The National Center on Child Abuse and Neglect estimated that more than 100,000 cases of sexual abuse occur annually. See National Center on Child Abuse and Neglect, supra, at 2. Other estimates have reached as high as 200,000 to 500,000 sexual assaults per year for female children only. See Schultz, The Child Sex Victim: Social, Psychological and Legal Perspectives, 52 Child Welfare 147, 148 (1973).

2. See Flammang, Interviewing Child Victims of Sex Offenders, in The Sexual Victimology of Youth 175, 177 (L. Schultz ed. 1980); MacFarlane, Sexual Abuse of Children, in The Victimization of Women 86, 87 (1978); Schultz, supra note 1, at 149.

3. See Stevens & Berliner, Special Techniques for Child Witnesses, in The Sexual Victimology of Youth 246, 248 (L. Schultz ed. 1980).

4. The ages of the victims range from early infancy (one or two months) to 17 or 18 years. Sgroi, Sexual Molestation of Children, Children Today, May-June 1975, at 18, 20.

5. See Collins, supra note 1, at C1, col. 1 (excerpt from an interview with Dr. Gene Abel, Director of the Sexual Behavior Clinic of the New York State Psychiatric Institute):

For the most part parents have told their children to stay away from men who are wearing raincoats and carrying candy. . . . But none of our patients [sex offenders of children] wear raincoats and carry candy. They come from all walks of life and all socioeconomic categories, and they look just like the neighbor next door. They may even be the neighbor next door.

6. See D. Finkelhor, Sexually Victimized Children 73 (1979); MacFarlane, supra note 2, at 86; Sgroi, supra note 4, at 20; Stevens & Berliner, supra note 3, at 246.

7. In a 1969 study of 250 cases of child sex abuse that had been reported to New York City's protective services, less than one percent of the molesters were sent to jail. Collins, supra note 1, at C10, col. 5.

Only 50% of the sex offenders (238 men) in the Sexual Behavior Clinic at the New York State Psychiatric Institute had ever spent time in jail. These men had committed a total of 16,666 acts of child molestation, an average of 68.3 molestations per offender. Id. at C1, col. 1, C10, col. 1.

8. See Stevens & Berliner, supra note 3, at 248; infra notes 47-49 and accompanying text.

9. See MacFarlane, supra note 2, at 87, 88; Schultz, supra note 1, at 149; infra notes 44-46 and accompanying text.

ant.[10] Even when the child does appear in court and testifies, he or she is often met with skepticism and disbelief.[11] Consequently, to establish the guilt of the defendant, many prosecutors have tried to introduce the out-of-court statements of the victim into evidence through the testimony of witnesses who heard the statements.[12] Since the hearsay rule[13] generally prohibits the introduction of these statements, an exception to the rule is often sought.[14] Courts have used a variety of approaches in determining whether an exception should apply.

This Note argues that the various approaches that have been taken by the courts to child hearsay statements in sex abuse cases are unsatisfactory. Given the unusual circumstances attendant to child sex abuse and the special characteristics of its young victims, the rationale of the hearsay rule and its exceptions requires that an alternative approach be employed to assess the admissibility of child hearsay statements. The Note begins by examining the traditional bases of the hearsay rule and the underlying logic of its exceptions. After analyzing the need for and reliability of out-of-court statements by children in such cases, the Note reviews and then critiques the various ways courts have treated these hearsay declarations. The Note concludes that these approaches inadequately assess the probative value of child hearsay statements in sex abuse cases. Instead, it proposes the adoption of an analysis similar to that embodied in a recently enacted Washington statute. The statute admits a child's out-of-court declaration if the time, content, and circumstances of the statement provide sufficient indicia of reliability.[15]

I. BACKGROUND LAW

A. *The Hearsay Rule*

Hearsay consists of "[out-of-court] statement[s] . . . offered in evidence to prove the truth of the matter asserted."[16] Under traditional formulations of

---

10. See Libai, The Protection of the Child Victim of a Sexual Offense in the Criminal Justice System, *in* The Sexual Victimology of Youth 187, 233 (L. Schultz ed. 1980); MacFarlane, supra note 2, at 99–100; infra notes 60–62 and accompanying text.

11. See Brown v. United States, 152 F.2d 138, 139 (D.C. Cir. 1945); Fitzgerald v. United States, 443 A.2d 1295, 1299 (D.C. 1982); Stevens & Berliner, supra note 3, at 252.

12. See, e.g., United States v. Nick, 604 F.2d 1199 (9th Cir. 1979) (federal government attempts to introduce testimony of child's mother as to statement made by child after allegedly being sodomized by his babysitter); State v. Boodry, 96 Ariz. 259, 394 P.2d 196 (1964) (state tries to introduce testimony of child's mother and neighbor as to statements made by the child after her alleged rape); infra notes 72–115, 123–35, 141–53 and accompanying text.

13. The hearsay rule prohibits the introduction into evidence of testimony or written evidence of a statement made out of court when the statement is being offered as an assertion to show the truth of the matters asserted therein. See E. Cleary, McCormick on Evidence 579–86 (2d ed. 1972) [hereinafter cited as McCormick].

14. See infra notes 72–115, 123–35, 141–53, and accompanying text.

15. The statute also requires that the hearing on admissibility be conducted outside the presence of the jury and either that the child testify at the proceeding or, if the child is unavailable, corroborative evidence of the act be provided. 1982 Wash. Legis. Serv. ch. 129, § 2 (West).

16. Fed. R. Evid. 801(c); accord McCormick, supra note 13, at 584. Such statements may be oral or written and may even incorporate nonverbal conduct if the conduct was intended to be an assertion. Fed. R. Evid. 801(a).

the hearsay rule, evidence concerning these statements is barred from use in court unless the original declarant testifies in court, where he may be cross-examined as to the grounds of his out-of-court assertion and as to his qualifications to make the assertion.[17]

The rule against admission of hearsay statements stems from the long-established belief that cross-examination is the best vehicle for discovering the truth and that the most reliable statements come from the witness stand.[18] By questioning in court the person who made the original statement, the trier of fact can detect and eliminate any inaccuracies in the witness's perception, memory, and narration of the event.[19] The opportunity to put the declarant under oath and to observe his or her demeanor is another traditional reason for requiring an appearance in court.[20]

B. *Exceptions to the Hearsay Rule*

Despite the primacy attached to cross-examination, exceptions to the hearsay rule have long existed in evidentiary law.[21] The reasons for allowing hearsay to be used are twofold. First, reliability of certain hearsay statements can be assured even without cross-examination of the original declarant.[22] Trustworthiness can be inferred from the fact that the statement was made under or subjected to certain conditions that insure a degree of reliability comparable to that found in a cross-examined statement.[23] Moreover, the recurring need for hearsay evidence constitutes another justification for allow-

---

17. See Fed. R. Evid. art. VIII advisory committee note; 5 Wigmore, Evidence in Trials at Common Law 12 (J. Chadbourn rev. 1974) [hereinafter cited as 5 Wigmore]; McCormick, supra note 13, at §§ 579-81.

18. See Ohio v. Roberts, 448 U.S. 56, 64-65 (1980); California v. Green, 399 U.S. 149, 159 (1970); Fed. R. Evid. art. VIII advisory committee note; 5 Wigmore, supra note 17, at 32 (cross-examination "is beyond any doubt the greatest legal engine ever invented for the discovery of truth.").

19. See G. Lilly, An Introduction to the Law of Evidence 159 (1978); McCormick, supra note 13, at 581-82.

20. See California v. Green, 399 U.S. 149, 158 (1970); McCormick, supra note 13, at 582. But see 5 Wigmore, supra note 17, at 10 (oath is merely incidental to cross-examination and is not an essential justification for the hearsay rule).

21. See 5 Wigmore, supra note 17, at 158.

22. See id. at 252:
There are many situations in which it can be easily seen that such a required test [of cross-examination] would add little as a security, because its purposes had been already substantially accomplished. If a statement has been made under such circumstances that even a skeptical caution would look upon it as trustworthy . . . it would be pedantic to insist on a test whose chief object is already secured.
See also Fed. R. Evid. art. VIII advisory committee note ("Common sense tells that much evidence which is not given under . . . [traditionally required] conditions may be inherently superior to much that is.").

23. See 4 J. Weinstein & M. Berger, Weinstein's Evidence, ¶ 800[01], at 800-11 (1981 & Cum. Supp. 1982) [hereinafter cited as Weinstein's Evidence] (credibility of declarant depends upon the opportunity declarant had to observe event, circumstances surrounding the statement, and declarant's relationship to the case; excluding statements merely because they have not been given in court cripples judicial process).

ing its use in contravention of the hearsay rule.[24] Such need is usually found in situations where the declarant is dead or otherwise unavailable for cross-examination,[25] or where the statements contain unique evidentiary value, unobtainable from other sources.[26]

These two principles, trustworthiness and necessity, thus serve as the underlying rationales for exceptions to the hearsay rule.[27] In applying these two principles, judges over time have set aside certain classes of hearsay statements that possess similar or identical guarantees of trustworthiness.[28] The class-exception system constitutes the general framework under which hearsay statements are evaluated for their credibility, although in many jurisdictions the trial judge retains the power to admit evidence that falls outside a specific class exception but nevertheless is still reliable and necessary.[29] Today, the class-exception system exists in statutory form at the federal level[30] and in some states,[31] as well as in common law form in others.[32]

C. *Constitutional Constraints on the Use of Hearsay Statements*

Despite the widespread acceptance of hearsay rule exceptions, their use is constitutionally restricted. The sixth amendment requires that "[i]n all criminal prosecutions, the accused shall enjoy the right . . . to be confronted with the witnesses against him."[33] This provision has never been read to exclude the

---

24. See Fed. R. Evid. art. VIII advisory committee note ("[W]hen the choice is between evidence which is less than best and no evidence at all, only clear folly would dictate an across-the-board policy of doing without.").

25. 5 Wigmore, supra note 17, at 253.

26. Id.

27. See Fed. R. Evid. 803 & 804 advisory committee notes; Cornelius v. State, 12 Ark. 782, 804 (1852); Garwood v. Dennis, 4 Binn. 314, 328 (Pa. 1811).

28. Fed. R. Evid. art. VIII advisory committee note; 5 Wigmore, supra note 17, at 253-55 ("the exceptions have been established casually in the light of practical experience, and with little or no effort . . . at generalization or comprehensive planning. The courts have had in mind merely to sanction certain situations as a sufficient guarantee of trustworthiness.").

29. See, e.g., Fed. R. Evid. 803(24) & 804(b)(5); Ariz. R. Evid. 803(24) & 804(b)(6); S.D. R. Evid. 19-16-35; Wyo. R. Evid. 803(24), 804(b)(6). But see Note, Residual Exception to the Hearsay Rule, 10 Loy. U. Chi. L.J. 611, 613-14 (1979) (Illinois retains a rigid common law system of hearsay exceptions; evaluation of evidence is restricted to the framework of these established exceptions.).

30. The Federal Rules of Evidence contain 24 exceptions to the hearsay rule that can be invoked regardless of whether the declarant is available for cross-examination. These exceptions include present sense impressions, recorded recollections, records of regularly conducted activity, and public records and reports. See Fed. R. Evid. 803. There are five additional exceptions in the Federal Rules that can be used only if the declarant is unavailable. These include former testimony and statements against interest. See Fed. R. Evid. 804.

31. See, e.g., Me. R. Evid.; Mont. R. Evid.; Okla. Stat. Ann. tit. 12 §§ 2803(24), 2804(5) (1980); Wyo. R. Evid. 803(24) & 804(b)(6). Approximately 22 states have statutory rules of evidence similar to the Federal Rules; the remaining states possess common law rules of evidence. See 4 Weinstein's Evidence, supra note 23, art. VIII.

32. See, e.g., People v. Robinson, 73 Ill. 2d 192, 383 N.E.2d 164 (1978) (court applies excited utterance exception); People v. Egan, 78 A.D.2d 34, 434 N.Y.S.2d 55 (1980) (court admits statements as declarations against penal interest). State hearsay exceptions, both statutory and common law, closely parallel the federal statutory exceptions.

33. U.S. Const. amend. VI.

admission of all hearsay evidence,[34] yet it has nonetheless placed significant limits on the use of such evidence.[35]

Although the Supreme Court has been reluctant to lay down principles that would determine the constitutionality of all hearsay exceptions under the confrontation clause,[36] admitting a declarant's out-of-court statements in situations where the declarant is available as a witness probably does not violate the confrontation clause.[37] However, when the declarant is not testifying and is unavailable to be cross-examined, the use of hearsay exceptions must fulfill certain constitutional requirements. In this context, to be admitted, the hearsay statement must either fall within a firmly rooted hearsay exception[38] or, if the statement does not qualify for any exception, present particularized guarantees of trustworthiness.[39]

II. Application of Hearsay Principles to Children's Hearsay Statements in Sex Abuse Cases

The principles underlying the hearsay rule require that an out-of-court statement be admissible only if the requisite need and reliability can be shown.[40] Because of the unique circumstances of child sex abuse, hearsay statements of the victim are especially necessary to establish the guilt of the defendant.[41] In addition, the reliability of such statements must be evaluated with careful attention to these circumstances. Even though out-of-court declarations by the victim may not be inherently reliable, they are, at the very least, as reliable as his or her in-court statements, and moreover, trustworthiness can ultimately be determined by looking to circumstantial indicia of reliability.[42]

A. Need for Children's Hearsay Statements

The unusually compelling need for children's hearsay statements in sex abuse cases is demonstrated primarily by the fact that the statements often constitute the only proof of the crime.[43] Physical corroboration is rare, for the

---

34. See Ohio v. Roberts, 448 U.S. 56, 64 (1980); Mattox v. United States, 156 U.S. 237, 243 (1895).

35. See Mancusi v. Stubbs, 408 U.S. 204 (1972); Lilly, supra note 19, at 275.

36. California v. Green, 399 U.S. 149, 162 (1970).

37. Id. at 158–61.

38. Ohio v. Roberts, 448 U.S. 56, 66 (1980).

39. Id.

40. See supra notes 16–39 and accompanying text.

41. See infra notes 43–51 and accompanying text.

42. See infra notes 52–71, 108–15 and accompanying text.

43. See Joint Hearings on SB 4461 before the Washington State Senate Judiciary Comm. and Washington State House Ethics, Law & Justice Comm., 47th Leg., 1982 sess. 23 (January 28, 1982) (child's hearsay statements are usually the only evidence in a child molesting case) (testimony of Lucy Berliner, social worker, Sexual Assault Center in Seattle, Washington) (transcript on file at the office of the Columbia Law Review) [hereinafter cited as Joint Hearings]; infra notes 44–51 and accompanying text.

crimes committed are predominantly nonviolent in nature.[44] Most crimes consist of petting, exhibitionism, fondling, and oral copulation, activities that do not involve forceful physical contact.[45] The lack of physical corroboration can also be attributed to the fact that most children, for a variety of reasons, do not resist their attackers and succumb easily.[46]

In addition, witnesses other than the victim and perpetrator are rare; people simply do not molest children in front of others.[47] Most often, the offender is a relative or close acquaintance of the child[48] who is likely to have many opportunities to be alone with the child.[49]

Finally, since a child's memory fades rapidly over time, the account given closer in time to the actual event is the one more likely to be accurate.[50] The

---

44. See Flammang, supra note 2, at 177:
Types of offenses run the totality of the continuum of the human sexual experience. The offenses include homosexuality, sodomy, incest, normally accepted acts of intercourse, various methods of oral copulation, and numerous incidents of sex play. The latter is most frequently encountered, due to the physical differences between the victim and the adult offender and the pain that is likely to occur during the act of penetration.
See also MacFarlane, supra note 2, at 87; Schultz, supra note 1, at 149; Joint Hearings, supra note 43, at 22–23 (testimony of Lucy Berliner, social worker, Sexual Assault Center in Seattle, Washington) (child sex abuse basically consists of nonviolent molestation).

45. See, e.g., Haley v. State, 157 Tex. Crim. 150, 151, 247 S.W.2d 400, 401 (1952); Flammang, supra note 2, at 177.

46. See MacFarlane, supra note 2, at 88:
Children are accessible targets for a number of reasons. They have been conditioned to comply with authority; they are in subordinate positions and are fearful of threats; they are intensely curious; they are susceptible to bribes and the promise of reward. In addition, children are often naive with regard to social norms and values, and . . . may respond willingly to intimate and gentle contact which they may associate with feelings of being loved . . . . Thus, the use of physical violence is rare because it isn't necessary; children by their very nature make ideal victims of sexual exploitation.
Even when physical injury is inflicted, there is a chance that it may not be diagnosed as related to sex abuse due to the unwillingness of many parents and physicians to entertain the possibility that a child has been sexually assaulted.
Recognition of sexual molestation in a child is entirely dependent on the individual's inherent willingness to entertain the possibility that the condition may exist. Unfortunately, willingness to consider diagnosis of suspected child molestation frequently seems to vary in inverse proportion to the individual's level of training . . . . The lack of preparation and willingness of many physicians to assist patients with sexual problems in general has often been noted. When the patient is a child, these deficiencies are extremely serious.
Sgroi, Sexual Molestation of Children, supra note 4, at 21; see also R. Brant & V. Tisza, The Sexually Misused Child, *in* The Sexual Victimology of Youth 46 (L. Schultz ed. 1980).

47. See Joint Hearings, supra note 43, at 23 (testimony of Lucy Berliner, social worker, Sexual Assault Center in Seattle, Washington).

48. See Finkelhor, supra note 6, at 73; MacFarlane, supra note 2, at 86; Sgroi, supra note 4, at 20; Stevens & Berliner, supra note 3, at 246; Joint Hearings, supra note 43, at 21 (testimony of Steve Adkins, detective, Special Assault Section of King County Police Department) (in King County, Washington, stepfathers constitute the highest percentage of sex offenders).

49. See United States v. Nick, 604 F.2d 1199, 1201 (9th Cir. 1979) (babysitter sexually assaults three-year-old victim in privacy of locked bedroom); State v. Ritchey, 107 Ariz. 552, 553–54, 490 P.2d 558, 559–60 (1971) (family friend molests two sisters while on an outing); Oldham v. State, 167 Tex. Crim. 644, 646, 322 S.W.2d 616, 618 (1959) (neighbor in his own house molests child who had come to play with neighbor's dogs).

50. See A.D. Yarmey, The Psychology of Eyewitness Testimony 204–05 (1979) (children possess inferior long-term and short-term memories when compared to adults); Stevens & Berliner, supra note 3, at 254 (child's memory of details blurs quickly). But see Altemeyer, Fulton & Berney, Long-Term Memory Improvement: Confirmation of a Finding by Piaget, 40 Child

child's inability to recollect details is especially significant in light of the great lapse of time between the commission of the crime and the trial.[51]

B. *Reliability of Children's Hearsay Statements*

Whether out-of-court statements by children are intrinsically reliable is questionable. Some courts and commentators hold that such statements, standing alone, are trustworthy. Two justifications are commonly offered. First, it is highly unlikely that children persist in lying to their parents or other figures of authority about sex abuse.[52] Second, children do not have enough knowledge about sexual matters to lie about them.[53] In contrast, other courts and commentators, focusing on the well-established tendency of children to fantasize and tell stories, have concluded that these statements are not inherently reliable.[54]

Nevertheless, in child sex abuse cases, the victim's out-of-court statements may, in fact, be more trustworthy than his or her in-court testimony. Requiring a child victim to testify in a sex abuse case adversely affects his or her perception[55] and memory[56] and yields poor and unconvincing evidence. The courtroom experience is extremely traumatic and stressful for most children,[57] despite the steps taken to alleviate this problem.[58] Children are fre-

---

Dev. 845 (1969) (study finds that memories of kindergarten children improved over a period of six months).

51. See United States v. Jones, 477 F.2d 1213 (D.C. Cir. 1973) (eight- to nine-month lapse between incident and trial); People v. Debreczeny, 74 Mich. App. 371, 253 N.W.2d 776 (1977) (20-month lapse between date of defendant's arrest and commencement of trial); Stevens & Berliner, supra note 3, at 248 (average time for adjudication of child sex abuse cases in Seattle is six months).

52. Stevens & Berliner, supra note 3, at 250.

53. See Wold v. State, 57 Wis. 2d 344, 357-58, 204 N.W.2d 482, 491 (1973); Williams v. State, 145 Tex. Crim. 536, 549, 170 S.W.2d 482, 490 (1943). See also Flammang, supra note 2, at 184 (details about sexual acts are not within the common experiential knowledge of a child).

54.
> A woman's uncorroborated tale of a sex offense is not more reliable than a man's. A young child's is far less reliable. "It is well recognized that children are more highly suggestible than adults. Sexual activity, with the aura of mystery that adults create about it, confuses and fascinates them. Moreover they have, of course, no real understanding of the serious consequences of the charges they make . . . ."

Wilson v. United States, 271 F.2d 492, 492-93 (D.C. Cir. 1959) (citing Guttmacher & Weihofen, Psychiatry & the Law 374 (1952)); accord United States v. Wiley, 492 F.2d 547, 550 (D.C. Cir. 1973); Brown v. United States, 152 F.2d 138, 139 (D.C. Cir. 1945).

55. See infra notes 57-65 and accompanying text; cf. Yarmey, supra note 50, at 208-09 (citing 1977 study that found that children are adversely affected by the stress inherent in making identifications from lineups, in contrast to identifications made from colored slides; 12% accuracy compared to 29% accuracy).

56. Live testimony thus exacerbates a child's loss of memory over time. See supra note 50 and accompanying text.

57. See Joint Hearings, supra note 43, at 24 (testimony of Lucy Berliner, social worker, Sexual Assault Center in Seattle, Washington) (child froze in court despite pretrial confidence; testimony disjointed and jumbled); Libai, supra note 10, at 194-95 (description of "legal process trauma" experienced by children); MacFarlane, supra note 2, at 99; Stevens & Berliner, supra note 3, at 254-55.

58. Some courts, recognizing the trauma exerted on the child, have refused to require the child to testify in certain situations. See State v. Boodry, 96 Ariz. 259, 264-65, 394 P.2d 196, 200,

quently subjected to long and extended series of questions and to hostile attacks on their credibility.[59] The stress is intensified if the victim must face the accused again,[60] or if he or she must testify against a close relative,[61] a situation that often occurs in sex abuse cases.[62] Under these circumstances, children, if they reply at all, often give confused and inaccurate answers.[63] Children are susceptible to leading questions[64] and often tailor their replies to appease the examining attorney.[65]

Consequently, in light of the unusual need for child hearsay statements in sex abuse cases,[66] as well as their potentially superior trustworthiness to in-court testimony,[67] the traditional reasons for barring use of such hearsay statements[68] become less compelling. If circumstantial guarantees of trustworthiness are present, the out-of-court declaration should be admitted.[69] Any

---

cert. denied, 379 U.S. 949 (1964). But see Ketcham v. State, 240 Ind. 107, 113, 162 N.E.2d 247, 249-50 (1959) ("[T]he delicacies of the situation should not be permitted to outweigh the fact that a man's liberty and reputable life is at stake. The consequential embarrassment is a small price to pay in return for a showing of the witness' understanding of the details."; quoting Riggs v. State, 235 Ind. 499, 503, 135 N.E.2d 247, 249 (1956)).

59. See Schultz, supra note 1, at 150; Stevens & Berliner, supra note 3, at 255. See also State v. Berry, 101 Ariz. 310, 314, 419 P.2d 337, 341 (1966) (noting defense counsel's vigorous attempts to extract inconsistencies in six-year-old child's testimony by use of calendar dates; court finds no fatal variance between charge set forth and evidence at trial).

60. See Joint Hearings, supra note 43, at 24 (testimony of Lucy Berliner, social worker, Sexual Assault Center in Seattle, Washington) (speaker suggests that judges should allow children to sit away from the defendant to lessen courtroom trauma).

61.

> This author will never forget the look on the face of a 9-year-old incest victim when her father was brought into the courtroom with chains and handcuffs around his hands and waist. With support and reassurance from concerned professionals and family members, she had, up until that point, coped remarkably well with the rigors of the judicial process. Her only comment before she withdrew into a spasmodic, twitching episode . . . was "I did *that* to my Daddy?"

MacFarlane, supra note 2, at 99.

62. See, e.g., State v. Duncan, 53 Ohio St. 2d 215, 216, 373 N.E.2d 1234, 1235 (1978) (stepfather); State v. Boodry, 96 Ariz. 259, 261, 394 P.2d 196, 197, cert. denied 379 U.S. 949 (1964) (father); People v. Baker, 251 Mich. 322, 323, 232 N.W. 381, 382 (1930) (father).

63. Joint Hearings, supra note 43, at 8-9 (testimony of Mary Kay Barbieri, Chief, Criminal Division, King County Prosecutor's Office) (child's testimony is often confused, disjointed and punctuated by long, painful silences).

64. Yarmey, supra note 50, at 200 (children are afraid of authority and will want to please adults by giving the "correct" answer).

65. See McCormick, supra note 16, at 10; Yarmey, supra note 50, at 213 (citing studies showing children's sensitive reactions to suggestive questions).

66. See supra notes 43-51 and accompanying text.

67. See supra notes 55-65 and accompanying text.

68. See supra notes 16-20 and accompanying text.

69. See infra notes 108-15 and accompanying text. In examining the underlying rationale for each of the established exceptions to the hearsay rule, it can be argued that the compelling need for children's hearsay statements, alone, justifies their admission. See 5 Wigmore, supra note 17, at 254:

> These two principles—necessity and trustworthiness—are only imperfectly carried out in the detailed rules under the exceptions . . . . The two principles are not applied with equal strictness in every exception; sometimes one, sometimes the other, has been chiefly in mind. In one or two instances one of them is practically lacking.

prejudice to the defendant caused by attempts to introduce unreliable child hearsay statements[70] could be avoided by requiring the judge to make the evidentiary ruling outside the presence of the jury.[71]

III. Judicial Approaches to the Problem of Child Hearsay Statements in Sex Abuse Cases

Courts, in practice, have evaluated and admitted child hearsay statements using a variety of approaches and exceptions to the hearsay rule. For the most part, these judicial approaches have not properly dealt with the unique circumstances surrounding child sex abuse.

A. *Spontaneous Exclamation Exception*

1. *Description.* The hearsay statements of child victims of sex crimes have almost uniformly been handled under the spontaneous exclamation exception to the hearsay rule.[72] The underlying rationale of the exception is that under certain circumstances extreme excitement or shock may still the declarant's capacity to reflect and contrive.[73] Any statement arising during this

---

70.
In a trial for sexual assault, a child's out of court testimony is often the sole and crucial evidence the state has. The issue usually arises before a jury so that the witness is led up to the point of testifying concerning hearsay statements. Then objection is interposed by defense counsel. The trial judge is faced with a situation where so much of the foundation has already been presented to a jury that nothing will remove the impact of the witness' testimony and the inferences to be drawn therefrom.
Anderson, Children's Out-of-Court Statements Under Rule 908.03 of the Wisconsin Rules of Evidence, 47 Wisc. Bar. Bull. 47, 54 (1974).
71. The Federal Rules of Evidence state that evidentiary rulings should be made outside the presence of the jury "when the interests of justice require or, when an accused is a witness, if he so requests." Fed. R. Evid. 104(c); see also Fed. R. Evid. 103(c) ("In jury cases, proceedings shall be conducted, to the extent practicable, so as to prevent inadmissible evidence from being suggested to the jury by any means, such as making statements or offers of proof or asking questions in the hearing of the jury."). Many states have similar provisions. See, e.g., S.D. Codified Laws Ann., § 19-9-9 (verbatim version of Fed. R. Evid. 104(c)); Wyo. R. Evid. 104(c) (same).
In light of the strong societal feelings against child sex offenders, a hearing out of the presence of the jury may well indeed be essential to the protection of the defendant's rights. See Slough & Knightly, Other Vices, Other Crimes, 41 Iowa L. Rev. 325, 333–34 (1936):
One need not display an imposing list of statistics to indicate that community feelings everywhere are strong against sex offenders. Murderers and thieves may be evil persons, but in common parlance they are not degenerate or perverted, and their crimes are not unnatural and detestable. In the eyes of the layman, the normal person may kill or steal, but only the queer and the abnormal will stoop to the libidinous crimes of incest, sodomy, and rape. Once the accused has been characterized as a person of abnormal bent, driven by biological inclination, it seems relatively easy to arrive at the conclusion that he must be guilty, he could not help but be otherwise.
See also People v. Burton, 55 Cal. 2d 328, 340–41, 359 P.2d 433, 11 Cal. Rptr. 65, 69 (1961) (court must be wary of jury's tendency to be easily swayed by improper evidence in sexual assault cases); Anderson, supra note 70, at 54 (recommending that rulings on child hearsay statements in sex abuse cases be made outside the hearing of the jury).
72. The author has found only four states that have looked beyond the spontaneous declaration exception: Michigan, Wisconsin, Washington and Kansas. See infra notes 123-35, 141-53, 164-65, 189 and accompanying text.
73. See Lancaster v. People, 200 Colo. 448, 615 P.2d 720, 722 (1980); State v. Messamore, 2 Hawaii App. 643, 639 P.2d 413, 418 (1982); Fed. R. Evid. 803(2) advisory committee note; 6 J.

period is thus assumed to be free of conscious fabrication and is considered a sincere and trustworthy response.[74] The exception also entails an element of necessity. Once the condition of shock is over, subsequent utterances by the declarant may not possess the same superior assurance of reliability due to the declarant's regained capability to reflect and distort.[75]

The use of the spontaneous exclamation exception in child sex abuse cases is virtually indistinguishable from its use in cases involving adults. First, there must be a sufficiently startling occurrence that produces, or is likely to produce, the requisite shock or nervous excitement in the child declarant.[76] Second, the resultant shock or nervous excitement must affect the child at the time the statement is made.[77] Although this requirement has been phrased in a variety of ways, all interpretations emphasize the importance of the absence of "reasoned reflection" and premeditation.[78] Finally, the courts have required that the time lapse between the incident and the statement be relatively brief.[79]

Wigmore, Evidence in Trials at Common Law 195 (J. Chadbourn rev. 1976) [hereinafter cited as 6 Wigmore]. The spontaneous exclamation exception is also known as the "excited utterance," see Fed. R. Evid. 803(2), or "res gestae" exception. See Robinson v. State, 232 Ga. 123, 129, 205 S.E.2d 210, 214–15 (1974); Oldham v. State, 167 Tex. Crim. 644, 646–47, 322 S.W.2d 616, 618–19 (1959).

74. See supra note 73; Harnish v. State, 9 Md. App. 546, 549, 266 A.2d 364, 365 (1970) ("[T]he basis for the admission of declarations under the *res gestae* rule is the belief that spontaneous and instinctive utterances, made without opportunity or time for reflection or deliberation, are more likely to produce a true and accurate picture of the transaction or event . . . .").

75. See 6 Wigmore, supra note 73, at 199 (the superior trustworthiness of these extrajudicial statements creates a necessity of resorting to them for unbiased testimony).

76. See State v. Ritchey, 107 Ariz. 552, 555, 490 P.2d 558, 561 (1971) (exception requires a "startling event"); People v. Orduno, 80 Cal. App. 3d 738, 746, 145 Cal. Rptr. 806, 810 (1978) (there must be "some occurrence startling enough to produce nervous excitement and render the utterance spontaneous and unreflecting"), cert. denied, 439 U.S. 1074 (1979). Most courts assume, however, that the alleged sexual assault constitutes such an occurrence, especially for a young child. See People v. Miller, 58 Ill. App. 3d 156, 161, 373 N.E.2d 1077, 1080 (1978).

77. Compare People v. Stewart, 39 Colo. App. 142, 145, 568 P.2d 65, 68 (1977) (child was found to be still in a state of shock when she reported incident to the police), and Wheeler v. United States, 211 F.2d 19, 24 (D.C. Cir. 1953) (sufficient evidence existed to show that child was still highly distraught and in shock when she spoke), cert. denied, 347 U.S. 1019 (1954), with Ketcham v. State, 240 Ind. 107, 112, 162 N.E.2d 247, 249 (1959) (utterance was not made under "uncontrolled domination of the senses"; story was reluctantly drawn out by questions).

78. See Bass v. State, 375 So.2d 540, 543 (Ala. Crim. App. 1979) (statement must be "the reflex product of the immediate sensual impressions, unaided by retrospective mental action") (quoting McElroy's Ala. Evid. § 265.01(11) (1977)); People v. Orduno, 80 Cal. App. 3d 738, 746, 145 Cal. Rptr. 806, 810 (1978) (utterance must be made "while the nervous excitement may be supposed still to dominate and the reflective powers to be yet in abeyance"), cert. denied, 439 U.S. 1074 (1979); Ketcham v. State, 240 Ind. 107, 112, 162 N.E.2d 247, 249 (1959) (utterance must be made under "the immediate and uncontrolled domination of the senses"); Oldham v. State, 167 Tex. Crim. 644, 647, 322 S.W.2d 616, 619 (1959) (declarations must be "the natural and spontaneous outgrowth of the main fact and must exclude the idea of premeditation").

Some courts in older cases drew a line between statements given in response to questions and statements given without prompting. See Smith v. United States, 215 F.2d 682, 683 (D.C. Cir. 1954); Ketcham v. State, 240 Ind. 107, 112, 162 N.E.2d 247, 249 (1959). Recent decisions, however, have not found the distinction compelling. See Fitzgerald v. United States, 443 A.2d 1295, 1304 (D.C. 1982).

79. See State v. Ritchey, 107 Ariz. 552, 555–56, 490 P.2d 558, 561–62 (1971).

In applying these standards, several courts have barred the introduction of narratives by

This requirement, in essence, is merely an additional assurance that the statements have been made spontaneously, before the child has had time to contrive and misrepresent.[80]

In *State v. Boodry*[81] and *People v. Miller*,[82] the children's statements were admitted under the spontaneous exclamation exception. Both courts found that the sexual acts committed constituted sufficiently startling events[83] and that the children spoke spontaneously and without fabrication within minutes of the alleged assault.[84] By contrast, in *Ketcham v. State*,[85] a child's hearsay statement was excluded for lack of spontaneity.[86] This finding was supported by the fact that the child did not report the incident until two hours after the alleged attack and had to be repeatedly questioned in order to bring out the full story.[87]

2. *Inadequacy of Spontaneous Exclamation Exception in Child Sex Abuse Cases.* The analytic framework of the spontaneous exclamation exception in child sex abuse cases and the exception's criteria of trustworthiness are built on the premise that the declarant has the psychology, behavior, and experience of an adult and reacts accordingly. Invocation of the exception in this context assumes that the rationale, criteria, and application of the exception are identical for the statements of both children and adults.[88] This view, however, is unfounded. By treating child declarants as adults, the exception fails to take into account the special circumstances surrounding child sex

---

children, stating that such relation of past events does not contain the requisite spontaneity. See Brown v. United States, 152 F.2d 138, 139 (D.C. Cir. 1945); State v. Shambo, 133 Mont. 305, 310, 322 P.2d 657, 660 (1958). But see Comment, Excited Utterances and Present Sense Impressions as Exceptions to the Hearsay Rule in Louisiana, 29 La. L. Rev. 661, 669 (1969) (arguing that form of statement is irrelevant).

80. See 6 Wigmore, supra note 73, at 202–03. Since the crucial element that buttresses the reliability of such declarations is their spontaneity, the authorities and the case law are concerned that the time span between the event and the making of the statement be very short. State v. Messamore, 2 Hawaii App. 643, 639 P.2d 413, 418 (1982). Generally, courts have not applied this requirement strictly, see Beausoliel v. United States, 107 F.2d 292, 295 (D.C. Cir. 1939); Williams v. State, 145 Tex. Crim. 536, 548–49, 170 S.W.2d 482, 490 (1943), but most are still wary of admitting statements made after a significant delay without a special showing that the child was still under emotional stress. See State v. Wilson, 20 Or. App. 553, 559–60, 532 P.2d 825, 828 (1975) (event producing excited state of declarant was ongoing; victim fled from father and told first person she encountered what had happened); State v. Pace, 301 So. 2d 323, 326 (La. 1974) (child was in company of defendant until she returned home); Haley v. State, 157 Tex. Crim. 150, 151-52, 247 S.W.2d 400, 401 (1952) (defendant remained in child's home until the following morning).

81. 96 Ariz. 259, 394 P.2d 196, cert. denied, 379 U.S. 949 (1964).

82. 58 Ill. App. 3d 156, 373 N.E.2d 1077 (1978).

83. Id. at 161, 373 N.E.2d at 1080; State v. Boodry, 96 Ariz. 259, 264-65, 394 P.2d 196, 200, cert. denied, 379 U.S. 949 (1964).

84. *Boodry*, 96 Ariz. at 264-65, 394 P.2d at 200; *Miller*, 58 Ill. App. at 160-61, 373 N.E.2d at 1080.

85. 240 Ind. 107, 162 N.E.2d 247 (1959).

86. Id. at 112, 162 N.E.2d at 249.

87. Id. at 109, 112, 162 N.E.2d at 248, 249.

88. See supra notes 72–87 and accompanying text.

abuse.[89] It ignores the unusual need for child hearsay statements and, in addition, fails to analyze properly their reliability.[90]

The major weakness of the exception in this context stems from its undue reliance on spontaneity as an indicator of trustworthiness, to the exclusion of other equally valid indicia of reliability.[91] This emphasis on spontaneity is improper for two reasons. First, most children do not view a sexual episode as shocking[92] or even as particularly unusual.[93] Children thus often do not recount the event with the shock or emotion required under the exception. Children are simply not as highly sexualized or moralized as adults. They may not know what has happened to them is wrong.[94] This may be especially true if the child has been involved in an incestuous relationship. A parental imprimatur on the entire situation may often cause the child to view everything as normal.[95] A sexual incident may not be traumatic for other reasons as well. Often, the victims themselves are searching for warmth and affection. "For some, it represents the first time they experience what they perceive to be recognition or special attention from the parent or parent figure."[96] Sexual relationships of substantial duration between children and adults are not uncommon.[97]

---

89. See supra notes 43–65 and accompanying text.

90. Id.

91. See infra notes 108–15 and accompanying text.

92. See Finkelhor, supra note 6, at 65 (only 26% of women assaulted as children surveyed felt shock; 20% felt surprised; 8% remember feeling pleasure); Landis, supra note 1, at 98 (only 12.9% of men and 25.3% of women surveyed viewed experience as shocking); Schultz, supra note 1, at 149.

93. T. McCahill, L. Meyer & A. Fischman, The Aftermath of Rape 44 (1979) ("In many cases, the nature of the event (or events) is merely confusing. Whereas the event is disturbing to the victim, it is perhaps no more disturbing than so many other aspects of a child's life.").

94.
[C]hildren have only a dim sense of adult sexuality. What may seem like a horrible violation of social taboos from an adult perspective need not be so to a child. A sexual experience with an adult may be something unusual, vaguely unpleasant, even traumatic at the moment, but not a horror story. Most children's sexual experiences involve encounters with fondlers and exhibitionists, . . . and "it is difficult to understand why a child, except for its cultural conditioning, should be disturbed at having its genitals touched, or disturbed at seeing the genitals of other persons."
Finkelhor, supra note 6, at 31, quoting A. Kinsey, Sexual Behavior in the Human Female 121 (1953). See also Joint Hearings, supra note 43, at 23 (testimony of Lucy Berliner, social worker, Sexual Assault Center in Seattle, Washington) (children act normally because they are not taught what child molesting is).

95. See People v. Taylor, 66 Mich. App. 456, 460, 239 N.W.2d 627, 629 (1976):
She [the victim] testified further that she never told anyone because her father said that "it wouldn't be right" to tell, and that she felt that "it was private" and thought that "he could get in trouble." In her words: "Because, you know, I mean he never told me it was really wrong, because he was my father and everything."
See also Joint Hearings, supra note 43, at 25 (testimony of Brian Leavitt) (testifying witness was raped and molested repeatedly by stepfather; did not discover such behavior was wrong until sex education teacher told him).

96. MacFarlane, supra note 2, at 88–89.

97. See People v. Taylor, 66 Mich. App. 456, 457, 239 N.W.2d 627, 628 (1976) (father had sexual relations with daughter for four years on a regular basis); Joint Hearings, supra note 43, at 25 (testimony of Brian Leavitt) (testifying witness was raped and molested by stepfather for one to one-and-one-half years); Finkelhor, supra note 6, at 3; Schultz, supra note 1, at 149–50.

This childhood perspective on sexual experiences naturally does not produce the shock or excitement that the law presumes to exist after such an event. Quite often, the incident is related as part of the day's activities without any indication from the child that it was traumatic or unusual. For example, in *Brown v. United States*[98] the three-year-old victim calmly reported her assault in school that day during the course of normal dinnertime conversation. The statement was subsequently excluded for lack of spontaneity.[99]

Second, a significant delay frequently precedes the child's statement, thereby violating the time requirement of the spontaneous exclamation exception.[100] Even when a child is aware of the nature of his or her assault, a report of the event may still not be instantly forthcoming.[101] This delay may be caused by a variety of factors: the victim's fears of not being believed,[102] feelings of confusion and guilt,[103] efforts to forget,[104] and threats against the victim by the defendant.[105] Consequently, a child often keeps silent until something compels him or her to relate what has happened. For example, in one case[106] the five-year-old victim broke silence about his prior sexual assault to prevent being sent to the defendant's house again.[107]

The spontaneous exclamation exception thus unnecessarily bars a significant proportion of probative evidence that should be admitted. By relying solely on spontaneity, the exception ignores the presence of other cogent

---

98. 152 F.2d 138 (D.C. Cir. 1945).

99. Id. at 138; see also Smith v. United States, 215 F.2d 682, 683 (D.C. Cir. 1954) (child spent the time between the alleged offense and the telling of it to her mother in a normal manner in the household); Oldham v. State, 167 Tex. Crim. 644, 646, 322 S.W.2d 616, 618 (1959) (child relates incident in asking for a glass of chocolate milk).

Indeed, many child psychologists note that children are traumatized more by the reactions of their family and society to the incident than by the incident itself. See MacFarlane, supra note 2, at 87; National Center on Child Abuse & Neglect, supra note 1, at 5; Renshaw & Renshaw, Incest, *in* Traumatic Abuse and Neglect of Children at Home 420 (1980).

100. See supra notes 79-80 and accompanying text.

101. See Joint Hearings, supra note 43, at 22 (testimony of Doris Stevens, Director, Sexual Assault Center in Seattle, Washington) ("[T]he younger the victim is and the closer the relationship is to the assailant, the more likely it is to be a longer period of time [before the child reports the incident]. Most children do not report immediately.").

102. Id. at 23.

103. See Stevens & Berliner, supra note 3, at 251; Schultz, supra note 1, at 150; National Center on Child Abuse and Neglect, supra note 1, at 2.

104. See Joint Hearings, supra note 43, at 23 (testimony of Lucy Berliner, social worker, Sexual Assault Center in Seattle, Washington).

105. See Fitzgerald v. United States, 443 A.2d 1295, 1298 (D.C. 1982); Ketcham v. State, 240 Ind. 107, 109, 162 N.E.2d 247, 248 (1959); People v. Bonneau, 323 Mich. 237, 239, 35 N.W.2d 161, 161-62 (1948); see also Joint Hearings, supra note 43, at 19 (testimony of Steve Adkins, Detective, Special Assault Section of King County Police Department) (children feel great fear from even the mildest of threats).

A child may not spontaneously relate the event for other reasons as well. He or she may want to protect younger siblings, see MacFarlane, supra note 2, at 90, or may fear blame for the incident, see National Center on Child Abuse and Neglect, supra note 1, at 2.

106. Harnish v. State, 9 Md. App. 546, 266 A.2d 364 (1970).

107. Id. at 365; see also State v. Messamore, 2 Hawaii App. 643, 639 P.2d 413, 416 (1982) (child unable to control her urination as a result of being raped; tells mother what happened in order to avoid being spanked for urinating on the stairs); People v. Taylor, 66 Mich. App. 456, 460-61, 239 N.W.2d 627, 629-30 (1976) (victim reports being sexually assaulted by her father

circumstantial guarantees of trustworthiness, and the fact that the requisite need for and reliability of children's hearsay statements can be established independently of a showing of shock. To determine accuracy, circumstances such as the age of the child,[108] his or her physical and mental condition,[109] the exact circumstances of the alleged event,[110] the language used by the child,[111] the presence of corroborative physical evidence,[112] the relationship of the accused to the child,[113] the child's family, school, and peer relationships,[114] and the reliability of the testifying witness,[115] can be examined.

3. *Attempts to Mitigate the Harshness of the Spontaneous Exclamation Exception.* Some courts, recognizing the flaws inhering in a mechanical application of the spontaneous exclamation exception to child hearsay statements in sex abuse cases,[116] have attempted to mitigate the arbitrariness of the rule.

---

after being told that her younger sister had told others of being sexually molested by father as well).

108. See Beausoliel v. United States, 107 F.2d 292, 295 (D.C. Cir. 1939) (reflective powers of a young child less likely to be used in sex abuse situation); State v. Ritchey, 107 Ariz. 552, 556, 490 P.2d 558, 562 (1971); Smith v. State, 6 Md. App. 581, 587, 252 A.2d 277, 281 (1969) (tender age of child makes it unlikely that exciting influence of event had subsided quickly); Williams v. State, 145 Tex. Crim. 536, 549, 170 S.W.2d 482, 490 (1943) (tender age of victim makes it unlikely that she knew anything about sexual matters).

109. See United States v. Iron Shell, 633 F.2d 77, 86 (8th Cir. 1980), cert. denied, 450 U.S. 1001 (1981); State v. Wilson, 20 Or. App. 553, 559, 532 P.2d 825, 828 (1975).

110. See State v. Pace, 301 So. 2d 323, 326 (La. 1974); Haley v. State, 157 Tex. Crim. 150, 151–53, 247 S.W.2d 400, 401–02 (1952) (delay in reporting incident due to the fact that child was in the company of the defendant for an extended period of time; child reported assault at first available opportunity).

111. See United States v. Nick, 604 F.2d 1199, 1204 (9th Cir. 1979) ("The childish terminology has the ring of verity and is entirely appropriate to a child of his tender years."); Williams v. State, 145 Tex. Crim. 536, 549, 170 S.W.2d 482, 490 (1943) (childlike manner in which statement was related was entirely appropriate and natural for the victim; disproves notion that statement was premeditated); Joint Hearings, supra note 43, at 9 (testimony of Mary Kay Barbieri, Chief, Criminal Division in King County Prosecutor's Office) (children's statements are often phrased in language that tells a jury that the event occurred).

112. See United States v. Nick, 604 F.2d 1199, 1204 (9th Cir. 1979) (sperm on pants, medical examination); Soto v. Territory, 12 Ariz. 36, 40, 94 P. 1104, 1105 (1908) (lacerated and bleeding rectum); Johnson v. State, 201 Tenn. 11, 13, 296 S.W.2d 832, 833 (1956) (bruises around rectum); Bertrang v. State, 50 Wis. 2d 702, 705–06, 184 N.W.2d 867, 868–69 (1971) (blood on panties).

113. See United States v. Nick, 604 F.2d 1199, 1204 (9th Cir. 1979) (victim knew defendant-babysitter well, not likely to mistake his assailant); People v. Taylor, 66 Mich. App. 456, 460, 239 N.W.2d 627, 629 (1976) (delay in reporting assault is natural when father is the perpetrator; victim likely to have no sense of outrage) (citing People v. Baker, 251 Mich. 322, 326, 232 N.W.2d 381, 383 (1930)).

114. See People v. Price, 33 Misc. 2d 476, 479, 226 N.Y.S.2d 460, 463 (N.Y. Ct. Spec. Sess. 1962) (hearsay statement was not made "in the setting of a hate-filled controversy where the child finds itself involved as a partisan, which setting so often renders children's testimony untrustworthy and even dangerous"); Haley v. State, 157 Tex. Crim. 150, 154, 247 S.W.2d 400, 402 (1952) (child had been ignored by her mother, natural for her to tell neighbors about incident).

115. See United States v. Nick, 604 F.2d 1199, 1204 (9th Cir. 1979) (mother not likely to forget her child's simple shocking seven-word statement; mother was also subjected to cross-examination); Bertrang v. State, 50 Wis. 2d 702, 708, 184 N.W.2d 867, 870 (1971); Joint Hearings, supra note 43, at 8 (testimony of Mary Kay Barbieri, Chief, Criminal Division in King County Prosecutor's Office) (relationship between defendant and testifying witness important in determining reliability of child's statement); see also infra notes 132–35 and accompanying text.

116. See supra notes 91–107 and accompanying text.

Although ostensibly applying the exception, they have gone beyond its established limits and have admitted statements which would normally be excluded under traditional formulations of the spontaneous exclamation exception.

For example, in *Smith v. State*,[117] the Maryland Court of Special Appeals admitted the hearsay statement of a four-year-old rape victim despite the fact that four-and-one-half to five hours had elapsed before she spoke to her mother about the incident.[118] The court ignored the fact that the child was calm at the hospital, hours before she made her statement,[119] and that at trial, the examining doctor had characterized the child's demeanor as "placid."[120]

However, in avoiding the harsh results of the spontaneous exclamation exception in this manner, courts have virtually destroyed the integrity of the exception, stretching it far beyond its traditional bounds,[121] and creating much uncertainty in its application. What courts are in fact doing is looking to various circumstantial guarantees of trustworthiness, of which spontaneity is just one.[122]

B. *Tender Years Exception*

1. *Description*. The Michigan courts have also attempted to escape the arbitrary strictures of the spontaneous exclamation exception through the development of a "tender years" exception specifically applicable to out-of-court statements made by child victims of sex crimes.[123] Although the exception has been recently eliminated by the adoption of the Michigan Rules of

---

117. 6 Md. App. 581, 252 A.2d 277 (1969).

118. Id. at 583-85, 252 A.2d at 278-79.

119. Id. at 583, 252 A.2d at 278.

120. Id. Similarly in State v. Ritchey, 107 Ariz. 552, 490 P.2d 558 (1971), the Arizona Supreme Court allowed the admission of hearsay statements by two sisters, four and six years of age, who had been molested by a family friend. Id. at 555-56, 490 P.2d at 559-60. The statements were accepted under the spontaneous exclamation exception despite the fact that the children did not exhibit any shock or nervous excitement and were merely subdued in their manner. Id. at 555, 490 P.2d at 561; see also People v. Stewart, 39 Colo. App. 142, 145, 568 P.2d 65, 68 (1977) (court admits statement of a six-year-old victim made to police officer two hours after sexual assault, even though child had opportunity to tell others earlier); State v. Noble, 342 So. 2d 170, 172-73 (La. 1977) (court admits statement of four-year-old victim made two days after rape); Haley v. State, 157 Tex. Crim. 150, 151-52, 247 S.W.2d 400, 401 (1952) (court admits statement of four-and-one-half-year-old victim made more than eight hours after rape).

121. See Joint Hearings, supra note 43, at 9 (testimony of Mary Kay Barbieri, Chief, Criminal Division in King County Prosecutor's Office) (Washington courts have extended the excited utterance exception for children in sex abuse cases).

122. See supra notes 108-15 and accompanying text.

123. See, e.g., People v. Turner, 112 Mich. App. 381, 316 N.W.2d 426 (1982), vacated, 332 N.W.2d 150 (Mich. 1983); People v. Dermartzex, 29 Mich. App. 213, 185 N.W.2d 33 (1970), aff'd, 390 Mich. 410, 213 N.W.2d 97 (1973). The exception has been expressly confined to these situations. See People v. Washington, 84 Mich. App. 750, 753-54, 270 N.W.2d 511, 512 (1978) (court refuses to apply "tender years" exception to hearsay statements of young child who witnessed murder of parents; exception limited to sex crime situations). However, the Michigan courts, in at least one case, have extended the exception to child witnesses of sex crimes. See People v. Lovett, 85 Mich. App. 534, 543-45, 272 N.W.2d 126, 129-30 (1978).

Evidence,[124] its genesis and development is still instructive in the area of child hearsay statements in sex abuse cases.

The tender years exception has been characterized as a variation of the spontaneous exclamation exception,[125] but is, in fact, markedly different. The requirement of contemporaneity is dispensed with entirely. The exception admits statements of young victims regardless of how much time has elapsed between the assault and the statement.[126] The delay, however, must be properly explained either by fear instilled in the child or by another "equally effective circumstance."[127] The underlying rationale appears to be the assumption that the child is under continuing duress throughout the entire period.[128] Moreover, the tender years exception allows hearsay to be introduced only for the purposes of corroborating the child's in-court testimony.[129] The exception was first recognized in *People v. Gage*,[130] where the court admitted the hearsay statements of a ten-year-old victim of sexual assault that were made approximately three months after the incident.[131]

By merely requiring that the delay be adequately explained, the tender years approach properly recognized that spontaneity is not the sole indicator of trustworthiness in evaluating children's statements. Michigan courts used the exception to incorporate more appropriate criteria of reliability by broadly

---

124. See People v. Kreiner, 415 Mich. 372, 329 N.W.2d 716, 717 (1982) (tender years exception to the hearsay rule no longer exists).

125. See People v. Baker, 251 Mich. 322, 326, 232 N.W. 381, 383 (1930) ("the admissibility of details of complaint, in the case of very young girls, has been permitted on a liberal extension of the res gestae doctrine"); People v. Turner, 112 Mich. App. 381, 383, 316 N.W.2d 426, 427 (1982) ("[T]he tender years exception is a species of the res gestae exception."), vacated, 332 N.W.2d 150 (Mich. 1983).

126. See People v. Gage, 62 Mich. 271, 275, 28 N.W. 835, 836 (1886) ("[T]he lapse of time occurring after the injury, and before complaint made, is not the test of admissibility.. . ."); infra note 127 and accompanying text.

127. People v. Baker, 251 Mich. 322, 326, 232 N.W. 381, 383 (1930); see also People v. Bonneau, 323 Mich. 237, 240, 35 N.W.2d 161, 162 (1948) (delay excusable due to defendant's threats); People v. Debreczeny, 74 Mich. App. 371, 394, 253 N.W.2d 776, 778 (1977) (delay adequately explained by fact that child interviewer at police station was off duty; statement was made at earliest opportunity the following morning); People v. Dermartzex, 29 Mich. App. 213, 218, 185 N.W.2d 33, 35 (1970), aff'd, 390 Mich. 410, 213 N.W.2d 97 (1973) (delay properly explained by fear engendered in victim by defendant; court notes that defendant was a large man of about 225 pounds and that victim's parents lived in Canada).

128. See People v. Gage, 62 Mich. 271, 275, 28 N.W. 835, 836-37 (1886):

> The female outraged was a girl of tender years . . . and through fear caused by threats made by the accused she refrained from telling her parents of the outrage until they heard it from others whom she had told. She appears to have been under a sort of duress, caused by fear of the whipping which the respondent had impressed upon her mind would befall her if she told her parents, and it was with great reluctance she finally disclosed the facts to her mother, caused by the fear respondent had engendered in her mind.

See also People v. Edgar, 113 Mich. App. 528, 317 N.W.2d 675 (1982).

129. See People v. Kreiner, 415 Mich. 372, 329 N.W.2d 716, 719 (1982) (exception permits hearsay only to corroborate the testimony of the complainant); People v. Taylor, 66 Mich. App. 456, 461, 239 N.W.2d 627, 630 (1976) (hearsay testimony corroborating the details of the alleged statutory rape is permissible under the tender years exception).

130. 62 Mich. 271, 28 N.W. 835 (1886).

131. Id. at 273-74, 28 N.W. at 835-36.

interpreting what constitutes an "equally effective circumstance" for purposes of justifying the delay. Such circumstances have been read to include the presence of threats by the offender,[132] the absence of the child's parents at the time of the assault,[133] the relationship of the offender to the child,[134] and the nature and duration of sexual relations between the child and offender.[135]

2. *Inadequacy of the Tender Years Approach.* Despite the flexibility and sensitivity of the Michigan courts towards the statements of child sex abuse victims, the tender years exception, as it was employed, is flawed. It ignores the unique problems posed by child hearsay statements in these situations and fails to require the presence of sufficient assurances of reliability.

The major shortcoming of the tender years approach is that in many situations the exception allowed impermissible bootstrapping; statements, whose delay was explained solely by the child's hearsay statement itself rather than by independent corroborative evidence, were admitted under the exception. For example, in *People v. Edgar,*[136] the court justified admitting a victim's out-of-court statement made one week after the event because the child's hearsay statement alleged threats of whipping by the defendant.[137] The court ignored the fact that children's statements are not inherently truthful,[138] and that a child's memory is likely to fade quickly over time.[139] While the reliability of the assertion itself may be one factor indicating its admissibility, it cannot be the only factor. To allow the content of the hearsay statement to determine its own validity merely begs the question.[140]

C. *The Residual Exception*

1. *Description.* Another approach that has been used to determine the admissibility of child hearsay statements is the residual hearsay exception. The exception has been employed in Wisconsin[141] and is embodied in sections

---

132. See People v. Bonneau, 323 Mich. 237, 240, 35 N.W.2d 161, 162 (1948); People v. Gage, 62 Mich. 271, 275, 28 N.W. 835, 837 (1886); People v. Edgar, 113 Mich. App. 528, 534, 317 N.W.2d 675, 678 (1982).

133. See People v. Dermartzex, 29 Mich. App. 213, 218, 185 N.W.2d 33, 35 (1970), aff'd, 390 Mich. 410, 213 N.W.2d 97 (1973).

134. See People v. Taylor, 66 Mich. App. 456, 460, 239 N.W.2d 627, 629 (1976).

135. Id.

136. 113 Mich. App. 528, 317 N.W.2d 675 (1982).

137. Id. at 530-31, 317 N.W.2d at 676-78; see also People v. Bonneau, 323 Mich. 237, 239, 35 N.W.2d 161, 162 (1948) (child's statement alleges that defendant "would get after her" if she told); People v. Gage, 62 Mich. 271, 273, 28 N.W. 835, 836 (1886) (child's statement reported threats by defendant of whipping).

138. See supra notes 52-54 and accompanying text. See also Anderson, supra note 70, at 51 (there is no reason for attaching any trustworthiness to that part of the out-of-court statement relating to the reasons for the delay unless there are other independent facts to render the statement reliable).

139. See supra notes 50-51 and accompanying text.

140. When the child's in-court testimony corroborates her hearsay statements, the bootstrapping problem remains unsolved. The hearsay statement still has no guarantee of reliability independent of the child.

141. See Bertrang v. State, 50 Wis. 2d 702, 184 N.W.2d 867 (1971); see also Thomas v. State, 92 Wis. 2d 372, 377, 284 N.W.2d 917, 921 (1979) (state attempts to admit hearsay statement of 16-

908.03(24) and 908.045(6) of the Wisconsin Rules of Evidence.[142] The exception, which parallels rules 803(24) and 804(b)(5) of the Federal Rules of Evidence,[143] admits hearsay statements falling outside the enumerated exceptions if they possess "comparable circumstantial guarantees of trustworthiness."[144]

The Wisconsin courts have employed the residual approach to go beyond the limits of the spontaneous exclamation exception and, like the Michigan courts, have looked for indicia of reliability more suitable for young children. In *Bertrang v. State*,[145] the Supreme Court of Wisconsin admitted the hearsay statement of a nine-year-old victim made two days after she was sexually assaulted by the defendant.[146] In assessing the trustworthiness of the statement, the court looked at the age of the child,[147] the nature of the assault,[148] the presence of physical evidence of the assault,[149] the relationship of the child to the defendant,[150] and the spontaneity of the statement.[151]

Because of its flexibility, the residual exception is superior to the judicial approaches to child hearsay statements examined thus far. Unlike the excited utterance exception, the rule allows the court to look to indicia of reliability in addition to spontaneity, which by itself does not specifically address the special nature of sex abuse cases.[152] Moreover, the residual approach requires that these indicia be independent of the hearsay statement, thereby preventing the bootstrapping problems of the tender years exception.[153]

---

year-old mentally deficient victim of rape under rule 908.03(24); court allows statement in as a prior consistent statement under 908.01(4)(a)).

142. Both rules state: "A statement not specifically covered by any of the foregoing exceptions but having comparable circumstantial guarantees of trustworthiness [is admissible]." Wis. R. Evid. 908.03(24), 908.045(6). Rule 908.03(24) applies whether or not the declarant is available to testify; rule 908.045(6) can be used only when the declarant is unavailable. Cf. Fed. R. Evid. 803(24), 804(b)(5) (residual exceptions under the federal rules).

143. The Wisconsin Rules of Evidence were modeled after the Federal Rules of Evidence, see Wis. R. Evid., 59 Wis. 2d Rp. (Foreword by Chief Justice Hallows); the federal advisory committee notes to the Federal Rules were accordingly included for informational purposes, see id. at R2.

144. Wis. R. Evid. 908.03(24), 908.045(6).

145. 50 Wis. 2d 702, 184 N.W.2d 867 (1971).

146. Id. at 708, 184 N.W.2d at 870.

147. Id. at 706, 184 N.W.2d at 869.

148. Id. at 708, 184 N.W.2d at 870.

149. Id.

150. Id.

151. Id. at 707–08, 184 N.W.2d at 869–70. The court also stated that the reliability of the assertions themselves and the reliability of the testifying witness could also be considered in determining the admissibility of a child's statement. Id. at 708, 184 N.W.2d at 870.

Although purporting to apply the spontaneous exclamation exception, id. at 706–08, 184 N.W.2d at 869–70, the court in *Bertrang* went far beyond the traditional limitations of the exception; the statement was made after a two-day time lapse and was prompted by direct questioning by the victim's mother. Id. at 705–06, 184 N.W.2d at 868–69. See Mitchell v. State, 84 Wis. 2d 325, 332, 267 N.W.2d 349, 352 (1978) (statements in *Bertrang* "were of a type normally covered by a specific exception [spontaneous utterance], but the facts presented did not satisfy the requirements of the specific exception"). In fact, the Judicial Council Committee used *Bertrang* as a basis for establishing the residual exception in the Wisconsin Rules of Evidence and as an example of how the exception should properly be employed. Wis. R. Evid. 908.03(24) judicial council committee note.

152. See supra notes 91–107 and accompanying text.

153. See supra notes 136–39 and accompanying text.

2. *Inadequacy of the Residual Exception.* Despite the potential application of the residual exception to child hearsay statements in child sex abuse cases, the availability of the exception is sharply limited. The exception was never intended to create formal class exceptions to the hearsay rule and cannot be applied to child hearsay statements as a group.[154] Rather, it was intended to be used rarely and only in exceptional circumstances.[155] Thus, the mere availability of the residual exception does not guarantee that courts will not resort to the more traditional analyses that thus far have proved inadequate.[156]

Even if the residual approach is used in the form of a class exception for child hearsay statements, there is great potential for judicial abuse of discretion. Beyond requiring the presence of circumstantial guarantees of trustworthiness, the exception, as it exists in Wisconsin, provides no guidance to the courts in considering the special circumstances of these statements.[157] The open-ended nature of the residual approach is simply not suited for class exceptions, including child hearsay statements in sex abuse cases. These exceptions require more particularized standards of need and trustworthiness.[158]

IV. SOLUTION: WASHINGTON STATUTORY EXCEPTION

The unique nature of child sex abuse cases imposes rigorous demands on courts when assessing the admissibility of child hearsay statements. Not only must the courts be sensitive to the critical need for these statements,[159] but they must also address the various reliability problems posed by the statements.[160] This is essential if the underlying principles of the hearsay rule are to be followed[161] and the defendant's rights under the confrontation clause

---

154. See Wis. R. Evid. 908.03(24) federal advisory committee note, 59 Wis. 2d R301–02 (1973) (exception does not contemplate an unfettered exercise of judicial discretion; it should be used only to treat new and presently unanticipated situations).

155. See Wis. R. Evid. 908.03(24) federal advisory committee note, 59 Wis. 2d R301–02 (1973). Cf. S. Rep. No. 1277, 93rd Cong., 2d Sess. 20, reprinted in 1974 U.S. Code Cong. & Ad. News 7051, 7066 ("The residual exceptions are not meant to authorize major judicial revisions of the hearsay rule . . . ."); 4 Weinstein's Evidence, supra note 23, ¶ 803(24)[01], at 803-296 (emphasis added):

> Congress did not wish to see the courts create new, formal exceptions to the hearsay rule except by the formal method of promulgation by the Supreme Court subject to the veto of Congress . . .[;] it authorized *individual case decisions* admitting hearsay not within the precise bounds of a recognized exception.

156. See supra notes 72–140 and accompanying text.

157. See Wis. R. Evid. 908.03(24) and 908.045(6). Indeed, some commentators have noted that the *ordinary*, as opposed to class, application of the *federal* residual exception, which is more detailed than its Wisconsin counterpart, has resulted in widely varying standards of trustworthiness and need among the circuits. See Yasser, Strangulating Hearsay: The Residual Exceptions to the Hearsay Rule, 11 Tex. Tech. L. Rev. 587, 597, 603–04 (1980); Note, The Residual Exceptions to the Hearsay Rule in the Federal Rules of Evidence: A Critical Examination, 31 Rutgers L. Rev. 687, 707 (1978); see also Note, The Federal Courts and the Catchall Hearsay Exceptions, 25 Wayne L. Rev. 1361, 1377 (1979) (recommending that trial courts' discretion under the residual exception be restricted to prevent standards of trustworthiness from falling too low).

158. See supra notes 21–32 and accompanying text.

159. See supra notes 43–51 and accompanying text.

160. See supra notes 52–71 and accompanying text.

161. See supra notes 16–32 and accompanying text.

protected.[162] None of the approaches examined above, however, has adequately met these demands.[163]

An approach that properly addresses the need for children's hearsay statements, realistically and effectively ensures their trustworthiness, and poses no threat to defendants' rights, is found in a newly enacted Washington statute. The statute establishes a specific hearsay exception for child declarants in sex abuse cases:[164]

> A statement made by a child when under the age of ten describing any act of sexual contact performed with or on the child by another, not otherwise admissible by statute or court rule, is admissible in evidence in criminal proceedings in the courts of the state of Washington if:
>
> (1) The court finds, in a hearing conducted outside the presence of the jury that the time, content, and circumstances of the statement provide sufficient indicia of reliability; and
>
> (2) The child either:
>
> (a) Testifies at the proceedings; or
>
> (b) Is unavailable as a witness: *Provided*, That when the child is unavailable as a witness, such statement may be admitted only if there is corroborative evidence of the act.
>
> A statement may not be admitted under this section unless the proponent of the statement makes known to the adverse party his intention to offer the statement and the particulars of the statement sufficiently in advance of the proceedings to provide the adverse party with a fair opportunity to prepare to meet the statement.[165]

A. *Analysis of Washington Statutory Exception*

The Washington exception addresses the special nature of child hearsay statements in sex abuse cases in several ways. First, unlike the spontaneous exclamation exception, admissibility is not conditioned upon the fulfillment of one inflexible criterion of trustworthiness.[166] The exception permits the courts to look to other pertinent and persuasive indicia of reliability, indicia which have in fact been recognized as suitable guarantees of trustworthiness in these cases.[167] This allows a broad range of reliable statements to be admitted that would otherwise be summarily excluded because they failed to meet the requirements of the spontaneous exclamation exception. For example, in *Ketcham v. State*,[168] the court might have decided differently[169] if instead of focusing on spontaneity, its attention had been directed to the fact that there

---

162. See supra notes 33–39 and accompanying text.
163. See supra notes 72–158 and accompanying text.
164. 1982 Wash. Legis. Serv. ch. 129, § 2 (West).
165. Id.
166. See supra notes 88–115 and accompanying text.
167. See supra notes 108–15, 132–35, 145–51 and accompanying text.
168. 240 Ind. 107, 162 N.E.2d 247 (1959).
169. See supra notes 85–87 and accompanying text (child's statement in *Ketcham* was excluded for lack of spontaneity; requirements of the excited utterance exception not met).

was physical evidence of the assault[170] and that the defendant had been seen alone with the child around the time of the alleged crime.[171]

While the exception permits the court to examine a variety of indicia indicating reliability, the exception avoids the bootstrapping problem of the tender years exception.[172] The statute requires the court to examine not only the content of the out-of-court declaration, but the time and circumstances surrounding the statement as well.[173] Moreover, the exception requires the presence of corroborative evidence if the child is unavailable to testify.[174]

The Washington statute is also superior to the residual exception approach, as adopted in Wisconsin. The statute requires courts to look for alternative indicia of reliability if the statement falls outside all of the established class exceptions.[175] It therefore ensures that courts will not be limited to traditional hearsay analyses. The exception, in effect, is a class one, intended to prevent children's hearsay statements from being arbitrarily evaluated and excluded.[176] The residual exception, in contrast, does not provide this guarantee of judicial scrutiny. Since it was never intended as a catch-all for any class of statements,[177] there is no assurance that courts will not continue to resort to the conventional—and flawed—approaches.

In addition, the Washington exception mitigates the possibility of judicial abuse of discretion and provides detailed guidance to the courts seeking to apply it.[178] It prescribes specific substantive rules to determine how child hearsay statements should be assessed, as well as procedural rules governing the exception's operation.[179]

Finally, the statute goes to great lengths to prevent prejudice to the defendant. All rulings on the admissibility of child hearsay statements must, under the exception, be made outside the hearing of the jury.[180] Given the emotional nature of child sex abuse[181] and the potential prejudicial effects of foundation testimony,[182] this additional requirement represents a significant advance over all the other approaches.

---

170. Ketcham v. State, 240 Ind. 107, 112, 162 N.E.2d 247, 249 (1959) (physician testified as to bruises and injuries around the pelvis and vagina of the child).

171. Id.

172. See supra notes 136–40 and accompanying text.

173. 1982 Wash. Legis. Serv. ch. 129, § 2 (West).

174. Id.

175. Id.

176. See Joint Hearings, supra note 43, at 9 (testimony of Mary Kay Barbieri, Chief, Criminal Division in King County Prosecutor's Office) (excited utterance exception too limited despite efforts of Washington courts to stretch its requirements; much trustworthy evidence still excluded).

177. See supra notes 154–56 and accompanying text.

178. See supra notes 157–58 and accompanying text.

179. See 1982 Wash. Legis. Serv. ch. 129, § 2 (West).

180. Id.

181. See People v. Burton, 55 Cal. 2d 328, 340–41, 359 P.2d 433, 437, 11 Cal. Rptr. 65, 69 (1961) (court must be wary of jury's tendency to be easily swayed by improper evidence in sexual assault cases); Slough & Knightly, Other Vices, Other Crimes, 41 Iowa L. Rev. 325, 333–34 (1956) (community feelings are strong against sex offenders); supra notes 70–71 and accompanying text.

182. See Anderson, supra note 70, at 54 (in most child sex abuse cases, much foundation evidence will be already introduced before an objection to the hearsay statement is interposed; the impact of this foundation testimony upon the jury is impossible to remove).

B. *Constitutionality*

The Washington exception was carefully drafted to avoid any confrontation clause problems.[183] In fact, it appears to go beyond the constitutional requirements set forth by the Supreme Court.[184] The exception demands that the hearsay statement contain "sufficient indicia of reliability" whether or not the child is available to testify.[185] Such indicia have been required by the Supreme Court only when the declarant is unavailable.[186] If the declarant testifies, the sixth amendment imposes no such standard of trustworthiness.[187] In addition, the Washington exception requires the concurrent presence of corroborative evidence if the child is unavailable to testify.[188] The Supreme Court merely requires that the statement contain "adequate indicia of reliability;" independent corroboration is not necessary under the confrontation clause.[189]

CONCLUSION

Thus far, courts have improperly analyzed the hearsay statements of children in child sex abuse cases. A new approach is needed, one which is sensitive to the special circumstances of child sex abuse and its victims. This Note proposes that the newly adopted Washington statute serve as a model for other states. Using this approach not only provides a means by which the probative value of child hearsay statements can be cogently assessed, but also ensures proper protection for the accused.

Judy Yun

---

183. See Joint Hearings, supra note 43, at 2–7.

184. See Ohio v. Roberts, 448 U.S. 56 (1980); California v. Green, 399 U.S. 149 (1970); supra notes 33–39 and accompanying text.

185. 1982 Wash. Legis. Serv. ch. 129, § 2 (West).

186. See Ohio v. Roberts, 448 U.S. 56, 66 (1980); supra note 39 and accompanying text.

187. See California v. Green, 399 U.S. 149, 158–59 (1970) (any inaccuracies in declarant's prior statement are exposed by cross-examination).

188. 1982 Wash. Legis. Serv. ch. 129, § 2 (West); see also Joint Hearings, supra note 43, at 10 (testimony of Mary Kay Barbieri, Chief, Criminal Division in King County Prosecutor's Office) (discussing what type of corroboration satisfies the exception; such corroboration includes the presence of venereal disease or medical trauma).

189. See Ohio v. Roberts, 448 U.S. 56, 66 (1980); see also supra notes 33–39 and accompanying text; Joint Hearings, supra note 43, at 6 (testimony of Mary Kay Barbieri, Chief, Criminal Division in King County Prosecutor's Office) (corroborative evidence requirement goes beyond what the Constitution requires).

Kansas has recently enacted a statutory exception for child hearsay statements similar to Washington's. See Kan. Stat. Ann. ch. 60, art. 460 § dd (Supp. 1982). However, the Kansas exception is noticeably more relaxed in its admissibility standards. A statement need only be "apparently reliable" if the child is unavailable as a witness. Id. Doubts concerning the statement's trustworthiness affect the *weight* of the statement rather than its admissibility. Id. Therefore, although the exception is a much-needed liberalization of present evidentiary law, it is of questionable constitutional validity. See supra notes 33–39 and accompanying text.

Journal of Social Issues, Vol. 40, No. 2, 1984, pp. 109–123

Child Witnesses and the First Amendment: A Psycholegal Dilemma

Gary B. Melton
University of Nebraska—Lincoln

There have been a number of recent proposals for procedural reforms to protect child victims in their role as witnesses. The Supreme Court's decision in Globe Newspaper Co. v. Superior Court *suggests both the constitutional limits of these reforms and some circumstances in which social-science evidence in unlikely to be given weight by the judiciary.* Globe *is particularly interesting with respect to the latter issue because its judgment appeared to turn on perceptions of empirical data. The Court's use of these data is analyzed, and suggestions are made for future research about children's involvement as witnesses. It is argued that attention might be better paid to making the present system more responsive to the needs of child witnesses than to attempting major procedural changes.*

In recent years increasing attention has been paid to the problem of victims being placed "on trial," especially in sex-offense cases. It is typically argued that the process of investigation and trial results in an exacerbation of psychological trauma and embarrassment. The victim often must describe, and in a sense relive, the traumatic event repeatedly, and defense counsel may suggest that the victim stimulated or participated in the offense (Holmstrom & Burgess, 1973). This emotional fallout of the legal process may be heightened by the requirement of testimony in open court; the victim may feel on display as he or she is forced to recall painful memories, defend against suggestions of having stimulated the offense, and confront the defendant. This feeling of public humiliation may be exacerbated by the presence of the press in the courtroom and the specter of future publicity.

This article is based on a paper presented at the meeting of the American Psychology–Law Society, Chicago, October 1983.

Correspondence regarding this article may be addressed to Gary B. Melton, Department of Psychology, University of Nebraska–Lincoln, 209 Burnett Hall, Lincoln, NE 68588.

These untoward side effects of the legal process take on particularly profound meaning when the victim is a child. Although there is little direct evidence, the traumatic effects of police interrogation and courtroom testimony would appear especially severe for child victims. Children are less likely than adults to have the cognitive skills necessary to organize the experience. Prosecutors and police may have special difficulty in communicating with child victims and offering them emotional support and preparation for the various steps in the legal process, including testimony. Also, to the extent that delays in the legal process result in "marking time" for the child and his or her family until the event can be put behind them (Burgess & Holmstrom, 1978), the process may result in a temporary plateau in the child's development. However, there may be reason to modify procedures for children's testimony even if these hypotheses as to especially traumatic effects of the legal system on child victims are invalid. The historic duty of the state as *parens patriae* to protect children may give special significance to whatever negative effects the legal process has on victims generally. In short, the state's interest in punishing and incapacitating child molesters may come into conflict paradoxically with its interest in promoting the healthy socialization of children and protecting them from trauma.

Starting from such a premise, there have been a number of proposals for special procedures in trials of defendants charged with sex offenses against children. Some proposals involve procedures that are supplements to, rather than fundamental changes of, existing criminal procedure. The recently enacted Victim and Witness Protection Act (1982), for example, requires the Department of Justice to develop specific procedures to make victims more comfortable and less subject to fear or embarrassment during the legal process (e.g., separate waiting rooms, victim counseling services, specially trained law enforcement officers, involvement of the victim in prosecutorial decision-making). The provision of special programs and materials (e.g., Lewis & Greenwood, 1979) to prepare child witnesses for the legal process is of a similar genre. Such reforms make the present system more responsive to the needs of child victims; they do not challenge prevailing criminal procedure.

Several proposals for substantial changes in procedure are more troublesome. Generally, these proposals aim to make criminal procedures less stressful for child witnesses by (a) eliminating or reducing the size of the audience during the child's testimony, and/or (b) removing the defendant during the child's testimony. Thus, for example, some states permit videotaped depositions by child victims of sex offenses to avoid the presumed trauma of testimony in open court (Arizona Revised Statutes, 1978/1982; Florida Statutes, 1979/1983; Montana Code, 1977/1981; New Mexico Statutes, 1978). At its most extreme, Israel provides by statute (Law of Evidence, 1955) for the appointment of child mental-health professionals as special youth examiners whose report of the child's discussion of the offense is admissible as evidence (see Reifen, 1958,

1973, for a description of the implementation of this statute). Under Israeli law, neither open testimony nor confrontation by the defendant is required in cases of sex offenses against children.

Libai (1969) and Parker (1983) have proposed less radical procedures, which they believe are consonant with the American constitutional system. To avoid the child's directly facing the defendant or the public, the Libai–Parker proposal calls for the development of special courtrooms for children. These courtrooms would be informal (e.g., without an imposing judicial bench) and would be equipped with a one-way mirror, behind which could be the defendant, friends and family, and representatives of the public. The defendant could communicate with his or her attorney by means of a "bug-in-the-ear." To minimize the amount of time that the child and the child's family are in limbo, the judge could order a videotaped pretrial deposition, which would be shown to the trier of fact when the case finally went to trial. The deposition would be taken in the children's courtroom. Parker's (1983) modification of the Libai proposal also provides for prohibition of publication of the child's name and address (through use of Jane or John Doe appellations on public court records) and for potential closure of the courtroom. Closure would occur only if the trial judge found a compelling state interest in doing so in the particular case.

The American proposals attempt to strike a balance between the interests of the child, and the rights of the defendant and the public. However, the privacy interests of the child victim are likely to carry less weight in a balancing test than the rights of the defendant, which are constitutionally protected and therefore fundamental. Thus, even these "moderate" reforms raise a number of constitutional issues, with respect to the protection of the defendant's Sixth Amendment right to confrontation of witnesses, the defendant's Sixth Amendment right to public trial, and the public's First Amendment right (through the press) to access to the trial process (see Melton, 1980, 1981, for a detailed discussion). For example, the proposals for the use of one-way mirrors or closed-circuit television with electronic communication between the defendant and counsel arguably preserve the defendant's right to confrontation by providing the opportunity for his or her indirect participation in cross-examination. However, such a procedure would fail on constitutional grounds if the Sixth Amendment requires *face-to-face* confrontation (*Kirby v. United States,* 1899, p. 55; *Mattox v. United States,* 1895, pp. 243–244; *Snyder v. Massachusetts,* 1934, p. 106; *United States v. Benfield,* 1979). It is likely that the right to confrontation applies as an element of due process even in civil abuse proceedings because of the potential stigma and loss of parental rights attached to a finding of abuse, although the standard for attenuating the right to confrontation in family court is likely to be lower than in a criminal trial where the Sixth Amendment applies (*In re S. Children,* 1980).

Preservation of the defendant's right to a public trial is somewhat less problematic. There is ample precedent for limiting the size of the audience when child victims of sex offenses testify (*Geise v. United States*, 1958; *Melanson v. O'Brien*, 1951). Similar authority exists for removing spectators who do not have a direct interest in the case. They may be removed to protect the dignity of testifying rape victims (*Aaron v. Capps*, 1975; *Harris v. Stephens*, 1966; *United States ex rel. Latimore v. Sielaff*, 1977). The interests of the defendant in a public trial may be met by having present, at a minimum, the defendant, counsel, and the defendant's family and friends (*In re Oliver*, 1948). This small audience could presumably be removed from the courtroom itself and placed behind a one-way mirror so that the child need not face them.

However, the circumstances in which actual closure of the courtroom to spectators is permissible may be quite limited, as illustrated by a recent Supreme Court case (*Globe Newspaper Co. v. Superior Court* [*Globe III*, 1982]) which considered the scope of the First Amendment right to a public trial. *Globe* is interesting not only because of its implications for consideration of reforms in procedures governing testimony by child victims: it is also noteworthy because the holding in the case turned at least superficially on the interpretation of psychological evidence.

Globe v. Superior Court

Globe involved the test of the constitutionality of a Massachusetts statute barring anyone not "having a direct interest in the case" from the courtroom during testimony by a minor victim of a sex offense (Massachusetts General Laws, 1923/1972). The Supreme Judicial Court of Massachusetts had twice considered the *Globe's* objection to being excluded from a trial of a defendant who had been charged with the forcible rape and forced unnatural rape of three girls who were minors (ages 16, 16, 17) at the time of trial. Relying exclusively on an analysis of the statute in the context of the common law, the Supreme Judicial Court in *Globe I* (1980) held that the interests supported by the closure statute *required* exclusion of the press only during the testimony of the victims; exclusion during the rest of the trial was a matter of the trial judge's discretion. The court interpreted the statute as intended "to encourage young victims of sexual offenses to come forward; once they have come forward, the statute is designed to preserve their ability to testify by protecting them from undue psychological harm at trial" (*Globe I*, 1980, p. 369). Beyond this general concern with the statute as facilitative of the administration of justice, the court also identified a legislative intent to shield minors from public degradation.

The *Globe* appealed to the United States Supreme Court, which summarily vacated the judgment of the Massachusetts court and remanded the case (*Globe* remand, 1980) for reconsideration in the light of *Richmond Newspapers, Inc. v. Virginia* (1980), which had made clear for the first time that public access to criminal trials is guaranteed by the First Amendment. On reconsideration, the

Massachusetts Supreme Judicial Court affirmed its earlier decision. Although acknowledging "a temporary diminution" of "the public's knowledge about trials" (*Globe II*, 1981, p. 781), the court held that a case-by-case determination of the propriety of closure would defeat the state's legitimate interests:

> Ascertaining the susceptibility of an individual victim might require expert testimony and would be a cumbersome process at best. Only the most exceptional minor would be sanguine about the possiblity that the details of an attack may become public. An examiner would have to distinguish between natural hesitancy and cases of particular vulnerability. To the extent that such a hearing is effective, requiring various psychological examinations in some depth, the victim will be forced to relive the experience. So, too, the families of youthful victims will be uncertain whether the reporting of a sexual assault will expose a child to additional trauma caused by the preliminary hearing as well as to public testimony at the trial. (*Globe II*, 1981, pp. 779–780)

Globe again appealed to the U.S. Supreme Court (*Globe III*, 1982). The Supreme Court reversed the Massachusetts court, 6-3. Writing for the majority, Justice Brennan held the Massachusetts statute to be violative of the First Amendment, in that mandatory closure was broader than necessary to meet compelling state interests. Justice O'Connor wrote separately to emphasize her belief that the holdings in both *Richmond Newspapers* and *Globe* applied only to criminal trials. Chief Justice Burger, joined by Justice Rehnquist, dissented on the merits of the case, and Justice Stevens dissented on the ground that the issue was moot because the trial in the case at hand had been completed.

Justice Brennan began the analysis of the merits of the case by reiterating the constitutional basis for the access of the press and the general public to criminal trials, as developed in *Richmond Newspapers*. Having emphasized the constitutional values at stake, Justice Brennan argued that any attenuation of the access of the press must be based on a "weighty" state interest: "It must be shown that the denial [of access] is necessitated by a compelling government interest, and is narrowly tailored to serve that interest" (*Globe III*, 1982, p. 2620).

The majority analyzed the state interests purported to be served by the closure statute to be "reducible to two: the protection of minor victims of sex crimes from further trauma and embarrassment; and the encouragement of such victims to come forward and testify in a truthful and credible manner" (*Globe III*, pp. 2620–2621). Justice Brennan acknowledged the former interest—protection of the minor victim—as compelling. However, he also argued that the statute was too broad in its scope. While there might be justification for closure of the courtroom during testimony by *some* minor victims, there was insufficient justification for *mandatory* closure. Citing Massachusetts Justice Wilkins's concurring opinion in *Globe II* (1981), Justice Brennan noted that some minor victims might *want* publicity of the trial so that they could expose the heinous behavior of the defendant; others might simply not be bothered by the presence of the press. Moreover, the incremental protection gained by the victim might be quite small. Massachusetts already permitted publication of the victims' names in the court record, which is available to the press.

The majority found the second state justification—facilitation of justice in cases of sexual crimes against minors—to be without merit, in that "no empirical support" had been produced to support the assertion that the closure statute would increase reporting of offenses. Indeed, in view of the minimal shield against publicity offered by the closure statute, Justice Brennan found the "claim speculative in empirical terms, but . . . also open to serious question as a matter of logic and common sense" (*Globe III*, 1982, p. 2622). Moreover, even if the assertion withstood empirical scrutiny, the majority regarded it as insufficiently compelling to overcome a constitutional interest, because such a claim "could be relied on to support an array of mandatory closure rules designed to encourage victims to come forward: Surely it cannot be suggested that minor victims of sex crimes are the *only* crime victims who, because of publicity attendant to criminal trials, are reluctant to come forward and testify" (*Globe III*, 1982, p. 2622). With respect to the assertion that the closure statute would improve the quality of minor victims' testimony, Justice Brennan noted that the Court has presumed *openness* to improve testimony. Starting from such a presumption, only a showing of improved testimony by *all* child victims would justify mandatory closure in his view.

The Chief Justice, joined by Justice Rehnquist, quarreled with the majority on a variety of points in *Globe III*. Most basically, they criticized the majority's interpretation of *Richmond Newspapers* (1980) as overly broad. Perhaps getting to the crux of the disagreement, the dissenters also expressed their disgust at the result of *Globe:* specifically, that while "states are permitted . . . to mandate the closure of all proceedings in order to protect a 17-year-old charged with rape, they are not permitted to require the closing of part of criminal proceedings in order to protect an innocent child who has been raped or otherwise sexually abused" (*Globe III*, 1982, p. 2623).[1]

Beyond these differences in analysis, about half of Chief Justice Burger's opinion was devoted to an attack on the majority's perception of the empirical realities. He regarded the Massachusetts statute as a rational expression of "the Commonwealth's overriding interest in protecting the child from the severe—possibly permanent—psychological damage" of testimony before representatives of the press (*Globe III*, 1982, p. 2626).

---

[1]Chief Justice Burger may have overstated the limits of privacy in delinquency proceedings. In states in which the juvenile respondent has at least a conditional right to a public trial, or the public has at least a conditional right of access, open delinquency proceedings may still be possible (ABA/IJA, 1980, §§ 6.1–6.13; *R.L.R. v. State*, 1971; *State ex rel, Oregonian Publishing Co.*, 1980). Where privacy of delinquents has conflicted with the constitutional rights of the press or of criminal defendants in criminal trials, the privacy interest has been outweighed (*Davis v. Alaska*, 1974; *Oklahoma Publishing Co. v. District Court*, 1977; *Smith v. Daily Mail Publishing Co.*, 1979).

The Chief Justice claimed further that the reality of such severe psychological damage was "not disputed" (*Globe III*, 1982, p. 2626) and cited six authorities that he claimed supported such a view. With respect to the majority's allegation of the lack of empirical evidence to support the second interest alleged by the state—improvement of reporting and prosecution of sex offenses against children—Chief Justice Burger responded with a rather circular argument: only by permitting experimentation by the states can such data be generated. Such an argument, carried to its logical conclusion, would justify any state intrusion into a constitutionally protected zone if there *might* be a state interest of compelling proportion. Regardless, the Chief Justice was convinced that the "reality of human experience" "cavalier[ly] disregard[ed]" by the majority showed that the statute would "prevent the risk of severe psychological damage caused by having to relate the details of the crime in front of a crowd which inevitably will include voyeuristic strangers," perhaps including "a live television audience, with reruns on the evening news. That ordeal could be difficult for an adult; to a child, the experience can be devastating and leave permanent scars" (*Globe III*, 1982, p. 2626). Rejecting case-by-case consideration of closure, the Chief Justice asserted that the "mere possibility" of testimony before the press would be enough to deter many parents and children from reporting sex offenses (*Globe III*, 1982, p. 2626).

The Use and Abuse of the Social Sciences

Globe presents an interesting example of the use and significance of social-science evidence in an appellate case. Indeed, if taken literally, had the majority found a substantially stronger link between the closure statute and the protection of child victims, the result in *Globe* would have been different, given the same analysis. (We shall see, however, that no empirical evidence could have met the majority's standard.)

Moreover, the division of the Court on the interpretation of the social-science evidence is surprising, at least on the surface. The advocates of greater attention to the social sciences in *Globe* are not the Court's liberals but Chief Justice Burger and Justice Rehnquist, neither of whom has expressed much affection for the social sciences in the past (see, e.g., *Ballew v. Georgia*, 1978, opinion of Justice Powell, concurring in the judgment, joined by Chief Justice Burger and Justice Rehnquist; *Craig v. Boren*, 1976, opinion of Justice Rehnquist, dissenting).

Close examination of the Burger–Rehnquist argument in *Globe III* shows no new affinity for empiricism, however. First, the Chief Justice apparently made no systematic examination of the relevant social-science literature. The extralegal authorities he cited had all been previously cited in *Globe I* (1980) by the Massachusetts Supreme Judicial Court, and these authorities were cited without critical analysis of their findings. Specifically, Chief Justice Burger cited six authorities in support of his assertions concerning the "devastating" trauma for child victims of testimony in open court. Two of these citations (Berger, 1977; Libai, 1969) were of nonempirical law-journal articles, and a third citation (Bohmer & Blumberg, 1975) was of an unsystematic, impressionistic law-journal "study." (In that regard, social scientists wishing to disseminate their work to legal policy-makers are reminded of the need to publish their findings in journals accessible through the *Index to Legal Periodicals;* see Tanke & Tanke, 1979). One of the citations was of a secondary source (Katz & Mazur, 1979), and another citation was of a report of a committee of the American Psychiatric Association (Hilberman, 1976), which made a series of assertions about the problems of child victims in the legal system without supporting data.

The only one of the treatises actually presenting data was Holmstrom and Burgess's (1978) volume on institutional responses to rape victims. Burgess and Holmstrom, a nurse/sociologist research team, pioneered in the study of victims, including minor victims, of sexual assault. Combining a counseling program with research purposes, they acted as participant–observers, and they reported rich anecdotal data. However, there are substantial methodological problems in their work. Their interviews were unstructured and presumably affected by Burgess and Holmstrom's preconceptions and their counseling motive. Where quantified data are reported, they make no mention of the reliability of ratings, even though some of the categories are quite subjective. Even if one assumes that failure to recognize these limitations in Burgess and Holmstrom's work was a lack of social-science sophistication rather than an uncritical eye, the Chief Justice still can be criticized for citing their findings about *adults'* responses to the legal system. He overlooked their book on *child* victims of sexual assault (Burgess, Groth, Holmstrom, & Sgroi, 1978), which includes a chapter by Burgess and Holmstrom on the experiences of child victims and their families in the legal system. Rather than examine these findings, the Chief Justice assumed that "certainly the impact on children must be greater" (*Globe III,* 1982, p. 2626, footnote 7). Although, as already noted, such a hypothesis is plausible, it does not stand on intuition alone. Indeed, particularly for young children, there is also reason to believe that children's responses might be less severe on the average than are adults'. The typical case of sexual abuse is nonviolent (Finkelhor, 1979). Provided that parents and others do not overreact, and that they are supportive of the child during the legal process, it may well be that the experience will carry little trauma (see also Berliner & Barbieri, 1984).

Second, the "empirical" evidence on which the Chief Justice relied to support the state's assertion that the closure statute increased reporting of sex offenses against children was nothing more than his intuition: "the reality of human experience" (*Globe III,* 1982, p. 2626). It is noteworthy that the state admitted in oral argument before the Supreme Court that no evidence existed to support its claim (*Globe* argument, 1982). Despite this lack of data, Chief Justice Burger drew a number of unequivocal psychological conclusions, as he has in several other cases involving purported severe harm to minors (e.g., *H. L. v. Matheson*, 1981; *Parham v. J. R.*, 1979; see Melton, 1983b, 1984a, for commentary). In short, it is likely that the citation of social-science authorities was in support of assumptions already made. Put in such a light, the uncritical citation of the extralegal authorities is unsurprising. Chief Justice Burger probably began his analysis with an a priori concept of minors as extremely vulnerable (and, therefore, properly subject to adult authority), a view he has expressed in a number of contexts (Melton, 1983a, 1984a).

Third, the use of empirical evidence which the Chief Justice recommended in *Globe* was fundamentally conservative, in that it was intended for the purpose of *supporting* the rationality of state action. Particularly when coupled with the lack of critical analysis of this evidence, such use of empirical evidence is reminiscent of the first "Brandeis briefs" (appellate briefs citing extralegal authority), which were used to establish the *existence*, not the *validity*, of social facts that might have served as the bases for legislative action (Rosen, 1972). That is, the argument was based on the existence of social-science authority that might have been used by the legislature to provide a rational basis for policy, even if the assumptions did not withstand careful scrutiny. Consequently, there was no real need for analysis of the evidence by Chief Justice Burger and Justice Rehnquist, because the real analysis in their view concerned the legitimacy of the state's purposes, not the validity of the assumptions underlying these purposes.

Although the use of the social sciences by Chief Justice Burger appears half-hearted at best, the majority in *Globe* seems little more enthusiastic. On its face, Justice Brennan's analysis starts from a premise that state infringements on constitutional rights must be justified by empirical evidence—indicating that the state purpose is indeed compelling and that the statute narrowly serves this purpose (i.e., that the purpose could not be served by a more narrowly drawn measure). In this regard, the majority opinion is straightforward in setting forth a strong presumption against reforms that intrude upon constitutionally protected zones. Nonetheless, on close reading of the opinion, it is difficult to imagine *any* social-science evidence that would have supported a compelling state interest served by a mandatory closure statute. Noting that the Supreme Court had precedents for the premise that open trials produce better testimony, Justice Brennan argued that a mandatory closure statute could be justified only if it could be shown that "closure would improve the quality of testimony of *all* minor victims" (*Globe III*, 1982, p. 2622, footnote 26)—an impossible task. Rather than raise a meaningless call for empirical evidence, the majority would have been clearer if it had simply indicated that open trials are supported by fundamental values inherent in American criminal justice and that broad attacks on this tradition will not be sustained. Moreover, the citation of earlier opinions in which the positive relationship between openness and quality of testimony had been assumed also clouds the issue. Because it is consistent with constitutional values, this statement of "fact" has taken on precedential value of its own (cf. Perry & Melton, in press). Reliance on *precedent* hardly establishes the truth-value of a proposition. Again, honesty demands reliance on the real value bases of the opinion when, in fact, the empirical premise is essentially unrebuttable.

In short, analysis of the debate in *Globe* about the merit of empirical evidence does little to promote faith that the Supreme Court will make good use of social-science data to examine assumptions about "social fact" that underlie its opinions. *Globe* does suggest the kind of case in which social-science evidence is likely to carry little probative weight. Where fundamental legal values are at issue, empirical arguments are likely to be overcome by a priori assumptions. This conclusion does not abrogate the need for honesty as to the real bases of judicial opinions; it does, however, suggest to social scientists areas where their work is unlikely to influence judicial decision-making. There may be some instances in which fundamental interests are in conflict and in which the courts look to other factors to tip the balance. However, it is important to note that such attention to empirical data is unlikely to occur in *Globe*-style cases. Although the right of the public to access to criminal trials is fundamental, witnesses' interest in privacy is not (*Press-Enterprise Co. v. Superior Court,* 1984). Moreover, empirical evidence is irrelevant to the question of whether such an interest merits constitutional protection, at least within the current framework of the Constitution. Despite the majority's call for more data in *Globe,* it seems clear that no data could have been sufficiently compelling to overcome the public's interest if applied to all cases.

Implications for Procedural Reform

Having considered the nature of the *Globe* analysis, it is important to look at its result. Returning to the issue posed initially in this article, what lesson does *Globe* teach with respect to the possibilities of procedural reform to protect child victims in the legal process? The answer is clear: where the interests of child witnesses, as a class, conflict with the constitutional rights of the defendant or the public, the latter will generally prevail. This principle does not preclude procedural modifications in *specific* cases where there is compelling justification, however (cf. *Press-Enterprise Co. v. Superior Court,* 1984). With respect to the access of the press, for example, the Supreme Court had indicated in *Richmond Newspapers* (1980) that the courtroom could be closed if the trial judge determined "an overriding interest articulated in findings" (p. 581). The Court did not specify the nature of the findings required, however. This ambiguity was clarified somewhat in *Globe.* With respect to child victims, the Court indicated that "the factors to be weighed are the minor victim's age, psychological maturity and understanding, the nature of the crime, the desires of the victim, and the interests of parents and relatives'' (*Globe III*, 1982, p. 2621). The Court gave no further guidance as to the calculus to be employed in deciding whether to curtail press access in particular cases.

Presumably, the *Globe* factors also would apply in other instances in which an individual child victim/witness of a crime other than a sexual offense seeks closure of the courtroom. If there were reasons to expect particularly profound trauma and embarrassment, closure might be justified, at least in the case of children, regardless of the crime. However, it is important to note that the existing statutory provisions in some states for procedural aberrations (e.g., videotaped depositions) all apply exclusively to victims of sex crimes. Also, the broader the class to which such procedures are applied, the stronger the justification must be.

For the longer term, the *Globe* holding suggests some directions for research relevant to the protection of child victims. First, consistent with the case-by-case inquiry that *Globe* permits, researchers might try to identify the individual and situational factors determinative of, or at least correlated with, psychological harm of open testimony. As an initial step, studies of the factors accounting for the reactions of child victims to the legal process, at both debriefing and long-term follow-up points, might provide information relevant to the decision about which cases merit some procedural aberration. Such data might also suggest situations of child victimization that particularly demand preventive intervention.

Second, *Globe* indicates that broad procedural reforms to protect child witnesses are unlikely to pass constitutional scrutiny. Consequently, researchers might better spend their energy studying ways in which the present system might be made more responsive.[2] At a minimum, research is needed to identify children's perceptions of the nature of the criminal process, the roles of attorneys, and so forth. Such data are lacking even for "normal" children who have no contact with the legal system (Grisso & Lovinguth, 1982). In the present context, systematic understanding of children's experience would seem to be a prerequisite to preparing children of various ages and backgrounds for the legal process. Attention needs to be given to children's understanding of the range of steps in the investigation and prosecution of alleged offenders against children, not just of the trial phase.

---

[2]In that regard, care must be taken to ensure that the reforms are not themselves stress-inducing. For example, the Federal Victim and Witness Protection Act (1982) and similar victim-protection legislation in some states require the preparation of a victim impact assessment as part of the presentence investigation. The required scope of the assessment—psychological, medical, social, economic—is such that victims might ultimately be placed under greater scrutiny than offenders, even though the purpose of the assessment is to consider factors relevant to restitution and retribution for the victims.

Indeed, reports of child sexual abuse rarely reach a criminal trial. Rogers (1980) tracked 261 cases over a two-year period in the District of Columbia in which the police had been called on a complaint of sexual abuse of a child. Eighty-five percent (223) of the cases were referred for prosecution. Warrants or custody orders were denied by the prosecutor in one-third (32 adult and 41 juvenile) of these cases, most commonly because of a lack of corroborating evidence. Of the cases that ultimately went to court during the period of the study, 28% (2 adults and 22 juvenile cases) were dismissed, and a guilty plea was obtained in 62% (21 adults and 32 juvenile cases). Thus, only 8 of the 261 cases actually went to trial, and 5 of these cases were in closed juvenile delinquency proceedings. Although the data from a single jurisdiction may be unrepresentative, there is reason to believe that the nation-wide probability of sexual abuse cases reaching a criminal trial is even lower. Plea bargaining is ubiquitous in most jurisdictions (Department of Justice, 1983). Moreover, authorities may choose to file civil child abuse complaints instead of criminal charges, unlike the apparent practice in the District of Columbia.

Finally, both the vacuum in relevant data (but see Burgess & Holmstrom, 1978; DeFrancis, 1969) and the infrequency of open testimony by child victims suggest that attempts at substantial procedural reform are premature. As indicated above, even basic descriptive information on children's responses to attorneys—and vice versa—is lacking. Moreover, the assumption that open, confrontational testimony is traumatic for child victims of sexual offenses has yet to be validated. At least for some child victims, the experience may be cathartic (Berliner & Barbieri, 1984; Pynoos & Eth, 1984; Rogers, 1980); it provides an opportunity for taking control of the situation (cf. Melton & Lind, 1982) and achieving vindication. Particularly, in view of the constitutional values at stake, would-be reformers have an obligation to go beyond conventional wisdom and show that reforms are both needed and likely to be beneficial.

The reasoning of the Supreme Court in *Globe* would have been more elegant had it limited its analysis to the breadth of the public's constitutional right of access to criminal trials. Once that right was found applicable, the evidence needed to establish a compelling state interest in closing trials involving child victim/witnesses was much weightier than the scant psychological-research literature currently available on the topic. This is not to say that psychologists have no role in facilitating the protection of child witnesses. Rather, the task should be viewed as one of *incremental* research and reform, rather than a broad attack upon constitutionally protected interests.

The most effective strategy would be to identify special vulnerabilities of child witnesses who have particular psychological or demographic characteristics, and then to test specific interventions or procedural changes to reduce trauma or foster adaptation in those groups. The problem is an *ecological* one in the strictest sense (cf. Bronfenbrenner, 1974). It involves the interaction of the developing child's psychological characteristics with various legal procedures and other aspects of the situation (e.g., perceived parental attitudes). For some children, it may be that minor interventions (e.g., acquainting the child with the physical layout of the courtroom; a friendly word from the judge) will have significant effect on both the quality of the child's testimony and the level of stress experienced by the child. Without attention to such specific relations between psychosocial variables and legal procedures, global assertions about harm are unlikely to provide information probative for legal decision-making or useful for clinical prevention.

References

Aaron v. Capps, 507 F.2d 685 (5th Cir. 1975).

American Bar Association/Institute of Judicial Adminstration. (1980). *Juvenile justice standards relating to adjudication.* Cambridge, MA: Ballinger.

Ariz. Rev. Stat. Ann. § 12-2312 (1982) (enacted 1978).

Ballew v. Georgia, 435 U.S. 223 (1978).

Berger, V. (1977). Man's trial, woman's tribulation: Rape cases in the courtroom. *Columbia Law Review, 77,* 1–103.

Berliner, L., & Barbieri, M. A. (1984). Legal testimony by child victims of sexual assault. *Journal of Social Issues, 40*(2), 125–137.

Bohmer, C., & Blumberg, A. (1975). Twice traumatized: The rape victim and the court. *Judicature, 58,* 390–399.

Bronfenbrenner, U. (1974). Developmental research, public policy, and the ecology of childhood. *Child Development, 45,* 1–5.

Burgess, A. W., Groth, A. N., Holmstrom, L. L., & Sgroi, S. M. (Eds.). (1978). *Sexual assault of children and adolescents.* Lexington, MA: Lexington Books.

Burgess, A. W., & Holmstrom, L. L. (1978). The child and family in the court process. In A. W. Burgess, A. N. Groth, L. L. Holmstrom, & S. M. Sgroi (Eds.), *Sexual assault of children and adolescents* (pp. 205–230). Lexington, MA: Lexington Books.

Craig v. Boren, 429 U.S. 190 (1976).

Davis v. Alaska, 415 U.S. 308 (1974).

DeFrancis, V. (1969). *Protecting the child victim of sex crimes committed by adults.* Denver: American Humane Association.

Department of Justice, Bureau of Justice Statistics (1983). *Report to the nation on crime and justice: The data.* Washington, DC: Author.

Finkelhor, D. (1979). *Sexually victimized children.* New York: Free Press.

Fla. Stat. Ann. § 918.17 (West Supp. 1983) (enacted 1979).

Geise v. United States, 262 F.2d 151 (9th Cir. 1958).

Globe Newspaper Co. v. Superior Court, 401 N.E.2d 360 (Mass. 1980) (*Globe I*).

Globe Newspaper Co. v. Superior Court, *summarily vacated and remanded,* 449 U.S. 894 (1980) (*per curiam*) (*Globe* remand).

Globe Newspaper Co. v. Superior Court, 401 N.E.2d 260 (Mass. 1981) (*Globe II*).

Globe Newspaper Co. v. Superior Court, 50 U.S.L.W. 3795 (U.S. April 6, 1982) (*Globe* argument).

Globe Newspaper Co. v. Superior Court, 102 S.Ct. 2613 (1982) (*Globe III*).

Grisso, T., & Lovinguth, T. (1982). Lawyers and child clients: A call for research. In J. S. Henning (Ed.), *The rights of children: Legal and psychological perspectives* (pp. 215–232). Springfield, IL: Charles C. Thomas.

Harris v. Stephens, 361 F.2d 888 (9th Cir. 1966), *cert. denied,* 386 U.S. 964 (1966).

Hilberman, E. (1976). *The rape victim.* New York: Basic Books.

H. L. v. Matheson, 450 U.S. 398 (1981).

Holmstrom, L. L., & Burgess, A. W. (1973). Rape: The victim goes on trial. In I. Drapkin & E. Viano (Eds.), *Victimology: A new focus, Vol. 3: Crimes, victims, and justice* (pp. 31–47). Lexington, MA: Lexington Books.

Holmstrom, L. L., & Burgess, A. W. (1978). *The victim of rape: Institutional reactions.* New York: Wiley.

In re Oliver, 333 U.S. 257 (1948).

In re S. Children, 102 Misc. 1015, 424 N.Y.S.2d 1004 (Fam. Ct. 1980).

Katz, S., & Mazur, M. A. (1979). *Understanding the rape victim: A synthesis of research findings.* New York: Wiley.

Kirby v. United States, 174 U.S. 47 (1899).

Law of Evidence Revision (Protection of Children) Law 5715–1955 § 4. 9 Laws of the State of Israel (auth. trans. 1955).

Lewis, C., & Greenwood, M. (1979). *Testifying: An informational booklet for children.* Brooklyn, NY: Brooklyn Victim Services Agency.

Libai, D. (1969). The protection of the child victim of a sexual offense in the criminal justice system. *Wayne Law Review, 15,* 977–1032.

Mass. Gen. Laws Ann. Ch. 278, 16A (West 1972) (enacted 1923).

Mattox v. United States, 156 U.S. 237 (1895).

Melanson v. O'Brien, 191 F.2d 963 (1st Cir. 1951).

Melton, G. B. (1980). Psycholegal issues in child victims' interaction with the legal system. *Victimology, 5*(3/4), 274–284.

Melton, G. B. (1981). Procedural reforms to protect child victim/witnesses in sex offense proceedings. In J. Bulkley (Ed.), *Child sexual abuse and the law* (pp. 184–198). Washington, DC: American Bar Association.

Melton, G. B. (1983a). Children's competence to consent: A problem in law and social science. In G. B. Melton, G. P. Koocher, & M. J. Saks (Eds.), *Children's competence to consent* (pp. 1–18). New York: Plenum.

Melton, G. B. (1983b). Minors and privacy: Are legal and psychological concepts compatible? *Nebraska Law Review, 62,* 455–493.

Melton, G. B. (1984a). Developmental psychology and the law: The state of the art. *Journal of Family Law.*

Melton, G. B. (1984b). Family and mental hospital as myths: Civil commitment of minors. In N. D. Reppucci, L. A. Weithorn, E. P. Mulvey, & J. Monahan, *Children, law, and mental health* (pp. 151–167). Beverly Hills, CA: Sage.

Melton, G. B., & Lind, E. A. (1982). Procedural justice in family court: Does the adversary model make sense? In G. B. Melton (Ed.), *Legal reforms affecting child and youth services* (pp. 65–83). New York: Haworth.

Mont. Code Ann. §§ 46-15-401 to -403 (1981) (enacted 1977).

N.M. Stat. Ann. § 30-9-17 (1978).

Oklahoma Publishing Co. v. District Court, 430 U.S. 308 (1977) *(per curiam).*

Parham v. J.R., 442 U.S. 584 (1979).

Parker, J. Y. (1983). The child witness versus the press: A proposed legislative response to *Globe v. Superior Court. Albany Law Review, 47,* 408–465.

Perry, G. S., & Melton, G. B. (in press). The precedential value of judicial notice of social facts: Parham as an example. *Journal of Family Law.*

Press-Enterprise Co. v. Superior Court, 104 S. Ct. 819 (1984).

Pynoos, R. S., & Eth, S. (1984). The child as witness to homicide. *Journal of Social Issues, 40*(2), 87–108.

R.L.R. v. State, 487 P.2d 27 (Alaska 1971).

Reifen, D. (1958). Protection of children involved in sexual offenses: A new method of investigation in Israel. *Journal of Criminal Law, Criminology, and Police Science, 49,* 222–229.

Reifen, D. (1973). Court procedures in Israel to protect child-victims of sexual assault. In I. Drapkin & E. Viano (Eds.), *Victimology: A new focus, Vol. 3: Crimes, victims, and justice* (pp. 67–72). Lexington, MA: Lexington Books.

Richmond Newspapers, Inc. v. Virginia, 448 U.S. 555 (1980).

Rogers, C. M. (1980, September). *Child sexual abuse and the courts: Empirical findings.* Paper presented at the meeting of the American Psychological Association, Montreal.

Rosen, P. (1972). *The Supreme Court and social science.* Urbana: University of Illinois Press.

Smith v. Daily Mail Publishing Co., 443 U.S. 97 (1979).

Snyder v. Massachusetts, 291 U.S. 97 (1934).

State ex rel. Oregonian Publishing Co. v. Diez, 613 P.2d 23 (Or. 1980).

Tanke, E. D., & Tanke, T. J. (1979). Getting off a slippery slope: Social science in the judicial process. *American Psychologist, 34,* 1130–1138.

United States ex rel. Latimore v. Sielaff, 561 F.2d 691 (7th Cir. 1977).

United States v. Benfield, 593 F.2d 815 (8th Cir. 1979).

Victim and Witness Protection Act, Pub. L. 97–291, 96 Stat. 1248 (1982).

Evidentiary and Procedural Trends in State Legislation and Other Emerging Legal Issues in Child Sexual Abuse Cases

Josephine A. Bulkley*

I. Introduction

Since the early 1980's, a number of states have undertaken statutory reform efforts to improve the handling of child sexual abuse cases in the legal system. Legislative reform in a few areas had begun earlier, including a trend to abolish the corroboration requirement and to abolish competency tests for children.[1] For example, in 1981, a dozen states had eliminated competency qualifications of child witnesses; by 1985, 23 states had made this change, nearly twice the number of states in a four year period. The reasons motivating the recent reform movement seem to be the greater awareness and reports of child sexual abuse, the increasing number of cases being prosecuted with children as witnesses in court, and wide circulation of the ABA's *Recommendations for Improving Legal Intervention in Intrafamily Child Sexual Abuse Cases* with its range of suggestions regarding state legislative action and other innovations in legal intervention. An additional reason for some of the reforms relates to changes in attitudes regarding children and their abilities.

The new legislation affecting the prosecution of child abuse cases is designed to serve three basic purposes — to modify legal procedures to be more sensitive to child victims, to improve prosecution and conviction rates, and to provide treatment in special programs for the offender, child and family. First, literature is replete with documentation by mental health clinicians, child welfare professionals, prosecutors, children's attorneys, and other legal experts who stress that children suffer additional psychological harm by in-

* Project Director, Child Sexual Abuse Law Reform Project, National Legal Resource Center for Child Advocacy and Protection, Washington, D.C.
   1. Bulkley, *Recommendations for Improving Legal Intervention in Child Sexual Abuse Cases*, Recommendations 4.1 and 4.2 and *Commentary*, American Bar Association, Washington, D.C. (1982).

645

sensitive legal procedures.[2] Second, until recent years, criminal proceedings often were not initiated (particularly in incest cases) due to a variety of reasons, including lack of eyewitnesses or physical evidence and perceptions that children were not credible witnesses.[3] Finally, since the 1970's, however, a number of specialized incest treatment programs have developed around the country, some of which were funded for several years by the National Center on Child Abuse and Neglect to provide training to professionals in other jurisdictions. These programs vary in terms of treatment philosophy and their involvement with the legal system.

Although the effectiveness of programs that provide alternative dispositions for offenders and their families should be explored, this article deals only with reforms to minimize trauma and improve prosecutions. This article will deal with two of these reforms that have generated a significant amount of legislative activity — special hearsay exceptions for complaints of sexual abuse by child victims and videotaping or closed-circuit television procedures for taking a child's testimony outside the courtroom. Legislative efforts in other areas, such as videotaped interviews, competency, expert testimony, civil protective orders or many other ideas outlined, for example, in the ABA's *Recommendations* are not examined here.[4] Appendix A, however, contains a list of states that have adopted statutes in the following areas: videotaped testimony, closed-circuit television testimony, videotaped interviews, special hearsay exceptions, and the abolition of competency requirements.

II. The Problems Defined

As some researchers suggest, new research relating to children in the legal system would be helpful in a number of areas.[5] These

2. L. Berliner & D. Stevens, *Advocating for Sexually Abused Children in the Criminal Justice System*, in Sexual Abuse of Children: Selected Readings, National Center on Child Abuse and Neglect (1980); De Francis, *Protecting the Child Victim of Sex Crimes*, American Humane Association (1969); MacFarlane, *Sexual Abuse of Children*, in The Victimization of Women 81 (J. Chapman and M. Gates eds. 1978); Sgroi, *Introduction: A National Needs Assessment for Protecting Child Victims of Sexual Assault*, in Sexual Assault of Children and Adolescents xv (A. Burgess et al. eds. 1978); *Child Sexual Abuse and the Law*, American Bar Association (J. Bulkley ed. 1981).
3. K. MacFarlane & J. Bulkley, *Treating Child Sexual Abuse: An Overview of Current Program Models*, in Social Work and Child Sexual Abuse 69, J. of Soc. Work & Hum. Sexuality, Vol. 1 No. 2 (1982) (hereinafter cited as *Treating Child Sexual Abuse*).
4. These and other areas, however, were analyzed at the ABA's March 1985 National Policy Conference on Legal Reforms in Child Sexual Abuse Cases, and in that conference's report, *Papers from a National Policy Conference on Legal Reforms in Child Sexual Abuse Cases* (June, 1985).
5. *See* G. Melton, *Child Witnesses and the First Amendment: A Psychological Dilemma*, in The Child Witness 109, J. Soc. Issues Vol. 40 No. 2 (G. Goodman ed. 1984); G. Melton, *Testimony on the Subject of Child Sexual Abuse Victims in the Courtroom* before the U.S. Senate Subcommittee on Juvenile Justice, Committee on the Judiciary, May 22, 1984.

646

areas include the effects of pretrial investigation and the trial itself on the child's performance as a witness; determining what factors may make some children more vulnerable, e.g., age, type of abuse, relationship of child to perpetrator, threats, young age, sex; determining what aspects of the legal process (such as repeated pretrial questioning, delays, testifying in open court, or in front of the defendant) cause greatest trauma, inhibit reporting, or contribute to a child's retraction or refusal to testify; and what if any long term effects legal intervention produces upon children. The experience of numerous professionals throughout the country who have frequent contact with children have fueled the recent legislative reform movement.

In 1981, the National Center on Child Abuse and Neglect (NCCAN) reported that the average age of a child victim of sexual abuse was between 11 and 14 years of age; however, it also was noted that more recent program information showed a higher percentage of sexually abused children under age 12, and one program showed that ⅓ of the victims were under age six.[6] Recent revelations about sexual abuse of pre-school age children in child care forces us to accept the fact that very young children are at risk. Further, it must now be acknowledged that in addition to parental sexual abuse, a significant amount of sexual abuse is committed by adults outside of the home. These new problems also raise new legal concerns. In cases involving offenders who are not parents, such as teachers, day care providers, or babysitters, the criminal justice system is more likely to be involved than when the offender is a parent. Although more incest cases also are being prosecuted in many jurisdictions, a juvenile court child protection proceeding sometimes is the only legal intervention in an incest case. Even if criminal prosecution occurs in an incest case, a special program may exist for offenders who plead guilty, where they may obtain specialized treatment along with the child and family under a sentence of work-release or probation.[7] The child in a non-incest case therefore has a greater chance of having to testify in a criminal proceeding, since more prosecutions and fewer guilty pleas are likely. In cases with young victims, there may be greater problems in proving the abuse and consequently, greater trauma to the child.

Although one may accept the need to reform laws and legal procedures, the assumptions and purposes underlying proposals need to be examined, and the legal and practical consequences should be an-

---

6. *Child Sexual Abuse: Incest, Assault and Sexual Exploitation,* at 3 National Center on Child Abuse and Neglect (Rev. April, 1981).

7. *See Innovations in the Prosecution of Child Sexual Abuse Cases,* American Bar Association (J. Bulkley ed. 1981); *Treating Child Sexual Abuse, supra* note 3.

alyzed thoroughly before states adopt innovative approaches. It is wise to proceed with caution in order to protect against reversals of convictions by appeals courts based on a statute's unconstitutionality, to prevent backlash and failure of legislatures to enact reforms for fear they will be found unconstitutional by the judiciary, and to ensure that reforms are narrowly drawn to apply only in cases where it has been shown that a particular child would be injured by a particular legal procedure.

III. Approaching the Problems

A state may want to consider adopting a range of legislative alternatives that permit a court to decide "on a case-by-case basis whether the state's legitimate concern for the well-being of the minor victim necessitates"[8] the use of a particular evidentiary or procedural approach. As the U.S. Supreme Court stated in *Globe Newspaper Co. v. Superior Court*, a case-by-case determination "ensures that the constitutional right of the press and public to gain access to criminal trials will not be restricted except where necessary to protect the State's interest."[9] In addition to avoiding constitutional challenges — whether they involve the first amendment or the rights of a defendant in criminal trials — a statute that provides "a narrowly tailored means of accommodating the state's asserted interest"[10] also assures that an approach is used only when clearly necessary. In *Globe Newspaper*, a statute permitting mandatory closure of the courtroom during the testimony of child sexual abuse victims in a criminal trial was held to be overly broad, since it would apply whether or not the victim sought to have closure and even if the victim would not suffer injury if the proceeding was open to the press or public.

Indeed, research and clinical evidence suggests that children, like adults, react differently to being victimized and react differently to the aftermath and the judicial process.[11] Mandating an approach for all children could also be interpreted as degrading; although efforts should be made to protect children, efforts also should be directed to treating them equally as adults, where appropriate. Reform laws abolishing competency requirements for children often reflect such an attitude.

It may be wiser to enact reforms in the treatment of child sex-

---

8. Globe Newspaper Co. v. Superior Court, 457 U.S. 596, 608 (1982).
9. *Id.*
10. *Id.*
11. L. Berliner & M. K. Barbieri, *The Testimony of the Child Victim of Sexual Assault*, in the Child Witness 125, 135, *supra* note 5; Libai, *The Protection of the Child Victim of a Sexual Offense in the Criminal Justice System*, 15 WAYNE L. REV. 977, 1015 (1969); G. Melton, *Child Witnesses and the First Amendment*, *supra* note 5.

648

ual abuse cases as part of a broader package of special procedures for *any victim of crime* who is shown to have specific vulnerabilities or who is likely to be psychologically harmed by particular legal procedures. On the one hand, concern for safeguarding the well-being of young victims may justify special treatment; on the other hand, many other potentially vulnerable populations, such as developmentally disabled elderly persons, adult persons who have a history of psychiatric problems, or adult persons who were victimized in an extremely traumatic crime also may deserve special procedures to reduce the trauma they experience in the criminal justice system.

Although it might be better for states to develop a comprehensive legislative scheme for all vulnerable crime victims, this approach has its shortcomings. First of all, legislatures tend to deal with single issues and to consider laws that address a specific current problem. Secondly, it seems improbable that the more radical reforms proposed in child sexual abuse cases could be available for a much larger category of all vulnerable crime victims. Nevertheless, the idea of developing special procedures by statute for young victims may lead other groups to lobby for similar reforms.

Perhaps a more fertile area for research is one involving the need to study and compare the effects of victimization and legal intervention on a variety of crime victims. One risk with establishing special approaches for child witnesses without procedures available for other witnesses is that a social policy of special treatment for a particular group necessarily excludes other potentially eligible groups in society. If children do not suffer greater harm than certain other crime victims, or if other criminal cases are equally difficult to prove, it seems unwise to develop approaches solely for children. Furthermore, it may be wise to limit the use of evidentiary and procedural innovations to cases in which the young victim is, for example, under ten years of age. Many statutes that provide for testimony by videotape or television cover children up to 16, 17 or 18 years of age.[12] Lowering the applicable age limit might eliminate a lot of children who may be traumatized, but it may be one method of ensuring that special approaches are used only in the most serious cases or extraordinary circumstances.

IV. State Legislation Creating a Special Hearsay Exception for a Child's Complaint of Sexual Abuse

One evidentiary reform attracting attention by state legislatures is the creation of a special exception to the hearsay rule to permit a child victim's complaint of sexual abuse to be admitted into evi-

---

12.   Alaska, Arkansas, California, Montana, New Mexico, South Dakota, Wisconsin.

dence. Traditionally, such a statement is hearsay and may not be admitted to prove the truth of the assertion unless it falls within an existing hearsay exception. State codes include a variety of exceptions for admitting these statements, including the following: (1) excited utterances or *res gestae*; (2) statements to physicians; (3) statement of present bodily feelings or symptoms or present sense impressions; (4) necessity exception; (5) prior consistent statements (if the child is available to testify); and (6) residual exception.[13] A child's prompt complaint also may be admitted not as proof of the truth of the statements but to corroborate the child's in-court testimony to rebut an inference of silence inconsistent with the abusive act.[14] Yet some states have not adopted all the above exceptions,[15] and a child's statement may not meet the strict requirements of a particular traditional exception.

Because of the need for such statements as evidence (direct evidence or other circumstantial evidence may be minimal, and a statement may not fit within an existing exception) eleven states have adopted by statute a special hearsay exception. (See Appendix A for list of states.) Although the language and organization of the provisions vary, most statutes allow a child victim's statement to be admitted if: (1) either the child testifies or is found to be unavailable; and (2) the court finds the statement to be reliable. Only Illinois and Vermont allow such statements to corroborate the child's in-court testimony. Iowa allows statements to be admitted only in juvenile court child abuse adjudication proceedings and does not require unavailability or reliability.

Four statutes (Indiana, Minnesota, South Dakota and Washington) require corroboration or other evidence of the act, in addition to requiring unavailability of the child and reliability of the statement before it may be admitted. The purpose of requiring other evidence in addition to the statement when the child victim's testimony is not available is to prevent a conviction based upon evidence of the child's statements alone. The appropriate statutory language should indicate that after a court finds both unavailability and reliability, and admits the statement into evidence, there may not be a conviction un-

---

13. J. Bulkley, *Evidentiary Theories for Admitting a Child's Out-of-Court Statement of Sexual Abuse at Trial,* in Child Sexual Abuse and the Law 153 (J. Bulkley, ed. 1981).

14. *Id.* For more in-depth discussion of the new special exceptions, *see* Skoler, *New Hearsay Exceptions for a Child's Statement of Sexual Abuse,* 18 J. MAR. L. REV. 1 (1984); *Sexual Abuse of Children — Washington's New Hearsay Exception,* 58 WASH. L. REV. 813 (1983); *A Comprehensive Approach to Child Hearsay Statements in Sex Abuse Cases,* 83 COLUM. L. REV. 1745 (1983); J. Pierron, *The New Kansas Law Regarding Admissibility of Child-Victim Hearsay Statements,* J. Kan. Bar Assn. 88 (Summer, 1983). *See also Papers from a National Policy Conference on Legal Reforms in Child Sexual Abuse Cases,* American Bar Association (June 1985).

15. *See, .e.g.,* KAN. STAT. ANN. § 60-460 (1982) with an exhaustive array of statutory hearsay exceptions.

650

less other evidence exists in addition to the child's statement. As discussed below, this may not be necessary, since a prosecution is unlikely to be commenced with only the child's statement. On the other hand, a state may want to include this requirement to ensure that defendants receive a fair trial.

Under the new exceptions, if the child testifies at trial, the prior statement can be admitted as substantive evidence; however, the child's testimony is sufficient to convict without the statement, and the statement merely serves to corroborate the in-court testimony. In cases where the child cannot testify, the necessity for these statements is much greater. Situations where the child may not be able to testify include cases involving extremely young victims (such as two or three-year olds) who may not be able to communicate or remember what happened to them, or other children who would be highly traumatized emotionally from testifying or intimidated by the defendant into not testifying.[16] As noted above, the problem with these cases is that if the child does not testify and the sole evidence is the victim's out-of-court statement, it is unlikely that the state would bring a case. But where circumstantial evidence in addition to the statement is available, a prosecutor could decide that there is sufficient evidence to convict the defendant beyond a reasonable doubt.

Despite the hope that these new exceptions bring toward increasing the number of prosecutions and convictions, in cases where the child does not testify and is not subject to cross-examination, admissibility of statements under the new exceptions may be jeopardized under the confrontation clause of the sixth amendment.[17] The confrontation clause has been interpreted as a rule of preference for "face-to-face confrontation at trial," requiring the "personal presence of the witness at trial, enabling the trier to observe his demeanor as an aid in evaluating his credibility and making false accusation more unlikely because of the presence of the accused and the solemnity of the occasion."[18] If, however, the declarant's live testimony in court cannot be obtained, principles of necessity and public policy have been invoked to admit some hearsay statements.[19]

It would be not enough, however, for the prosecutor simply not to call or produce the child victim to testify at trial. Indeed, the U.S. Supreme Court in the 1980 decision of *Ohio v. Roberts* held that to satisfy the confrontation clause, the "prosecution must either produce, or demonstrate the unavailability of, the declarant whose state-

---

16. *See* L. Berliner & M.K. Barbieri, *supra* note 11; U.S. v. Carlson, 547 F.2d 1346 (8th Cir. 1976); State v. Sheppard, I 0822-12-83 (N.J. Super. Ct. Sept. 27, 1984).
17. U.S. Const. amend. VI.
18. McCormick, Evidence § 252, at 606 (1972).
19. Mattox v. U.S., 156 U.S. 237 (1895).

ment it wishes to use against the defendant."[20] Thus as noted earlier, if the child is available and testifies at trial, the statement may be admitted under a special exception as a prior consistent statement with no further inquiry.

If a prosecutor chose not to produce the child victim as a witness, however, two requirements must be met under *Ohio v. Roberts* to satisfy the confrontation clause. In addition to unavailability the statement must possess indicia of reliability. Both of these requirements are discussed in greater detail below.

A. *Unavailability*

Most of the new hearsay exceptions require a showing of the declarant's unavailability before the statement may be admitted. Traditional categories of unavailability include death, absence, physical disability, mental infirmity or insanity, failure of memory, refusal to testify, privilege, or supervening disqualification.[21] Unavailability of the witness at trial also is a requirement for admitting hearsay under certain traditional exceptions, including dying declarations, statements against interest, and former testimony. (Most exceptions allow hearsay to be admitted even if the declarant does not testify at trial.)

There is, however, a higher standard of unavailability for constitutional purposes. The Supreme Court has addressed the issue only in the context of a declarant's absence from the jurisdiction, holding that the prosecution must make a "good faith effort" to obtain the presence of the witness at trial.[22] The Court also has indicated in the *Ohio v. Roberts* decision that the "lengths to which the prosecution must go to produce the witness is a question of reasonableness."[23] Until the Supreme Court decides the issue, this is the only guide for courts in deciding what is a sufficient showing of unavailability to satisfy the confrontation clause.

In child sexual abuse cases, a child is likely to be unavailable under the categories of mental infirmity (which may encompass psychological harm),[24] failure of memory,[25] refusal to testify (based on threats of harm to the child by the defendant),[26] and incompe-

---

20. Ohio v. Roberts, 448˙ U.S. 55, 65 (1979).
21. McCORMICK, EVIDENCE § 253, at 608 (1972).
22. Barber v. Page, 390 U.S. 719 (1968).
23. Ohio v. Roberts, 448 U.S. at 74.
24. *See* People v. Stritzinger, 34 Cal.3d 441, 668 P.2d 738 (1983); Hochheiser v. Superior Court, No. 5005940 (Cal. Ct. App. Nov. 9, 1984) (affirmed during week of Feb. 11, 1985 by California Supreme Court); People v. Gomez, 103 Cal. Rptr. 80, 26 Cal. App.3d 225 (1972); Warren v. U.S., 436 A.2d 821, (D.C. 1981).
25. *See* U.S. v. Iron Shell, 633 F.2d 77 (8th Cir. 1980); State v. McCafferty, #14350 (S.D. Oct. 3, 1984); State v. Slider, No. 12888-4-I (Wash. Ct. App. Sept. 24, 1984).
26. *See, e.g.*, Rice v. Marshall, 709 F.2d 1100 (6th Cir. 1983); U.S. v. Carlson, 547

tency.[27] Rather than declare a child incompetent, courts have sometimes established a special type of unavailability for very young child sexual abuse victims who cannot be meaningfully cross-examined, although they are present at trial and take the witness stand.[28] Thus, prosecutors may be able to obtain admission of statements both in cases where the child does not take the witness stand at all, or where the child "freezes up" on the stand, and becomes unavailable because of failure of memory, or simply a refusal or inability to continue testifying. Showing unavailability, however, may not always be easy. One court, for example, found that the evidence presented established only that the witnesses' mental, emotional, and physical condition rendered her ability to testify merely inconvenient and *not* relatively impossible.[29]

One special exception statute in Indiana specifically defines unavailability of a child sexual abuse victim, providing that a child is unavailable if:

> (i) a psychiatrist has certified that the child's participation in the trial would be a traumatic experience; (ii) a physician has certified that the child cannot participate in the trial for medical reasons; or (iii) the court has determined that the child is incapable of understanding the nature and obligation of an oath.[30]

States that have adopted or are considering special exceptions should include definitions or refer to other sections of their code regarding unavailability.[31] How unavailability should be shown also should be specified, including the requirement of a hearing on the issue and the making of a trial record. A hearing should be held, for example, on a child's incompetency if that is the basis of unavailability alleged by the prosecutor. Holding a hearing ensures factual support for the trial court's finding and gives an appellate court a basis with which to uphold the trial court's determination.

California courts have held that unavailability due to psychological harm can be established only by an expert, not a lay witness.[32] Thus, when seeking to admit statements when the child is alleged to be unavailable due to severe psychological harm from testifying, a

---

F.2d 1346 (8th Cir. 1976); State v. Sheppard, #0822-12-83 (N.J. Super. Sept. 27, 1984).

27. *See* Indiana statute, Appendix A; State v. Ryan, No. 50216-1 (Wash. S. Ct. Nov. 26, 1984).

28. U.S. v. Iron Shell, 633 F.2d 77 (8th Cir. 1980); U.S. v. Nick, 604 F.2d 1199 (9th Cir. 1979); State v. McCafferty, #14350 (S.D. Oct. 3, 1984).

29. People v. Williams, 155 Cal. Rptr. 414 (1979).

30. *See* Appendix A.

31. Warren v. U.S., 436 A.2d 821 (D.C. 1981). This case notes that nineteen states have statutes with mental infirmity as a category of unavailability and includes an excellent discussion on psychological harm from testifying as an unavailability basis for admitting prior testimony.

32. *See, e.g.,* People v. Stritzinger, 34 Cal.3d 441, 668 P.2d 738 (Cal. 1983).

653

mental health professional who has had direct experience with the child should testify to emotional problems of the child and that such problems would be seriously exacerbated by testifying in court. Indiana's statute is a good example of specifying a requirement for expert testimony, although California has added a category of unavailability that defines an expert as "a physician, surgeon, psychiatrist, licensed psychologist, licensed clinical social worker, or licensed marriage family or child counselor."[33]

B. Reliability

As noted previously, in order to protect an accused's constitutional right to confront witnesses, a second requirement also must be met before a child's statement may be admitted under the new exceptions. In *Ohio v. Roberts*, the U.S. Supreme Court indicated that after a witness is shown to be unavailable, a statement may be admitted only if it has "sufficient indicia of reliability"; such reliability "can be inferred without more in a case where the evidence falls within a *firmly rooted hearsay exception. In other cases, the evidence must be excluded, at least absent a showing of particularized guarantees of trustworthiness."[34] Thus, if a statement does not fall within a "firmly rooted exception," a court can nevertheless admit the statement under a special exception if the statement is shown to possess particularized guarantees of trustworthiness.

As with the showing of unavailability, factors showing trustworthiness may not be easy to establish. Indeed, it is preferable for prosecutors to seek admissibility of hearsay statements of child sexual abuse victims under one or more of the long-standing or accepted exceptions. A court would be likely to admit a statement under a traditional exception in order to avoid making particularized findings of trustworthiness. South Dakota's statute, for example, makes a statement admissible under the *new* exception only if it is not admissible under any other statute or exception.[35]

In seeking admissibility under the new exception, a prosecutor should first attempt to show that the statement satisfied one or more criteria cited in the U.S. Supreme Court's decision in *Dutton v. Evans*.[36] The *Dutton* criteria are: (1) The statement contains no express assertion of past fact; (2) cross-examination could not show the declarant's lack of knowledge; (3) the possibility of declarant's faulty recollection is remote; and (4) the circumstances surrounding the

---

33. Cal. Evid. Code § 240 (amended and effective January 1, 1985, Assem. Bill No. 3840, Stats. 1984, ch. 401).
34. Ohio v. Roberts, 448 U.S. at 66 (emphasis added).
35. *See* S.D.C.L.A. § 19-16-38 (1984).
36. Dutton v. Evans, 400 U.S. 74 (1970).

654

statement are such that there is no reason to suppose the declarant misrepresented the defendant's involvement.

Courts have held that all four *Dutton* factors need not be present in order to admit a statement over confrontation objections, and in fact, if other factors indicate reliability, a statement need not satisfy any of the elements.[37] Prosecutors also should marshall facts to satisfy criteria cited by other courts as indicating a statement's trustworthiness, including the following:

(1) whether there is an apparent motive to lie;

(2) the general character of the declarant;

(3) whether more than one person heard the statements;

(4) whether the statements were spontaneous or directly responsive to questions;

(5) the timing of the declaration;

(6) the relationship of speaker and declarant;

(7) the child's young age makes it unlikely the child fabricated where the statement represents a graphic account beyond the child's experience;

(8) the nature and duration of the abuse;

(9) the relationship of declarant and defendant;

(10) the statement has a "ring of verity" and terminology appropriate to the child's age;

(11) the child was suffering pain or distress when making statement; and

(12) extrinsic evidence exists to show defendant's opportunity to commit the act complained of in child's statement;

(13) certainty that the statement was made, based on an assessment of the child's credibility in court;]

(14) assurance of personal knowledge of the event;

(15) partiality of the child because of interest, bias, coercion or corruption.[38]

V. Alternative Approaches for Avoiding the Child Victim's Testimony in Open Court Where Necessary to Prevent Severe Emotional Trauma or When the Child is Otherwise Not Available as a Witness

The ABA *Recommendations* state the following regarding the testimony of child sexual abuse victims:

1.4.4. Child's Testimony

> In criminal cases, a child sexual abuse victim should testify at preliminary hearings or grand jury proceedings only if needed. Where necessary to prevent trauma to the child, procedures

---

37. U.S. v. Perez, 658 F.2d 654 (8th Cir. 1981).

38. *See* U.S. v. Perez, 658 F.2d at 661 n. 6; U.S. v. Iron Shell, 633 F.2d at 87; U.S. v. Nick, 604 F.2d at 1199; State v. Ryan, No. 50216-1; State v. McCafferty, #14350 (S.D. Oct. 3, 1984); Bertrang v. State, 50 Wis. 2d 702, 184 N.W.2d 867 (1971).

should be developed to avoid the need for the child's testimony in open court in criminal and civil trials, taking into account any constitutional limitations.

Testifying in a formal courtroom at a criminal trial in front of the defendant, jury, judge and an audience of spectators, and being subjected to direct and cross-examination often is cited as one of the most intimidating and stressful aspects of the legal process for children.[39] Although such an experience also may be anxiety-producing for adults, adults generally have developed coping mechanisms to deal with such situations. Further, adults have a general understanding of the purpose and operation of our legal system and should be better able to withstand and deal with a defense attorney's efforts to discredit their testimony.

The choice of alternatives for taking a child's testimony should depend upon the needs and problems of a particular child. For some children, testifying in front of the defendant may not be as traumatic as sitting on the witness stand in a formal courtroom with an audience full of strangers and the press or with the jury present. A videotaped deposition with the defendant present may be the proper mechanism for such a child. In juvenile court child protection cases there is no jury and the public is excluded, and in some cases, a child may be interviewed in the judge's chambers (generally with the parent alleged to have committed the abuse present). This would provide a less formal setting in which the child may be examined and cross-examined. Other children may not be disturbed by testifying in the presence of the public or the jury, but terrified of facing the defendant. Still other children may only require an advocate, close friend or relative in order to feel less traumatized. Finally, some children may find testifying a helpful experience in dealing with the abuse and may not be traumatized at all.

For the above reasons, legislatures adopting innovative approaches should not mandate a particular approach for all child victims, such as excusing all children from testifying, closing the courtroom in all cases when a child testifies, or preventing the child from seeing the defendant in all cases during the child's testimony. Indeed, the U.S. Supreme Court in *Globe Newspaper Co. v. Superior Court* held that mandatory exclusion of the press during the testimony of a child sexual abuse victim was violative of the first amendment.[40]

A number of states have enacted or are considering legislation allowing alternatives for taking the testimony of a child sexual abuse

---

39. *See* sources cited *supra* note 2.
40. 457 U.S. 596 (1982).

656

victim in order to prevent the child from having to testify in open court at trial, including testimony by videotape or closed-circuit television. States, however, should adopt legislation allowing the use of such alternatives. A California appeals court skirted the constitutional issues and disallowed the use of closed-circuit television for taking a child's trial testimony because specific authorization for such a procedure had not been granted by state statute, a necessity given the serious constitutional issues raised by the procedure.[41] Other courts, however, have allowed such alternatives without legislative authority, or at least have addressed the constitutional issues despite the absence of legislation.[42] For example, where no legislative authority existed, some courts have allowed a child sexual abuse victim to testify in court with the defendant hidden from the child's view, although courts have held such a procedure to be violative of the defendant's right of confrontation.[43]

A. Videotaped Testimony or Deposition

States seem to be most interested in statutes to allow videotaping of a child's testimony. In 1982, the ABA's Child Sexual Abuse Project found that four (4) states allowed videotaped testimony. By 1985, fourteen (14) states had statutes permitting videotaped trial or preliminary hearing testimony. (See Appendix A for states.) Six (6) of the 14 statutes permit the videotape to be made or admitted into evidence at trial only if the court finds that the child's testimony in open court would cause severe emotional trauma.[44] Three (3) of these statutes allow either the videotape to be made or to be admitted at trial if the court finds the child to be "medically unavailable" because testimony would cause emotional trauma, or otherwise "unavailable" as defined in a state's evidence code sections relating to the admissibility of hearsay or prior testimony.[45] The remaining statutes simply give the court discretion to order the making of the videotape. Thirteen (13) specifically allow cross-examination or questioning of the child by the defendant or his lawyer.

Twelve (12) statutes require the physical presence of the defen-

---

41. Hochheiser v. Superior Court, No. 5005940 (Cal. Ct. App. Nov. 9, 1984).

42. See U.S. v. Benfield, 593 F.2d 815 (8th Cir. 1979) (videotaped deposition with defendant in a different room and not seen by witness); State v. Sheppard #10822-12-83 (N.J. Super. Sept. 27, 1984) (closed-circuit television); State v. Hutchins, 286 So. 2d 244 (Fla. 1973) (videotaped deposition). See also Washington Post, Nov. 14, 1984 "Judge Says Girl, 4 Must Face Father in Sex Abuse Trial" disallowing closed circuit television as a violation of the defendant's right to confront witnesses.

43. See State v. Strable, 313 N.W. 2d 497 (Iowa 1981) (upheld); Herbert v. Superior Court, 172 Cal. Rptr. 850 117 Cal. App.3d 132 (1981) (struck down).

44. California, Colorado, Florida, Maine, South Dakota, and Wisconsin (Florida and Wisconsin only require a finding by the court when the videotape is made).

45. California, Colorado and South Dakota.

dant in the room where the videotaping takes place; the statutes in Kentucky and Texas *mandate* that the defendant be hidden from the child's view, although the defendant must be able to see and hear the child. The age of the child varies by statute, although all provisions allow videotaping of children under 12 years of age.

B. Live Testimony of the Child by Closed-Circuit Television

Three (3) states, Kentucky, Louisiana, and Texas, have statutes permitting closed-circuit television of a child's testimony. (See Appendix A.) All of these laws are structured along similar lines. During the trial, the child is questioned by the prosecutor and defense attorney (with a support person allowed to be present) in a room outside the courtroom, which is televised to the judge, jury and public in the courtroom. The defendant must be able to "observe and hear the testimony of the child in person," but the child may not see or hear the defendant. Only Louisiana conditions the use of this procedure "when justice so requires."

A bill in California, which has passed the state senate, proposes *two-way* television of the child's testimony, which may be utilized if psychological harm to the child from testimony in open court is shown. Under this bill, the child would be in a room outside the courtroom, and the judge, jury, defendant, and both attorneys would be in the courtroom. The child would be able to see the courtroom by television, and the people in the courtroom can see the child by television, and only a support person would be permitted with the child. This proposal thus differs from the other laws by allowing the child to see the courtroom and the jury, judge, public and defendant, but permits the questioning to occur by television rather than in the child's presence.

C. Potential Constitutional and Other Problems With Alternative Procedures for Taking a Child's Testimony

The above statutory alternatives may create a number of constitutional violations, many of which have been analyzed by various law journal articles.[46] As noted earlier, careful consideration of these issues is advised in order to avoid reversals of convictions and to prevent retrials. When a significant number of states have passed legislation dealing with an area of great concern to the public such as child sexual abuse, the natural inclination to follow the trend should

---

46. *See* Brakel, *Videotape in Trial Proceedings: A Technological Obsession*, 61 ABA J. 956 (Aug. 1975); Doret, *Trial by Videotape — Can Justice Be Seen to be Done?*, 47 Temp. L.Q. 228 (1973-74); Comment, *Libai's Child Courtroom: Is is Constitutional?*, 7 J. Juv. L. 31 (1983); Comment, *The Criminal Videotape Trial: Serious Constitutional Questions*, 55 OR. L. REV. 567 (1976); *An Evaluation of Video-Tape Trials*, 26 Stan. L. Rev. 619 (1974).

658

be tempered by evaluating the issue in terms of both its constitutionality as well as its practicality.

The constitutional issues raised by the new videotaping and closed-circuit television statutes include the defendant's right to a fair trial under the due process clause of the fourteenth amendment,[47] the defendant's sixth amendment right to a public trial and to a trial by jury,[48] the defendant's sixth amendment right to confront witnesses,[49] and the public's (and press') first amendment right to attend criminal trials.[50] Commentators have suggested that the defendant's jury trial right may be infringed, even if the videotaping is shown to the jury later, because it interferes with the jury's decisionmaking function by distorting or not fully conveying evidence, especially a witness' demeanor; it denies the jury's power at common law to question witnesses; and "it compromises the integrity of the court."[51]

The defendant's right to a fair trial under the 14th amendment due process clause "traditionally has required judge and jury to be unbiased and evidence to be trustworthy."[52] The use of videotaping may prevent the jury from making an accurate and unbiased decision decision if the videotaping medium prejudicially alters or does not convey evidence. Moreover, the truth-eliciting aspects of the jury trial are removed when videotaping is used, enhancing the possibility of unfairness or perjury.[53]

As with the jury trial right, the defendant's right to a public trial and the right of the press and public to attend criminal trials may be infringed even if the videotape is shown later to the public. Commentators have cited a number of reasons to support this contention, such as the fact that witnesses "may speak more truthfully if placed before the scrutiny of their peers," and that confidence in judicial remedies may lead to public skepticism of judicial processes if the videotaping is done privately.[54]

The first amendment right of access to criminal trials by the press and public has been analyzed in depth elsewhere.[55] The issue has reached the U.S. Supreme Court, which held in *Globe Newspaper* that mandatory closure of the courtroom during the victim's testimony violated the first amendment. Statutes in many states allow

---

47. U.S. CONST. amend. XIV.
48. U.S. CONST. amend. VI.
49. *Id.*
50. U.S. CONST. amend. I.
51. 55 OR. L. REV. at 578.
52. *Id.* at 582.
53. *Id.* at 583.
54. *Id.* at 573.
55. *See* Parker, *The Child Witness Versus the Press: A Proposed Legislative Response to Globe v. Superior Court*, 47 ALB. L. REV. 408 (1983); G. Melton, *supra* note 5.

closure within the discretion of the court, which should pass constitutional muster. Videotaped testimony shown later to the press and public also should not be violative of the first amendment as long as they are not *mandated* by statute.

The defendant's sixth amendment right to confront witnesses in a criminal trial also may be violated unless certain requirements are met before using videotaped testimony or closed circuit television. Generally, closed circuit television or videotaping of the child's testimony is sought where it is believed that if the child testifies, she will suffer serious emotional harm or will be so terrified that she will refused to talk or will "freeze up" because of the courtroom setting or personal threats by the defendant. Depositions frequently have been used in situations where it is impossible to obtain the witness' personal presence at trial. One commentator notes three types of unavailability: the witness is not available for legal process (e.g. death, absence); available for process, but not available for actual attendance (e.g., illness); or available for process and attendance but not available for testifying. It is the third category that justifies videotaping or television for taking the child's testimony.[56]

Necessity is the basic principle for the use of depositions and former testimony at trial and for the use of closed circuit television. If the witness's testimony in court cannot be had, "it will be lost entirely for the purposes of doing justice if it is not received in the form in which it survives and can be had. The only inquiry then, need be: Is his testimony in court unavailable?"[57] Thus, in order to admit videotaped testimony in lieu of the child's testimony in court, the requirement of unavailability first must be met. As with special hearsay exceptions, unavailability categories include death, absence, physical or mental disability, incompetency at trial, failure of memory, and refusal to testify.[58] As some statutes provide, severe psychological trauma to the child from testifying also may be a proper ground, although statutes that allow a videotaped deposition to be admitted based on any of the above grounds of unavailability are preferable.

As noted earlier, *Ohio v. Roberts* also requires that the deposition possess indicia of reliability, either by falling within a traditional hearsay exception or having particularized guarantees of trustworthiness.[59] In analyzing the videotaping legislation, both requirements of *Ohio v. Roberts* must be considered. The eight (8) statutes that do not require unavailability to be demonstrated proba-

---

56. WIGMORE, WIGMORE ON EVIDENCE § 1402 at 204 (1974).
57. *Id.* at 203.
58. *See* text accompanying note 21, *supra.*
59. *See* text accompanying note 34, *supra.*

660

bly violate the confrontation clause. Those statutes that require a finding of the child's unavailability, and require the testimony to be taken in accordance with the state's hearsay exception for former testimony should be constitutional. Statutes requiring a showing of unavailability and cross-examination in the defendant's presence also should satisfy confrontation requirements. Cross-examination and the defendant's presence clearly fulfill the trustworthiness requirement, and courts have allowed videotaped depositions in other cases where a witness was unable to attend the trial where these elements were present.[60] As discussed below, however, statutes that attempt to hide the defendant from the child's view may not be constitutional under the confrontation clause of the U.S. Constitution or under state constitutions if the defendant's right to be confronted with the witnesses against him is considered a right to physical, face-to-face confrontation with the witness.

The closed-circuit television laws in Kentucky and Texas do not require a showing similar to unavailability. Louisiana allows the procedure "when justice so requires." Since testimony by television should not be considered hearsay, unavailability may not be the test. Nevertheless, courts may require a showing of necessity or "extraordinary" or other circumstances similar to unavailability to justify restriction of a constitutional right.[61] The California Supreme Court recently upheld the *Hochheiser* decision which borrowed language from the *Globe* case and stated that "a compelling state interest" must be shown to permit two-way television.

The videotaping and closed-circuit television statutes in Kentucky, Louisiana, and Texas also do not permit the child to see the defendant, although the defendant must be in the room and be able to see the child. The issue is whether cross-examination without physical confrontation of the child is sufficient to satisfy the trustworthiness requirement. If confrontation is interpreted to mean that the witness and defendant must face each other physically, as some courts have held,[62] these statutes would be unconstitutional. The purpose underlying the face-to-face requirement is that the witness is less likely to make a false accusation while in the presence of the accused. This purpose clearly is not met if the child cannot see the defendant, even though the defendant can see the child. Moreover, almost half the state constitutions give the defendant a right to meet witnesses against him "face-to-face," which may be literally inter-

---

60. U.S. v. Singleton, 460 F.2d 1148, 1153 (2d Cir. 1972); State v. Hewett, 545 P. 2d 1201, 1204 (Wash. 1976); State v. Hutchins, 286 So. 2d at 246.
61. U.S. v. Benfield, 593 F.2d at 822; Hochheiser v. Superior Court, No. B005940, at 28.
62. Herbert v. Superior Court, 172 Cal. Rptr. 850 (Cal. Ct. App. 1981); U.S. v. Benfield, 593 F.2d at 822.

preted by courts; indeed, a trial court in Kentucky recently struck down the state's videotaping statute because it does not permit face-to-face confrontation of the child witness and the defendant as required by the Kentucky constitution.[63]

The above closed circuit television or videotaping provisions may guarantee trustworthiness by providing an opportunity for cross-examination, permitting the defendant to see the child, and showing the videotape or televising the testimony to the jury and public, despite the fact that the child cannot see the accused. A trial court in New Jersey upheld an approach where the defendant was in the courtroom with the judge, jury and public, who could view the child by a television monitor, although the child had no view into the courtroom.[64] Further, in a child sexual abuse prosecution, the Iowa Supreme Court allowed the defendant to be hidden from the view of the child witness during the child's testimony and rejected a confrontation challenge because there was cross-examination and the jury could observe the demeanor of the witness while testifying.[65] Unlike the Iowa situation, with the above videotaping and television laws, the child is not testifying in open court in the presence of the judge and jury. The jury does *not* have the opportunity to observe the child's demeanor *during* the videotaped deposition or preliminary hearing, although they may view it later. Although the jury may see the child testifying on television with the closed-circuit television approach, the problems cited earlier with distorted or excluded evidence are still present. As the *Hochheiser* decision noted, " . . . use of closed circuit television may affect the jurors' impressions of the witness demeanor and credibility."

It is possible that a court may hold that cross-examination alone fulfills the trustworthiness requirement, and satisfies the confrontation clause without the defendant's physical presence. One commentator notes:

> If there has been a cross-examination, there has been a confrontation. The satisfaction of the right of cross-examination disposes of any objection based on the so-called right of confrontation.[66]

Professor Wigmore further states that requiring the witness' personal appearance enables the jury and judge to observe the demeanor of the witness while testifying; it does not mean the opponent and wit-

---

63. Commonwealth v. Willis, No. 84CR346 (Ky. Cir. Ct. Feb. 20, 1985); *See* WIGMORE, WIGMORE ON EVIDENCE § 1397, at 155 for a list of state constitution confrontation clauses.
64. State v. Sheppard, #10822-12-83 (N.J. Super. Sept. 27, 1984).
65. State v. Strable, 313 N.W. 2d 497 (Iowa 1981).
66. WIGMORE, 5 WIGMORE ON EVIDENCE § 1396, at 154.

ness must be confronted, but that the witness must be present before the tribunal.[67] This element can be satisfied by videotaping or television (albeit with the drawbacks noted above).

If however, a court considers face-to-face confrontation indispensable, two-way closed-circuit television may be valid as long as confrontation is interpreted to mean that the defendant and witness only must see each other. The Supreme Court of Missouri allowed two-way closed circuit television for an expert's testimony, holding that while the witness was not *physically* present in the courtroom, "his image and voice were there . . . for the defendant to see and hear and, by the same means, simultaneously for him to be seen and heard by the witness."[68] In a 1979 case, moreover, a videotaped deposition was held to be unconstitutional where physical face-to-face confrontation was absent, although the court noted: "Today's decision should not be regarded as prohibiting the development of electronic video technology in litigation. . . . [W]here the procedure more nearly approximates the traditional courtroom setting, our approval might be forthcoming."[69] The court went on to say, "It is possible that face-to-face confrontation through two-way closed circuit television might be adequate," although concern was expressed that no showing of "extraordinary circumstances" was made in the Missouri decision.[70] Although at least one Florida trial court is known to have allowed two-way television in a child sexual abuse proceeding,[71] the recent *Hochheiser* California Supreme Court decision noted serious constitutional problems with two-way television, including violations of the defendant's right to a jury trial and a fair trial, as well as of the right of confrontation.

Another potential problem is that some statutes do not require a finding of unavailability at the time of trial when the videotape is sought to be admitted in lieu of the personal appearance of the child, but only require a finding of unavailability to make the videotape. To satisfy the confrontation clause, it may be that unavailability must be established not just at the time of the taking of the videotape, but at trial, particularly if the witness' condition may have changed.[72] Colorado requires a showing of unavailability both to make and to admit the videotape. Many state criminal procedure rules require

---

67. *Id.*
68. Kansas City v. McCoy, 525 S.W. 2d 336 (Mo. 1975).
69. U.S. v. Benfield, 593 F.2d at 821-22.
70. *Id.* at 822 n. 11.
71. *See Papers from a National Policy Conference on Legal Reforms in Child Sexual Abuse Cases, supra* note 14.
72. McCORMICK, EVIDENCE § 253, at 612-13 (1972). Indeed, U.S. v. Benfield noted its concern that only a marginal showing of unavailability was made at trial and no new evidence was presented. The court said "an additional showing of the witness' mental condition and availability on the trial date would have been a much better practice." 593 F.2d at 817 n. 4.

663

two showings.[73]

One problem that requires attention is that most statutes that allow pre-trial depositions or videotaping of preliminary hearing testimony do not permit an additional deposition if new evidence is discovered between the original videotape and the trial. (South Dakota, however, allows a second tape). Unless the videotaping occurs *during* the trial, moreover, an additional deposition frequently may be necessary, which would result in one more time a child must be questioned. Thus, states may want to consider requiring the videotaping *after* the trial has begun, as is required in Florida's statute, to avoid greater trauma to a child who is forced to be fully cross-examined a second time when unavailability is not established prior to trial.

VI. Conclusion and Emerging Issues

A number of areas relating to child victims in the legal system remain to be explored. This article addresses a few issues designed to help improve prosecutions of child sexual abuse and to prevent psychological trauma to children who testify.

Cases of child sexual abuse are being litigated in various judicial forums. In addition to civil child protection actions which may be filed in cases involving a parent, other possible legal actions include civil protective order proceedings, custody and divorce actions, and civil tort suits seeking money damages against perpetrators or against institutions, such as school systems, for hiring or maintaining an employee who sexually abuses children. These suits are becoming more prevalent, and many of them have resulted in settlements of hundreds of thousands of dollars for the victims.[74] Several attorneys have developed law practices or reputations in handling these cases.[75]

When child sexual abuse is an issue in a custody case, significant problems are presented. Conflicts between the parents must be considered when examining an allegation of sexual abuse in divorce cases. In some cases, it has been alleged that courts believe that the mother is vindictive by alleging sexual abuse, and award custody or generous visitation privileges to the father, who in fact may have sexually abused the child. On the other hand, cases now are coming to light in which it is believed that some parents have manipulated their child into claiming sexual abuse to prevent the other parent from having contact with or custody of the child. Moreover, when an

---

73. *See, e.g.*, McCORMICK, EVIDENCE § 253, at 612 n. 55, § 613 n. 56; WIGMORE, 5 WIGMORE ON EVIDENCE § 1411 (1974).

74. The ABA's Child Sexual Abuse Law Reform Project has a file with pleadings from a substantial lawsuit in Louisiana, as well as newspaper articles of a major lawsuit settled in Virginia and several others around the U.S.

75. L.A. Times, May 21, 1982, "Incest: The Victim Fights Back, Some File Suits for Damages."

allegation is made, how it is handled in the family court in a custody proceeding may be problematic, since judges may not be as knowledgeable about sexual abuse of children as their counterparts in juvenile or criminal court. In many custody cases, whether the parent sexually abused the child often is not separately proven or determined. Thus, in Maryland, a bill was enacted into law in 1984 requiring the court in a divorce or custody case to make a finding by a preponderance of the evidence regarding a sexual abuse allegation before it makes a custody award to either parent.[76] A survey of practices as well as legal research and analysis in this area would be helpful to domestic relations lawyers and family court judges.

Greater awareness and prosecutions mean that statistically more children may retract their stories (although some actually may be false retractions). Hopefully, this should result in more careful and thorough investigations before cases are filed. Further, as with *any other crime*, there will be some false reports or witnesses who lie. As one commentator has noted in discussing one of the questionable assumptions underlying the corroboration requirement for child sex offense prosecutions (now abolished in all jurisdictions):

> . . . It is estimated that most sexual offenses are never reported to the authorities. Those authorities who support the assumption cite only isolated examples of false complaints, many of which were by persons suffering from severe psychiatric disturbances. Existing statistics indicate that the frequency of "false" reports for sex offenses approximates the frequency of false reports for other crimes.[77]

Indeed, at least one researcher notes that "there is little correlation between age and honesty . . . children are no more prone to lying than adults."[78]

Although much as been learned and many changes made during the last five to ten years, reforms are still needed. New methods to protect children nevertheless must be considered in the context of our constitutional system that values liberty and assumes an individual innocent until proven guilty by the state. The current media attention focusing on the problems involving child witnesses eventually will die down. At that time, there may be greater objectivity and recognition that the current reform movement contributed to more effective handling of cases, more guilty persons prosecuted and convicted and, hopefully, fewer children traumatized.

---

76. Md. Code Ann. § 9-101 Family Law Article (Oct. 1, 1984).
77. D. Lloyd, *The Corroboration of Sexual Victimization of Children*, in Child Sexual Abuse and the Law 103, American Bar Association (J. Bulkley ed. 1981).
78. G. Melton, J. Bulkley & D. Wulkin, *Competency of Children as Witnesses*, in Child Sexual Abuse and the Law, *supra* note 77 at 125, 136-38.

Chart 1

States With Statutes For Videotaping
And Closed-Circuit Television Of A Child's Testimony
As of May, 1985**

| *Videopated Testimony* | *17 States* |
State	Citation
Alaska	ALASKA STAT. § 12.45.047 (1982)
Arizona	ARIZ. REV. STAT. ANN. § 12-2311 (1978)
Arkansas	ARK. STAT. ANN. §§ 43-2035 to 2037 (1981, 1983)
California[1]	CAL. PENAL CODE § 1346 (1983)
Colorado	COLO. REV. STAT. § 18-3-413
Florida	FLA. STAT. § 918.17 (1984)
Kansas	(Recently enacted)
Kentucky	KY. REV. STAT. § 421.350 (1984)
Iowa	(Recently enacted)
Maine	ME. REV. STAT. ANN. tit. 15, §1205 (1983)
Montana	MONT. CODE ANN. §§ 46-15-401 to 403 (1977)
New Mexico	N.M. STAT. ANN. § 30-9-17 and N.M. R. Cr. P.R. 29.1 (1980)
New York[2]	(Recently enacted — No cite yet)
Oklahoma[3]	(Recently enacted)
South Dakota[1]	S.D. CODIFIED LAWS ANN. § 23A-12-9 (1983)
Texas	TEX. CRIM. PROC. CODE ANN. § 38.071 (1983)
Wisconsin	WIS. STAT. § 967.04(7) (1983)

Bills Pending

Delaware
District of Columbia
Massachusetts
Michigan
Missouri

Ohio
South Carolina
Utah
Vermont

Chart 2

| *Closed Circuit T.V.* | *4 States* |
State	Citation
Kentucky	KY. REV. STAT. § 431.350(3) (1984)
Louisiana	LA. REV. STAT. 15:260 (1984)
Maryland[3]	(Recently enacted)
Texas	TEX. CODE CRIM. PROC. ANN. art. 38.071(3) (1983)

Bills Pending

California (passed State Senate)
Ohio

Chart 3

States With A Special Hearsay Exception for a Child's
Statements of Sexual Abuse — 11 States

State	Citation
Arizona	Ariz. Rev. Stat. Ann. § 13-1416 (1984-85)
Colorado	Colo. Rev. Stat. § 18-3-411(3)
Illinois	Ill. 83rd Gen. Assem. P.A. 83-1067 Sec. 115-10 and Ill. Stat. Ann. Ch. 37, § 704-6(4)(c)
Indiana	Ind. Code § 35-37-4-6 (1984)
Iowa (Juvenile Court Only)	Iowa Code Ann. § 232.96(6) (1984-85)
Kansas	Kan. Stat. Ann. § 60-460(dd) (1982)
Minnesota	Minn. Stat. § 595.02(3) (1984)
South Dakota	S.D. Codified Laws Ann. § 19-16-38 (1984)
Utah	Utah Code Ann. § 76-5-411 (1983)
Vermont	(Recently enacted)
Washington	Wash. Rev. Code § 9A.44.120 (1982)

Chart 4

Special Exception for Videopated Interviews of Child Sexual Abuse Victims — 4 States

State	Citation
Iowa (Juvenile Court Only)	Iowa Code § 232.96(6)(Supp. 1984).
Kentucky	Ky. Rev. Stat. § 421.350(1)(2) (1984)
Louisiana	La. Rev. Stat. 15:440.1-.6 (1984)
Texas	Tex. Code Crim. Proc. Ann. art. 38.071(1), (2) (1983)

Chart 5

States With Statutes or Rules Eliminating Competency Qualification of Children — 23 States

State	Citation
Arizona	ARIZ. REV. STAT. ANN. § 12-2202
Arkansas	ARK. STAT. ANN. § 28-1001
Colorado (sex abuse only)	COLO. REV. STAT. § 13-90-106(1)(b)
Delaware	R. Evid. 601
Florida	FLA. STAT. § 90.601
Iowa	IOWA CODE § 622.1
Maryland	MD. CTS. & JUD. PROC. CODE ANN. § 9-101
Michigan	MICH. STAT. ANN. § 27A.2163
Mississippi	MISS. CODE ANN. § 13-1-3
Missouri	MO. REV. STAT. § 491.060(2)
Nebraska	NEB. REV. STAT. § 27-601
Nevada	NEV. REV STAT. § 50.015
New Jersey	N.J. REV. STAT. § 2A:81-1
New Mexico	R. Evid. 601
North Dakota	R. Evid. 601
Oklahoma	OKLA. STAT. § 12-2601
Oregon	OR. REV. STAT. § 40.310
Pennsylvania	PA. STAT. ANN. § 42-5911 (Purdon)
South Dakota	S.D. CODIFIED LAWS ANN. § 19-14-1
Utah (sex abuse only)	UTAH CODE ANN. §§ 78-24-2; 76-5-410
Washington	WASH. REV. CODE § 5.60.050
Wisconsin	WIS. STAT. § 906.01
Wyoming	WYO. STAT. § 1-138

*Information for these charts was obtained through research by the ABA's Child Sexual Abuse Law Reform Project (including the help of the project's law clerk, Carl Jenkins) and from a legislative survey prepared for a report of a recent project on child victim legal reforms by ABT Associates, Boston, Massachusetts (the final report will be available in the spring, 1985, and will be known as *When the Victim is a Child: Issues for Judges and Prosecutors*).
**Some apply in both criminal and civil cases, and some in all child abuse cases, but most cover criminal child sex offense cases only.
¹Videotaped preliminary hearing testimony for use at trial.
²Videotaped testimony for use at Grant Jury proceeding.
³These laws were passed immediately before the publication of this article.

0091-4169/88/7903-759
THE JOURNAL OF CRIMINAL LAW & CRIMINOLOGY
Copyright © 1988 by Northwestern University, School of Law

Vol. 79, No. 3
Printed in U.S.A.

SIXTH AMENDMENT—DEFENDANT'S RIGHT TO CONFRONT WITNESSES: CONSTITUTIONALITY OF PROTECTIVE MEASURES IN CHILD SEXUAL ASSAULT CASES

Coy v. Iowa, 108 S. Ct. 2798 (1988)

I. INTRODUCTION

In *Coy v. Iowa*,[1] the United States Supreme Court held that a one-way mirror placed between the thirteen-year-old victims of an alleged sexual assault and the defendant during the victims' testimony at trial violated the defendant's sixth amendment[2] right to confront the witnesses against him.[3] In the Supreme Court of Iowa, defendant Coy had challenged his sexual assault conviction on the grounds that the placing of the one-way mirror, in accordance with an Iowa statute,[4] between himself and the children testifying at his trial violated his constitutional right to confront the witnesses against him and his constitutional right to due process.[5] The Supreme Court of Iowa held that the defendant's rights were not violated by the screen.[6] On appeal to the United States Supreme Court, Coy again argued that his constitutional rights were violated. The United States Supreme Court reversed the lower court

---

[1] 108 S. Ct. 2798 (1988).

[2] The sixth amendment provides in pertinent part: "[i]n all criminal prosecutions, the accused shall enjoy the right . . . to be confronted with the witnesses against him." U.S. CONST. amend. VI.

[3] *Coy*, 108 S. Ct. at 2799, 2802.

[4] The relevant Iowa provision provides in pertinent part:

The court may require a party be confined [sic] to an adjacent room or behind a screen or mirror that permits the party to see and hear the child during the child's testimony, but does not allow the child to see or hear the party. However, if a party is so confined, the court shall take measures to insure that the party and counsel can confer during the testimony and shall inform the child that the party can see and hear the child during the testimony.

IOWA CODE ANN. § 910A.14 (West 1987).

[5] State v. Coy, 397 N W 2d 730, 730-31 (Iowa 1986), *rev'd*, 108 S. Ct. 2798 (1988).

[6] *Id.* at 734.

decision.[7]

This Note argues that the Supreme Court was correct in deciding that in this case the defendant's rights were violated. However, this Note, in agreement with the concurring opinion, endorses a narrow interpretation of *Coy*. Although the sixth amendment confrontation rights include the right to the face-to-face meeting denied in this case, this right is not absolute and is subject to exceptions. Moreover, while the use of protective devices like the screen at issue in *Coy* is justifiable as a public policy exception to the right to confrontation, a court should require a case-specific showing of necessity before permitting the use of these devices. Since there was no such showing in *Coy* to justify the infringement of the defendant's confrontation right, the violation of this right was unconstitutional.

II. FACTUAL BACKGROUND

The defendant, John Avery Coy, lived with his girlfriend in a residential neighborhood next door to one of the victims.[8] On the afternoon of August 2, 1985, Coy, sitting in a lawn chair in his back yard, watched as C.B., one of the thirteen-year-old victims, constructed a makeshift tent in her back yard in preparation for a camp out.[9] The tent was not visible from the street, but was visible from Coy's home.[10] C.B. and her friend, thirteen-year-old N.C., went to sleep in the tent at about 10:00 or 11:00 p.m.[11] During the night, a man crawled into the tent, grabbed the girls by the throat and threatened them, warning them not to scream.[12] The man ordered the girls to take off all their clothes except their underwear.[13] He fondled their breasts and vaginal areas and took off their underwear, which he placed in a white bag he had brought with him.[14] After removing his own clothing, he ordered the girls to perform oral sex on him and then to kiss each other.[15] They obeyed.[16] He also urinated into one of the cups which the girls had brought out to the tent with them.[17] Before leaving, the man warned the girls not to tell anyone what had happened, and tied the girls with their

---

[7] *Coy*, 108 S. Ct. at 2803.
[8] Brief for Appellee at 3, Coy v. Iowa, 108 S. Ct. 2798 (1988)(No. 86-6757).
[9] *Id.*
[10] *Id.*
[11] *Id.*
[12] *Id.*
[13] *Id.*
[14] *Id.*
[15] *Id.* at 4.
[16] *Id.*
[17] *Id.*

sweatpants.[18]

After the girls untied themselves, they went into the house to report the incident to C.B.'s parents, who called the police and took the girls to the hospital for an examination.[19] C.B.'s father told the police that he suspected Coy, and Coy was arrested on an unrelated charge.[20] The girls could not identify their attacker because at the time of the assault he appeared to be wearing a nylon stocking over his head, and he shined a flashlight in their eyes.[21] The girls' flashlight with Coy's fingerprints was found in Coy's garage and the cup into which the attacker urinated was found in the garbage just inside Coy's back door.[22]

At the beginning of Coy's trial, the State of Iowa made a motion to allow the victims to testify either via closed-circuit television or behind a screen.[23] A recently enacted Iowa statute approved the use of such devices.[24] Coy objected to the use of the screen, arguing that the girls could not identify him as their attacker, and that the screen violated his sixth amendment right to confront the witnesses against him.[25] He also contended that the screen created an inference of guilt, thereby violating his fourteenth amendment right to a fair trial.[26]

The court rejected the state's request to employ closed-circuit

---

[18] *Id.* The man stated that if the girls "told anyone what had happened, they would go through a lot." *Id.*

[19] *Id.*

[20] *Id.* The father suspected Coy because "only Coy had a vantage point to see the tent." *Id.* When arrested, Coy was wearing a wrist watch, pushed midway up his arm, with the face of the watch turned inward. *Id.* The girls testified that the intruder was wearing a watch midway up his arm, with the face turned inward. *Id.* at 5.

[21] Coy v. Iowa, 108 S. Ct. 2798, 2806 n.1 (Blackmun, J., dissenting).

[22] Brief for Appellee at 5. Coy testified that on the morning following the assault he found the flashlight and cup discarded at the corner of his driveway and took them inside. Brief for Appellant at 8, Coy v. Iowa, 108 S. Ct. 2798 (1988)(No. 86-6757). In addition, the girls stated that immediately after their attacker left the tent, they heard a nearby motorcycle start up and drive away. The defendant did not own a motorcycle, nor had he operated one in the area. During the search of the defendant's residence, the police did not find a mask or clothing that matched the description given by the girls, nor did they find the girls' panties. *Id.*

[23] *Coy,* 108 S. Ct. at 2799.

[24] *Id. See supra* note 4 for the text of the Iowa statute.

[25] Brief for Appellant at 3-4. *See supra* note 2 for the text of the sixth amendment. Defense counsel's argument that the girls could not identify their assailant implied that testifying in the defendant's presence would not be traumatic for the girls. Brief for Appellant at 4 n.6. The State countered that even if the girls could not identify their attacker, they would be traumatized by the presence of the defendant because they assumed he was guilty from the fact that he was charged. *Id.*

[26] *Coy,* 108 S. Ct. at 2799. The fourteenth amendment provides in pertinent part, "nor shall any State deprive any person of life, liberty, or property, without due process of law." U.S. CONST. amend. XIV § 1.

television but permitted a screen to be used only during the girls' testimony.[27] During the girls' testimony, the lighting in the courtroom was dimmed and a one-way mirror was set up in front of the table where Coy sat.[28] The mirror allowed the defendant to hear and dimly see the witnesses, but the witnesses were only able to hear the defendant.[29] In addition, the mirror allowed the rest of the courtroom, including judge, jury, and spectators, to see and hear both the witness and the defendant.[30] The witnesses were told that the defendant could see and hear them while they were testifying.[31] The trial court twice instructed the jury that the mirror was used in accordance with a recent Iowa statute.[32] Both after the girls testified and at the close of the state's case, Coy moved for a mistrial based on the prejudicial impact the screening device had upon his trial.[33] These motions were overruled.[34]

After jury trial, Coy was convicted on two counts of engaging in lascivious acts with a child.[35] On appeal to the Supreme Court of Iowa, Coy contended that the screen violated his sixth amendment right to confront his accusers.[36] Coy argued that the trial court was constitutionally required to find that the screen was necessary before permitting its use.[37] He also argued that the screen was prejudicial and therefore a violation of his right to a fair trial guaranteed by the fourteenth amendment.[38] The Iowa Supreme Court affirmed Coy's conviction and held that a finding of necessity was not constitutionally required because Coy's confrontation rights were not violated.[39] The court also held that the screen was not prejudicial and

---

[27] Brief for Appellant at 4.

[28] Brief for Appellee at 9-10.

[29] Brief for Appellant at 5-6.

[30] *Coy*, 108 S. Ct. at 2806 (Blackmun, J., dissenting).

[31] *Id.* (Blackmun, J., dissenting).

[32] Brief for Appellee at 11-12.

[33] Brief for Appellant at 7.

[34] *Id.*

[35] State v. Coy, 397 N.W.2d 730, 730 (Iowa 1986), *rev'd*, 108 S. Ct. 2798 (1988). Coy was convicted of violating § 709.8(1) of the Iowa code which provides:

> It is unlawful for any person eighteen years of age or older to perform any of the following acts with a child with or without the child's consent unless married to each other, for the purpose of arousing or satisfying the sexual desires of either of them:
>   1. Fondle or touch the pubes or genitals of a child.
>   2. Permit or cause a child to fondle or touch the person's genitals or pubes.
> . . . .
> Any person who violates a provision of this section shall, upon conviction, be guilty of a class "D" felony.

Iowa Code Ann. § 709.8(1) (West 1985).

[36] *Coy*, 108 S. Ct. at 2800.

[37] State v. Coy, 397 N.W.2d at 730.

[38] *Coy*, 108 S. Ct. at 2800.

[39] State v. Coy, 397 N.W.2d at 733-34. The court stated that "the issue of necessity

thus the defendant was not denied his right to a fair trial.[40]

On appeal to the United States Supreme Court, Coy again argued that the use of the screen, over his objections and without a finding that its use served an essential state interest, was a violation of his fourteenth amendment right to a fair trial and his sixth amendment confrontation right.[41] Coy also contended that the Iowa Supreme Court's error was not harmless and therefore required reversal.[42] The United States Supreme Court considered the issue of whether Coy's sixth amendment right to confrontation and Coy's fourteenth amendment right to a fair trial were violated by the use of the screen.[43]

III. THE MAJORITY OPINION

The majority opinion, delivered by Justice Scalia,[44] rejected the Iowa Supreme Court's ruling and held for the defendant Coy.[45] Justice Scalia stated that the right to face-to-face confrontation violated in *Coy* is an essential element of the confrontation clause.[46] Justice Scalia added that certain rights guaranteed by the confrontation clause, such as the right to cross-examine or to restrict the admissibility of out-of-court statements, may be subjected to exceptions in the face of "other important interests."[47] However, the majority declined to comment on whether the right to face-to-face confrontation is subject to exceptions and whether the interest at issue in *Coy* of protecting the child witnesses was sufficient to justify an exception.[48] The majority stated that even if an exception to the face-to-face confrontation right were to be allowed, such an exception would be permitted only after a case-specific showing that the exception was necessary.[49] The majority held that since no case-specific showing of necessity was made in *Coy*, the defendant's sixth amendment right was violated.[50]

---

arises when a witness is unavailable for trial and a party seeks to introduce some prior statement or testimony of that witness . . . . Here, both girls were present at trial and testified under oath." *Id.* at 734.

[40] *Id.* at 735.

[41] Brief for Appellant at 11, 31.

[42] *Id.* at 41.

[43] *See Coy*, 108 S. Ct. at 2799, 2800, 2803.

[44] Justice Scalia was joined by Justices Brennan, Marshall, O'Connor, Stevens and White.

[45] *Coy*, 108 S. Ct. at 2803.

[46] *Id.* at 2801.

[47] *Id.* at 2802.

[48] *Id.* at 2803.

[49] *Id.*

[50] *Id.*

The opinion first stated that the defendant's sixth amendment right was violated because the confrontation clause guarantees the defendant face-to-face confrontation with the witnesses.[51] After noting several historical examples of the right of confrontation,[52] the majority conceded that most judicial treatment of the confrontation clause has dealt either with the admissibility of out-of-court statements or restrictions upon the scope of cross-examination.[53] The majority pointed out that judicial treatment of the right to cross-examination and the right to be present during testimony, rather than the right to face-to-face confrontation, exists because "there is at least some room for doubt (and hence litigation) as to the extent to which the Clause includes th[e] [former] elements."[54] The majority stated that, because confrontation is defined as a face-to-face encounter,[55] the right to face-to-face confrontation is a literal requirement and hence the most essential element of the confrontation right.[56] The other elements of the right are judicially mandated components of the right and hence not as well established as the right to face-to-face confrontation, which is a literal requirement of the amendment.[57]

The majority explained that the right to face-to-face confrontation serves a symbolic as well as a functional purpose.[58] Traditionally, noted the Court, a face-to-face confrontation between accuser and accused gives the appearance of fairness which satisfies the public's feelings of what is just.[59] The rationale behind this sentiment is that "it is always more difficult to tell a lie about a person 'to his face' than 'behind his back.' "[60] Moreover, the Court posited, "even if the lie is told, it will often be told less convincingly."[61]

---

[51] *Id.* at 2800.

[52] Justice Scalia referred to a quote from the Roman Governor Festus, who stated that the accused must be allowed to meet his accusers "face to face." *Id.* (citing *Acts* 25:16). In addition, Justice Scalia stated that "[i]t has been argued that a form of the right of confrontation" pre-dated the right to jury trial in England. *Coy*, 108 S. Ct. at 2800 (citing Pollitt, *The Right of Confrontation: Its History and Modern Dress*, 8 J. PUB. L. 381, 384-387 (1959)).

[53] *Coy*, 108 S. Ct. at 2800.

[54] *Id.*

[55] The majority cited the Latin roots of the word "confront" to support its definition of confrontation as a face-to-face encounter. The word, noted the majority, is derived from the prefix "con" which means "against" or "opposed" and the noun "frons" which means "forehead." *Id.*

[56] *Id.* at 2801.

[57] *Id.* at 2800-01.

[58] *Id.* at 2801.

[59] *Id.* at 2801-02.

[60] *Id.* at 2802.

[61] *Id.*

In a footnote, the majority addressed the minority's discussion of Dean Wigmore's treatment of the confrontation right.[62] While conceding Wigmore's conclusion that the confrontation right's purpose was to provide for cross-examination, the majority stated that simply because cross-examination is one purpose of the confrontation right, the fulfillment of this purpose does not automatically discharge the right.[63] Moreover, the majority added that "Wigmore did mention . . . that a secondary purpose of confrontation is to produce 'a certain subjective moral effect . . . upon the witness.' "[64]

Having stated that the right to physical, face-to-face confrontation is an essential element of the sixth amendment confrontation right, the majority then turned to the question of whether this right was violated in *Coy*.[65] The Court reasoned that because the screen's sole purpose was to obstruct the witness' view of the defendant, Coy's right to face his accusers was violated.[66] Justice Scalia noted that some elements of the confrontation right, such as the right to cross-examine, the right to exclude out-of-court statements, and the right to face-to-face confrontation at proceedings other than trial, are subject to certain exceptions because they are "reasonably implicit" elements of the right.[67] These rights are not explicitly contained in the sixth amendment, but rather are incidents of the confrontation right, or traditional evidentiary rules covered by the amendment.[68] However, the right to face-to-face confrontation is "the right narrowly and explicitly set forth in the Clause" and a literal requirement of the sixth amendment.[69] Therefore, the Court explained, while the implicit elements of the right, such as the right to cross-examine, may be subject to exceptions, the right to face-to-face confrontation is absolute, as it is the most explicit and essential element of the confrontation right.[70] The Court, therefore, concluded that the mere existence of exceptions to the non-literal ele-

---

[62] *Id.* at 2801-02 n.2.

[63] *Id.* (citing 5 J. WIGMORE, EVIDENCE § 1397, at 158 (J. Chadbourn rev. ed. 1974)). In support of this proposition, the Court noted that the right to a jury trial is similarly not discharged merely because "the accused is justly convicted and publicly known to be justly convicted—the purposes of the right to jury trial." *Id.*

[64] *Id.* (quoting 5 J. WIGMORE, *supra* note 63, § 1395, at 153). The majority conceded that Wigmore also asserted "without support, that this effect 'does not arise from the confrontation of the *opponent* and the witness,' but from 'the witness' presence before the *tribunal*' . . ." *Id.* (quoting 5 J. WIGMORE, *supra* note 63, § 1395, at 154)(emphasis in original).

[65] *Id.* at 2802.

[66] *Id.*

[67] *Id.*

[68] *Id.* at 2800-01.

[69] *Id.* at 2802.

[70] *Id.* at 2803.

ments of the clause does not support the argument that exceptions may be made to the right to face-to-face confrontation.[71]

However, the Court declined to determine whether the right to face-to-face confrontation is subject to exceptions,[72] stating that if exceptions existed, the right would be subject to only those exceptions "necessary to further an important public policy."[73] The Court went on to note that if compelling state interests existed which necessitated exceptions infringing upon the right to face-to-face confrontation, the prosecution had failed to establish the existence of any such interests in *Coy*.[74] The prosecution's suggestion that the statute permitting the screen's use created a "legislatively imposed presumption of trauma" to a child victim compelled to testify in open court was rejected by the majority.[75] The Court stated that "[s]ince there have been no individualized findings that these particular witnesses needed special protection, the judgment here could not be sustained by any conceivable exception."[76]

Finally, the Court recognized that the trial court's violation of Coy's confrontation right, like other confrontation clause violations, was subject to a harmless error analysis and remanded the case to the court below to conduct this analysis.[77] The Court added that

---

[71] *Id.*

[72] The Court stated: "[w]e leave for another day, however, the question whether any exceptions [to the confrontation right] exist." *Id.* at 2803.

[73] *Id.* The majority referred to Ohio v. Roberts, 448 U.S. 56 (1980). *Coy*, 108 S. Ct. at 2803. *Roberts* stated that "competing interests, if 'closely examined' . . . may warrant dispensing with confrontation at trial." *Roberts*, 448 U.S. at 64 (quoting Chambers v. Mississippi, 410 U.S. 294, 295 (1973))(citations omitted). In *Roberts*, the Court suggested that the "necessities of the case" and the interests of "effective law enforcement" are such competing interests. *Roberts*, 448 U.S. at 64. The Court in *Chambers* identified these interests as "other legitimate interests in the criminal trial process." *Chambers*, 410 U.S. at 295.

[74] *Coy*, 108 S. Ct. at 2803.

[75] *Id.* The Court explained that the presumption underlying the Iowa statute was not sufficient to support such a novel exception to the confrontation right as the exception advocated by the prosecution stating that: "[e]ven as to exceptions from the normal implications of the Confrontation Clause, as opposed to its most literal application, something more than the type of generalized finding underlying such a statute is needed when the exception is not 'firmly . . . rooted in our jurisprudence.' " *Id.* (quoting Dutton v. Evans, 400 U.S. 74, 91 (1970)).

[76] *Id.*

[77] *Id.* at 2803. The Court cited Delaware v. Van Arsdall, 475 U.S. 673 (1986), for the principle that certain constitutional errors may be found to be "harmless beyond a reasonable doubt." *Coy*, 108 S. Ct. at 2803 (citing *Van Arsdall*, 475 U.S. at 681). In *Van Arsdall*, the Court held that "the constitutionally improper denial of a defendant's opportunity to impeach a witness for bias, like other Confrontation Clause errors, is subject to harmless error analysis" and remanded the analysis to the lower court, as did the Court in *Coy*. *Van Arsdall*, 475 U.S. at 684. The *Van Arsdall* Court explained that in Chapman v. California, 386 U.S. 18, 24 (1967), *reh'g denied*, 386 U.S. 987 (1967), "the Court rejected

because the violation of Coy's confrontation right required that the lower court's judgment be reversed, a discussion of the defendant's contention that the screen violated his right to a fair trial was unnecessary.[78]

IV. CONCURRING OPINION

In her concurring opinion,[79] Justice O'Connor agreed with Justice Scalia that the defendant's sixth amendment right to confront the witnesses against him was violated by the use of the screen.[80] However, although Justice Scalia declined to determine whether the physical right to face-to-face confrontation was absolute, Justice O'Connor departed from the majority by arguing that the right, like other elements of the confrontation clause, is subject to exceptions.[81] Justice O'Connor asserted that "in an appropriate case . . . procedural devices designed to shield a child witness from the trauma of courtroom testimony" may be used.[82] The concurrence agreed with the majority that these devices should be permitted only after a case-specific showing of necessity, which was absent in *Coy*.[83] Thus, while the concurring opinion did not conflict with the majority's stance, it extended the majority's holding to permit the use of protective devices when there is a case-specific showing of necessity.[84]

After emphasizing the gravity of the problem of child abuse and sexual assault, Justice O'Connor discussed the difficulties inherent in the prosecution of such cases, such as the lack of witnesses besides the victim and the trauma suffered by child witnesses.[85] She referred to other procedural devices aimed at protecting child witnesses, including one-way or two-way closed circuit television,

---

the argument that all federal constitutional errors, regardless of their nature or the circumstances of the case, require reversal of a judgment of conviction." *Van Arsdall*, 475 U.S. at 681. The Court, in *Van Arsdall*, reasoned that the Constitution entitles the defendant to a fair, but not a perfect, trial; and that certain errors may be "harmless" in terms of their effect on the fact finding process. *Id*. As articulated in *Van Arsdall*, the *Chapman* principle, which has been reaffirmed repeatedly, is that "an otherwise valid conviction should not be set aside if the reviewing court may confidently say, on the whole record, that the constitutional error was harmless beyond a reasonable doubt." *Id*.

78 *Coy*, 108 S. Ct. at 2803. Accordingly, the Court did not reach the question of whether the screen was prejudicial. *Id*.

79 Justice White joined in Justice O'Connor's concurring opinion.

80 *Coy*, 108 S. Ct. at 2803 (O'Connor, J., concurring).

81 *Id*. (O'Connor, J., concurring).

82 *Id*. (O'Connor, J., concurring).

83 *Id*. at 2805 (O'Connor, J., concurring).

84 *Id*. (O'Connor, J., concurring).

85 *Id*. at 2803-04 (O'Connor, J., concurring).

which broadcast the child's testimony to the jury from a room in which only the judge, counsel, technicians, and in some cases the defendant, are present.[86] Justice O'Connor suggested that these devices would present no violation of the confrontation right if the testimony is given in the presence of the defendant or if the defendant can see the countenance of the witness through two-way closed circuit television.[87]

Justice O'Connor then indicated her agreement with Justice Scalia on the issue of whether face-to-face confrontation is guaranteed by the sixth amendment,[88] affirming that "the [Confrontation] Clause embodies a general requirement that a witness face the defendant."[89] However, Justice O'Connor added that this requirement, like the other requirements of the confrontation clause, is not absolute.[90] Even if certain protective devices are violative of the confrontation clause, Justice O'Connor stated, they should be permitted if necessary "to further an important public policy."[91] She then stated that the protection of child witnesses was such a policy.[92]

The concurrence agreed "with the Court that more than the type of generalized legislative finding of necessity present here is required" to allow use of a confrontation-violative procedure.[93] Thus, reversal of Coy's conviction was mandated. However Justice O'Connor noted that "if a court makes a case-specific finding of necessity, as is required by a number of state statutes, . . . the Confrontation Clause may give way to the compelling state interest of protecting child witnesses," and the use of protective devices would be permitted.[94]

V. DISSENTING OPINION

Justice Blackmun's dissent[95] treated two undecided issues of the majority opinion: whether exceptions to the "literal" confrontation right exist,[96] and whether the screen had a prejudicial impact

---

[86] *Id.* at 2804 (O'Connor, J., concurring).

[87] *Id.* (O'Connor, J., concurring).

[88] *Id.* (O'Connor, J., concurring).

[89] *Id.* (O'Connor, J., concurring).

[90] *Id.* (O'Connor, J., concurring).

[91] *Id.* at 2805 (O'Connor, J., concurring).

[92] *Id.* (O'Connor, J., concurring).

[93] *Id.* (O'Connor, J., concurring).

[94] *Id.* (O'Connor, J., concurring)(citations omitted).

[95] Chief Justice Rehnquist joined in Justice Blackmun's dissent.

[96] *Coy,* 108 S. Ct. at 2808 (Blackmun, J., dissenting).

upon Coy's fourteenth amendment right to a fair trial.[97] Justice Blackmun concluded that: the confrontation right does not mandate, but merely manifests " 'a preference for face-to-face confrontation at trial;' "[98] the "preference" for face-to-face confrontation is subject to exceptions involving essential state interests;[99] the protection of child witnesses qualifies as such a state interest;[100] a specific showing that an essential state interest is present is unnecessary and the showing in *Coy* was sufficient;[101] and finally, the use of the screen was not prejudicial to Coy's right to a fair trial.[102]

Justice Blackmun began by asserting that the confrontation clause's primary purpose is to prevent the use of depositions or *ex parte* affidavits in lieu of live testimony and to ensure that the witnesses testify under oath and in the presence of the defendant.[103] In addition, the clause ensures that the witnesses are subject to cross-examination and that the jurors are able to observe the witnesses' demeanors as they testify.[104] Justice Blackmun pointed out that these purposes were fulfilled in *Coy* and that the screen's only effect was obstruction of the witness' view of the defendant.[105]

The dissent clashed[106] with the majority over Dean Wigmore's treatment of the confrontation right.[107] The dissent pointed out that, according to Wigmore, " '[t]here was never at common law any

---

97 *Id.* at 2809-10 (Blackmun, J., dissenting).

98 *Id.* at 2808 (Blackmun, J., dissenting)(quoting Ohio v. Roberts, 448 U.S. 56, 63 (1980)).

99 *Id.* (Blackmun, J., dissenting)(citations omitted).

100 *Id.* (Blackmun, J., dissenting).

101 *Id.* at 2809 (Blackmun, J., dissenting).

102 *Id.* at 2810 (Blackmun, J., dissenting).

103 *Id.* at 2805 (Blackmun, J., dissenting). Justice Blackmun relied on Kentucky v. Stincer, 107 S. Ct. 2658 (1987)(citing Mattox v. United States, 156 U.S. 237, 242-243 (1895)).

104 *Coy*, 108 S. Ct. at 2805 (Blackmun, J., dissenting)(citing *Mattox*, 156 U.S. at 242-43).

105 *Id.* at 2806 (Blackmun, J., dissenting).

106 A lesser clash between the majority and the dissent began with the dissent's observation that the face-to-face element of the confrontation right is not essential since blind witnesses are allowed to testify and they cannot, as the witnesses in *Coy*, see the defendant. *Id.* at 2808 (Blackmun, J., dissenting). The majority responded that the dissent's contention is "no more true than that the importance of the right to live, oral cross-examination is belied by the possibility that speech and hearing-impaired witnesses might have testified." *Id.* at 2802 n.2. The dissent then countered that a deaf or mute witness who could not be cross-examined would also not be able to testify in the first place. The dissent added that "[m]ore importantly, if a deaf or mute witness were completely incapable of being cross-examined (as blind witnesses are completely incapable of seeing a defendant . . .), I should think a successful Confrontation Clause challenge might be brought against whatever direct testimony they did offer." *Id.* at 2808 n.4 (Blackmun, J., dissenting).

107 *Id.* at 2807 (Blackmun, J., dissenting).

recognized right to an indispensable thing called confrontation *as distinguished from cross-examination.*' "[108] The dissent also noted Wigmore's statement that the purpose of the confrontation right was to provide for cross-examination and to permit the court to view the witness' demeanor.[109] The dissent employed Wigmore's discussion in arguing that face-to-face confrontation is not an absolute, nor even a " 'secondary and dispensable' " requirement of the confrontation clause.[110]

This right, Justice Blackmun asserted, may be departed from "if it is justified by a sufficiently significant state interest."[111] Justice Blackmun stated that the significance of the state's interest in protecting child witnesses lies not only in shielding the child witness from further trauma, but also in ensuring effective testimony, which may be impossible to obtain from an overwhelmed and traumatized child witness.[112] Justice Blackmun articulated his view that this state interest outweighed the "preference" for allowing the witness to see the defendant during the testimony.[113]

Justice Blackmun also stated that a specific showing of necessity should not be required to justify the use of screens and similar devices.[114] In support of this, Justice Blackmun noted that other exceptions to the confrontation clause[115] are generally admissible under the Federal Rules of Evidence without any special showing of necessity.[116] Responding to the majority's assertion that the Iowa procedure is not "firmly . . . rooted in our jurisprudence,"[117] Justice Blackmun stated that a "firm rooting in jurisprudence" was not a requirement for an exception to the face-to-face confrontation right.[118] The requirement that an exception be firmly rooted in our jurisprudence, noted Justice Blackmun, is only imposed in the case of out-of-court statements, where reliability, not necessity, is ques-

---

[108] *Id.* (Blackmun, J., dissenting)(quoting 5 J. WIGMORE, EVIDENCE § 1397, at 158 (J. Chadbourn rev. ed. 1974))(emphasis in original).

[109] *Id.* (Blackmun, J., dissenting)(quoting 5 J. WIGMORE, *supra* note 108, §§ 1397, 1399 at 158, 199)

[110] *Id.* (Blackmun, J., dissenting)(quoting 5 J. WIGMORE, *supra* note 108, § 1399, at 199).

[111] *Id.* at 2808 (Blackmun, J., dissenting).

[112] *Id.* at 2809 (Blackmun, J., dissenting).

[113] *Id.* (Blackmun, J., dissenting).

[114] *Id.* (Blackmun, J., dissenting).

[115] The exceptions to which Justice Blackmun referred included statements of a co-conspirator, excited utterances, and business records. *Id.* at 2809 n.6 (Blackmun, J., dissenting).

[116] *Id.* at 2809 (Blackmun, J., dissenting).

[117] *Id.* at 2803.

[118] *Id.* at 2809 (Blackmun, J., dissenting).

tioned.[119] Because the testimony at issue was under oath, in view of the jury, and subject to cross-examination, it was deemed reliable and no specific showing of reliability or necessity was required.[120]

Finally, the dissent rejected the defendant's argument that the screen was prejudicial, a question the majority declined to reach.[121] Justice Blackmun pointed out that the screen was not a brand of guilt,[122] especially as the jury was instructed to draw no inferences from the use of the screen.[123] Finally, Justice Blackmun noted that there are other practices, which single out the accused from all others in the courtroom, that are permissible.[124]

VI. ANALYSIS

Although the majority was inaccurate in stating that face-to-face confrontation is the most essential requirement of the sixth amendment confrontation right,[125] the majority and concurring opinions were correct in holding that the right to face-to-face confrontation is an important element of the sixth amendment confrontation right. While the majority declined to comment on the susceptibility of the confrontation right to exceptions,[126] the concurring opinion was correct in stating that the right to face-to-face confrontation, like other elements of the confrontation right, is subject to exceptions

---

[119] *Id.* (Blackmun, J., dissenting).

[120] *Id.* (Blackmun, J., dissenting).

[121] *Id.* at 2810 (Blackmun, J., dissenting).

[122] *Id.* (Blackmun, J., dissenting). Previous cases have held that practices such as clothing the defendant in prison garb or having the defendant shackled and gagged brand the defendant with a mark of guilt. *See* Estelle v. Williams, 425 U.S. 501, 505 (1976)(clothing the defendant in prison garb prejudicial); Illinois v. Allen, 397 U.S. 337, 344 (1970)(having the defendant shackled and gagged prejudicial). Coy argued that the use of the mirror, which was accompanied by a dimming of the courtroom lights and a shining of bright lights on the mirror, created a dramatic, eerie effect, and indicated to the jury that the defendant was guilty. *Coy*, 108 S. Ct. at 2810 (Blackmun, J., dissenting).

[123] *Coy*, 108 S. Ct. at 2810 (Blackmun, J., dissenting). The trial court instructed the jury as follows:

> It's quite obvious to the jury that there's a screen device in the courtroom. The General Assembly of Iowa recently passed a law which provides for this sort of procedure in cases involving children. Now, I would caution you now and I will caution you later that you are to draw no inference of any kind from the presence of that screen. You know, in the plainest of language, that is not evidence of the defendant's guilt, and it shouldn't be in your mind as an inference as to any guilt on his part. It's very important that you do that intellectual thing.

Id. (Blackmun, J., dissenting)(quoting Joint Appendix at 17, Coy v. Iowa, 108 S. Ct. 2798 (1988)(No. 86-6757))(citation omitted).

[124] The dissent cited Holbrook v. Flynn, 475 U.S. 560, 567 (1986), in which four uniformed state troopers sitting behind the defendant throughout the trial were held not inherently prejudicial. *Coy*, 108 S. Ct. at 2810 (Blackmun, J., dissenting).

[125] *Coy*, 108 S. Ct. at 2800.

[126] *Id.* at 2803.

relating to essential state interests.[127] The protection of child witnesses from the trauma of facing the defendant, as articulated by
Justice O'Connor in her concurring opinion,[128] and the enhance-
ment of the truth-finding process, which the one-way mirror provides, are policy interests justifying an exception to the
confrontation right. However, as Justice O'Connor stated, the use
of these procedural devices should be allowed only where there has
been a case-by-case showing of necessity.[129] Because there was no
such showing in *Coy,* the defendant's confrontation right was
violated.[130]

A.   FACE-TO-FACE CONFRONTATION AS AN ELEMENT OF THE
     CONFRONTATION RIGHT

Although support, in the form of factually analagous cases, for a
finding that physical face-to-face confrontation is an element of the
confrontation right is not extensive, support for the opposite conclusion is equally sparse. Whether the defendant has a right, guaranteed by the sixth amendment, to physically face the witness, thus
was a question of first impression for the Supreme Court. The cases
referred to in the majority opinion concern other aspects of the confrontation right, such as the well-established hearsay rules. None of
the cases cited deal with the defendant's right to physically face the
witness.[131] Therefore, as the majority conceded, most judicial treatment of the confrontation right concerns the right to be present
during testimony and to cross-examine.[132]

---

[127] *Id.* at 2804 (O'Connor, J., concurring).

[128] *Id.* at 2805 (O'Connor, J., concurring).

[129] *Id.* (O'Connor, J., concurring).

[130] *Id.* (O'Connor, J., concurring).

[131] For example, the leading case, California v. Green, 399 U.S. 149 (1970), involved
prior statements by a witness. In *Green,* the Court held that the confrontation clause was
not violated when prior statements made by a witness at a preliminary hearing and to a
police officer were admitted to prove the truth of the matter contained therein. *Id.* at
152-53. A look at the facts of the other cases which the majority used to support the
inclusion of the face-to-face confrontation right in the sixth amendment right reveals
little similarity between these cases and *Coy.* For example, in Ohio v. Roberts, 448 U.S.
56 (1980), the Court held that, when the witness was unavailable, admission of a transcript of the witness' testimony at a preliminary hearing did not violate the sixth amendment confrontation right. *Id.* at 66. Dutton v. Evans, 400 U.S. 74 (1970), involved a
witness who testified as to the statements of a co-conspirator. The Court upheld the
admission of this hearsay. *Id.* at 89-90. Kirby v. United States, 174 U.S. 47 (1899), held
the admission of prior convictions of defendants violative of the sixth amendment. *Id.* at
54. Pennsylvania v. Ritchie, 480 U.S. 39 (1987), also a child sexual assault case, differed
substantially from *Coy.* In *Ritchie,* the Court held that the confrontation clause was not
violated when the defendant was refused access to a confidential file which he sought for
purposes of cross-examination. *Id.* at 51-54.

[132] *Coy,* 108 S. Ct. at 2800.

However, the Court cannot conclude that the right to face-to-face confrontation is an undeniable element of the right simply because the Court has never had occasion to address the issue of whether face-to-face confrontation is required by the sixth amendment. The fact that the right to face-to-face confrontation has not been the subject of litigation does not mean that it is an undisputed element of the confrontation right. Judicial opinions concerning cross-examination and the other confrontation rights are more prevalent because these are the issues upon which defendants have commonly appealed their convictions; this does not reflect a belief of the Court that the right to cross-examination is somehow less essential than the right to face-to-face confrontation.

While a comparison of the facts of the other confrontation clause cases with those of *Coy* does not offer much support for inclusion of the face-to-face confrontation right in the sixth amendment right, an analysis of the language of the confrontation clause cases does support this principle.[133] Moreover, the Supreme Court's past discussions of the relationship between the hearsay rules and the confrontation clause lend further support for the majority's holding. As the Court pointed out in Green, the hearsay rules and the confrontation clause are somewhat parallel.[134] In *Green*, the Court outlined the three purposes of the confrontation right, which it held were fulfilled by the admission of prior statements of a witness present at trial and subject to cross-examination.[135] The purposes of the confrontation right, as delineated by the *Green* court, are that confrontation: "1) insures that the witness will give his statements under oath . . .; (2) forces the witness to submit to cross-examination . . .; [and] (3) permits the jury that is to decide the defendant's fate to observe the demeanor of the witness . . . thus aiding the jury in assessing his credibility."[136]

---

[133] For example, in *Ritchie*, the Court stated that "[t]he Confrontation Clause provides two types of protection for a criminal defendant: the right physically to face those who testify against him, and the right to conduct cross-examination." *Ritchie*, 480 U.S. at 51 (citation omitted). In *Green*, Justice Harlan, concurring, stated that the confrontation clause confers "a right to meet face to face all those who appear and give evidence at trial." *Green*, 399 U.S. at 175 (Harlan, J., concurring). The Court also stressed that the "literal right to 'confront' the witness at the time of trial" formed "the core of the values furthered by the Confrontation Clause." *Id.* In Mattox v. United States, 156 U.S. 237 (1895), the Court stated that the confrontation right consists essentially of the defendant "seeing the witness face to face" and cross-examination. *Id.* at 244. Moreover, in *Kirby*, the Court stated that the defendant must be allowed to see the witness. *Kirby*, 174 U.S. at 55.

[134] *Green*, 399 U.S. at 155.

[135] *Id.* at 158-59.

[136] *Id.* at 158.

Although these purposes of the confrontation right, which are also the purposes of the hearsay rules, were fulfilled in *Coy*, the confrontation clause guarantees more than just protection against the admission of hearsay. The dissent was inaccurate when it suggested that the confrontation clause merely guarantees the enforcement of the hearsay rules.[137] As the Court stated in *Green*:

> [w]hile it may readily be conceded that hearsay rules and the Confrontation Clause are generally designed to protect similar values, it is quite a different thing to suggest that the overlap is complete and that the Confrontation Clause is nothing more or less than a codification of the rules of hearsay and their exceptions as they existed historically at common law. Our decisions have never established such a congruence; indeed, we have more than once found a violation of confrontation values even though the statements in issue were admitted under an arguably recognized hearsay exception.[138]

While the use of the one-way mirror in *Coy* fulfilled the three *Green* requirements, it nevertheless prevented face-to-face confrontation between the witnesses and the defendant. The screen completely obstructed the witnesses' view of the defendant and somewhat impeded the defendant's view of the witnesses.[139] The majority's contention that it is harder to lie about a person when facing that person, while not strongly substantiated, is persuasive. As pointed out by the Court in *Jay v. Boyd*,[140] " '[a]n honest witness may feel quite differently when he has to repeat his story looking at the man, whom he will harm greatly by distorting or mistaking the facts.' "[141] The California Court of Appeals for the Third Circuit observed in *Herbert v. Superior Court*,[142] that "[m]ost believe that in some undefined but real way recollection, veracity, and communica-

---

[137] *Coy*, 108 S. Ct. at 2807-08 (Blackmun, J., dissenting).

[138] *Green*, 399 U.S. at 149, 155-56.

[139] *Coy*, 108 S. Ct. at 2799. Coy argued that the screening barrier obstructed his view of the witnesses and their reactions as they testified and thus hindered his assistance of counsel during examination. Brief for Appellant at 36, Coy v. Iowa, 108 S. Ct. 2798 (1988)(No. 86-6757). Coy cited the trial court, which stated, after testing the device, that "[i]t is possible to dimly see a person seated in the witness chair" and later added that "[y]ou can see the features of the person seated in the witness chair, but it is dark." *Id.* at 36 n.44 (quoting Joint Appendix at 10-11, Coy v. Iowa, 108 S. Ct. 2798 (1988)(No. 86-6757)). Coy added that defense counsel was also unable to view the witnesses clearly unless he moved away from the defendant's table, thus restricting Coy's access to counsel during cross-examination. *Id.* at 36.

[140] 351 U.S. 345 (1956)(denial of deportation suspension to alien based on confidential information not disclosed to the alien upheld).

[141] *Id.* at 375-76 (Douglas, J., dissenting)(quoting Z. CHAFEE, THE BLESSINGS OF LIBERTY 35 (1956)).

[142] 117 Cal. App. 3d 661, 172 Cal. Rptr. 850 (1981)(confrontation rights of defendant in child sexual assault case violated when the defendant was seated so he could not see the complaining witness during her testimony).

tion are influenced by face-to-face challenge."[143] These principles provide an underlying rationale for the Court's inclusion of the face-to-face right in the confrontation clause.[144]

The dissent's argument that the law reflects merely a preference for, rather than a requirement of, face-to-face confrontation is unsupported. The dissent emphasized the Court's statement in *Ohio v. Roberts*[145] that the Confrontation Clause embodies "a preference for face-to-face confrontation at trial.'"[146] However, this statement must be viewed in light of its accompanying footnote quoting *California v. Green*.[147] This footnote quoted *Green* in affirming the essential nature of the "literal right to 'confront' the witness."[148] Therefore, although the face-to-face confrontation right is not the most important element of the sixth amendment right, it is nevertheless a required element.

B.   THE RIGHT TO FACE-TO-FACE CONFRONTATION IS NOT ABSOLUTE

The fact that the right to face-to-face confrontation is not the most essential element of the confrontation clause supports the conclusion that the face-to-face confrontation right is subject to exceptions, as are other elements of the confrontation right. Although the majority declined to resolve this issue, the concurring opinion accurately concluded that there are constitutionally permissible exceptions to the defendant's right to physically face the witness.[149]

The Supreme Court has stated more than once that even the most well established elements of the confrontation clause, such as the right to cross-examination, are subject to exceptions.[150] Prior recorded testimony of an unavailable witness is an example of such exceptions. In *Roberts*, the witness' " 'whereabouts were entirely un-

---

[143] *Id.* at 670, 172 Cal. Rptr. at 855 (quoting U.S. v. Benfield, 593 F.2d 815, 821 (8th Cir. 1979)).

[144] *Coy*, 108 S. Ct. at 2802.

[145] 448 U.S. 56 (1980).

[146] *Coy*, 108 S. Ct. at 2808. (Blackmun, J., dissenting)(quoting *Roberts*, 448 U.S. at 63).

[147] 399 U.S. 149 (1970).

[148] *Roberts*, 448 U.S. at 63 n.5 (quoting *Green*, 399 U.S. at 157). *Roberts* quoted the Court's statement in *Green* that "it is this literal right to 'confront' the witness at the time of the trial that forms the core of the values furthered by the Confrontation Clause." *Green*, 399 U.S. at 157.

[149] 108 S. Ct. at 2804-05 (O'Connor, J., concurring).

[150] In Mattox v. United States, 156 U.S. 237, 244 (1895), the Court stated that constitutional safeguards like the confrontation right "must occasionally give way to considerations of public policy and the necessities of the case." *Id.* at 243. In Chambers v. Mississippi, 410 U.S. 294 (1973), the Court stated that, "[o]f course, the right to confront . . . is not absolute and may, in appropriate cases, bow to accommodate other legitimate interests in the criminal trial process." *Id.* at 295.

known' "[151] and the prosecution sought admission of hearsay consisting of a transcript of the witness' testimony at a preliminary hearing.[152] The Court held the transcript admissible as an exception to the confrontation right.[153]

Another constitutionally permissible exception to the confrontation right involves prior inconsistent and out-of-court statements of a testifying witness. In *Green*, the witness was available and, in fact, testified at the trial.[154] After testifying at trial inconsistently with his testimony at a preliminary hearing, the witness' "memory was 'refreshed' by his preliminary hearing testimony," parts of which were read by the prosecutor.[155] The Court held that the admission of excerpts from the testifying witness' testimony at a preliminary hearing was not unconstitutional where the witness was subject to cross-examination at both proceedings.[156]

A third example of exceptions to the confrontation right is the admissibility of a co-conspirator's statements. In *Dutton v. Evans*,[157] a witness testified as to statements made to him by a fellow prisoner, who was a co-conspirator of the defendant.[158] The statements incriminated the defendant.[159] The Court held the statements admissible[160] in accordance with a Georgia statute which provided that, "[a]fter the fact of conspiracy shall be proved, the declarations by any one of the conspirators during the pendency of the criminal project shall be admissible against all."[161]

The *Coy* majority stated that because the face-to-face confrontation right is the most literal element of the sixth amendment right it should not be subject to exceptions.[162] The Court seemed to be

---

[151] *Roberts*, 448 U.S. at 61 (quoting State v. Roberts, 55 Ohio St. 2d 191, 194, 378 N.E.2d 492, 495 (1978), *rev'd*, 448 U.S. 56 (1980)).

[152] *Id.* at 58.

[153] *Id.* at 77. In a similar case, Mancusi v. Stubbs, 410 U.S. 204 (1971), the previous trial testimony of a witness who had moved to Sweden was held admissible as an exception to the confrontation right, because the Court found the witness unavailable. *Id.* at 209, 216.

[154] *Green*, 399 U.S. at 152.

[155] *Id.*

[156] *Id.* at 158.

[157] 400 U.S. 74 (1970).

[158] *Id.* at 77-78.

[159] *Id.*

[160] *Id.* at 77-78, 89-90.

[161] GA. CODE ANN. § 38-306 (1954). The co-conspirator exception was also applied in United States v. Inadi, 475 U.S. 387 (1986)(admission of the out-of-court statements of a non-testifying co-conspirator upheld), and Bourjaily v. United States, 107 S. Ct. 2775 (1987)(admission of the out-of-court statements of a co-conspirator did not violate confrontation clause).

[162] Coy v. Iowa, 108 S. Ct. 2798, 2803 (1988).

arranging the confrontation rights on a spectrum, ranging from least established to most established. However, while the face-to-face confrontation right may be the most literal element of the sixth amendment right, it has also been the least litigated and had not, until *Coy* been the subject of a ruling by the Court. If the Court's spectrum rationale is to be applicable in determining the susceptibility of the confrontation right to exceptions, the fact that the face-to-face confrontation right is the least substantiated element of the sixth amendment confrontation right leads to the conclusion that the right at issue in *Coy* is actually the most susceptible to exceptions.[163]

C. PROTECTIVE MEASURES SERVE A STATE INTEREST JUSTIFYING
    EXCEPTIONS TO THE CONFRONTATION RIGHT

An interpretation of the majority opinion as holding that, even if the right to face-to-face confrontation were subject to exceptions in the interest of public policy, the protection of child sexual assault victims is not such a policy would ignore a grave societal problem. In fact, the majority never actually stated that the protection of child witnesses is not a public policy sufficiently important to justify exceptions to the confrontation right. The opinion merely stated that

---

[163] The majority's view that the exceptions to the confrontation clause involving non-literal rights, such as the right to cross-examine or to exclude out-of-court statements, are distinguishable from the exception advocated by the state in *Coy* is flawed in another respect. The majority held that it is permissible to erode the right to cross-examine and the right to exclude out-of-court statements, but that the right to physically face the defendant, as a literal requirement of the clause, is less susceptible to exceptions. *Id.* at 2803. However, the same hearsay exceptions which infringe on the right to cross-examine and the right to exclude out-of-court statements also infringe on the literal element of the clause—the right to physically face the witness. Justice O'Connor made this observation in her concurrence in *Coy,* when she stated:

> [i]ndeed, virtually all of our cases approving the use of hearsay evidence have implicated the literal right to "confront" that has always been recognized as forming "the core of the values furthered by the Confrontation Clause," and yet have fallen within an exception to the general requirement of face-to-face confrontation.

Id. at 2804-2805 (O'Connor, J., concurring)(quoting California v. Green, 399 U.S. 149, 157 (1970)(citations omitted). For example, in *Dutton,* as well as the other cases involving the co-conspirator exception, the defendant was denied the opportunity to cross-examine and to exclude the out-of-court statements of a co-conspirator whose statements to a testifying witness were admitted at the defendant's trial. *Dutton,* 400 U.S. at 77-78. In this case, the defendant was also denied the opportunity to face the co-conspirator whose out-of-court statements were used against him. In *Roberts,* the defendant was denied the opportunity to cross-examine at trial the unavailable witness whose preliminary hearing testimony was being admitted. *Roberts,* 448 U.S. at 58-59. The defendant was also denied the opportunity to face the witness at trial. However, in both cases the Court allowed the exception. *Id.* at 77. These cases demonstrate that the Court has permitted the right to physically face the defendant, along with the non-literal elements of the confrontation clause, to be infringed.

because the prosecution did not demonstrate that the use of the screen in *Coy* was necessary, the existence of an essential state interest was not established.[164] Therefore, the majority left undecided the issue which the concurring and dissenting opinions decided affirmatively: that because the public policy served by protective devices such as the screen in *Coy* is an essential state interest, the defendant's right to physically face the witnesses can be violated in certain cases to protect child victims of sexual assault.[165]

The Court has not developed a comprehensive scheme or set of factors to be used in formulating exceptions to the confrontation clause. In *Roberts*, the United States Supreme Court commented, "[t]he Court has not sought to 'map out a theory of the Confrontation Clause that would determine the validity of all' " hearsay exceptions.[166] However, an analysis of the public policies that the Court has determined justify exceptions to the confrontation clause rights supports a conclusion that the state's interest in protecting child witnesses is such a public policy. The application of constitutional criminal procedural safeguards must consider balancing the rights of the individual against the "rights of the public" in preventing "a manifest failure of justice."[167] The most prominent public policies which the Court has stated support the established exceptions to the confrontation right are the policies of "effective law enforcement"[168] and "accurate factfinding."[169] Additionally, the Court has referred to "other legitimate interests in the criminal trial process" which justify exceptions to the confrontation right.[170]

The public policy of protecting child witnesses from the trauma of courtroom testimony justifies an exception to the confrontation right to permit the use of a protective device such as that used in *Coy*. By increasing the probability that a child victim will be willing to testify and will testify accurately against the sexual offender, devices such as the *Coy* screen increase the likelihood that a sexual abuser will be convicted. The screen in *Coy* and other procedural devices designed to shield the child witness therefore represent the policy of "effective law enforcement"[171] and "accurate fact-finding."[172] Moreover, the protection of the child witness from the

---

164 *Coy*, 108 S. Ct. at 2803.
165 *Id.* at 2803 (O'Connor, J., concurring); *Id.* at 2809 (Blackmun, J., dissenting).
166 *Roberts*, 448 U.S. at 64-65 (quoting California v. Green, 399 U.S. 149, 162 (1970)).
167 Mattox v. United States, 156 U.S. 237, 243, 244 (1895).
168 *Roberts*, 448 U.S. at 64.
169 Bourjaily v. United States, 107 S. Ct. 2775, 2782 (1987).
170 Chambers v. Mississippi, 410 U.S. 284, 295 (1973).
171 *Roberts*, 448 U.S. at 64.
172 *Bourjaily*, 107 S. Ct. at 2782.

trauma of facing the defendant can most certainly be considered as within the class of "other legitimate interests in the criminal trial process."[173] Therefore, the use of the screen serves a public policy which strongly justifies a marginal infringement of the defendant's confrontation right.

In *Globe Newspaper Co. v. Superior Court*,[174] the Court hinted at its willingness to permit infringements on constitutional rights for the purpose of protecting child witnesses.[175] The *Globe* Court held that a Massachusetts statute[176] which mandated the exclusion of the press and general public, under all circumstances, from the court-room, during the testimony of a minor victim at a sex offense trial violated the first amendment.[177] The *Globe* Court stated that the interest of "safeguarding the physical and psychological well-being of a minor" victim testifying regarding a sexual assault was a compelling interest which would justify a violation of the first amendment right of the press and general public to access to trials under certain circumstances.[178] While striking the statute as unconstitutional, the Court nonetheless supported the exclusion of the press and general public if the trial court determines "on a case-by-case basis whether closure is necessary to protect the welfare of a minor victim."[179] The Court's determination in *Globe* that the interest of protecting child sexual assault victims from the trauma of testifying was a "compelling one,"[180] justifying an infringement of the first amendment when necessary, strongly supports the conclusion that the same interest justifies an infringement of the sixth amendment confrontation right.

Procedural devices designed to ease the trauma to the child victim of sexual assault are necessary to secure both the testimony of the victim and the veracity of the testimony, thereby facilitating the conviction of sexual offenders of children, which furthers the goals

---

[173] *Chambers*, 410 U.S. at 295.

[174] 457 U.S. 596 (1982).

[175] *Id.* at 607-609.

[176] The statute provided:

At the trial of a complaint or indictment for rape, incest, carnal abuse or other crime involving sex, where a minor under eighteen years of age is the person upon, with or against whom the crime is alleged to have been committed . . . the presiding justice shall exclude the general public from the court room [sic], admitting only such persons as may have a direct interest in the case.

MASS. GEN. LAWS ANN. ch. 278, § 16A (West 1981).

[177] *Globe*, 457 U.S. at 610-11. The first amendment states in pertinent part: "[c]ongress shall make no law . . . abridging the freedom of speech, or of the press . . . ." U.S. CONST. amend. I.

[178] *Globe*, 457 U.S. at 607-08.

[179] *Id.* at 608.

[180] *Id.* at 607.

of "effective law enforcement"[181] and "accurate fact-finding."[182] These goals are particularly important because of the gravity of the problem of child sexual abuse. In 1985, there were an estimated 113,000 cases of officially reported child sexual abuse.[183] Moreover, there is evidence that the actual incidence of sexual abuse of children is much more extensive than the officially reported statistics indicate.[184] Studies demonstrate that two-thirds of all sexually abused children suffer identifiable emotional disturbance and fourteen percent of all victims become severely disturbed.[185] Child sexual abuse has been linked with depression, learning difficulties, sexual promiscuity, runaway behavior, hysterical seizures, and compulsive rituals,[186] although the effects vary from child to child.[187]

---

[181] *Roberts*, 448 U.S. at 64.

[182] *Bourjaily*, 107 S. Ct. at 2782.

[183] This figure was compiled by the American Humane Association (AHA), based on reports from state child-protective agencies. Donnelly, *Child Sexual Abuse*, 1 CONG. QUARTERLY'S EDITORIAL RES. REP. 490, 492 (1987).

[184] *Id.* For example, 54% of 930 San Francisco women surveyed in a random sampling reported experiencing sexual abuse prior to the age of eighteen. A similar study of 521 Boston men and women revealed that 15% of women and 6% of men reported past sexual abuse. Additionally, 12% of women and 3% of men in a survey of 2000 Texans reported sexual abuse as children. *Id.*

[185] Weiss & Berg, *Child Victims of Sexual Assault: Impact of Court Procedures*, 21 J. AM. ACAD. CHILD PSYCHIATRY 513, 514 (1982).

[186] J. CONTE, A LOOK AT CHILD SEXUAL ABUSE 22 (1986). A recent study organized the impact of child sexual abuse into a model identifying four specific effects of the abuse: traumatic sexualization, betrayal, powerlessness and stigmatization. Finkelhor & Browne, *The Traumatic Impact of Child Sexual Abuse: A Conceptualization*, 55 AM. J. ORTHO-PSYCHIATRY 531-37 (1985). Traumatic sexualization occurs when a child's sexual development is misdirected by the abuse in an "interpersonally dysfunctional fashion." *Id.* at 531. This phenomenon results in "inappropriate repertoires of sexual behavior, . . . misconceptions about [the child's] . . . sexual self-concepts, and . . . unusual emotional associations to sexual activities." *Id.* Betrayal refers not only to betrayal by offenders who are trusted family members or friends but also to betrayal by family members who are unwilling to believe or protect the victim. The disillusionment and hostility resulting from this betrayal can lead to acquiescence in other abusive relationships, aversions to all relationships, marital problems, antisocial behavior or delinquency. Powerlessness arises from the invasion of the child's body against the child's will. The condition is exacerbated by coercion and manipulation. Powerlessness, particularly for males, leads to an unusual need to control or dominate others. Stigmatization results from negative feelings of shame and guilt communicated to the child victim by the offender and society. Stigmatization may result in the victim's engaging in alcohol abuse, criminal behavior, or prostitution. *Id.* at 531-39.

[187] Victims of a single incident, such as the victims in *Coy*, generally experience acute anxiety, phobic reactions and depression. Weiss & Berg, *supra* note 185, at 514. Sexually abused adolescents can become suicide risks and younger children may exhibit regressive phenomena such as bed-wetting, separation concerns and clinging, infantile behavior. *See id.* at 514. *See also* D. WHITCOMB, E. SHAPIRO, L. STELLWAGEN, WHEN THE VICTIM IS A CHILD: ISSUES FOR JUDGES AND PROSECUTORS 15-16 (1985)(describing effects of abuse and factors contributing to variation in child responses). If the offender is never apprehended, the effects of the abuse are aggravated due to the child's fear of

The impact of sexual abuse can be long lasting. Many incest victims experience psychological disturbance even twenty years after the assault.[188] Some child abuse victims grow up to become offenders themselves.[189]

Procedural reform in the prosecution of child sexual assault cases is needed because, despite the gravity of the problem of child sexual abuse, the offenders are often never convicted due to the societal, institutional, and procedural barriers which impede the reporting, investigating and prosecuting of these crimes.[190] As the Court pointed out in *Pennsylvania v. Ritchie*,[191] "[c]hild abuse is one of the most difficult crimes to detect and prosecute, in large part because there often are no witnesses except the victim."[192] Bringing the abuse to the attention of the authorities is the first obstacle to the successful prosecution of child sexual assault cases.[193] Once action is taken on a reported incident, difficulties arise in the investigation of the report. Multiple questionings of the child, often by untrained parties, place a great strain upon the child and are one of the most traumatic aspects of the process.[194] Questioning by investigators who treat children as they treat adults and employ leading questions often prompts children to alter their stories, rendering it difficult for authorities to ascertain the facts.[195] Because of these problems, and because child sexual assault cases are traditionally hard to win, prosecutors are generally reluctant to take on child sex-

---

repeated incidents or threats of reprisal by the offender. Weiss & Berg, *supra* note 185, at 514. Assaults by family members, which, according to some estimates, comprise three quarters of the cases, Donnelly, *supra* note 183, at 492, are additionally accompanied by deep feelings of guilt over the " 'trouble'. . . [the child] 'caused' the family." Weiss & Berg, *supra* note 185, at 514.

[188] Goodman, *Child Witnesses: Conclusions and Future Directions for Legal Practice*, 40 J. Soc. Issues 157, 167 (1984).

[189] J. Conte, *supra* note 186, at 23.

[190] Donnelly, *supra* note 183, at 493-96.

[191] 480 U.S. 39 (1987).

[192] *Id.* at 60.

[193] Many child victims are either too embarassed to speak out or too afraid to speak out as a result of threats from the offender. D. Whitcomb, E. Shapiro, L. Stellwagen, *supra* note 187, at 4. Victims of sexual abuse by family members often will not report the abuse because of loyalty to or fear of hostility and rejection from the offender and the family. Berliner & Barbieri, *The Testimony of the Child Victim of Sexual Assault*, 40 J. Soc. Issues 125, 128 (1984). Children who tell their stories to family members or other trusted figures are often not believed. *Id.* at 127. Even when children are believed, the children and their families may be hesitant to report the crime because of fear of the trauma to the victim which may be inflicted by the criminal justice system. *Id.* at 128. Moreover, when the crimes are reported, overburdened child protection agencies, which are often responsible for initial investigations, are sometimes forced to ignore many reports. Donnelly, *supra* note 183, at 494.

[194] D. Whitcomb, E. Shapiro, L. Stellwagen, *supra* note 187, at 100.

[195] Donnelly, *supra* note 183, at 494-96.

ual abuse cases.[196] Recently, however, these attitudes have been changing.[197]

Once a case is brought to trial, further problems arise. The credibility of child witnesses may be questioned because of misconceptions about the competency of child witnesses with regard to memory deficits, levels of suggestibility, or ability to distinguish between fact and fantasy.[198] However, several studies have disproved these misconceptions.[199] Nevertheless, even completely honest children can sometimes be ineffective witnesses.[200] Children frequently have problems providing a coherent narrative of events, often in response to the stress of interrogation.[201] These problems are aggravated when, as often is the case, the crime "involves many separate acts, occurring over a long period of time" and reported only much later.[202] "An abused child's inability to provide investigators with basic details of time, place and physical description often results in the case being dropped."[203]

Cases may also be dropped when the adverse effects of police interrogation, court delays, and, in cases of incest, family pressures, cause the victim to recant.[204] Because the victim is often the only witness, the victim's testimony is essential to successful prosecution of the offender.[205] For instance, in one case where a twelve-year-old girl was gang raped by five teenagers, the charges were dropped against one of the offenders because the victim could not go through with a second trial.[206] In another case in which an eleven-year-old boy was sodomized by two men, the boy's parents decided

---

[196] *Id.* at 497.

[197] *Id.*

[198] Bulkley, *Legal Proceedings, Reforms and Emerging Issues in Child Sexual Abuse Cases*, 6 BEHAVIORAL SCI. & L. 153, 155 (1988).

[199] *See id.* at 155. Studies reveal that there is little support for the assertion that child reports of abuse are unreliable. Berliner & Barbieri, *supra* note 193, at 127. Evidence shows that children do not tend to fantasize about things outside of their realm of normal experience. Landwirth, *Children as Witnesses in Child Sexual Abuse Trials*, 80 PEDIATRICS 585, 586 (1987). The evidence also indicates that children are more likely to underreport the amount and type of abuse, as opposed to exaggerating such abuse. Berliner & Barbieri, *supra* note 193, at 127. Moreover the validity of child reports is supported by the relatively high rates of confessions by offenders. *Id.* Another commentator states that "[f]alse allegations by either children or adults [of sexual assault] remain rare events," which can be avoided by "proper investigatory technique[s]." Quinn, *The Credibility of Children's Allegations of Sexual Abuse*, 6 BEHAVIORAL SCI. & L. 181, 195 (1988).

[200] Donnelly, *supra* note 183, at 494.

[201] *Id.* at 494-495.

[202] Berliner & Barbieri, *supra* note 193, at 129.

[203] Donnelly, *supra* note 183, at 495.

[204] Weiss & Berg, *supra* note 185, at 516.

[205] Bell, *Working with Child Witnesses*, PUB. WELFARE 5, 6 (Winter 1988).

[206] Weiss & Berg, *supra* note 185, at 516. One of the offenders was tried separately,

not to prosecute because they were concerned about the traumatic effects of a court trial.[207] The boy had shown signs of emotional disturbance following the incident and was beginning to recover when the parents made the decision not to prosecute.[208] In *State v. Sheppard*,[209] an attorney, who had reviewed between seventy-five and eighty cases of child abuse as a member of a "charge" committee in the prosecutor's office, testified that nearly ninety percent of the child abuse cases were dismissed because children could not cope with the prospect of facing the defendant, relatives and strangers in a courtroom.[210] The attorney told of one instance in which a case of sexual assault of a twelve-year-old girl was dropped because a psychiatrist advised that "the child could not testify without having a total emotional breakdown."[211]

Because the problems at the pre-trial stages of a sexual assault case result in so few incidents of sexual assault actually being prosecuted, it is especially important that once a case reaches trial, the child is afforded the protection that will allow him or her to testify accurately and without undergoing excessive trauma.[212] The gravity of the child sexual abuse problem and its devastating effects on child victims necessitates the prosecution of these crimes to deter the offenders and vindicate the victims.[213] Because of the multitude of

---

because of his status as an adult. Therefore, the victim was required to be present at two trials. *Id.*

[207] *Id.*

[208] *Id.*

[209] 197 N.J. Super. 411, 484 A.2d 1330 (1984).

[210] *Id.* at 417, 484 A.2d at 1333.

[211] *Id.* at 418, 484 A.2d at 1333. Another attorney with substantial experience in the prosecution of child abuse cases testified that out of the thirty or forty cases he had handled, he was able to complete a trial in only one. *Id.* at 417, 484 A.2d at 1333.

[212] Donnelly, *supra* note 183, at 494-496, 497. The many problems involved in sexual assault cases which prevent offenders from being brought to justice comprise an underlying rationale for placing special emphasis on convicting sexual offenders against children. Sexual abusers of children are most likely undeterred by the criminal penalties of child sexual assault because of the problems in the prosecution of child sexual abuse cases. For example, potential offenders are aware that children often do not speak out, that children's reports of abuse are often not believed, and that children are often too traumatized by the assault and its aftermath to testify. Because the chances that a sexual offender against a child will be convicted are relatively small, the potential offender is not as deterred by the possibility of being caught as perpetrators of other crimes might be. One who rapes, kidnaps or assaults an adult does not know, as does one who sexually assaults children, that psychological, societal and institutional barriers will contribute to preventing him from being brought to justice.

[213] The existence of these problems in the criminal justice system seems to lend support to the arguments of some mental health professionals who advocate the diversion of child sexual abuse cases from the criminal justice system to juvenile or family court, or voluntary treatment programs. These experts believe that offenders have psychological disorders that call for treatment rather than punishment. Berliner & Barbieri, *supra*

problems which characterize the investigation and prosecution of these crimes, procedural reforms are needed.[214] Devices such as the mirror in *Coy* ease the trauma to the child of facing the defendant during testimony, thereby encouraging the child witness to testify. Facilitating the child's testimony is especially important because the

---

note 193, at 129. *See also* J. BULKLEY, CHILD SEXUAL ABUSE: LEGAL ISSUES AND APPROACHES i (1981). Additional controversy over whether child sexual abuse should be prosecuted where the abuser is a parent is generated by concern over the trauma to the family. Bulkley, *supra* note 198, at 154. Other professionals argue that the criminal justice system provides the "concrete symbol . . . [which] sanctions the total unacceptability of such behavior." J. BULKLEY, *supra* note 213, at i. "Most child sexual abusers know that they are breaking the law and can be held legally responsible." Berliner & Barbieri, *supra* note 193, at 128. In addition, sexual offenders rarely seek mental-health treatment voluntarily. *Id.* Often offenders that are in voluntary treatment drop out. J. BULKLEY, *supra* note 213, at ii. The criminal court has the coercive power that alternative methods of addressing the problems of child sexual assault do not have. Bulkley, *supra* note 198, at 157. Moreover, there still remains the problem of false accusations, which the criminal justice system, through its procedural safeguards, is designed to ferret out. *Id.* Therefore, the criminal justice system, with its specialized fact finding process and deterrent effect, remains the best corrective forum for the problem of child sexual abuse. Once an offender has been convicted, the law can then "be used effectively as a leverage, even when the goal of all concerned is treatment rather than punishment." Berliner & Barbieri, *supra* note 193, at 128.

214 Other reforms of courtroom procedure implemented in some jurisdictions include provisions to: 1) liberalize the competency requirements of minor witnesses; 2) require speedy trials of sexual assault cases; 3) establish special hearsay exceptions for the child victim's out-of-court statement of abuse; 4) close the courtroom to the press or public during the child's testimony; and 5) permit greater use of expert testimony. Brief of Amicus Curiae The American Bar Association at 12, Coy v. Iowa, 108 S. Ct. 2798 (1988)(No. 86-6757). In addition, early docketing of cases involving child victims/witnesses addresses the problems of delays in prosecution of child sexual assault cases. Goodman, Jones, Pyle, Prado-Estrada, Port, England, Mason & Rudy, *The Emotional Effects of Criminal Court Testimony on Child Sexual Assault Victims: A Preliminary Report,* in PROCEEDINGS FROM THE INTERNATIONAL CONFERENCE ON CHILD WITNESSES: DO THE COURTS ABUSE CHILDREN? (in press) [hereinafter Goodman]. To address problems at the investigative stages, states have passed reporting laws, which "establish a comprehensive legislative scheme for child protection designed to encourage reports of abuse . . ., to designate one agency to handle reports, and to offer services to children and families." Bulkley, *supra* note 198, at 158. Some communities have established programs which address the problems arising in child sexual assault cases before and during the prosecution of the cases. *See generally* AMERICAN BAR ASSOCIATION NATIONAL LEGAL RESOURCE CENTER FOR CHILD ADVOCACY AND PROTECTION, INNOVATIONS IN THE PROSECUTION OF CHILD SEXUAL ABUSE CASES (1981)(providing descriptions of several county and municipal programs for handling child sexual abuse cases). For example, in Seattle, a program called the Sexual Assault Center contributed to the implementation of new approaches to handling child sexual abuse cases. A special children's interviewing room instead of the police station, and joint interviews to avoid multiple interrogations were introduced. In addition, sensitive questioning techniques designed to reduce trauma to the child and enhance information gathering represent another area of possible reform. J. BULKLEY, *supra* note 213, at 13. A guardian ad litem, or legal representative, can work with the prosecutor to represent the child's interests and ensure that the child is handled sensitively. *Id.* at 14.

child victim is often the only witness to the crime.[215] Against this background, it is clear that the public policy of prosecuting crimes of sexual assault on children justifies a marginal infringement upon the defendant's right of confrontation.

In addition to the public policy of bringing sexual offenders to justice, the *Coy* screen and other similar devices serve the interest of protecting the child victim from the further trauma of testifying under the stare of the defendant, which is certainly one of the other "legitimate interests in the criminal trial process."[216] The line separating the adverse effects upon the child resulting from the actual abuse and the adverse effects upon the child resulting from involvment in the legal process is difficult to demarcate. However, evidence suggests that involvement in court proceedings intensifies the trauma to child sexual assault victims.[217] A recent study of child sexual assault victims involved in criminal proceedings demonstrated that children who testified in court showed a larger increase in overall behavioral disturbance than those children who did not testify in court.[218] The fear of facing the defendant is only one of the factors that contributes to the traumatic effect of courtroom testimony,[219] heightening the "emotional fallout of the legal process."[220] However, one study found that the most frequently mentioned fear of child victims of sexual assault was facing the defendant.[221] "[T]o a child who does not understand the reason for confrontation, the anticipation and experience of being in close proximity to the defendant can be overwhelming."[222] If a child is attempting to recover from the traumatic effects of sexual abuse, seeing the offender in the courtroom "may reactivate or intensify the clinical symptoms seen at onset or may produce new ones."[223]

---

215 *See supra* note 205 and accompanying text.

216 Chambers v. Mississippi, 410 U.S. 284, 295 (1973).

217 D. WHITCOMB, E. SHAPIRO, L. STELLWAGEN, *supra* note 187, at 17. One commentator stated: "[f]or a child, testifying in court may be the most traumatic experience of her involvment in the legal process." J. BULKLEY, *supra* note 213, at 13.

218 Goodman, *supra* note 214. Empirical research regarding children's reactions to court involvement is in its early stages. *Id.*

219 D. WHITCOMB, E. SHAPIRO, L. STELLWAGEN, *supra* note 187, at 17-18.

220 Melton, *Child Witnesses and the First Amendment: A Psychological Dilemma*, 40 J. SOC. ISSUES 109, 109 (1984).

221 D. WHITCOMB, E. SHAPIRO, L. STELLWAGEN, *supra* note 187, at 17. A recent study focused on the effects of court testimony on child sexual assault victims. Although not all children expressed negative feelings about other aspects of courtroom testimony such as talking to the judge or talking to the defense attorney, a significantly larger number of children expressed negative feelings about seeing the accused in court. Goodman, *supra* note 214.

222 D. WHITCOMB, E. SHAPIRO, L. STELLWAGEN, *supra* note 187, at 17-18.

223 Weiss & Berg, *supra* note 185, at 516.

Moreover, after going through the trauma of testifying, a child victim can be especially devastated by an acquittal for the defendant. Children often do not understand why the process has not resulted in a just outcome.[224]

The introduction of protective devices in cases of child sexual assault will not set a precedent for infringing on the defendant's sixth amendment confrontation right in cases involving adults. The particular need for using protective devices with child witnesses stems from the fact that child victims are inherently different from adult victims. A child does not understand why he or she must repeat his or her story to police, social workers, doctors, prosecutors, and the court and this further aggravates the child's feelings of helplessness.[225] Children are particularly affected by cross-examination, which they also do not understand.[226] Moreover, child victims who testify are overwhelmed by certain physical attributes of the courtroom or the figure of the judge.[227] Some children also may experience anxiety when they are asked questions which cause them to fear they have done something wrong.[228]

In addition, the rationale underlying the need for face-to-face confrontation does not apply to children in the same way that it applies to adults. The majority contends that the "Confrontation Clause does not, of course, compel the witness to fix his eyes upon the defendant; he may studiously look elsewhere, but the trier of fact will draw its own conclusions."[229] This represents a choice for the child between looking at the defendant and experiencing the resulting trauma, and trying not to look at the defendant, thereby increasing the jury bias against the child's credibility. A truthful child who is terrified in the presence of the defendant will of course avoid looking at the defendant, thereby decreasing his or her chances of being believed. On the other hand, the use of protective procedures for child witnesses may enhance truth telling. In *State v. Sheppard*,[230] a forensic psychiatrist explained this while testifying for the

---

[224] Berliner & Barbieri, *supra* note 193, at 135.

[225] D. WHITCOMB, E. SHAPIRO, L. STELLWAGEN, *supra* note 187, at 18.

[226] *Id.* Even an adult victim who thoroughly comprehends the importance of careful investigation and procedural safeguards in the criminal justice system would feel frustration, pain, and helplessness at the delays and complexities of the system. Children, on the other hand, do not understand why they have to be questioned so many times, why they have to reveal and relive the painful details of their experience to strangers, why the legal process takes so long, and, in some cases, why their attacker has not been punished. *Id.* at 17-18.

[227] *Id.*

[228] *Id.* at 19.

[229] Coy v. Iowa, 108 S. Ct. 2798, 2802 (1988).

[230] 197 N.J. Super. 411, 484 A.2d 1330 (1984).

state at a hearing in response to the state's application to employ closed-circuit television during the testimony of the child sexual assault victim. The psychiatrist stated that while an adult witness will be prompted by the traditional court setting to tell the truth, the "opposite is true of a child, particularly when the setting involves a relative."[231] In addition to the fear, anxiety and trauma caused by the courtroom, the child also has mixed feelings about his or her testimony. For the accused, he or she feels anger as well as care. The child feels guilt as well as satisfaction in response to the prospect of convicting the defendant.[232] "These mixed feelings . . . mitigate the truth, producing inaccurate testimony."[233] On the other hand, the more relaxed atmosphere provided by devices such as the mirror may result in the child giving a clearer and more complete description of the abuse.[234]

Although there are other possible reforms which address the problems of child witnesses, many of these other procedural reforms pose the same type of constitutional questions raised by the screen in *Coy*. Videotaped testimony, closed-circuit television, and the admission of prior statements by the child concerning the abuse all attempt to protect the child. Iowa is, in fact, unusual in permitting the use of the one-way mirror.[235] The screen used in *Coy* is actually the least intrusive of these methods. Closed-circuit television does not allow the defendant to be present with counsel during the child's testimony and cross-examination without forcing the witness to testify under the defendant's stare. It thus presents a choice between having the defendant in the same room as the witness or having only defendant's counsel present with the witness. However, placing the defendant in a separate room from the witness in this manner also separates the defendant from his counsel during cross-examination.[236]

Devices such as the one-way mirror in *Coy* serve the essential state interests of prosecuting sexual offenders of children and protecting the child victim of sexual assault from the trauma of viewing

---

[231] *Id.* at 416, 484 A.2d at 1332.

[232] *Id.*

[233] *Id.*

[234] Donnelly, *supra* note 183, at 499.

[235] Twenty-five states permit a loosening of the hearsay ban when a child has disclosed sexual abuse to a trusted adult and the prosecutor wishes the adult to testify as to the hearsay. Thirty-four states permit videotaped testimony of a child in lieu of live testimony. In addition, twenty-five states allow closed-circuit television testimony. Donnelly, *supra* note 183, at 496; Wyo. Stat. § 7-11-408 (1987).

[236] An additional advantage to the one-way mirror is that it is less costly and simpler to implement. American Bar Association, Guidelines for the Fair Treatment of Child Witnesses in Cases Where Child Abuse is Alleged 25 (Approved Draft, 1985).

the defendant during testimony. Because these interests justify infringing the defendant's right to face-to-face confrontation, the use of these devices constitutes a constitutionally permissible exception to the confrontation right.

D.   A SHOWING OF NECESSITY AS A PREREQUISITE

While protective devices should be allowed as exceptions to the confrontation right, a showing of necessity should be required for their use. This view is in accord with the majority and concurring opinions,[237] and with several state legislatures which have incorporated the requirement of necessity into their states' protective procedure statutes.[238] In *Ohio v. Roberts*,[239] the Court outlined an approach for permitting exceptions to the confrontation right.[240] The Court stated that "in conformance with the Framers' preference for face-to-face accusation, the Sixth Amendment establishes a rule of necessity."[241] The *Roberts* Court explained that if the prosecution wishes to introduce hearsay, it must be demonstrated that the declarant is unavailable and that the statement is reliable.[242] Moreover, in *Chambers v. Mississippi*,[243] the Court emphasized that the "denial" or "diminution" of the right to confront by competing interests "requires that the competing interest be closely examined."[244] The *Chambers* rule suggests that if an exception to the

---

[237] *See* Coy v. Iowa, 108 S. Ct. 2798, 2803 (1988); *id.* at 2805 (O'Connor, J., concurring).

[238] For example, Florida provides for the use of closed-circuit television in sexual assault cases involving children under age sixteen "[u]pon motion and hearing in camera and upon a finding that there is a substantial likelihood that the child will suffer at least moderate emotional or mental harm if required to testify." FLA. STAT. § 92.54(1) (1987). Massachusetts requires that a court ordering the use of a protective procedure must find "by a preponderance of the evidence at the time of the order that the child witness is likely to suffer psychological or emotional trauma as a result of testifying." MASS GEN. L. ch. 278, § 16D(b)(1) (1986). New Jersey requires that there be a "substantial likelihood" of "severe emotional or mental distress" for the use of closed-circuit testimony to be permitted. N.J. STAT. ANN. § 2A:84A-32.4(b) (West Supp. 1988). California provides extensive guidelines for making a finding of necessity, delineating the factors to be considered. CAL. PENAL CODE § 1347(d)(1) (West Supp. 1988). States that do not require a finding of necessity before the use of protective devices include Connecticut, Kansas, Kentucky, and Louisiana. *See, e.g.*, CONN. GEN. STAT. § 54-86g (Supp. 1987); KAN. STAT. ANN. § 38-1558 (1986); KY. REV. STAT. ANN. § 421-350(1)(3) (Baldwin 1986); LA. REV. STAT. ANN. § 15:283 (West Supp. 1987).

[239] 448 U.S. 56 (1980).

[240] *Id.* at 64-65.

[241] *Id.* at 65.

[242] *Id.*

[243] 410 U.S. 284 (1973).

[244] *Id.* at 295 (citing Berger v. California, 393 U.S. 314, 315 (1969)).

confrontation right is being invoked, a particularized showing justifying the exception must be made.

Globe Newspaper Co. v. Superior Court[245] also supports the requirement of a showing of necessity in the context of protecting child witnesses.[246] The *Globe* Court held the Massachusetts statute unconstitutional because the statute mandated exclusion in all cases.[247] The Court stated that "as compelling as that interest [of protecting minor victims of sexual assault] is, it does not justify a *mandatory* closure rule, for it is clear that the circumstances of the particular case may affect the significance of the interest."[248] The Court stated that a trial court should determine whether exclusion is necessary based on such factors as the victim's age, the victim's psychological maturity and understanding, the nature of the crime, the victim's wishes, and the interests of parents and relatives.[249]

The Court pointed out that the particular circumstances in *Globe* may have led to a finding that closure was unnecessary, had the trial court not been limited by the statute's provision of mandatory exclusion.[250] The Court noted that the names of the victims in *Globe* were already publicly known, and that, according to the prosecuting attorney, the victims stated that they wouldn't object to the press being present during their testimony provided that the press would not interview them or publish their names, photographs or personal information.[251] The Court added that child victims "could be protected just as well by requiring the trial court to determine on a case-by-case basis whether the State's legitimate concern for the well-being of the minor victim necessitates closure" as by requiring mandatory closure in all cases.[252] The Court discussed the rationale for a finding of necessity by explaining that "[s]uch an approach ensures that the constitutional right of the press and public to gain access to criminal trials will not be restricted except where necessary to protect the State's interest."[253]

Similarly, in allowing an exception to the confrontation right for cases of child sexual assault, courts must be careful to ensure that case-specific inquiries are made into the necessity of a protec-

---

[245] 457 U.S. 596 (1982).

[246] *Id.* at 609.

[247] *Id.* at 608, 610-611.

[248] *Id.* at 607-608 (emphasis in original).

[249] *Id.* at 608.

[250] *Id.* at 609

[251] *Id.* at 599 n.5.

[252] *Id.* at 609.

[253] *Id.*

tive device.[254] A case-specific finding is especially justified in the context of child protective exceptions because of variation among victims in reacting to both the sexual assault and the involvement in the judicial process. There is evidence that some children "appear unharmed by the criminal justice system."[255] One study concluded that "the opportunity to testify in juvenile court may exert a protective effect on the child victim."[256] This study suggested that testimony may be therapeutic for the child victim because it gives the child an opportunity to express his or her feelings and experiences and to counteract his or her sense of powerlessness.[257] However the therapeutic effect of the testimony may vary from child to child,[258] just as most studies have shown that some sexually abused children have far more serious reactions to the abuse than others.[259] One commentator stated:

> [p]sychiatric opinions and studies emphasize that each child victim reacts to an offense and its aftermath in his own individual way. . . . Thus, there can be no more justification for excusing all child victims from testifying than for imposing the duty on all of them. Each case merits its own individual decision.[260]

---

[254] As the Court suggested in *Globe*, Courts can consider several factors in determining whether the use of a protective procedure is necessary. *Id.* at 608. The child's age, fear of the defendant, handicap or disability, reaction to previous interviews, past history of abuse, and relationship to the defendant are important factors. Brief of Amicus Curiae The American Bar Association at 16, Coy v. Iowa, 108 S. Ct. 2798 (1988)(No. 86-6757). However, care is warranted in ensuring that an inquiry into the necessity of a protective device does not subject the child to further trauma. For example, "it would be self-defeating to subject the child to a grueling *voir dire* examination or, *after* the child has been called to testify, to delay the proceedings while this issue is being resolved." *Id.* at 17 (emphasis in original). Even a psychiatric evaluation of the child to determine the need for protective procedures is unnecessary as this determination can be made by referring to parents and other relatives, a child-victim advocate, a social worker, or the child's therapist. *Id.* at 18.

[255] D. WHITCOMB, E. SHAPIRO, L. STELLWAGEN, *supra* note 187, at 15-18.

[256] Runyan, Everson, Edelsohn, Hunter, & Coulter, *Impact of Legal Intervention on Sexually Abused Children*, 113 J. PEDIATRICS 647, 652 (1988)(studying impact on child sexual abuse victims of foster care placement of victims, criminal prosecution of the offender, and testimony by the victims in either criminal or juvenile court). The authors cautioned against applying these results to criminal court testimony. *Id.*

[257] *Id.* at 652. *See also* Berliner & Barbieri, *supra* note 193, at 135 ("the experience of testifying in court can have a therapeutic effect for the child victim").

[258] Runyan, Everson, Edelsohn, Hunter, & Coulter, *supra* note 256, at 650.

[259] J. CONTE, *supra* note 186, at 22-23. Some of the factors that affect the impact of the abuse on the child are: the age of the child; the age and gender of the offender; whether physical force was used; the frequency, severity and duration of the abuse; the relationship of the offender to the child; the number of the offenders; the number of problems exhibited by the child's family; and the relationship of the child to his or her siblings. *Id.*

[260] Libai, *The Protection of the Child Victim of a Sexual Offense in the Criminal Justice System*, 15 WAYNE L. REV. 977, 1009 (1969)(citations omitted). Careful attention to the underlying factors thought to aggravate the impact of child abuse is necessitated by the fact that psychological problems resulting from child sexual abuse often may not be immediately

Caution in permitting the use of these devices is further warranted by the fact that the danger of convicting innocent defendants of sexual abuse is not remote. There is evidence that children are sometimes manipulated by adults who encourage them to make false accusations of sexual assault.[261] For example, a mother involved in a custody dispute with the father may prompt the child to make false accusations of abuse.[262] Due to most children's level of suggestibility and desire to please adults, leading questions by interrogators may encourage a child to describe things that never happened.[263] Critics of procedural devices aimed at protecting child witnesses express concerns that these devices set precedents which may further erode constitutional protections for the accused.[264] The possibility of false accusations of sexual assault heightens the importance of procedural safeguards in cases of sexual assault. While the protection of child witnesses is an important goal, the rights of the accused must be protected as well. A rule of necessity which permits an infringement of a defendant's constitutional right only when necessary to protect the child witness, increases the protection of the accused's rights.

The *Coy* dissent, however, in light of its opinion that the confrontation right is not violated by protective devices, disagreed, and advocated that protective devices should be used even without a particularized showing of necessity.[265] The dissent pointed to other exceptions to the confrontation clause which do not require a showing of necessity.[266] For example, in *United States v. Inadi*,[267] the

---

apparent. Problems may not show up until later in the victim's life. J. CONTE, *supra* note 186, at 23. Therefore, a finding of a lack of necessity based on the child's appearance at the time of trial may not be appropriate.

[261] Donnelly, *supra* note 183, at 496. One study found that forty-five percent of reports of sexual abuse are unsubstantiated, although that number may include truthful reports which were unprovable. A more detailed survey in Denver reached a finding of only 8% untruthful allegations. *Id.* at 494. In one case, a man in the process of getting a divorce was accused of sexually abusing his two young daughters. Although the man was acquitted, he was still being denied the opportunity to see his children two years later. *Id.* at 491. Another man was accused of molestation by a friend of his daughter. Although the jury decided that the incident as described by the girl was physically impossible and acquitted the defendant, the financial and personal costs to him were substantial. *Id.* at 494. A group of parents who claim to have been falsely accused of sexual and other abuse have joined in an organization called Victims of Child Abuse Laws, Inc. (VOCAL). *Id.* at 493.

[262] *Id.* at 496. One study found that child abuse charges are made in three percent of custody disputes. *Id.*

[263] Donnelly, *supra* note 183, at 496.

[264] *Id.* at 493.

[265] Coy v. Iowa, 108 S. Ct. 2798, 2809 (Blackmun, J., dissenting).

[266] *Id.* at 2809 (Blackmun, J., dissenting). The dissent pointed out that "statements of a co-conspirator, excited utterances, and business records are all generally admissible

Court held that a specific showing that the witness was unavailable was not required,[268] and in *Bourjaily v. United States*,[269] the Court held that an independent showing of the reliability of evidence violative of the sixth amendment was also not required.[270] The *Bourjaily* Court's reasoning was based on the Court's statement in *Roberts* that in the case of a " 'firmly rooted hearsay exception,' " an independent inquiry into reliability is not necessary.[271] However, the *Roberts* decision also stated that "[i]n other cases, the evidence must be excluded, at least absent a showing of particularized guarantees of trustworthiness."[272] Moreover, the requirement of a showing of unavailability was not rescinded by *Inadi*, rather, it was deemed applicable to prior testimony and not to co-conspirator statements.[273] Therefore, *Inadi* and *Bourjaily* affirmed that a particularized showing of necessity is required, except in the case of a firmly rooted exception to the confrontation right. In those cases of exceptions not firmly rooted, "case-specific inquiry into the applicability of the rationale supporting the rule that allows"[274] the exception is necessary.

The shocking nature of child sexual assault cases leads to emotional demands for reform. However, because of the complex nature of the problem and the danger of infringing on the rights of the innocent, care is required in the implementation of these reforms. The inclusion of a rule of necessity as an exception to the confrontation right in child sexual assault cases constitutes this type of care.

---

under the Federal Rules of Evidence without case-specific inquiry into the applicability of the rationale supporting the rule that allows their admission." *Id.* at 2809 n.6 (Blackmun, J., dissenting). However, these examples are much more clearly definable exceptions than the one at issue in *Coy*. For example, the business record exception, FED. R. EVID. 803(6), is a clearly-defined category to which the rationale underlying the exception would apply in every case fitting within the category. The category of child sexual assault victims who would be excessively traumatized by testifying in the presence of their attackers is a much more ambiguous category, since not all child sexual assault victims are excessively traumatized by testifying. *See supra* notes 255-257 and accompanying text. Therefore, the rationale underlying the exception would not apply to every child victim.

267 475 U.S. 387 (1986).
268 *Id.* at 394.
269 107 S. Ct. 2775 (1987).
270 *Id.* at 2782.
271 *Id.* at 2782-2783 (quoting Ohio v. Roberts, 448 U.S. 56, 66 (1980)).
272 *Roberts*, 448 U.S. at 66.
273 *Inadi*, 475 U.S. at 394-95, 400.
274 *Coy*, 108 S. Ct. at 2809 n.5 (Blackmun, J., dissenting).

E.   THERE WAS NO SHOWING OF NECESSITY IN *COY*

As the majority[275] and concurrence[276] stated, there was no showing of necessity in *Coy* to justify the use of the one-way mirror. The defendant pointed out that there was "no testimony or finding that the child witnesses were traumatized or would be harmed by testifying in . . . [the defendant's] presence."[277] "Neither girl expressed a preference for the use of the screen during her testimony."[278] The record was "silent as to any justification for infringement on appellant's right to confront adverse witnesses."[279] The defendant further argued that:

> [w]hile the trial judge allowed defense counsel to assert his constitutional objections to the screening barrier, the court provided no explanation for his ultimate ruling. He did not make specific findings of fact as to the need for a screening device at this trial, nor did he conduct an evidentiary hearing during which the child witnesses, their parents and relatives, or expert witnesses could provide some justification for the extraordinary courtroom structure.[280]

The defendant noted that neither witness identified him as the offender and that the testimony of both witnesses was clear and articulate.[281] Because there was no showing that the witnesses in *Coy* would have been traumatized by testifying while the defendant was within view, the use of the mirror was unnecessary.[282] The Court in *Coy* was correct in concluding that the defendant's right to confront the witnesses against him was violated.

CONCLUSION

Although the defendant's right to confront the witnesses against him face-to-face has never been the subject of a Supreme Court decision, the literal meaning of the confrontation clause and Supreme Court language in several cases establish that the right is, if not the most essential, at least an important element of the sixth amendment confrontation clause. Therefore, Coy's sixth amendment right was violated by the use of the one-way mirror. However, the right to a face-to-face encounter is, like the other confrontation rights, not absolute where substantial public policy interests justify exceptions. The twin goals of convicting sexual offenders against

---

275 *See id.* at 2803.
276 *Id.* at 2805 (O'Connor, J., concurring).
277 Brief for Appellant at 39, Coy v. Iowa, 108 S. Ct. 2798 (1988)(No. 86-6757).
278 *Id.* at 5.
279 *Id.* at 39-40.
280 *Id.* at 27.
281 *Id.* at 28.
282 *Coy,* 108 S. Ct. at 2803.

children and protecting child victims of sexual assault from excessive trauma are public policy interests which justify permitting the use of protective devices such as the screen in *Coy*. However, the use of such a device should only be permitted if a case-specific showing that the device is necessary is made. Because there was no such showing in *Coy*, the violation of the defendant Coy's confrontation right was unconstitutional.

The majority opinion in *Coy* leaves two questions unanswered: first, whether, if there were a showing of necessity, the right to physically face the witness would be subject to an exception for the purpose of protecting child witnesses; second, whether, if a protective procedure passed the sixth amendment test, the Court would hold it violative of due process as a prejudicial device.

With regard to the first issue, the decisions in *Coy* suggest that Justice Blackmun and Chief Justice Rehnquist would join Justices O'Connor and White to affirm a conviction in which a protective device was used on a showing of necessity. In such a case the holding would be determined by Justice Kennedy's vote.[283] As to the issue of prejudice, only Justice Blackmun addressed the issue. However, because Justices O'Connor and White stated that protective devices would be allowed on a showing of necessity, it appears that, according to this reasoning, the prejudicial question is not an obstacle to the constitutionality of protective devices. Therefore, the outcome of this issue hinges on the same factor as that determining the first issue.

In any case, *Coy* does not forbid the use of protective procedures in child sexual assault cases. In her concurring opinion, Justice O'Connor noted that "[w]hile I agree with the Court that the Confrontation Clause was violated in this case, I wish to make clear that nothing in today's decision necessarily dooms such efforts by state legislatures to protect child witnesses."[284] A conservative approach toward allowing procedural reforms which implicate constitutional rights should result in reforms of the entire system, including trial procedure, to protect child victims and to make the successful prosecution, deterrence and rehabilitation of the offenders more likely.

RACHEL I. WOLLITZER

---

[283] Justice Kennedy took no part in the decision in *Coy*.
[284] *Coy*, 108 S. Ct. at 2804 (O'Connor, J., concurring).

VIDEOTAPED CHILD TESTIMONY AND THE CONFRONTATION CLAUSE: ARE THEY RECONCILABLE?

I. INTRODUCTION

A majority of state legislatures in the United States have enacted statutes providing for the use of videotaped testimony at trial in cases involving allegations of sexual abuse of children.[1] Videotaped testimony is but one of many reform measures that have been introduced by courts, legislatures, and others involved in the administration of the criminal justice system,[2] in response to the rapid growth in the number of reported instances of child sexual abuse.[3] Other statutory reforms enacted to respond to evidentiary problems in sexual abuse cases include the elimination or modification of child competency restrictions,[4] the enactment of special hearsay exceptions,[5] and provisions allowing

---

1. Thirty-three state statutes provide for videotaping child testimony in sexual child abuse cases. These include: ALA. CODE § 15-25-2 (Supp. 1986); ALASKA STAT. § 12.45.047 (1984); ARIZ. REV. STAT. ANN. §§ 13-4251, 13-4253(B),(C) (Supp. 1986); ARK. STAT. ANN. §§ 43-2035-2037 (Supp. 1985); CAL. PENAL CODE § 1346 (West 1986); COLO. REV. STAT. §§ 18-3-413, 18-6-401.3 (1986); CONN. GEN. STAT. § 54-86q (Supp. 1987); DEL. CODE ANN. tit. 11, § 3511 (Supp. 1986); IND. CODE ANN. § 35-37-4-8(c), (d), (f), (g) (Burns 1986); IOWA CODE ANN. § 910A.14 (West Supp. 1985); KAN. STAT. ANN. § 24-3434 (1986); KY. REV. STAT. ANN. § 421.350(4) (Baldwin 1986); MASS. GEN. LAWS ANN. ch. 278, § 16D(b)(2) (West Supp. 1987); MINN. STAT. ANN. § 595.02(4) (West Supp. 1987); MISS. CODE ANN. § 13-1-407 (1986); MO. REV. STAT. § 491.675–491.690 (1986); MONT. CODE ANN. §§ 46-15-401–403 (1986); NEV. REV. STAT. § 174.227 (1986); N.H. REV. STAT. ANN. § 517:13-a (Supp. 1987); N.M. STAT. ANN. § 30-9-17 (1986); OHIO REV. CODE ANN. § 2907.41 (A), (B), (D), (E) (Baldwin Supp. 1987); OKLA. STAT. ANN. tit. 22, § 753(C) (West 1986); PA. STAT. ANN. tit. 42, §§ 5982, 5984 (Purdon 1986); R.I. GEN. LAWS § 11-37-13.2 (1986); S.C. CODE ANN. § 16-3-1530(G) (Law. Co-op. 1984); S.D. CODIFIED LAWS ANN. § 23A-12-9 (Supp. 1987); TENN. CODE ANN. § 24-27-116(d)–(f) (Supp. 1986); TEX. CRIM. PROC. CODE. art. 38.071 (Vernon Supp. 1987); UTAH CODE ANN. § 77-35-15.5(3)–(4) (Supp. 1987); VT. R. EVID. 807 (Supp. 1986); WIS. STAT. ANN. § 967.04(7)–(10) (West 1986); WYO. STAT. § 7-11-408 (1987).

2. *Children's Justice Act: Hearings on S.140 Before the Subcomm. on Children, Family, Drugs, and Alcoholism of the Senate Comm. on Labor and Human Resources,* 99th Cong., 1st. Sess. 82 (1985) (statement of Debra Whitcomb); *see also* Brief of Amicus Curiae Judge Charles B. Schudson, Coy v. Iowa, 108 S. Ct. 2798 (1988). In his brief Judge Schudson categorized these innovations into four broad categories: (1) the elimination or modification of child competency restrictions; (2) the enactment or interpretation of hearsay exceptions to allow a jury to learn of a child's disclosure or complaints; (3) broadening the admissibility of expert testimony; and (4) the use of courtroom techniques which help the child witness feel comfortable enough to testify. *Id.*

3. Christiansen, *The Testimony of Child Witnesses: Fact, Fantasy, and the Influence of Pretrial Interviews,* 62 WASH. L. REV. 705 (1987).

4. *See, e.g.,* MICH. STAT. ANN. § 27A.2163 (1985); MO. ANN. STAT. 491.060(2) (Vernon 1985); WIS STAT. § 27A.2163 (Callaghan 1985).

5. *See, e.g.,* ILL. ANN. STAT. ch 37, para. 704-6(4)(c) (Smith-Hurd 1985); IND. CODE § 35-37-4-6 (1985), MINN. STAT. § 595.02(3) (1985).

testimony of the child witness via one-way[6] or two-way closed circuit television.[7] These various reforms generally seek to achieve two goals: to make the legal process more sensitive to child witnesses who are allegedly victims of sexual abuse,[8] and to increase the success rate for the prosecution of child sexual abuse cases.[9] These are also the articulated goals of the Children's Justice Act,[10] through which the federal government has offered financial grants to states as an incentive to implement protective reforms for children in sexual abuse cases.[11]

Statutes permitting the use of videotaped testimony at trial potentially raise the issue of whether the defendant's sixth amendment right to confrontation[12] has been violated.[13] Some statutes explicitly require that the child witness not be able to see or hear the defendant while the child's deposition or testimony is being videotaped;[14] other statutes provide that the child witness may be prevented from seeing or hearing the defendant upon a finding by the court that the child is likely to suffer trauma as a result of further contact with the defendant.[15] In addition, almost half the statutes designed to protect abuse victims preclude the child witness from testifying at the trial or any proceeding at which the

---

6. *See, e.g.,* ALA. CODE § 15-25-3 (Supp. 1986); IND. CODE ANN. § 35-37-4-8 (Burns 1986); KAN. STAT. ANN. § 38-1558 (1986); R.I. GEN. LAWS § 11-37-13.2 (Supp. 1986).

7. *See, e.g.,* CAL. PENAL CODE § 1347 (West 1986); N.Y. CRIM. PROC. LAW § 65.00–65.30 (McKinney Supp. 1987); OHIO REV. CODE ANN. § 2907.41(C), (E) (Baldwin Supp. 1987).

8. Brief of Amicus Curiae The American Bar Association, Coy v. Iowa, 108 S. Ct. 2798 (1988).

9. Note, *The Testimony of Child Victims in Sex Abuse Prosecutions: Two Legislative Innovations,* 98 HARV. L. REV. 806, 808 (1985).

10. Children's Justice and Assistance Act of 1986, Pub. L. No. 99-401, 100 Stat. 903 (codified as amended at 42 U.S.C. § 5103(d) (Supp. 1987)).

11. 42 U.S.C. § 5103(d) (Supp. 1987).

12. U.S. CONST. amend. VI. "In all criminal prosecutions, the accused shall enjoy the right . . . to be confronted with the witnesses against him . . . ." *Id.*

13. The United States Supreme Court has held that a "face-to-face confrontation between the accused and accuser [is] 'essential to a fair trial in a criminal prosecution.' " Coy v. Iowa, 108 S. Ct. 2798, 2801 (1988) (quoting Pointer v. Texas, 380 U.S. 400, 404 (1965)). Every videotaping statute presently in force, however, contains at least one provision which technically infringes, to some degree, upon a defendant's constitutional right to confront the witnesses against him. *See infra* notes 14–17 and accompanying text.

14. The following statutes preclude the defendant from being seen or heard by the child witness during the child's videotaped deposition or testimony: ARK. STAT. ANN. §§ 43-2035–037 (Supp. 1985); CONN. GEN. STAT. § 54-86q (Supp. 1987); DEL. CODE ANN. tit. 11, § 3511 (Supp. 1986); KAN. STAT. ANN. § 24-3434 (1986); KY. REV. STAT. ANN. § 421.350(4) (Baldwin 1986); OKLA. STAT. ANN. tit. 22, § 753(C) (West 1986); PA. STAT. ANN. tit. 42, §§ 5982, 5984 (Purdon 1986); R.I. GEN. LAWS § 11-37-13.2 (1986); TEX. CRIM. PROC. CODE ANN. art. 38.071 § 3 (Vernon Supp. 1987).

15. The following statutes allow the defendant to be seen or heard by the child witness during the child's videotaped deposition or testimony, unless the court finds that the child will be further traumatized by the defendant's presence: MASS. GEN. LAWS ANN. ch. 278, § 16D(b)(2) (West Supp. 1987); MINN. STAT. ANN. § 595.02(4) (West Supp. 1987); MISS. CODE ANN. § 13-1-407 (1986); UTAH CODE ANN. § 77-35-15.5(3), (4) (Supp. 1987); WYO. STAT. § 7-11-408 (1987).

videotaped deposition or testimony is introduced.[16] Other states provide
that the child witness may be precluded from testifying in-person at the
trial or any other proceeding upon a finding by the court that the child
may be traumatized by the presence of the defendant.[17] Since these
provisions enable the child witness to avoid contact with the defendant
while the child testifies, they technically violate the defendant's right to
a face-to-face confrontation with the child witness[18] as guaranteed by
the sixth amendment.[19]

The United States Supreme Court has not considered a constitutional challenge with regard to the use of videotaped testimony of a
child witness.[20] Since there is a considerable degree of variation from
one statute to another,[21] it is not likely that a prospective determination
could be made as to whether videotaping statutes would pass constitutional muster categorically. Rather, such statutes must be analyzed in-
dividually to determine whether there are sufficient safeguards provided
in the statute to prevent the defendant in a child sexual abuse case
from being denied his constitutional right to be confronted with the
witnesses against him.[22] The incentive provided by the Children's Jus-

---

16. Of the thirty-three state statutes permitting the use of a child's videotaped deposition or
prior testimony at trial, fifteen statutes automatically preclude the child witness from testifying in
person at the trial or proceeding at which the videotaped deposition or prior testimony is admitted.
These statutes are: ARIZ. REV. STAT. ANN. §§ 13-4251, 4253(B), (C) (Supp. 1986); ARK. STAT.
ANN. §§ 43-2035–2037 (Supp. 1985); CONN. GEN. STAT. § 54-86q (Supp. 1987); DEL. CODE ANN.
tit. 11, § 3511 (Supp. 1986); KAN. STAT. ANN. § 24-3434 (1986); KY. REV. STAT. ANN. §
421.350(4) (Baldwin 1986); N.H. REV. STAT. ANN. § 517:13-a (Supp. 1987); OHIO REV. CODE
ANN. § 2907.41(A), (B), (D), (E) (Baldwin 1987); OKLA. STAT. ANN. tit. 22, § 753(C) (West
1986); PA. STAT. ANN. tit. 42, §§ 5982, 5984 (Purdon 1986); R.I. GEN. LAWS § 11-37-13.2 (1986);
TENN. CODE ANN. § 24-27-116(d), (e), (f) (Supp. 1986); TEX. CRIM. PROC. CODE ANN. art.
38.071, § 3 (Vernon Supp. 1987); UTAH CODE ANN. § 77-35-15.5(3), (4) (Supp. 1987); WIS.
STAT. ANN. § 967-04(7)–(10) (West 1986).

17. Eight statutes preclude the child witness from testifying in person at the trial or proceeding upon certain particularized findings by the court. These statutes are: ALA. CODE § 15-25-
2 (Supp. 1986); CAL. PENAL CODE § 1346 (West 1986); COLO. REV. STAT. §§ 18-3-413, 6-401.3
(1986); IND. CODE ANN. § 35-37-4-8(c), (d), (f), (g) (Burns 1986); MASS. GEN. LAWS ANN. ch.
278, § 16D(b)(2) (West Supp. 1987); S.D. CODIFIED LAWS ANN. § 23A-12-9 (Supp. 1987); VT.
R. EVID. 807 (Supp. 1986); WYO. STAT. § 7-11-408 (1987).

18. Coy v. Iowa, 108 S. Ct. 2798, 2800–01 (interim ed. 1988).

19. U.S. CONST amend. VI.

20. The Court has, however, addressed the issue of face-to-face confrontation with respect
to a similar child protective reform, the use of a screen placed between the defendant and child
witness during the child's testimony at trial. *Coy,* 108 S. Ct. 2798 (108 S. Ct. at 2798). The
procedure in question in *Coy* was found to violate the defendant's right to a face-to-face encounter
with the witness against him guaranteed to him by the sixth amendment. *Id.*

21. *Compare* ALASKA STAT. § 12.45.047 (1984) *and* NEV. REV. STAT. § 174.227 (1986)
(very few procedural guidelines) *with* OHIO REV. CODE ANN. § 2907.41 (Baldwin 1986) *and* VT.
R. EVID. 807 (Supp. 1986) (explicit procedural guidelines directed toward reducing potential
trauma to the child witness as well as preserving defendant's constitutional rights).

22. U.S. CONST. amend. VI.

tice Act to the states[23] to implement reform measures demonstrates a strong national commitment to deal with many of the problems of prosecuting child sexual abuse cases.[24] Despite the encouragement provided by Congress, however, these reform measures must not contravene the defendant's right to confront the witnesses against him,[25] or the statutes may be invalidated by the courts if challenged.[26]

The Ohio General Assembly has followed the national trend of enacting legislation to protect child witnesses.[27] In 1986, the Ohio legislature provided for the use of videotaped testimony in sex offense cases in which the alleged victim is a child under eleven years of age.[28] The constitutionality of the Ohio legislation provisions has not been challenged, but a recent United States Supreme Court decision, *Coy v. Iowa*,[29] should provide answers to many of the issues that would arise if a challenge is brought based upon the confrontation clause. Since the *Coy* decision may subject the Ohio legislation, as well as that of other states, to similar constitutional challenges, this comment will analyze the Ohio child witness legislation[30] in light of the United States Supreme Court's decision in *Coy* in order to determine the possibility of a

---

23. 42 U.S.C. § 5103(d) (Supp. 1987).

24. One commentator has suggested that the public response to the increase in reported instances of child sexual abuse has created "an atmosphere startlingly reminiscent of the Salem witch hunts and McCarthy's 'Red Scare.'" Feher, *The Alleged Molestation Victim, the Rules of Evidence, and the Constitution: Should Children Really be Seen and Not Heard?*, 14 AM. J. CRIM. L. 227, 227, 228–29 (1988). While the procedural reforms that have been implemented by the states may solve a great many problems in the prosecution of child sexual abuse cases, Feher asserts that they pose a significant threat of stripping the innocent defendant of his liberty in violation of his right to confront the witnesses against him. *Id.* at 229.

25. *See* Coy v. Iowa, 108 S. Ct. 2798, 2803 (interim ed. 1988)(exceptions to the confrontation clause may only be allowed when necessary to further an important public policy; something more than the generalized finding underlying a statute is needed when the exception is not rooted in our jurisprudence). United States v. Benfield, 593 F.2d 815 (8th Cir. 1979).

26. *Coy* 108. S. Ct. at 2803; *Benfield*, 593 F.2d at 822.

27. OHIO REV. CODE ANN. §§ 109.54, 2151.3511, 2907.41, 2937.11, 2937.15, 2945.49 (Baldwin 1986).

28. OHIO REV. CODE ANN. §§ 2907.41, 2937.11, 2945.49, 2151.3511 (Baldwin 1986).

29. *Coy*, 108 S. Ct. at 2798.

30. This article will focus primarily on § 2907.41 of the Ohio Revised Code. O.R.C. § 2907.41 addresses itself to "any proceeding in the prosecution of a charge of a violation of" certain child sex offenses. OHIO REVISED CODE ANN. § 2907.41(A)(1) (Baldwin 1986). Sections 2937.11, 2945.49 and 2151.3511 of the Ohio Revised Code address themselves to more specific circumstances. Section 2937.11, for example, deals with a preliminary hearing set pursuant to a felony violation of certain child sex offenses. *See id.* § 2937.11. Section 2945.49 deals with any trial on a charge of a felony violation of certain child sex offenses. *See id.* § 2945.49. Section 2151.3511 deals with proceedings in juvenile court involving a complaint in which a child is charged with a violation of certain child sex offenses. *See id.* § 2151.3511. Thus, while the statutes each relate to different circumstances, the language of each is similar, and Section 2907.41 is intended to relate to all proceedings that may take place regarding the child sex offenses designated therein. *See id.* § 2907.41.

successful constitutional challenge.

II. THE CONFRONTATION CLAUSE REQUIREMENT OF A FACE-TO-FACE ENCOUNTER BETWEEN DEFENDANT AND WITNESS

The confrontation clause of the sixth amendment guarantees a criminal defendant the right "to be confronted with the witnesses against him."[31] The United States Supreme Court has held that the right to confront witnesses is not only applicable to federal prosecutions, but is "likewise a fundamental right and is made obligatory on the States by the Fourteenth Amendment."[32] The application of the confrontation clause to the states was based upon a finding by the Court that "the right of confrontation and cross-examination is an essential and fundamental requirement for the kind of fair trial which is this country's constitutional goal."[33] Since the right of confrontation applies to the states as well as to the federal government,[34] state laws providing for the use of videotaped testimony in child sexual abuse cases must comply with the requirements of the confrontation clause of the sixth amendment.[35]

Two distinct rights are secured for a criminal defendant by the confrontation clause: "the right physically to face those who testify against him, and the right to conduct cross-examination."[36] While the United States Supreme Court has long recognized the right to a face-to-face meeting between defendant and witness under the confrontation clause,[37] the Court has more often been faced with cases pertaining to the right to cross-examine witnesses.[38] In *Coy v. Iowa*,[39] the Supreme Court observed that most of its encounters with the confrontation clause have concerned either the admissibility of out-of-court statements or restrictions on the scope of cross-examination.[40] As a result, the Court had little case law on which to rely in determining whether

---

31. U.S. CONST. amend. VI.

32. Pointer v. Texas, 380 U.S. 400, 403 (1965).

33. *Id.* at 405.

34. *Id.* at 403.

35. *See* United States v. Benfield, 593 F.2d 815 (8th Cir. 1979).

36. Pennsylvania v. Ritchie, 480 U.S. 39, 51 (1987) (plurality opinion) (quoting Delaware v. Fensterer, 474 U.S. 15 (1985)).

37. The right of a face-to-face meeting between defendant and witness was explicitly recognized by the Court as early as 1899. *See* Kirby v. United States, 174 U.S. 47 (1899). The *Kirby* Court stated that "a fact which can be primarily established only by witnesses cannot be proved against an accused . . . except by witnesses who confront him at trial, upon whom he can look while being tried." *Id.* at 55.

38. Coy v. Iowa, 108 S. Ct. 2798 (interim ed. 1988).

39. 108 S. Ct. 2798 (108 S. Ct. at 2798).

40. *Id.* at 2800.

the defendant's right to a face-to-face meeting was violated in *Coy*.[41]

Writing for the Court, Justice Scalia made a number of references to prior Supreme Court cases in order to support its holding in *Coy*. The Court found that the confrontation clause requires a face-to-face encounter between defendant and witness.[42] Only two of the references represent a clear holding of a majority of the Court.[43] These two references are to cases decided almost a century ago.[44] All other references made by the Court are either to statements made in a concurring opinion,[45] a dissenting opinion,[46] a plurality opinion,[47] or merely indirectly support the holding in *Coy*.[48] Despite these somewhat unsound precedents relied upon in *Coy*, the Court made it clear that the right to a face-to-face meeting between defendant and witness is a well-established principle.[49] Nevertheless, it is apparent from this rather weak foundation that the Supreme Court has only just begun to define the scope of the right to a face-to-face encounter embodied within the confrontation clause.[50]

---

41. *See infra* notes 42–48 and accompanying text.

42. *Coy*, 108 S. Ct. at 2800–02.

43. Kirby v. United States, 174 U.S. 47 (1899) (concerning the admissibility of prior convictions of codefendants to prove an element of an offense); *see also* Dowdell v. United States, 221 U.S. 325 (1911) (concerning a provision of the Phillipine Bill of Rights).

44. *See supra* note 43.

45. *Coy*, 108 S. Ct. at 2800 (" '[s]imply as a matter of English' it confers at least a 'right to meet face to face all those who appear and give evidence at trial' ") (quoting California v. Green, 399 U.S. 149, 175 (1970) (Harlan, J., concurring)).

46. *Coy*, 108 S. Ct. at 2800 ("[w]e have never doubted, therefore, that the Confrontation Clause guarantees the defendant a face-to face meeting with witnesses appearing before the trier of fact") (citing Kentucky v. Stincer, 107 S. Ct. 2658, 2669 (interim ed. 1987) (Marshall, J., dissenting)).

47. *Coy*, 108 S. Ct. at 2801 (" '[t]he Confrontation Clause provides two types of protections for a criminal defendant: the right physically to face those who testify against him, and the right to conduct cross-examination' ") (quoting Pennsylvania v. Ritchie, 480 U.S. 39, 51 (1987) (plurality opinion)).

48. *Coy*, 108 S. Ct. at 2801 ("we have described the 'literal right to confront the witness at the time of trial' as forming 'the core of the values furthered by the Confrontation Clause' ")(quoting *Green*, 399 U.S. at 157).

49. *Coy*, 108 S. Ct. at 2800 (construing Kirby v. United States, 174 U.S. 47, 55 (1899)).

50. Historically, the rules governing criminal proceedings have been effective in assuring that the requirement of a face-to-face encounter was met. Ensuring the criminal defendant's rights was accomplished in most cases because, by preserving the right to the opportunity for cross-examination, the right to a face-to-face encounter was, generally, inevitably preserved. Recently, though, technological advances have made it possible to obtain testimony by methods other than in the traditional courtroom setting. The recent widespread introduction of innovations such as videotaped testimony in criminal proceedings will undoubtedly provide the Court with additional opportunities to further define the right to a face-to-face encounter under the confrontation clause.

III.   *Coy v. Iowa*: The Confrontation Clause Requires That a Witness be Able to See the Defendant During Testimony

In *Coy v. Iowa*,[51] the United States Supreme Court found a procedure used by an Iowa state court in child sexual abuse cases to be an unconstitutional violation of the sixth amendment confrontation clause.[52] In *Coy*, the defendant was charged with sexually assaulting two thirteen-year-old girls while they were camping out in the backyard of the home next door to Coy's.[53] According to the children, their assailant entered the tent wearing a stocking over his head, shined a flashlight in their faces, and warned the girls not to look at his face.[54] Neither of the children was able to describe their assailant's face.[55] At the beginning of Coy's trial, the state moved to have the complaining witnesses testify either behind a screen or via closed-circuit television, pursuant to Iowa Code section 910A.14.[56] At the trial, a large screen was placed between Coy and the witness stand during the children's testimony.[57] After the lighting was adjusted, Coy could dimly perceive the child witnesses, but the children could not see Coy.[58] Over the defendant's vehement objection that the screen placed between himself and the complaining witnesses infringed upon his sixth amendment right to confront his witnesses, the trial court found that the procedure was not violative of any constitutional guarantees.[59] The Iowa Supreme Court affirmed Coy's conviction, finding that, since his ability to cross-examine the children was not impaired by the screen, there was no violation of the confrontation clause.[60]

Iowa Code section 910A.14[61] provides for the use of several protective procedures in child sexual abuse cases. One such procedure is the use of one-way closed-circuit television during the witness' testi-

---

51.   108 S. Ct. 2798 (1988).
52.   *Id.* at 2803.
53.   *Id.* at 2799.
54.   *Id.*
55.   *Id.*
56.   *Id.* The statute at issue in *Coy* provided, in part:

The court may require a party be confined to an adjacent room or behind a screen or mirror that permits the party to see and hear the child during the child's testimony, but does not allow the child to hear or see the party. However, if a party is so confined, the court shall take measures to insure that the party and counsel can confer during the testimony and shall inform the child that the party can see and hear the child during testimony.

Iowa Code § 910A.14 (1987).
57.   *Coy*, 108 S. Ct. at 2799.
58.   *Id.*
59.   *Id.* at 2800.
60.   *Id.*
61.   Iowa Code § 910A.14 (1987).

mony at trial.[62] Another procedure provided for in the Iowa statute is the use at trial of a videotaped deposition of the child witness.[63] A third procedure entails confining a defendant behind a screen or mirror that permits the defendant to see and hear the child during the child's testimony, but prevents the child from seeing or hearing the defendant.[64] The constitutionality of this third procedure was at issue in *Coy*.[65]

The narrow issue before the Court in *Coy* was whether the confrontation clause requires that a witness have the opportunity to see the defendant during the witness' testimony at trial in a criminal prosecution.[66] In establishing that the confrontation clause does, in fact, impose such a requirement, the *Coy* Court relied on not only its past decisions,[67] but also on a diversity of sources tracing "back to the beginnings of Western legal culture,"[68] including the Bible,[69] Shakespeare[70] and President Eisenhower.[71] The Court even went so far as to quote the common, everyday phrase, "look me in the eye and say that,"[72] in support of its holding that the word "confrontation," as it is used in the sixth amendment, includes a face-to-face meeting between the witness and the accused.[73] Hence, in *Coy* the Court held that, to satisfy the confrontation clause, it was not sufficient that the defendant was indirectly capable of seeing and hearing the witnesses as they testified before the jury, nor was it enough that the defendant had the op-

---

62. *Id.*

63. *Id.*

64. *Id.*

65. *Coy,* 108 S. Ct. at 2799.

66. *Id.*

67. *See supra* notes 42–48 and accompanying text.

68. *Coy,* 108 S. Ct. at 2800.

69. *Id.* ("[t]he Roman Governor Festus, discussing the proper treatment of his prisoner, Paul, stated: 'It is not the manner of the Romans to deliver any man up to die before the accused has met his accusers face to face, and has been given a chance to defend himself against the charges' ") (quoting Acts 25:16) *Id.*

70. *Coy,* 108 S. Ct. at 2800 ("Shakespeare was thus describing the root meaning of confrontation when he had Richard the Second say: 'Then call them to our presence - face to face, and frowning brow to brow, ourselves will hear the accuser and the accused freely speak . . . .' ") (quoting Richard II, act I, sc. 1).

71. "President Eisenhower once described face to face confrontation as part of the code of his home town of Abilene, Kansas. In Abilene, he said, it was necessary to '[m]eet anyone face to face with whom you disagree . . . In this country, if someone dislikes you, or accuses you, he must come up in front. He cannot hide behind the shadow.' " Pollitt, *The Right of Confrontation: Its History and Modern Dress,* 8 J. PUB. L. 381 (1959) (quoting press release of remarks made to the B'nai B'rith Anti-Defamation League, Nov. 23, 1953).

72. *Coy,* 108 S. Ct. at 2801. In support of the quotation from President Eisenhower's press release remarks *supra* note 71, Justice Scalia, the author of the majority opinion in *Coy,* stated that "[t]he phrase still persists, 'Look me in the eye and say that.' " *Coy,* 108 S. Ct at 2801.

73. *Id.* at 2802.

portunity to cross-examine the witnesses at trial.[74] Since the use of the screen at trial prevented the witnesses from viewing the defendant and it was successful in achieving its objective, the Court held that the procedure utilized in *Coy* to protect the witnesses resulted in a violation of the "defendant's right to a face to face encounter."[75]

Although the procedure used in *Coy* was found to violate the confrontation clause, the Court also held that the harmless error analysis of its decision in *Chapman v. California*[76] was applicable to the circumstances in *Coy*.[77] Thus, *Coy* was remanded to the Iowa Supreme Court for determination of whether the confrontation clause violation was harmless beyond a reasonable doubt.[78]

IV. Exceptions to the Confrontation Clause Requirement of a Face-to-Face Encounter Must be Necessary to Further an Important Public Policy

After the Court decided that the confrontation clause requires a face-to-face confrontation between the witness and the accused, the Court in *Coy v. Iowa*[79] addressed a second issue: whether there are any exceptions to the requirement of a face-to-face encounter under the confrontation clause.[80] In his majority decision, Justice Scalia acknowledged that exceptions to a face-to-face encounter might exist if it can be shown that the exception is necessary to further an important public policy.[81] Those whose opinions formed the plurality,[82] however, rejected Iowa's argument that the need to protect victims of sexual abuse was such an exception.[83] Although the state maintained that the statute created a "legislatively imposed presumption of trauma,"[84] a majority of the Court asserted that such a presumption would be insufficient to

---

74. The Court reversed the judgement of the Iowa Supreme Court, which had held that there was no violation of the confrontation clause because the defendant's ability to cross-examine the witnesses was not impaired by the use of the screen. *Id.* at 2803.

75. *Id.* at 2802.

76. 386 U.S. 18 (1967). In *Chapman* the Court held that a confrontation clause error will not result in the reversal of an "erroneously obtained judgment" unless the court finds that the error was harmless beyond a reasonable doubt. *Id.* at 24. This standard is based upon the original common law harmless error rule that the beneficiary of the error bears the burden of proving that no injury was sustained as a result of the error, and if this burden is not sustained then the judgment is reversed. *Id.* (citing 1 Wigmore, Evidence § 21 (3d. ed. 1940)).

77. *Coy,* 108 S. Ct. at 2803.

78. *Id.*

79. 108 S. Ct. 2798 (interim ed. 1988).

80. *Id.* at 2802–03.

81. *Id.* at 2803.

82. Justices Scalia, Brennan, Marshall and Stevens formed the plurality opinion, with Justices O'Connor and White concurring to provide a majority decision. *Id.* at 2799.

83. *Id.* at 2802.

84. *Id.* at 2803.

mandate any conceivable exception.[85] Instead, the Court reasoned that there must be an individualized finding that a particular witness needs special protection if an exception to the requirement of a face-to-face encounter is to be sustained.[86]

While the Supreme Court has, in the past, admitted certain exceptions to the confrontation clause, it has always done so with respect to implicit rights embodied within the clause.[87] The particular right addressed in *Coy*, on the other hand, was the explicit right to a face-to-face encounter between defendant and witness at trial.[88] The majority indicated that a different standard[89] is applicable to a right which is "narrowly and explicitly set forth in the [Confrontation] Clause."[90] While such a standard was not articulated in *Coy*,[91] the Court did hold that an exception to the confrontation clause requirement of a face-to-face encounter between the witness and the accused would at least require an individualized finding that a particular witness needs the special protection the exception provides.[92]

V. COMPATIBILITY OF THE OHIO STATUTE AND THE REQUIREMENT OF A FACE-TO-FACE ENCOUNTER

While the placement of a screen between defendant and witness in the courtroom is a clear violation of the right to a face-to-face encounter embodied within the confrontation clause after *Coy*, the taking of videotaped testimony pursuant to section 2907.41 of the Ohio Revised Code[93] does not appear to constitute such a clear violation.[94] On the

---

85. *Id.* Justices O'Connor and White agreed with the plurality on this point; however, they drew a distinction between the procedure at issue in *Coy,* the use of a screen placed between defendant and witness at trial, and procedures provided by other state statutes, such as the use of one or two-way closed circuit television during trial. *Id.* at 2805. Because those statutes do require a case-by-case finding of necessity in order to use the procedures set forth therein, such procedures might be permissible under the confrontation clause. *Id.*

86. *Id.* at 2803.

87. *Id.* Included among these implicit rights are the right to cross-examine, the right to exclude out-of-court statements, and the right to face-to-face confrontation *at some point in the proceedings other than the trial itself. Id.* at 2802–03 (emphasis added).

88. *Id.* at 2803. The "irreducible meaning of the [confrontation] clause" is the " 'right to *meet face to face* all those who appear and give evidence *at trial.' " Id.* (quoting California v. Green, 399 U.S. 149 (1970) (Harlan, J., concurring))(emphasis added).

89. *Id.* at 2803. Justice Scalia wrote: "Our cases suggest . . . that *even as to* exceptions from the normal implications of the Confrontation Clause, *as opposed to its most literal application*, something more than [a] generalized finding . . . is needed when the exception is not 'firmly . . . rooted in our jurisprudence.' " *Id.* (quoting Bourjaily v. United States, 107 S. Ct. 2775 (interim ed. 1987) (emphasis added)).

90. *Coy,* 108 S. Ct. at 2802.

91. *See id.* at 2803 ("(w)e leave for another day . . . the question whether any exceptions exist").

92. *Id,* at 2803.

93. OHIO REV. CODE ANN. § 2907.41 (Baldwin 1987).

one hand, a screen serves as a direct, unmistakable obstacle to the vision of one or more of the parties affected. The videotaping procedures provided for in Ohio Revised Code section 2907.41, on the other hand, allow both parties to observe each other while the child witness gives his or her testimony.[95] Even though the defendant is excluded from the room in which the child's deposition is taken,[96] the defendant is provided with a monitor in order to observe and hear the witness' testimony.[97] The child witness is also provided with a monitor by which he or she can observe the defendant while the witness testifies.[98] Thus, while the defendant and witness may not be literally face-to-face because they are not together in the same room while the witness testifies, there is no obstruction to the view of either party with respect to the other, as there was in *Coy v. Iowa*.[99]

Two provisions[100] within Ohio Revised Code section 2907.41[101] allow for the taking of a child's videotaped testimony for use in proceedings involving allegations of child sexual abuse. Section 2907.41(A)[102] sets forth procedures to be followed with respect to obtaining a videotaped deposition of the child witness.[103] A second provision of the Ohio statute, section 2907.41(D), allows for the videotaping of a child witness' testimony at the proceeding.[104] In other words, rather than providing for a videotaped deposition, which is taken at some time prior to the trial or other proceeding, section 2907.41(D) provides for the videotaping of the child witness' testimony on the day of the proceeding.[105]

Unlike the Iowa statute at issue in *Coy*,[106] these two provisions of section 2907.41 are subject to admissibility requirements set forth in section 2907.41(B) and section 2907.41(D) of the Ohio Revised Code.[107] According to the Court in *Coy*, an individualized finding that a child witness needs special protection could sustain an exception to

94. There were virtually no procedural requirements designed to ensure the preservation of a defendant's constitutional rights within the Iowa provision at issue in *Coy*. The Ohio statute to be analyzed here, on the other hand, is replete with such procedural protections.

95. OHIO REV. CODE ANN. § 2907.41(A)(2).

96. *Id.*

97. *Id.*

98. *Id.*

99. 108 S. Ct 2798, 2803 (interim ed. 1988).

100. OHIO REV. CODE ANN. § 2907.41(A), (D).

101. *Id.* § 2907.41.

102. *Id.* § 2907.41(A).

103. *Id.*

104. *Id.* § 2907.41(D).

105. *Id.* When the child witness is called to testify in the proceeding, the child's testimony is taken outside of the room in which the proceeding is being conducted. *Id.* The child's testimony is videotaped and subsequently replayed in the room where the proceeding is being conducted. *Id.*

106. IOWA CODE ANN. § 910A.14 (West Supp. 1985).

107. OHIO REV. CODE ANN. § 2907.41(B), (D).

the confrontation clause requirement of a face-to-face encounter.[108] The Iowa statute at issue in *Coy* did not require such a finding.[109] In fact, although the Iowa statute did give the court discretion in deciding whether to permit the use of the screen at trial,[110] it provided the court with absolutely no guidelines as to what factors it might consider in making such a determination.[111] Ohio Revised Code section 2907.41, on the other hand, provides the Ohio courts with a considerable number of procedural guidelines for conducting the videotaping of a child victim,[112] as well as guidelines for determining whether the use of such procedures are admissible.[113] Moreover, the Ohio statute explicitly requires, among other admissibility requirements, that an individualized finding be made that the child witness needs the special protection afforded by the videotaping procedure.[114] These guidelines and admissibility requirements appear to place the Ohio statute in a relatively favorable light in terms of meeting the standards set forth in *Coy* for an exception to the face-to-face encounter requirement of the confrontation clause.[115]

VI. Admissibility Requirements Under the Ohio Statute

The procedures set forth in both the deposition and testimony provisions are virtually identical.[116] One significant difference between the

---

108. *Coy*, 108 S. Ct. at 2803.

109. *See* Iowa Code Ann. § 910A.14.

110. *Id.* § 910A.14(1).

111. *See id.*

112. Ohio Rev. Code Ann. § 2907.41(A)(2), (O). The procedures for videotaping the child victim's testimony in proceedings is essentially the same as that used for videotaping the child victim test in depositions. *See id.* The person operating the recording equipment should be out of the child victim's sight and hearing. *Id.* Furthermore, when videotaping is conducted in a room outside the room where the proceeding takes place, the defendant shall be provided with an electronic means to communicate with his attorney. *Id.* § 2709.41(D); *see supra* notes 94–97 and accompanying text.

113. *Id.* at § 2907.41(A)(2)(a–c), (B)(1).

114. *Id.* at § 2907.41(B)(1)(b).

115. The Court's discussion in *Coy* strongly suggested that a standard might be applied to evaluate the validity of exceptions regarding a face-to-face encounter requirement in future cases of child sexual abuse where a statute designed to protect a child witness allegedly constitutes a violation of the confrontation clause. *Coy*, 108 S. Ct. at 2802–03. That standard is: (1) the exception must be necessary to further an important public policy, and (2) the necessity of the exception must be established by an individualized finding that the particular witness in each case needs the special protection created by the exception. *Id.* at 2803. At this point, prior to any other Supreme Court decision having been rendered on the subject, one can only speculate as to whether the Court will impose an additional standard on such an exception, as was indicated by the Court in *Coy. See supra* notes 80–82 and accompanying text.

116. Both provisions of the Ohio Revised Code allow the defendant to be present for the taking of the deposition or the testimony. Ohio Rev. Code Ann. § 2907.41(A)(2), (D) (Baldwin 1987). However, these provisions confine the defendant to a room separate than that in which either the deposition or the testimony is given. *Id.* § 2907.41(D). Both provisions provide the

two provisions, however, is that they are each subject to different requirements for admissibility.[117] Thus, section 2907.41 provides explicit requirements regarding the admissibility of the procedures for videotaping depositions as well as trial testimony.[118] The statute distinguishes between the two procedures for purposes of admissibility, indicating a recognition of the possibility that they might each affect a defendant's rights under the confrontation clause differently.

Section 2907.41(A), which governs videotaped depositions, makes it mandatory for a judge, upon motion by the prosecution, to order that a deposition of a child witness be videotaped.[119] However, the videotaped deposition is also subject to the admissibility requirements set forth in section 2907.41(B).[120] The videotaped deposition is admissible in a trial or other proceeding only if the testimony therein (or the part to be admitted as evidence) is not excluded by the hearsay rule[121] and the testimony is otherwise admissible under the Ohio Rules of Evidence.[122] The videotaped deposition will also be admissible if both of the two statutory requirements are fulfilled.[123] These requirements are: (1) that the defendant had an opportunity for cross-examination at the time when the deposition was taken,[124] and (2) that the judge determines that there is reasonable cause to believe that the child witness whose videotaped deposition was taken would experience serious emotional trauma as a result of participation in the proceeding.[125]

Unlike a videotaped deposition, the videotaping of a child witness' testimony at a proceeding is not mandatory upon request by the prosecution under the Ohio statute.[126] Rather, the use of such a procedure is at the discretion of the judge.[127] The judge's decision to allow the testi-

---

defendant and the child witness with monitors by which they can observe each other as the child gives the deposition or testimony. *Id.*

117. *Id.* § 2907.41(A)(2), (D).

118. *Id.*

119. *Id.* § 2907.41(A).

120. *Id.* § 2907.41(A)(2). "If the prosecution requests that a deposition to be taken under division (A)(1) of this section be videotaped, the judge *shall* order that the deposition be videotaped . . . ." *Id.* (emphasis added).

121. *Id.* § 2907.41(B)(1).

122. *Id.* The applicable Ohio Rules of Evidence are 801, 803 and 804. *Id.* The statute specifies that the testimony in question is not excluded by the hearsay rule if it is not hearsay under Evidence Rule 801; if it is within one of the Rule 803 exceptions to the hearsay rule, if the child whose deposition was videotaped is unavailable as a witness, as defined in Evidence Rule 804, and testimony is within the parameters set by rule 804. *Id.*

123. OHIO REV. CODE ANN. § 2907.41(B)(1)(a), (B)(1)(b).

124. *Id.* § 2907.41(B)(1)(a).

125. *Id.* § 2907.41(B)(1)(b).

126. *See id.* § 2907.41(D).

127. *Id.* ("The judge may issue such an order, upon motion of the prosecution, if the judge determines that the child victim is unavailable to testify in the room in which the proceeding is

mony to be videotaped must be based upon the judge's determination that the child is unavailable to testify in the same room with the defendant for at least one of three reasons set forth in section 2907.41(E).[128] The judge must find that (1) the child persistently refuses to testify despite judicial requests to do so;[129] (2) the child is unable to communicate about the alleged violation as a result of extreme fear, failure of memory, or another similar reason;[130] or (3) a substantial likelihood exists that the child will suffer serious emotional trauma as a result of testifying in the presence of the defendant.[131]

Pursuant to section 2907.41(D),[132] the videotaping of a child witness' testimony actually takes place at the proceeding.[133] Consequently, when the judge determines that the use of the procedure is permissible, the judge determines at the same time that the evidence is admissible at the proceeding. Therefore, the three factors set out above for determining a child witness' unavailability are also the factors for determining whether the testimony will be admissible at trial.

A comparison of the admissibility requirements for videotaped depositions with the admissibility requirements for videotaped testimony reveals that different standards are applicable to the admissibility of the evidence obtained in the two procedures. While the videotaping of a deposition is mandatory upon request by the prosecution,[134] its admissibility at a proceeding depends upon either its consistency with the common law or statutory hearsay rules,[135] or upon a particularized finding by the judge that the child witness is likely to experience serious emotional trauma by testifying in person at the proceeding.[136] This is a much broader standard than that applicable to the admissibility of videotaped testimony. While videotaped testimony is admissible at the

---

being conducted in the physical presence of the defendant . . . .").

128.   *Id.* § 2907.41(E).

129.   *Id.* § 2907.41(E)(1).

130.   *Id.* § 2907.41(E)(2).

131.   *Id.* § 2907.41(E)(3).

132.   *Id.* § 2907.41(D).

133.   *Id.* ("[t]he prosecution may file a motion with the judge requesting the judge to order the testimony of the child victim to be taken outside of the room in which the proceeding is being conducted and be recorded for showing in the room in which the proceeding is being conducted . . . .").

134.   *Id.* § 2907.41(A)(1).

135.   *Id.* § 2907.41(B)(1).

136.   *Id.* § 2907.41(B)(1)(b). In addition to the particularized finding that the child is likely to experience serious emotional trauma, admissibility also must meet the requirement that the defendant had an "opportunity and similar motive at the time of the taking of the deposition to develop the testimony by direct, cross, or redirect examination." *Id.* § 2907.41(B)(1)(a). Without both of these requirements fulfilled, the deposition is not admissible unless the testimony therein complies with the hearsay rules. *See supra* notes 101, 108, 109, 124 and accompanying text.

discretion of the judge,[137] it is only admissible upon the judge's determination that the child is considered unavailable as a witness for very specific reasons,[138] one of which is the substantial likelihood that the child witness will suffer serious emotional trauma as a result of testifying in person.[139]

The significance of this distinction drawn between the admissibility requirements of videotaped depositions and videotaped testimony under section 2907.41 is that it illustrates a recognition on the part of the Ohio legislature that a defendant's rights secured by the sixth amendment confrontation clause may very well be less seriously threatened by the videotaped deposition procedure than by videotaping the child witness' testimony at the proceeding.

For example, the provision allowing the child witness' deposition to be videotaped explicitly requires that the defendant's attorney be given the right to a full examination and cross-examination of the child whose deposition is being taken.[140] The provision allowing videotaped testimony at the proceeding,[141] on the other hand, does not explicitly set forth such a requirement.[142] Moreover, the videotaped deposition provision permits the attorney for the defendant to request that another deposition of the child witness be taken because new evidence material to the defense has been discovered.[143] This request can be made at any time prior to the end of the proceeding at which the original videotaped deposition is admitted.[144] There is no similar provision related to the videotaped testimony in the Ohio statute.[145] The differences between the two provisions[146] suggest that the Ohio legislature considered the potential injury that each of the procedures might infringe upon a defendant's rights under the confrontation clause.

VII. Conclusion

The United States Supreme Court has not yet had the opportunity

---

137. OHIO REV. CODE ANN. § 2907.41(D).

138. Id. § 2907.41(E). The reasons set forth in this section are limited to only several instances of unavailability as defined within Ohio Rule of Evidence 804. See supra notes 118–120 and accompanying text.

139. Id. § 2907.41(E). The child will likewise be considered unavailable when the child refuses to testify despite the court's request to do so, and when the child cannot communicate testimony regarding the alleged violations due to "extreme fear, failure of memory, or another similar reason . . . ." Id. § 2907.41(E)(1), (E)(2).

140. Id. § 2907.41(A)(1).

141. See id. § 2907.41(D).

142. Id.

143. Id. § 2907.41(A)(1).

144. Id.

145. See id. § 2907.41(D)

146. See supra notes 10–11 and accompanying text.

to address the issue of whether a statute providing for the use of video-taped testimony of a child witness in child sexual abuse cases meets the requirement of a face-to-face encounter embodied within the confrontation clause of the sixth amendment. Should the Court be faced with this issue regarding section 2907.41 of the Ohio Revised Code or a substantially similar statute, the fact that the statute requires that both parties be provided with monitors with which to view each other during the child witness' testimony will certainly present a less clear case of a confrontation clause violation than was presented to the Court in *Coy v. Iowa*.[147] This fact alone, however, might not be sufficient to sustain the constitutionality of the statute, since the Court could potentially hold that any technical violation of the defendant's right to a face-to-face encounter with the child witness will invalidate the statute.

In light of Congress' 1989 amendment of The Children's Justice Act,[148] which provides financial grants to states that enact child protective reforms, it appears likely that the Court will recognize that protecting victims of child abuse is an important public policy. While the Court was not willing to accept this argument in *Coy*, it is quite possible that the Court would reconsider such an argument if the statute in question requires a particularized finding that the child witness would experience serious emotional trauma by testifying in person. Section 2907.41 of the Ohio Revised Code specifically requires an individualized finding of serious emotional trauma to the child witness.[149] It also requires that both the defendant and child witness be able to see each other during the use of either procedure.[150] Moreover, virtually every state has confirmed the existence of an important public policy by enacting child protective reforms similar to those provided by the Ohio statute.[151] For these reasons, section 2907.41 stands a strong chance of withstanding constitutional scrutiny should it be challenged as violating the sixth amendment confrontation clause requirement of a face-to-face encounter between defendant and witness at trial.

Barbara Hobday Owens

---

147.   108 S. Ct. 2798 (interim ed. 1988).
148.   OHIO REV. CODE ANN. § 2907.41(B), (E).
149.   *Id.* § 2907.41(E)(3).
150.   *Id.* § 2907.41(A), (D).
151.   *See supra* notes 1–2 and accompanying text.

LEADING CASES

I. Constitutional Law

A. Criminal Law and Procedure

1. Confrontation Clause — Right to Confront Children in Child Abuse Cases. — In response to growing societal concern over child abuse,[1] many states have expanded traditional hearsay exceptions[2] or adopted statutes permitting child witnesses to testify on videotape[3] or by closed circuit television[4] in child sexual abuse cases. Applauded by child advocacy groups for facilitating prosecutions and protecting child victims from the trauma of facing their alleged abusers in court,[5] such provisions have also been invalidated[6] for depriving defendants of their sixth amendment right to confront their accusers.[7]

Last Term the Supreme Court considered the constitutionality of two of these developments: the admission at trial of a child's hearsay statements and the use of one-way closed circuit television to permit an alleged child abuse victim to give live testimony outside the accused's presence. In *Idaho v. Wright*,[8] the Court found admission of

---

[1] *See* SELECT COMM. ON CHILDREN, YOUTH & FAMILIES, ABUSED CHILDREN IN AMERICA: VICTIMS OF OFFICIAL NEGLECT, H.R. REP. No. 260, 100th Cong., 1st Sess. 1 (1987) (noting that reports of child abuse and neglect increased over 50% nationwide between 1981 and 1985).

[2] Children's out-of-court statements may be admissible at trial under traditional exceptions for excited utterances and statements for purposes of medical diagnosis or treatment and under residual hearsay exceptions similar to Federal Rules of Evidence 803(24) and 804(b)(5). *See* J. MYERS, CHILD WITNESS LAW AND PRACTICE §§ 5.31–.37, at 326–72 (1987). In addition, at least 20 states have adopted statutes specifically authorizing the admission of alleged child victims' hearsay statements in prosecutions for child sexual abuse. *See* Graham, *The Confrontation Clause, the Hearsay Rule, and Child Sexual Abuse Prosecutions: The State of the Relationship*, 72 MINN. L. REV. 523, 534 n.50 (1988) (citing statutes).

[3] Thirty-seven states authorize videotaped testimony by children in child abuse cases. *See* Maryland v. Craig, 110 S. Ct. 3157, 3167 n.2 (1990) (citing statutes).

[4] Twenty-four states allow alleged child abuse victims to testify via one-way closed circuit television. *See id.* at 3168 n.3 (citing statutes). Eight states permit testimony via two-way closed circuit television. *See id.* at 3168 n.4 (citing statutes).

[5] *See, e.g.*, Brief of Amici Curiae on Behalf of People Against Child Abuse, the Association for Childcare Excellence, the National Center for Missing and Exploited Children, and Rosie's Patrol at 7–18, *Craig* (No. 89-478).

[6] *See, e.g.*, Coy v. Iowa, 487 U.S. 1012, 1020–21 (1988) (holding that the placement of a one-way screen between a defendant and two child witnesses in a sexual assault trial violated the confrontation clause).

[7] The sixth amendment provides in relevant part: "In all criminal prosecutions, the accused shall enjoy the right . . . to be confronted with the witnesses against him." U.S. CONST. amend. VI. The confrontation clause was held applicable to state prosecutions in Pointer v. Texas, 380 U.S. 400 (1965).

[8] 110 S. Ct. 3139 (1990).

a child's hearsay statements unconstitutional but reaffirmed the principle that the confrontation clause does not absolutely bar admission of statements by out-of-court declarants. In *Maryland v. Craig*,[9] the more far-reaching decision, the Court for the first time squarely held that the right to a face-to-face meeting with witnesses who appear and testify at trial is also not absolute. Although *Craig* demonstrates the Court's willingness to consider the special needs of children when determining the scope of constitutionally protected rights, the Court's failure to limit the decision to children who are truly unable to communicate in the defendant's presence threatens unnecessarily to diminish the confrontation right.

Idaho v. Wright involved the admission in a child abuse trial of hearsay statements by a two-and-one-half-year-old child to an examining pediatrician.[10] The Supreme Court held that although the confrontation clause has never been interpreted to bar admission of all hearsay,[11] the doctor's testimony could not survive constitutional scrutiny. Writing for a 5–4 majority, Justice O'Connor[12] applied the two-part test announced in *Ohio v. Roberts*,[13] under which admission of hearsay at trial generally does not offend the confrontation clause if the declarant is shown to be "unavailable" to testify in court and the statement "bears adequate 'indicia of reliability.'"[14] An out-of-court statement satisfies the reliability requirement if it either "falls within a firmly rooted hearsay exception" or is supported by a showing of "particularized guarantees of trustworthiness."[15]

Focusing on the reliability requirement,[16] Justice O'Connor first observed that the trial judge admitted the doctor's statements pursuant to Idaho's residual hearsay exception,[17] which by definition is ad hoc

---

[9] 110 S. Ct. 3157 (1990).

[10] The trial judge allowed the pediatrician to testify that in response to his questions, the child had acknowledged abusive treatment of herself and her five-and-one-half-year-old sister. *See* Brief for Petitioner at 6–9, *Wright* (No. 89-260). Her statements were corroborated by physical and testimonial evidence that implicated the younger child's mother and father in the abuse. *See id.* at 5–6. Following the conviction of both parents, the mother appealed, contending that admission of the doctor's testimony violated her confrontation right. The Idaho Supreme Court agreed, reversed the conviction, and remanded the case. *See* State v. Wright, 116 Idaho 382, 775 P.2d 1224 (1989).

[11] *See Wright*, 110 S. Ct. at 3145 (citing Bourjaily v. United States, 483 U.S. 171, 182 (1987); *Pointer*, 380 U.S. at 407; Mattox v. United States, 156 U.S. 237, 243 (1895)).

[12] Justices Brennan, Marshall, Stevens, and Scalia joined Justice O'Connor's opinion.

[13] 448 U.S. 56 (1980).

[14] *Id.* at 66.

[15] *Id.*

[16] Because the trial judge found the child incapable of communicating to the jury, and defense counsel agreed, the Court assumed without deciding that the child was an "unavailable" witness. *Wright*, 110 S. Ct. at 3147.

[17] Rule 803 of the Idaho Rules of Evidence, which closely parallels Federal Rule 803, lists 22 categories of hearsay not excluded by the hearsay rule despite the declarant's availability as

and not firmly rooted.[18] She concluded that admission of the doctor's testimony violated the defendant's confrontation right because the prosecution did not show, by a totality of the circumstances surrounding the making of the out-of-court statements but excluding corroborative evidence, that the evidence was "so trustworthy that adversarial testing would add little to its reliability."[19]

Craig, the Term's second confrontation case, concerned the constitutionality of a Maryland statute that permits alleged child abuse victims to testify at trial by one-way closed circuit television if "[t]he judge determines that testimony by the child victim in the courtroom will result in the child suffering serious emotional distress such that the child cannot reasonably communicate."[20] Under the statutory procedure, the prosecutor and defense counsel examine and cross-examine the child witness in a separate room. In the courtroom, the judge, jury, and defendant observe the testimony on a video monitor, but the child witness cannot see them.[21]

In March 1987, Maryland invoked the procedure in its prosecution of a day care center owner charged with abusing a six-year-old child who attended the center.[22] In a two-day pretrial hearing, the trial judge heard the state's expert testimony regarding the degree of trauma several child witnesses who had attended the center would experience if required to testify in front of the defendant.[23] Without interviewing the children either in or outside the defendant's presence, the judge allowed the children to testify by one-way closed circuit television.[24] After conviction and an unsuccessful intermediate appeal,[25] the Maryland Court of Appeals reversed, holding that the trial

---

a witness. *See* IDAHO R. EVID. 803. It also provides a residual exception for other out-of-court-statements that have "equivalent circumstantial guarantees of trustworthiness," are "offered as evidence of a material fact," are more probative on the point for which they are offered than other reasonably obtainable evidence, and that serve the "general purposes of [the evidence] rules and the interests of justice." *Id.* 803(24).

[18] *See Wright*, 110 S. Ct. at 3147–48.

[19] *Id.* at 3149. The Court identified several factors that courts may properly consider in deciding whether a child's statement is sufficiently reliable, including the spontaneity of the statement and the use of terminology unexpected of a child of similar age. *See id.* at 3150. The majority found that the statements in this case failed to satisfy the reliability requirement because they largely responded to suggestive questions from the doctor. *See id.* at 3152–53.

In a dissent joined by Chief Justice Rehnquist and Justices White and Blackmun, Justice Kennedy agreed that children's hearsay statements must bear particularized guarantees of trustworthiness but disagreed with the majority's assertion that corroborative evidence should not be part of the reliability determination. *See id.* at 3153 (Kennedy, J., dissenting).

[20] MD. CTS. & JUD. PROC. CODE ANN. § 9-102(a)(1)(ii) (1989).

[21] *See id.* § 9-102(a)–(b).

[22] *See* Brief for Petitioner at 4, *Craig* (No. 89-478).

[23] *See id.* at 4–9.

[24] *See* Respondent's Brief at 2–4, *Craig* (No. 89-478).

[25] The Maryland Court of Special Appeals affirmed the conviction. *See* Craig v. State, 76 Md. App. 250, 544 A.2d 784 (1988).

judge should have questioned the children in the presence of the defendant in order to determine their inability to testify and should have considered the feasibility of less restrictive alternatives such as testimony by two-way closed circuit television.[26]

In a 5–4 decision handed down the same day as *Wright*, the Supreme Court in *Craig* established the facial validity of the Maryland statute. Again writing for the majority, Justice O'Connor[27] acknowledged that face-to-face confrontation is a "'core'" constitutional guarantee.[28] She nevertheless stressed that the confrontation clause actually consists of a bundle of rights — including physical presence, oath, cross-examination, and observation of the witness' demeanor by the trier of fact — that primarily ensures the reliability of the evidence admitted against criminal defendants.[29] Observing that the Court's precedents reflect only a *"preference* for face-to-face confrontation at trial,"[30] Justice O'Connor declined to declare the right of physical confrontation absolute. Instead, the Court held that the confrontation clause does not require a face-to-face meeting with witnesses who testify at trial if "denial of such confrontation is necessary to further an important public policy and . . . the reliability of the testimony is otherwise assured."[31]

Applying this standard, the Court first determined that the presence of three elements of the confrontation right — oath, cross-examination, and observation of the witness' demeanor — adequately ensures the reliability of testimony given under the Maryland statute.[32] Justice O'Connor next examined the question of public policy. Noting that the Court had previously sustained legislation designed to safeguard children "'even when the laws have operated in the sensitive area of constitutionally protected rights,'"[33] she concluded that the state's interest in protecting child witnesses from the trauma of testifying is sufficiently compelling to justify use of trial procedures that prevent children from viewing their alleged abusers.[34] Under the necessity requirement, the Court stated that the trial judge must find on a case-specific basis that the child, if required to testify before the defendant, would suffer "more than *de minimis*" emotional distress.[35] Concluding that as a constitutional matter the necessity determination

---

[26] *See* Craig v. State, 316 Md. 551, 566–68, 560 A.2d 1120, 1127–28 (1989).

[27] Chief Justice Rehnquist and Justices White, Blackmun, and Kennedy — the four dissenters in *Wright* — joined Justice O'Connor's opinion.

[28] *Craig*, 110 S. Ct. at 3164 (quoting California v. Green, 399 U.S. 149, 157 (1970)).

[29] *See id.* at 3163.

[30] *Id.* at 3165 (emphasis in original).

[31] *Id.* at 3166.

[32] *See id.*

[33] *Id.* at 3167 (quoting New York v. Ferber, 458 U.S. 747, 757 (1982)).

[34] *See id.* at 3169.

[35] *Id.*

could be made solely on the basis of expert testimony and without consideration of less restrictive alternatives,[36] the Court vacated the judgment and remanded the case.[37]

In dissent, Justice Scalia[38] criticized the Court for "fail[ing] so conspicuously to sustain a categorical guarantee of the Constitution against . . . prevailing current opinion."[39] Citing eighteenth- and nineteenth-century dictionaries and extending his textual interpretation of the confrontation clause in *Coy v. Iowa*,[40] Justice Scalia maintained that an unqualified right to face-to-face confrontation is "'the irreducible literal meaning of the [Confrontation] Clause.'"[41] He distinguished the Court's previous confrontation decisions because they involved admission of prior out-of-court statements, which the Constitution does not expressly prohibit, rather than contemporaneous out-of-court statements by witnesses who appear and testify at trial, which the Constitution plainly forbids.[42] Attacking both the necessity and state interest prongs of the majority's standard, Justice Scalia argued that a witness' unwillingness to testify cannot justify alternative trial procedures and that the state's real interest — convicting guilty child abusers — does not outweigh the corresponding interest in acquitting innocent defendants.[43] He emphasized, however, that these policy considerations are ultimately irrelevant, because the plain language of the confrontation clause, which guarantees a face-to-face meeting between accuser and accused "'[i]n *all* criminal prosecutions,'" permits no exceptions.[44]

By recognizing an exception to the right of physical confrontation, *Craig* answers a question left open three Terms ago in *Coy v. Iowa*.[45] *Coy* invalidated a statutory procedure allowing a one-way screen to be placed between the defendant and two child witnesses who testified against him in a child abuse trial. Writing for the *Coy* majority, Justice Scalia emphasized that a face-to-face meeting with accusers at trial is an essential confrontation right,[46] but he found the challenged procedure unconstitutional for the narrower reason that the trial judge made no individualized findings that the witnesses required special protection.[47] *Coy* expressly reserved the question whether such find-

---

[36] *See id.* at 3171.

[37] *See id.*

[38] Justices Brennan, Marshall, and Stevens joined Justice Scalia's dissent.

[39] *Id.* at 3171 (Scalia, J., dissenting).

[40] 487 U.S. 1012 (1988).

[41] 110 S. Ct. at 3173–74 (Scalia, J., dissenting) (quoting *Coy*, 487 U.S. at 1020–21).

[42] *See id.* at 3173.

[43] *See id.* at 3175–76.

[44] *Id.* at 3176 (quoting U.S. CONST. amend. VI (emphasis added)).

[45] 487 U.S. 1012 (1988).

[46] *See id.* at 1015–20.

[47] *See id.* at 1020–21.

ings would justify an exception to the right of physical confrontation.[48] In *Craig*, the Court answered this question affirmatively, and the unique problems presented by some child witnesses support the result. Because the decision rests on a broad statement of public policy rather than on the narrower doctrine of unavailability, however, lower courts will likely rely on *Craig* to further restrict the confrontation right in child abuse cases.

Craig signals the Court's readiness to look beyond the language of the confrontation clause to determine the scope of rights it affords criminal defendants. The majority properly rejected Justice Scalia's literal reading of the clause.[49] Justice Scalia has offered etymological evidence that "to confront" means to meet face-to-face[50] and has also concluded from early dictionary definitions of the word "witness" that "the witnesses against him" refers only to evidence given by declarants who actually testify at trial.[51] However, "the witnesses against him" could also refer to out-of-court declarants whose statements are used against the defendant at trial, and, as Justice O'Connor observed, confrontation could also mean "a clashing of . . . ideas" or "adversariness."[52] These propositions do not resolve the question whether the original meaning of the confrontation clause forecloses all exceptions to the right of physical confrontation. They do suggest, however, that the language of the clause is not so unambiguous that it should preclude consideration of the clause's underlying purposes.

For the *Craig* majority, the confrontation clause derives meaning not from a literal reading of the text, nor from inquiry into the framers' intent,[53] but from precedent. The Court's prior confrontation decisions recognize that the confrontation clause serves both functional and symbolic purposes.[54] Under the functional view, the confrontation right primarily "promotes reliability in criminal trials."[55] Under

---

[48] *See id.* at 1021 ("Whatever [the exceptions] may be, they would surely be allowed only when necessary to further an important public policy.").

[49] Justice Scalia's analysis, which in both *Craig* and *Coy* is more philological than historical, is consistent with the method of interpretation he has advocated elsewhere. *See* Scalia, *Originalism: The Lesser Evil*, 57 U. CIN. L. REV. 849, 856–64 (1989); *see also* Kannar, *The Constitutional Catechism of Antonin Scalia*, 99 YALE L.J. 1297, 1299, 1329–34 (1990) (discussing *Coy* and arguing that Justice Scalia "has upset ordinary political expectations" by applying a close textual analysis to both criminal procedure and other constitutional cases, even when such analysis produces conventionally "liberal" results).

[50] *See Coy*, 487 U.S. at 1016.

[51] *See Craig*, 110 S. Ct. at 3173 (Scalia, J., dissenting).

[52] 110 S. Ct. at 3163.

[53] Several authorities have concluded that the intent of the framers with respect to the confrontation clause cannot be conclusively determined from historical sources. *See, e.g.*, California v. Green, 399 U.S. 149, 174 (1970) (Harlan, J., concurring); Jonakait, *Restoring the Confrontation Clause to the Sixth Amendment*, 35 UCLA L. REV. 557, 569 n.46 (1988).

[54] *See* Lee v. Illinois, 476 U.S. 530, 540 (1986).

[55] *Id.*; *accord* Pennsylvania v. Ritchie, 480 U.S. 39, 52 (1987); Ohio v. Roberts, 448 U.S. 56, 65 (1980).

the symbolic view, the clause ensures that the criminal defendant's guilt or innocence is determined in an open, adversarial proceeding.[56] From this perspective, a face-to-face meeting between accuser and accused is "an essential and fundamental requirement for the kind of fair trial which is this country's constitutional goal."[57]

At first glance *Craig* appears consistent with these purposes. As Justice O'Connor argued, child witness testimony by closed circuit television remains reliable despite the absence of face-to-face confrontation because the child testifies under oath,[58] subject to cross-examination, and in such a way that the jury can observe the child's demeanor. Furthermore, empirical research suggests that in some cases questioning a fearful child witness outside the defendant's presence can actually enhance the reliability of the testimony.[59]

When read in conjunction with *Wright*, *Craig* can also be viewed as advancing the adversarial goals of the confrontation clause. A determination that Maryland's closed circuit television procedure violated the clause would have anomalously encouraged prosecutors in child abuse trials to rely more heavily on hearsay. Children's reliable out-of-court statements remain admissible after *Wright*,[60] and it makes little sense to exclude live, cross-examined testimony from the jury's consideration simply because a child is unable to communicate in front of the defendant. Given the Court's decision in *Wright*, *Craig* enhances fairness in child abuse prosecutions by affording the defendant a live contest with a witness whom the state in many instances would not otherwise produce at trial. Viewed in this light, the decision also serves the functional purpose of the confrontation clause by enabling the jury to determine the defendant's guilt or innocence on the basis of the better evidence.[61]

---

[56] *See* Jonakait, *supra* note 53, at 581–86 (1988); *The Supreme Court, 1987 Term — Leading Cases*, 102 HARV. L. REV. 143, 158 (1988) (discussing Coy v. Iowa, 487 U.S. 1012 (1988)).

[57] Pointer v. Texas, 380 U.S. 400, 405 (1965).

[58] Some states permit children to testify at trial despite their inability to swear an oath, *see, e.g.*, FLA. STAT. ANN. § 90.605(2) (West Supp. 1990), or to understand the obligation to testify truthfully, *see, e.g.*, People v. District Court, 791 P.2d 682, 685 (Colo. 1990) (en banc). Since *Craig* upheld the constitutionality of the Maryland statute in part because it requires testimony under oath, it remains unclear whether a child may constitutionally testify by closed circuit television without taking an oath.

[59] *See, e.g.*, Note, *Videotaping Children's Testimony: An Empirical View*, 85 MICH. L. REV. 809, 819–21 (1987); *see also Craig*, 110 S. Ct. at 3169–70 (citing additional authorities).

[60] The Court's refusal to require any minimum procedural safeguards in *Wright*, *see* 110 S. Ct. at 3148, affords lower courts latitude in finding children's out-of-court statements reliable. Moreover, *Wright* involved a residual hearsay exception, which, like the statutes described above in note 2, requires "particularized guarantees of trustworthiness" under the confrontation clause because it is not a "firmly rooted" exception. Ohio v. Roberts, 448 U.S. 56, 66 (1980). However, children's out-of-court statements may also be admissible under firmly rooted hearsay exceptions, *see* Graham, *supra* note 2, at 526–30, which do not require independent demonstrations of trustworthiness, *see* Bourjally v. United States, 483 U.S. 171, 182–83 (1987).

[61] *See Craig*, 110 S. Ct. at 3174 (Scalia, J., dissenting) ("'When two versions of the same

Nevertheless, these rationales are inadequate to explain fully the result in *Craig,* because in some circumstances closed circuit television testimony *disserves* the purposes underlying the confrontation clause by facilitating false accusations.[62] For this reason, the decision may best be understood not within the context of confrontation clause jurisprudence, but as an example of the Court's increasing willingness to interpret the Bill of Rights differently when children are concerned. Recently the Court has determined both that the Constitution sometimes guarantees less expansive individual liberties to children than to adults[63] and that a state's interest in children's welfare may limit the scope of other individuals' constitutional rights.[64] Because it allows states to dispense with the right of physical confrontation when necessary to protect child witnesses, *Craig* exemplifies the latter type of decision.

Society has a valid interest in safeguarding the psychological well-being of children. *Craig* remains problematic, however, because the Court failed to limit the scope of the exception it recognized. Because the constitutional rights of defendants who may stand falsely accused of child abuse must not be lightly abandoned, the Court should have clearly restricted exceptions to the right of physical confrontation to those situations in which a child witness' inability to communicate in the defendant's presence necessitates use of an alternative trial procedure.

The Maryland statute requires an individualized showing that a child witness, if forced to testify, will suffer serious emotional distress "such that the child cannot reasonably communicate."[65] Instead of

---

evidence are available, longstanding principles of the law of hearsay, applicable as well to Confrontation Clause analysis, favor the better evidence.'" (quoting United States v. Inadi, 475 U.S. 387, 394 (1986))). As Blackstone observed, "there is much more reason for the court to hear the narration of the child herself, than to receive it at second hand from those who swear they heard her say so." 4 W. BLACKSTONE, COMMENTARIES *214.

[62] *See Craig,* 110 S. Ct. at 3175–76 (Scalia, J., dissenting) (arguing that defendants have a heightened interest in securing reliable testimony in child abuse trials because of the likelihood that children, due to their susceptibility to suggestion, will make erroneous accusations).

[63] *See, e.g.,* Ohio v. Akron Center for Reproductive Health, 110 S. Ct. 2972, 2978–83 (1990) (upholding a parental notification statute generally requiring minors seeking abortions either to notify one parent or to follow a judicial bypass procedure); Hazelwood School Dist. v. Kuhlmeier, 484 U.S. 260, 270–73 (1988) (holding that high school officials may impose restrictions on school-sponsored student newspapers without violating students' freedom of speech).

[64] *See, e.g.,* Osborne v. Ohio, 110 S. Ct. 1691, 1695–97 (1990) (holding that although an individual has a first amendment right to view pornography in his own home, a state can constitutionally proscribe the possession and viewing of child pornography); Globe Newspaper Co. v. Superior Court, 457 U.S. 596, 607–11 & n.27 (1982) (stating that when an individualized showing of need is made, the first amendment right of the press and general public to attend criminal trials need not preclude a court from closing a trial during the testimony of a juvenile sex-offense victim).

[65] MD. CTS. & JUD. PROC. CODE ANN. § 9-102(a)(1)(ii) (1989).

focusing on the inability of some children to communicate in front of the defendant,[66] however, *Craig* held that "the state interest in protecting child witnesses from the trauma of testifying" by itself may justify allowing them to testify outside the accused's presence.[67] The Court did qualify its decision by stating that the confrontation clause permits testimony by one-way closed circuit television, "at least where such trauma would impair the child's ability to communicate."[68] Nevertheless, together with the Court's statement that the child's emotional distress satisfies *Craig's* necessity requirement if it is simply "more than *de minimis*,"[69] the broader language will likely encourage lower courts to uphold procedures for children's contemporaneous out-of-court testimony despite lower necessity thresholds than that of the Maryland statute.[70]

A better approach in cases involving closed circuit television testimony would be to require individualized findings that focus not on the harm the child will likely suffer in the defendant's presence, but on whether that harm affects his ability to give meaningful testimony. This approach would rest on firmer doctrinal foundation than a finding based solely on psychological harm. A child's inability to communicate in the accused's presence is the functional equivalent of "unavailability,"[71] and the Court has previously held that reliable substitutes for a witness' testimony do not violate the confrontation clause if the witness is unavailable to testify in court.[72] Moreover,

---

[66] Empirical studies indicate that although children often suffer trauma if required to testify in the defendant's presence, a substantial number are nonetheless able to convey accurately what they know at trial. *See* Brief for Amicus Curiae American Psychological Association in Support of Neither Party at 3, 9–11, *Craig* (No. 89-478). Only some child witnesses are likely to be so affected by fear of the defendant that face-to-face confrontation will render them incapable of communicating effectively to the jury.

[67] *See Craig*, 110 S. Ct. at 3169.

[68] *Id.* at 3170; *see also id.* at 3174 n.1 (Scalia, J., dissenting) (rejecting any broader interpretation of the majority opinion).

[69] *Craig*, 110 S. Ct. at 3169.

[70] *See, e.g.*, New Jersey v. Crandall, 120 N.J. 649, 577 A.2d 483 (1990) (relying on *Craig* to uphold N.J. REV. STAT. § 2A:84A-32.4 (1987), a closed circuit television provision that requires the trial court to find "a substantial likelihood that the [child] witness would suffer severe emotional or mental distress" if compelled to testify, *id.* § 2A:84A-32.4(b), but that does not require that this distress render the child unable to communicate in front of the defendant).

Most statutes authorizing child witness testimony by closed circuit television do not require the trial judge to find that the child is unable to communicate in the defendant's presence. Under some statutes, for example, the judge need only find that the child will suffer "moderate" or "unreasonable" emotional stress. *See* FLA. STAT. ANN. § 92.53(1) (West Supp. 1990) (requiring "at least moderate emotional or mental harm"); R.I. GEN. LAWS § 11-37-13.2 (Supp. 1989) (requiring "unreasonable and unnecessary mental or emotional harm"). Several others specify no minimum threshold. *See, e.g.*, ARIZ. REV. STAT. ANN. § 13-4253(A) (1989); KY. REV. STAT. ANN. § 421.350(3) (Michie/Bobbs-Merrill Supp. 1989).

[71] *Cf.* FED. R. EVID. 804(a) (listing several definitions of unavailability, including the declarant's lack of memory or persistent refusal to testify).

[72] *See* Ohio v. Roberts, 448 U.S. 56, 66 (1980); *see also* United States v. Inadi, 475 U.S.

this narrower rationale for limiting the right of face-to-face confrontation would better serve both the functional and symbolic goals of the confrontation clause. Limiting the trial court's inquiry to the child's unavailability as a witness acknowledges that in some cases questioning the child outside the defendant's presence may increase the accuracy of his testimony but that exceptions to the defendant's right of physical confrontation are tenable only when special circumstances render the adversarial process virtually meaningless.

For similar reasons, courts should also require a showing that the child cannot testify effectively in the defendant's presence before admitting the child's prior out-of-court statements at trial.[73] Although statutes authorizing the admission of children's hearsay statements generally oblige the state either to produce the child at trial or to prove him unavailable, these statutes typically fail to define unavailability[74] or do so in terms of the child's potential traumatization rather than his inability to testify.[75] Moreover, most traditional hearsay exceptions[76] demand no showing of unavailability. Nonetheless, enforcing a narrowly defined unavailability requirement in all these contexts would ensure that prosecutors do not circumvent the confrontation right by withholding children's testimony and introducing inferior hearsay evidence in its place.[77]

Relaxation of the unavailability requirement in child abuse cases threatens to weaken the confrontation rights of defendants who already come to trial severely stigmatized.[78] Because it did not clearly base *Craig* on the alleged victims' unavailability, the Supreme Court has enabled lower courts to limit further criminal defendants' con-

---

387, 394–95 (1986) (stressing that the unavailability requirement is appropriate for evidence that is "only a weaker substitute for live testimony").

[73] *See* Note, *The Testimony of Child Victims in Sex Abuse Prosecutions: Two Legislative Innovations*, 98 HARV. L. REV. 806, 818–19 (1985); *cf.* Nelson v. Farrey, 874 F.2d 1222, 1228 (7th Cir. 1989), *cert. denied*, 110 S. Ct. 835 (1990) ("[I]f [the child] were available yet not called, it would look as if the state were trying to circumvent the adversarial process gratuitously.").

[74] *See, e.g.*, ILL. ANN. STAT. ch. 38, para. 115-10(b)(2)(B) (Smith-Hurd Supp. 1990); WASH. REV. CODE § 9A.44.120(2)(b) (1985).

[75] *See, e.g.*, ALA. CODE § 15-25-32(b)(vi) (Supp. 1989).

[76] *See, e.g.*, FED. R. EVID. 803.

[77] It is unclear whether the Court's prior confrontation decisions require a showing of unavailability for children's hearsay statements. In United States v. Inadi, 475 U.S. 387 (1986), a case involving coconspirators' statements, the Court suggested that the *Roberts* unavailability requirement does not apply if the out-of-court statement derives independent evidentiary value from its context, the state's burden of proving the declarant's unavailability is heavy, and the benefit of such a requirement is slight. *See id.* at 394–400. Although children's hearsay statements often derive significance from the circumstances in which they are made, the burden of proving the child's unavailability is not onerous, and the benefit to the defendant — allowing him to confront the child if at all possible — is potentially great.

[78] *See* Brief Amicus Curiae of Victims of Child Abuse Laws (VOCAL) National Network in Support of Respondent at 3–7, *Craig* (No. 89-478).

frontation rights in the future. Courts will better serve the values underlying the confrontation clause by narrowly construing the public policy exception for child witnesses. By upholding exceptions to the confrontation right designed to facilitate child abuse prosecutions only when the child is truly incapable of communicating, courts can ensure that in this sensitive area of the law, "'the perception as well as the reality of fairness prevails.'"[79]

---

[79] Coy v. Iowa, 487 U.S. 1012, 1019 (1988) (quoting Lee v. Illinois, 476 U.S. 530, 540 (1986)).

Confrontation Clause Revisited:
Supreme Court Decisions
Idaho v Wright, and *Craig v Maryland*
An Attorney's Response

Louis Kiefer

On June 27, 1990 the United States Supreme Court issued two decisions which significantly impact on the practice of cases involving child sexual abuse. Both cases dealt with the Confrontation Clause of the United States constitution.

Based on these two cases, it is recommended that all interviews with alleged sexual assault victims be videotaped. Furthermore, since it may be necessary to determine whether the alleged child victim may testify in front of the accused, it may be necessary for the expert to examine the child in the presence of the accused.

Idaho v Wright 58 L.W.5036 found that the admission of the child's hearsay statements violated the Confrontation Clause.

The defendant was charged with two counts of lewd conduct with a minor, specifically her five and one-half and two and one-half-year-old daughters. At the trial it was agreed that the younger daughter was not "capable of communicating to the jury." One of the great logical legal inconsistencies is how any court can permit people to testify to what a person, who was then incompetent, said. It would seem that if the person was incompetent at the time of the utterance, and incompetent at the time of trial everything the person said would

Louis Kiefer is an attorney and can be contacted at 60 Washington Street, Suite 1403, Hartford, Connecticut 06106.

be inadmissible. However, that is not the law, and on occasion, the court will permit witnesses to testify as to competent statements made by incompetent people.

Thus, in the Idaho case, after it was agreed that the then three-year-old child was incompetent to testify, a pediatrician was called to the stand.

The following questioning between the pediatrician and the prosecutor occurred:

A. . . . I started out with basically, "Hi, how are you," you know, "What did you have for breakfast this morning?" Essentially a few minutes of just sort of chitchat.

Q. Was there response from Kathy to that first—those first questions?

A. There was. She started to carry on a very relaxed animated conversation. I then proceeded to just gently start asking questions about, "Well, how are things at home?," you know, those sorts. Gently moving into the domestic situation and then moved into four questions in particular, as I reflected in my records, "Do you play with daddy? Does daddy play with you? Does your daddy touch you with his pee-pee? Do you touch his pee-pee?" And again we then established what was meant by pee-pee, it was a generic term for genital area.

Q. Before you get into that, what was, as best you recollect, what was her response to the question, "Do you play with daddy?"

A. Yes we play—I remember her making a comment about yes we play a lot and expanding on that and talking about spending time with daddy.

Q. And "Does daddy play with you?" Was there any response?

A. She responded to that as well, that they played together in a variety of circumstances and, you know, seemed very unaffected by the question.

Q. And then what did you say and her response?
A. When I asked her "Does daddy touch you with his pee-pee," she did admit to that. When I asked, "Do you touch his pee-pee," she did not have any response.
Q. Excuse me. Did you notice any change in her affect or attitude in that line of questioning?
A. Yes
Q. What did you observe?
A. She would not—oh, she did not talk any further about that. She would not elucidate what exactly—what kind of touching was taking place, or how it was happening. She did, however, say that daddy does do this with me, but he does it a lot more with my sister than with me.
Q. And how did she offer that last statement? Was that in response to a question or was that just a volunteered statement?
A. That was a volunteered statement, as I sat and waited for her to respond, again after she sort of clammed-up, and that was the next statement that she made after just allowing some silence to occur.

These statements, offered for the truth, would appear to be hearsay and therefore not admissible. However, Idaho has, what is called a residual hearsay exception, which provides:

Rule 803. Hearsay exceptions: availability of declarant immaterial. The following are not excluded by the hearsay rule, even though the declarant is available as a witness . . . (24) Other exceptions. A statement not specifically covered by any of the foregoing exceptions but having equivalent circumstantial guarantees of trustworthiness, if the court determines that (A) the statement is offered as evidence of a material fact; (B) the statement is more probative on the point for which it is offered than any other evidence which the proponent can procure through reasonable efforts; and (C) the general purposes of these rules and the interests of justice will best be served by admission of the statement into evidence."

It should be noted that Rule 804 of the Federal Rules of Evidence is very similar.

After conviction, the Supreme Court of Idaho held that the admission of the pediatrician's testimony did not violate the residual hearsay rule.[2]

However, the Idaho court found that the admission of the inculpatory hearsay testimony violated respondent's federal constitutional right to confrontation because the testimony did not fall within a traditional hearsay exception and was based on an interview that lacked procedural safeguards.[3]

The court found the interview technique inadequate because "The questions and answers were not recorded on videotape for preservation and perusal by the defense at or before trial; and blatantly leading questions were used in the interrogation."

The statements also lacked trustworthiness because "This interrogation was performed by someone with a preconceived idea of what the child should be disclosing . . ." Noting that expert testimony and child psychology texts indicated that children are suscep-

tible to suggestion and are therefore likely to be misled by leading questions, the court found that "[t]he circumstances surrounding this interview demonstrate dangers of unreliability which because the interview was not [audio or video] recorded, can never be fully assessed."

The United States Supreme Court found that "The Confrontation Clause . . . bars the admission of some evidence that would otherwise be admissible under an exception to the hearsay rule."

The Court made a distinction between "firmly rooted hearsay exceptions"[4] and the residual hearsay exception which, by contrast, does not share the same tradition of reliability that supports the admissibility of statements under a firmly rooted hearsay exception.

Does this mean that all interviews should be videotaped and no leading questions should be asked? Not really, for several reasons. First of all, the Confrontation Clause is applicable to criminal due process of law and although the requirement of due process of law, recognized in civil cases, including juvenile, and family law, often has many of the same concepts, the confrontation clause is not automatically carried into other aspects of the law. Furthermore, the court suggested that each case would have to be decided on an ad hoc basis.

Also, it was an unusual decision where the three-and one-half-year-old child was found not to be competent to testify but her statements to the pediatrician were found, by the trial court, to be competent when made. Had the child testified the Confrontation Clause simply would not have applied.

Nevertheless, since one never knows who will be found competent or incompetent, or otherwise unavailable, and since one never knows whether the case which starts as a civil case will eventually turn into a criminal case, all evaluations, whether prosecution or defense orientated, should be recorded, unless of course, the standard of conduct is so outrageous, one would prefer no witnesses.

The case of *Maryland, Petitioner v. Sandra Ann Craig* 58 L.W.5044 was handed down the same day by the United States Supreme Court.[5]

The issue was a statutorily authorized procedure which permitted the court to order ". . . that the testimony of a child victim be taken outside the courtroom and shown in the courtroom by means of a closed circuit television if:

(i) The testimony is taken during the proceeding; and
(ii) The judge determines that testimony by the child victim in the courtroom will result in the child suffering serious emotional distress such that the child cannot reasonably communicate.
(2) Only the prosecuting attorney, the attorney for the defendant, and the judge may question the child,

. . . During the child's testimony by closed circuit television, the judge and the defendant shall be in the courtroom.

. . . This section may not be interpreted to preclude, for purposes of identification of a defendant, the presence of both the victim and the defendant in the courtroom at the same time.[6]

The procedure was followed and Sandra Craig, a day care operator was convicted of sexually abusing a six-year-old child. The Maryland State Court of Appeals reversed on the basis that the 6th Amendment to the United States Constitution requires a face to face confrontation.

The court found error in that the confrontation clause does not require confrontation if other due process traditions are followed including testimony under oath, and full cross-examination.

Under the statute the trial court was required to and did have an evidentiary hearing in which the judge found the child victim, if compelled to testify in the presence of the defendant, would suffer from serious emotional distress such that the child could not reasonably communicate.

The expert testimony in each case suggested that each child would have some or considerable difficulty in testifying in Craig's presence. For example, as to one child, the expert said that what "would cause him the most anxiety would be to testify in front of Mrs. Craig. . . ." The child "wouldn't be able to communicate effectively." As to another, an expert said she "would probably stop talking and she would withdraw and curl up." With respect to two others, the testimony was that one would "become highly agitated, that he may refuse to talk or if he did talk, that he would choose his subject regardless of the questions" while the other would "become extremely timid and unwilling to talk."

The court found that the procedure used "preserves all of the other elements of the confrontation right: the child witness must be competent to testify and must testify under oath; the defendant retains full opportunity for contemporaneous cross-examination; and the judge, jury, and defendant are able to view (albeit by video monitor) the demeanor (and body) of the witness as he or she testifies."

"If the State makes an adequate showing of necessity, the state interest in protecting child witnesses from the trauma of testifying in a child abuse case is sufficiently important to justify the use of a special procedure that permits a child witness in such cases to testify at trial against a defendant in the absence of face-to-face confrontation with the defendant."

"The requisite finding of necessity must of course be a case-specific one: the trial court must hear evidence and determine whether. . .closed circuit television procedure is necessary . . ." (Emphasis added).

While the defendant argued that the court had the duty to examine the child in the presence of the accused, the Supreme Court specifically refrained from limiting the proof to the judge's personal observations, although the court did say that ". . . we think such evidentiary requirements could strengthen the grounds for use of protective measures, we decline to establish, as a matter of federal constitutional law, any such categorical evidentiary prerequisites for the use of the one-way television procedure. *id. p 5050*

In the opinion of this author, the court, unknowingly has changed the traditional qualifications of witnesses. Prior to this decision a child, in order to be qualified to testify, had to "possess certain characteristics, including the capacity to observe, sufficient intelligence, adequate memory, the ability to communicate, an awareness of the difference between truth and falsehood, and an appreciation of the obligation to speak the truth.[7] The law now seems to say that the ability to communicate can be modified to say under certain circumstances and outside the presence of certain people.

However, under the Craig case, it appears that the defendant will be able to have an examination by experts, not only of the child for purposes of competency but also to determine the effect of the presence of the accused on the ability of the child to testify. Of course the best evidence of that will be to have the child "victim" interviewed by the expert in the presence of the accused.

Footnotes

(2) *State v. Giles*, 115 Idaho 984, 772 P.2d 191 (1989).

(3) *State v Giles*, 116 Idaho 382, 385, 775 P2 1224, 1227 (1989).

(4) Presumably the court is referring to such traditional exceptions as excited utterances, statements made for purposes of medical diagnosis and the like.

(5) Dr. Underwager and Ms. Wakefield had submitted a brief as *amicus curie*. See Vol.2, No.2 *Issues in Child Abuse Accusations*, IPT Spring 1990.

(6) Section 9-102 Courts and Judicial Proceedings Article of the Annotated Code of Maryland (1989).

(7) Meyers and Perry, *Child Witness Law and Practice* p.54.

The Best Evidence Produces the Best Law

Gail S. Goodman,* Murray Levine,* and Gary B. Melton†

In their comment in this issue, Underwager and Wakefield criticized the brief of the American Psychological Association (APA) in *Maryland v. Craig* (1990),[1] in which the Supreme Court held that the Sixth Amendment does not "prohibit use of a procedure that ensures the reliability of the evidence by subjecting it to rigorous adversarial testing and thereby preserves the essence of effective confrontation," whenever such action is "necessary to protect a child witness from trauma that would be caused by testifying in the physical presence of the defendant, at least where such trauma would impair the child's ability to communicate" (p. 3170). Contrary to Underwager and Wakefield's contention, *Craig* does not uphold "dispens[ing] with defendants' constitutional confrontation rights" (p. 234). Instead, the Court recognized *both* the seriousness of defendants' interests and the importance of protection of children from harm, and applied the general rule of constitutional analysis that fundamental rights may be abridged only when necessary to meet a compelling state interest.[2]

In that regard, the APA brief in *Craig*—like the APA's previous brief in *Kentucky v. Stincer* (1987)—carefully noted the risks that may be sufficiently grave to compel a special procedure in individual cases, but it also noted that those risks were not sufficiently widespread to justify a blanket infringement of defendants' rights. That perspective was consistent not only with the Court's ultimate holding in both cases but also with psychologists' ethical responsibilities both to "accord appropriate respect to the fundamental rights, dignity, and worth of all people" (APA, 1991, Principle D) and to "apply and make public . . . knowledge of psychology in order to contribute to human welfare," in part through "mitigat[ion of] the causes of human suffering" (APA, 1991, Principle F).

---

* State University of New York at Buffalo.
† Center on Children, Families, and the Law, University of Nebraska–Lincoln.

[1] The APA brief, which was reprinted as an appendix to Goodman, Levine, Melton, and Ogden's (1991) discussion, was the first to be prepared largely by a committee of the American Psychology–Law Society. David Ogden of Jenner & Block in Washington, DC, assisted in the preparation of the brief. We gratefully acknowledge that work as well as Ogden's helpful comments on an earlier version of this article. The page citations to the APA brief refer to the reprinted version (Goodman et al., 1991). Underwager and Wakefield also submitted a brief that set forth the arguments in the comment to which we are responding. Apparently the Supreme Court found their arguments unpersuasive.

[2] There is reason to believe both that *Craig* will be construed narrowly and that prosecutors will seldom seek to use procedures to limit face-to-face confrontation (see, e.g., *Commonwealth v. Ludwig*, 1991; Smith, 1991). Even in *Craig* itself, the Maryland Court of Appeals on remand from the U.S. Supreme Court (*Craig v. Maryland*, 1991) held that the trial court had failed to demonstrate necessity for use of closed-circuit testimony. Accordingly, the Court of Appeals again remanded the case for a new trial for Craig.

Summary of the Debate

Exaggeration

Underwager and Wakefield attacked the APA brief for purportedly (a) exaggerating the state of knowledge and (b) presenting evidence insufficiently valid to warrant the attention of legal policymakers. In regard to the former point, the exaggeration is Underwager and Wakefield's. In fact, the brief is much more circumspect than they describe. For example, Underwager and Wakefield simply misstated the brief when they wrote that the brief "does not present data to support its claim that fear of courtroom confrontation is characteristic of *most* children" (p. 236, emphasis added). Instead, we concluded that "in the presence of the defendant, *many* children are less communicative—and less accurate— witnesses" (p. 28, emphasis added). "Many children" is not "most children."

Similarly, Underwager and Wakefield described the brief as claiming that "face-to-face confrontation with the defendant is the *chief* source of trauma to children" (p. 236, emphasis added). No such assertion was made. To the contrary, we noted that some children are unharmed or even benefited by courtroom confrontation with their abusers (p. 21), that anxiety is not necessarily a marker of long-term harm or lack of satisfaction with the legal process (p. 22, Note 23), and that a number of factors, some of them unrelated to trial procedures, affect children's response to the legal process (p. 22, Note 24, and accompanying text).

What was stated was that "face-to-face confrontation is a *significant* factor in child victim-witnesses' distress" (p. 21, emphasis added), in fact a concern commonly expressed by children awaiting testimony. The brief documents that some children are adversely affected by testifying in a criminal court and facing the accused and that some children's abilities to reasonably communicate are thus inhibited. Underwager and Wakefield presented no evidence to counter those facts.

Underwager and Wakefield also claimed that "the APA brief presents statements derived only from clinical experience as authoritative" (p. 236). Again, we were careful to describe the nature of the evidence available. We pointed out that the research base is still being developed (pp. 24 & 29) and that, given ethical and practical constraints, research in this area is extremely difficult to conduct (p. 24, Note 28). Finkelhor and Browne's (1985; see also Browne & Finkelhor, 1986) formulation of "traumagenic dynamics" of child sexual abuse was explicitly identified as a theory "largely based on clinical experience and publications, and to a lesser degree on systematic research," and "subject to further test" (p. 24). We were careful to indicate that confrontation with a defendant *may* arouse fear, betrayal, a sense of powerlessness, and stigmatization, consistent with Finkelhor and Browne's theory.

Validity

Borrowing from Meehl's (1989) writings, Underwager and Wakefield argued that psychological theory, research, and procedures can be divided into *high and clear* versus *low and doubtful* validity and that information presented to courts should be only of the former type. That dichotomy is simplistic and reductionistic; certainly most psychological evidence falls between those extremes. Underwager and Wakefield ignored the basic concepts of *convergent* and *incremental* validity (cf. Ellsworth, 1990). The brief presented a combination of research and clinical evidence, all converging on the same conclusion, and research reported after the brief was submitted has further supported our position. By contrast, Underwager and Wakefield offered no scientific evidence supporting the traditional assumption that error is reduced by requiring children to testify face to face with the accused.

Regardless, Underwager and Wakefield's argument is logically flawed; if the goal is to reduce error, psychology that is less than high and clear still does a service as long as the error is reduced. It is noteworthy that the rule of evidence governing admissibility of expert opinions parallels psychology's concern with incremental validity (see Melton, Petrila, Poythress, & Slobogin, 1987).[3] The critical question is not whether an opinion carries a particular absolute level of validity. Instead, Federal Rule of Evidence 702 directs the court's attention to the question of whether the opinions presented have a foundation in specialized knowledge that will be of some assistance to the fact-finder. That approach is consistent with the law's preference not for *perfect* or even near-perfect evidence (such a demand would result in no evidence most of the time!) but instead for the *best* evidence available.

In that regard, clinical theories, like that of Finkelhor and Browne, offer "a framework for analyzing the emotional consequences of a possible face-to-face encounter between the child victim-witness and a defendant known to the child" (p. 24)—a framework that is derived from specialized knowledge and that may assist courts in conceptualizing the nature of the special risks faced by some children in the legal process. Underwager and Wakefield did not dispute that phenomena fitting our application of Finkelhor and Browne's work (e.g., a reexperience of a sense of betrayal by a trusted adult) have been observed and reported in the extensive literature on child sexual abuse, as cited by the latter authors. They did not debate the points—as indeed they could not—that the overwhelming majority of children who are sexually abused are victimized by someone whom they know and that trauma is particularly great when the abuser is a father or father figure.

Our formulation was buttressed by research on the variables associated with emotional distress after testimony (see Goodman, 1989) and more general psychological research on children's coping with stressful situations (a literature that provides support for many of the same indicators). In an instance in which the research base is developing and ethical constraints bar definitive experimental studies, such a description of existing research specifically on point in combination with other evidence that suggests the nature of the risk entailed is indeed the best available evidence.

---

[3] Of course, drafters of amicus briefs need not adhere to the rules governing expert testimony. Nonetheless, by analogy, such rules provide a useful framework for consideration of the merits of expert evidence brought to courts' attention through briefs.

The Factual Disputes

Effects of Testimony Face to Face with the Defendant

Underwager and Wakefield contended that there was no strong evidence that serious emotional trauma may be inflicted on children as a result of testimony face to face with the defendant. They noted that "the 1987 APA *Kentucky v. Stincer* brief concluded there were little [sic] data to support the proposition that face-to-face confrontation has more negative effects for child victims than it has for adults" (p. 234). They further contended (a) that a study conducted by Goodman and colleagues (Goodman et al., 1988; Goodman, Taub, Jones, England, & Prado, 1989) does not indicate that children who testify are at risk of enduring emotional distress and (b) that "there are no empirical studies which have focused exclusively on the psychological effects of child witnesses testifying in the presence of the defendant" (p. 234).

In the brief, we cited five studies of effects of legal involvement and testimony in criminal court, and we could have cited more (Oates & Tong, 1987). In addition, there is a substantial clinical and legal literature about children's adverse reactions to testimony about sexual assault and other serious crimes (e.g., MacDonald, 1971; Parker, 1982; Pynoos & Eth, 1984).

Random assignment of children in actual cases to various conditions of confrontation is ethically and legally impossible, but Goodman and colleagues (Goodman et al., 1988, 1989) did include measures of fear of the defendant in their study of children's reaction to testimony. Although Goodman and colleagues did not focus *exclusively* on psychological effects of face-to-face confrontation, they did study such effects; they just did so in the context of studying much more. Moreover, at the time of the brief, the Goodman and colleagues' study had been accepted following peer review for publication in a major scientific journal (Goodman et al., in press).

We also cited several laboratory studies showing that children's testimony is often inhibited by emotion when facing an accused person (e.g., Dent, 1977; Hill & Hill, 1987). Several more recent studies and reviews reinforce our conclusions (e.g., Cashmore & Bussey, 1990; Sas, 1990, 1991; Tidwell & Lipovsky, 1991). In a recent comprehensive review, Spencer and Flin (1990) concluded, "When children are required to give evidence from the courtroom, seeing the accused and fear of retribution from him are major causes of stress" (p. 293).

Confrontation, Arousal Level, and Reliability of Testimony

We also argued that vulnerable children who testify under conditions of high arousal are relatively unlikely to testify completely and relatively likely to refuse to testify. The effect of stress on children's memory is of obvious relevance here, but Underwager and Wakefield misconstrued the evidence presented. For example, they cited a chapter by Goodman, Rudy, Bottoms,and Aman (1990), which included description of a study in which high stress was associated with beneficial effects on children's memory (Goodman, Hirschman, Hepps, & Rudy, 1991). In citing Goodman et al.'s work, Underwager and Wakefield seemed befuddled by the fact that the brief presented a conclusion that stress can have adverse effects on children's testimony. They failed to recognize that Goodman et al.'s (1990) chapter discussed stress when witnessing an event, but that the brief referred to stress during retrieval. High levels of stress may operate very differently at encoding and retrieval; a distinction between the two is basic to most scientific conceptions of human memory.

Underwager and Wakefield cannot successfully dispute the scientific data indicating that the presence of the accused sometimes inhibits children's testimony. They ignored Dent's (1977) and Peters's (1988) findings and instead implied that Hill and Hill's (1987) study is the only one indicating that children are more likely to omit information in court when they are facing the accused. Moreover, they argued that the mock courtroom in Hill and Hill's study did what it should have done—reduce speculative error and increase accuracy. If so, then Hill and Hill's noncourt group should have shown significantly greater error than the court group, but such a pattern was not found. The thrust of the evidence was clear when the brief was written, but additional supportive results now are available (e.g., Bussey, Lee, & Grimbeck, in press; Peters, 1990; K. Saywitz, personal communication)—a point that Underwager and Wakefield failed to acknowledge in their comment.

The Limits of Expertise[4]

A final issue that Underwager and Wakefield raised regards the demands that *Craig* may place on psychologists. They concluded that "a psychologist cannot, as a responsible professional, testify that a child will be so seriously damaged by the sole factor of the defendant that the use of a videotaped testimony procedure is mandated"[5] (p. 241). Such a conclusion attacks a straw person. We did not claim that a psychologist acting as an expert witness should offer such an opinion, which would be a conclusion of law. Indeed, some would strenuously argue that such ultimate-issue opinions should be neither offered nor solicited (see Melton & Limber, 1989; Melton et al., 1987; see also Committee on Ethical Guidelines, 1991, § VII[F]).

The question remains, however, about the kinds of assistance that psychologists *can* offer to courts making case-by-case determinations of the need for a limitation of confrontation. The evidence that Underwager and Wakefield offered in opposition to provision of *any* opinions (e.g., reliability of DSM-IIIR diagnoses) is largely inapposite. A child's diagnosis has little relevance to a determination of risk related to courtroom procedures.

Instead, as argued in the brief, psychologists' opinions can be useful in providing courts with specialized knowledge that aids them in evaluating the risk to

---

[4] One of us has coauthored a manuscript providing a detailed discussion of the implications of *Craig* for forensic assessment (Small & Melton, 1991).

[5] Actually, *Craig* was focused on live closed-circuit testimony, not videotaped depositions.

a particular child. The approach used in the brief was illustrative. When examined in combination with clinical experience and factual testimony about the behavior that a child has demonstrated in analogous contexts, studies of (a) stress in childhood, (b) effects of the legal process, and (c) factors mediating the effects of sexual abuse provide a foundation for opinions about the circumstances under which children are at particular risk.

Such an approach is particularly useful, given the difficulty in generating a comprehensive data base on individual differences in response to various aspects of trial procedure.[6] Nonetheless, because such a data base is not available, experts should exercise appropriate caution in making any predictions about the effects of particular procedures. As in other contexts in which such a data base is not only unavailable but also extremely difficult to generate (e.g., conditions of child custody and visitation in divorce), psychologists may be most helpful to courts as expert investigators, who generate information about the emotional well-being and experiences of the child (see Melton et al., 1987; Weithorn & Grisso, 1987). In that regard, we note in the *Craig* brief that courts should consider not only expert testimony but also "testimony from parents, teachers, other confidants, or persons who have an opportunity to observe the child, sufficient to make an informed and fair decision that balances the State's interests in protecting a vulnerable child-witness and the truth-seeking process against the defendant's right to confrontation" (pp. 25–26).

CONCLUSION

Psychology bears a social responsibility to provide the best available evidence on important questions of legal policy whenever it can do so (APA, 1991, Principle F). It should proceed with caution, but it should not be disabled by a requirement for perfect evidence.[7] Point-by-point scrutiny of Underwager and Wakefield's criticisms shows not only that APA acted responsibly in presenting the best available evidence relevant to the Supreme Court's deliberation in *Maryland v. Craig,* but also that it acted with due care in doing so.

---

[6] Such a data base is difficult to generate, because of (a) low rates of use of special procedures, (b) the heterogeneity of sexually abused children, and (c) the ethical and legal problems that we have noted in research on the trial process. Given, though, the documented need for consideration of special procedures in some cases, courts will be assisted by the provision of information about analogous bodies of research (e.g., knowledge about factors mediating response to the trial process) as well as the concerns of particular child witnesses and their response in analogous situations.

[7] It is ironic that the most intense controversies about APA's amicus briefs have involved the briefs that had the clearest scientific grounding and that included the most extensive involvement of leading experts in the field (Bersoff, 1990). Taking into account the inherent limitations of the amicus process for full explication of a scientific literature (Melton, 1990) and considering the specious nature of most of the criticisms (as this article illustrates), it must be questioned whether many of the attempts to discredit APA briefs have served either justice or truth. Critics bear at least as much social and ethical responsibility for care in public statements and consideration of their likely consequences as does APA itself.

REFERENCES

American Psychological Association (1991, October). *Ethics code* (draft revision). Washington, DC: Author.

Bersoff, D. N. (1990, March). *APA and the Supreme Court: A ten-year retrospective*. Paper presented at the meeting of the American Psychology–Law Society, Williamsburg, VA.

Browne, A., & Finkelhor, D. (1986). Impact of child sexual abuse: A review of the research. *Psychological Bulletin, 99*, 66–77.

Bussey, K., Lee, K., & Grimbeck, E. J. (in press). Lies and secrets: Implications for children's reporting of sexual abuse. In G. S. Goodman & B. L. Bottoms (Eds.) *Understanding and improving children's testimony*. New York: Guilford.

Cashmore, J., & Bussey, K. (1990). Children's conception of the witness role. In J. Spencer, G. Nicholson, R. Flin, & R. Bull (Eds.), *Children's evidence in legal proceedings* (pp. 177–188). London: Hawksmere.

Committee on Ethical Guidelines for Forensic Psychologists. (1991). Specialty guidelines for forensic psychologists. *Law and Human Behavior, 15*, 655–665.

Commonwealth v. Ludwig, Pa. , 594 A.2d 281 (1991).

Craig v. Maryland, 322 Md. 418, 588 A.2d 328 (1991).

Dent, H. (1977). Stress as a factor influencing person recognition in identification parades. *Bulletin of the British Psychological Society, 30*, 339–340.

Ellsworth, P. (1990). To tell what we know or to wait for Godot. *Law and Human Behavior, 15*, 77–90.

Finkelhor, D., & Browne, A. (1985). The traumatic impact of child sexual abuse. *American Journal of Orthopsychiatry, 55*, 530–541.

Goodman, G. S. (1989). *The emotional effects on child sexual assault victims of testifying in criminal court*. Final report to the National Institute of Justice, Washington, DC.

Goodman, G. S., Jones, D. P. H., Pyle, E., Prado, L., Port, L., England, P., & Rudy, L. (1988). The child in court: A preliminary report on the emotional effects of criminal court testimony on child sexual assault victims. In G. Davies & J. Drinkwater (Eds.), *Proceedings from the Oxford conference on children in courts: Do the courts abuse children?* (pp. 46–54). Oxford, England: British Psychological Association.

Goodman, G. S., Levine, M., Melton, G. B., & Ogden, D. W. (1991). Child witnesses and the confrontation clause: The American Psychological Association brief in *Maryland v. Craig. Law and Human Behavior, 15*, 13–29.

Goodman, G. S., Pyle-Taub, E., Jones, D. P. H., England, P., Port, L., Rudy, L., & Prado, L. (in press). The effects of criminal court testimony on child sexual assault victims. *Monographs of the Society for Research in Child Development*.

Goodman, G. S., Rudy, L., Bottoms, B. L., & Aman, C. (1990). Children's memory and children's concerns: Issues of ecological validity in the study of children's eyewitness testimony. In R. Fivush & J. Hudson (Eds.), *Knowing and remembering in young children* (pp. 249–284). New York: Cambridge University Press.

Goodman, G. S., Taub, E., Jones, D. P. H., England, P., & Prado, L. (1989, August). Emotional effects of court involvement on children. In G. S. Goodman (Chair), *Child abuse victims in court*. Symposium presented at the American Psychological Association meeting, New Orleans.

Hill, P. E., & Hill, S. M. (1987). Videotaping children's testimony: An empirical view. *Michigan Law Review, 85*, 809–833.

Kentucky v. Stincer, 482 U.S. 730 (1987).

MacDonald, J. M. (1971). *Rape: Offenders and their victims*. Springfield, IL: Thomas.

Maryland v. Craig, 110 S.Ct. 3157 (1990).

Meehl, P. E. (1989). Law and the fireside inductions (with postscript): Some reflections of a clinical psychologist. *Behavioral Sciences and the Law, 7*, 521–550.

Melton, G. B. (1990). Knowing what we *do* know: APA and adolescent abortion. *American Psychologist, 45*, 1171–1173.

Melton, G. B., & Limber, S. (1989). Psychologists involvement in cases of child maltreatment: Limits of role and expertise. *American Psychologist, 44*, 1225–1233.

Melton, G. B., Petrila, J., Poythress, N. G., & Slobogin, C. (1987). *Psychological evaluations for the courts: A handbook for mental health professionals and lawyers.* New York: Guilford.

Oates, R., & Tong, L. (1987). Sexual abuse of children: An area with room for professional reforms. *Medical Journal of Australia, 147,* 544–548.

Parker, J. (1982). The rights of child witnesses: Is the court a protector or perpetrator? *New England Law Review, 17,* 643–717.

Peters, D. (1988, March). The effects of event-stress and stress during lineup identification on eyewitness accuracy in children. In D. Peters (Chair), *Children's eyewitness testimony.* Symposium presented at the American Psychology–Law Society meeting, Miami.

Peters, D. (1990, March). *Confrontational stress and children's testimony: Some experimental findings.* Paper presented at the American Psychology–Law Society meeting, Williamsburg, VA.

Pynoos, R., & Eth, S. (1984). The child witness to homicide. *Journal of Social Issues, 40*(2), 87–108.

Sas, L. (1990). *Reducing system-induced trauma for child sexual abuse victims through court preparation, assessment, and follow-up.* Unpublished manuscript, London Family Court Clinic.

Sas, L. (1991, August). Preparing sexually abused children for the stress of court: A controlled study. In G. S. Goodman (Chair), *Assessment, diagnosis, and support of child sexual abuse victims.* Invited symposium presented at the meeting of the American Psychological Association, San Francisco.

Small, M. A., & Melton, G. B. (1991). *Evaluation of child witnesses for confrontation by criminal defendants.* Manuscript submitted for publication.

Smith, B. (1991). *Prosecution of child maltreatment cases.* Progress report to the National Center on Child Abuse and Neglect, Washington, DC.

Spencer, J. R., & Flin, R. (1990). *The evidence of children.* London: Blackstone.

Tidwell, R., & Lipovsky, J. (1991). *Child victims and witnesses: A three-state profile.* Final report to the State Justice Institute (grant No. 88-11J-D-064).

Underwager, R., & Wakefield, H. (1992). Poor psychology produces poor law. Preceding paper, this issue, *Law and Human Behavior, 16,* 233–243.

Weithorn, L. A., & Grisso, T. (1987). Psychological evaluations in divorce custody: Problems, principles, and procedures. In L. A. Weithorn (Ed.), *Psychology and child custody determinations: Knowledge, roles, and expertise* (pp. 157–181). Lincoln: University of Nebraska Press.

ACKNOWLEDGMENTS

Bauer, Herbert. "Preparation of the Sexually Abused Child for Court Testimony." *Bulletin of the American Academy of Psychiatry and the Law* 11 (1983): 287–89. Reprinted with the permission of the *Bulletin of the American Academy of Psychiatry and the Law*. Courtesy of Yale University Law Library.

Fontana, Vincent J. "When Systems Fail: Protecting the Victim of Child Sexual Abuse." *Children Today* 13 (1984): 14–18. Reprinted with the permission of the U.S. Department of Health and Human Services. Courtesy of *Children Today*.

Claman, Lawrence, Janice C. Harris, Barton E. Berstein, and Robert Lovitt. "The Adolescent as a Witness in a Case of Incest: Assessment and Outcome." *Journal of the American Academy of Child Psychiatry* 25 (1986): 457–61. Reprinted with the permission of Williams & Wilkins.

Tedesco, John F., and Steven V. Schnell. "Children's Reactions to Sex Abuse Investigation and Litigation." *Child Abuse & Neglect* 11 (1987): 267–72. Reprinted with the permission of Elsevier Science Ltd. Courtesy of Yale University Law Library.

Hobson, Charles L. "Appointed Counsel to Protect the Child Victim's Rights." *Pacific Law Journal* 21 (1990): 691–730. Copyright 1990 by the University of the Pacific, McGeorge School of Law. Reprinted by permission. Courtesy of *Pacific Law Journal*.

Levin, Stephen. "Criminal Law—Evidence—Competency of Minor Witnesses—Obligation of Oath." *Duquesne Law Review* 11 (1972–73): 701–7. Reprinted with the permission of the *Duquesne University Law Review*. Courtesy of Yale University Law Library.

Goodman, Gail S. "Children's Testimony in Historical Perspective." *Journal of Social Issues* 40 (1984): 9–31. Reprinted with the permission of The Society for the Psychological Study of Social Issues. Courtesy of the *Journal of Social Issues*.

Melton, Gary B. "Sexually Abused Children and the Legal System: Some Policy Recommendations." *American Journal of Family Therapy* 13 (1985): 61–67. Reprinted with the permission of Brunner, Mazel, Inc. Courtesy of the *American Journal of Family Therapy*.

Nurcombe, Barry. "The Child as Witness: Competency and Credibility." *Journal of the American Academy of Child Psychiatry* 25 (1986): 473–80. Reprinted with the permission of Williams & Wilkins.

Lees-Haley, Paul R. "Innocent Lies, Tragic Consequences: The Manipulation of Child Testimony." *Trial Diplomacy Journal* 10 (1987): 23–26. Reprinted with the permission of John Wiley & Sons Inc. Courtesy of Yale University Law Library.

Miles, James R. "Corroboration of Infant's Testimony in Sex Crimes." *Ohio State Law Journal* 21 (1959): 137–39. Reprinted with the permission of the *Ohio State Law Journal*. Courtesy of Yale University Law Library.

Lane, Laura. "The Effects of the Abolition of the Corroboration Requirement in Child Sexual Assault Cases." *Catholic University Law Review* 36 (1987): 793–808. Reprinted with the permission of the *Catholic University Law Review*. Courtesy of the *Catholic University Law Review*.

Levine, Murray, and Lori Battistoni. "The Corroboration Requirement in Child Sex Abuse Cases." *Behavioral Sciences & the Law* 9 (1991): 3–20. Reprinted with the permission of John Wiley & Sons Ltd. Courtesy of Yale Univesity Law Library.

Yun, Judy. "A Comprehensive Approach to Child Hearsay Statements in Sex Abuse Cases." *Columbia Law Review* 83 (1983): 1745–66. Reprinted with the permission of the *Columbia Law Review*. Courtesy of Yale University Law Library.

Melton, Gary B. "Child Witnesses and the First Amendment: A Psycholegal Dilemma." *Journal of Social Issues* 40 (1984): 109–23. Reprinted with the permission of The Society for the Psychological Study of Social Issues. Courtesy of the *Journal of Social Issues*.

Bulkley, Josephine A. "Evidentiary and Procedural Trends in State Legislation and Other Emerging Legal Issues in Child Sexual Abuse Cases." *Dickinson Law Review* 89 (1985): 645–68. Reprinted with the permission of the Dickinson School of Law. Courtesy of the *Dickinson Law Review*.

Wollitzer, Rachel I. "Sixth Amendment—Defendant's Right to Confront Witnesses: Constitutionality of Protective Measures in Child Sexual Assault Cases." *Journal of Criminal Law & Criminology* 79 (1988): 759–94. Reprinted with the special permission of the Northwestern University School of Law, *Journal of Criminal Law & Criminology*. Courtesy of Yale University Law Library.

Owens, Barbara Hobday. "Videotaped Child Testimony and the Confrontation Clause: Are They Reconcilable?" *University of Dayton Law Review* 14 (1989): 361–76. Reprinted with the permission of the University of Dayton, Law School. Courtesy of the *University of Dayton Law Review*.

Student Case Note. "Confrontation Clause—Right to Confront Children in Child Abuse Cases." *Harvard Law Review* 104 (1990): 129–39. Reprinted with the permission of the Harvard University. Courtesy of Yale University Law Library.

Kiefer, Louis. "Confrontation Clause Revisited: Supreme Court Decisions *Idaho v. Wright* and *Craig v. Maryland*: An Attorney's Response." *Issues in Child Abuse Accusations* 2 (1990): 164–66. Reprinted with the permission of the Institute for Psychological Therapies. Courtesy of the Institute for Psychological Therapies.

Goodman, Gail S., Murray Levine, and Gary B. Melton. "The Best Evidence Produces the Best Law." *Law and Human Behavior* 16 (1992): 244–51. Reprinted with the permission of Plenum Press. Courtesy of Yale University Law Library.

Series Index by Author

Please Note: Numbers at the end of each entry refer to the volume in which the article appears.

Abrahams, N. et al., "Teachers' Knowledge, Attitudes, and Beliefs About Child Abuse and its Prevention" (1992) 10

Allen, M., "Child Maltreatment in Military Communities" (1975) 1

Allers, C.T., et al., "Unresolved Childhood Sexual Abuse: Are Older Adults Affected?" (1992) 4

Alter-Reid, K., et al.,"Sexual Abuse of Children: A Review of the Empirical Findings" (1986) 2

Ammerman, R.T., et al., "Consequences of Physical Abuse and Neglect in Children" (1986) 4

Apolinsky, S.R., et al., "Symbolic Confrontation with Women Survivors of Childhood Sexual Victimization" (1991) 5

Bauer, H., "Preparation of the Sexually Abused Child for Court Testimony" (1983) 8

Becker, J.V., et al., "Evaluation of Treatment Outcomes for Adult Perpetrators of Child Sexual Abuse" (1992) 6

Beitchman, J.H., et al., "A Review of the Short-Term Effects of Child Sexual Abuse" (1991) 4

Bergman, A.B., "Abuse of the Child Abuse Law" (1978) 3

Berlin, et al., "Effects of Statutes Requiring Psychiatrists to Report Suspected Sexual Abuse of Children" (1991) 10

Besharov, D.J., "'Doing Something' About Child Abuse: The Need to Narrow The Grounds for State Intervention" (1985) 10

———, "Putting Central Registers to Work" (1977) 10

———, "Representing Abused and Neglected Children: When Protecting Children Means Seeking Dismissal of Court Proceedings" (1981/2) 7

Bharam, D.M., "Statute of Limitations for Child Sexual Abuse Offenses: A Time For Reform Utilizing the Discovery Rule" (1989) 9

Bischoff, K.S., "The Voice of a Child: Independent Legal Representation of Children in Private Custody Disputes When Sexual Abuse Is Alleged" (1990) 9

Blumberg, M.L., "Child Sexual Abuse: Ultimate in Maltreatment Syndrome" (1978) 2

———, "Psychopathology of the Abusing Parent" (1974) 3

———, "Treatment of the Abused Child and the Child Abuser" (1977) 6

Borgman, R., "Antecedents and Consequences of Parental